Bill Herr

1996

Allied Aircraft Piston Engines of World War II

History and Development of Frontline Aircraft Piston Engines
Produced by Great Britain and the United States
during World War II

Graham White

Published by:
Society of Automotive Engineers, Inc.
400 Commonwealth Drive
Warrendale, PA 15096-0001
U.S.A.
Phone: (412) 776-4841
Fax: (412) 776-5760

Library of Congress Cataloging-in-Publication Data

White, Graham, 1945-
    The allied aircraft piston engines of World War II : history and
development of frontline aircraft piston engines produced by Great
Britain and the United States during World War II / Graham White.
       p.   cm.
    Includes bibliographical references and index.
    ISBN 1-56091-655-9 (hc)
      1. Airplanes, Military—United States—Motors—History.
2. Airplanes, Military—Great Britain—Motors—History. 3. World
War, 1939-1945—Equipment. I. Title.
TL701.W455   1995
629.134'352—dc20   95-20100
                                              CIP

Cover photo of Allison V-1710 F32 engine (courtesy of Allison Division, General Motors Corp.).

ISBN 1-56091-655-9

SAE Order No. R-154

This book is dedicated to my late Mom, Peggy White, and my Dad, Arthur White, who have always supported me in my various pursuits.

Foreword

As in chess, the course of history is determined by a few key moves—often by one false move, one fatal error of judgment. In war one's enemy is unlikely to grant a second chance, save by ineptitude.

In 1939, Germany invaded Poland, having already annexed Czechoslovakia. Britain and France, though far from prepared, fulfilled the threat and declared war on Germany. Arguably, the darkest phase of this century's history had begun. It was not at that time a world war. Indeed, it was a very European war, observed, often with journalistic impartiality, from the western side of the Atlantic.

Engineering has, for a long while, been a major contributor to military strength. In recent times the battles have been fought not only between armies, but between design offices, laboratories, test houses, and production lines. Germany had a fine reputation for engineering innovation, quality, and manufacture, and retained these, quite remarkably, until the final weeks of the war in Europe.

This book tells how this strength was countered, and how, with the entry into the war of the Japanese and consequently the United States toward the end of 1941, the engineering battle moved onto a broader front.

Since this book is about the Allied involvement in the struggle for aerial supremacy, or indeed for equality, it can never be more than half the story. It is, however, a part of the story that is not often told, and one that historians of classical or military background find hard to tell because every facet involves some technical development that may at the time have seemed quite trivial, but has in retrospect altered the course of history. In 1940 the outcome of the Second World War was far from certain.

There were many observers (possibly the fathers of those reading this book) who thought, and with some justification, that all of Europe would fall into the hands of Nazi Germany.

During that fine summer of 1940 the likelihood seemed very strong indeed. The Battle of Britain was never a foregone conclusion. Like the game of chess, it was a battle waiting for one side to make a mistake. Numerical superiority was with the Germans. Battle experience was with the Germans. That the battle would be fought over the South of England favored the British, since damaged aircraft could be recovered, and a rescued pilot could fight again. The effectiveness of British radar was a surprise to the attacking force, for without it the battle would have been lost. There was no way the RAF could have flown effective standing patrols.

The aircraft, however, were evenly matched. Both sides eventually withdrew one player each from the front line of daytime combat—the Germans, the Messerschmitt 110, which was out-performed by both the Hurricane and the Spitfire, and the British, the ill-conceived twin-seat Defiant.

Though both the Hurricane and the Spitfire were low-wing, single-seat, eight-gun fighters, their design concepts were different in many ways. They did, however, have one vital unit in common, and that was the engine. Had that engine not been available, had Camm and Mitchell, the respective design leaders of the Hurricane and the Spitfire, been obliged to rely on the next available alternative, there is little doubt that the Battle of Britain would have been lost. Operation Sealion, the German invasion of England, would have been put into effect. It is hard to imagine, despite Churchill's calls to what few arms the British had, how effective resistance could have been offered. Europe would have been in Axis hands. The rest is deep speculation, but the lessons of the Normandy beaches are enough to tell us that a counter-offensive from the American continent would have been decades away.

For a brief but crucial period of history, the survival of Europe, and indeed Western democracy, rested on the availability of one twelve-cylinder engine. The contribution to that engine's development by a small band of individuals was such that, had any one been eliminated, one knight or even one pawn lost in the game, the delicate balance of history's scales could have been inexorably tipped. The balance between catching and being caught was that delicate. Without Meredith's work on radiators, Miss Shilling's on carburetors, Hooker's on superchargers, the American Hamilton license for constant speed propellers (one could go on naming them), the battle might well have been lost.

The story of the piston engine in World War II is the story of the ending of an era—an era that was terminated by the acceleration of history. The piston engine never had the opportunity to reach its full development, for it had dawned on some by 1942 that the future lay with the jet. As a consequence of this, many who were involved with the piston engine changed horses, almost in midstream. Halford, who had been responsible for later efforts with the de Havilland Goblin gas turbine, abandoned the Napier Sabre, one of the last—and most powerful—aircraft piston engines. Hooker, somewhat reluctantly, left the Merlin to work with Whittle. Of the major builders, only Wright kept faith with the piston engine, getting as close to the ultimate in piston aero-engine development as engineering was to see, though this honorable, if short-sighted, conservatism was to cost them their very existence.

Had the war lasted three more years the jet engine would have been the decisive factor. In fact, the piston engine remained the key player. Only two jets had a measurable effect on the events of the war: the German Messerschmitt 262 and the British Gloster Meteor. The two were never to meet in battle.

The technology of the aircraft piston engine reached its climax against the accelerating ground-bass of war, often at the tempo of panic. This was particularly so for the European factories (which, in the context of this book, means the English factories), for these were prime targets for bombardment.

Just once in a while, and I hope not from SAE members, one is told that history is irrelevant to engineering. I dispute this: I have known engineers who may be indifferent to the foundations of their profession, but I have yet to find among them one who doesn't aspire to more than mediocrity.

Everything in engineering is interpretation. Interpretation is impossible without data. Data is history. History (and we don't need to haggle over semantics) is not the learning by rote of names and dates, any more than knowledge of a language is the ability to recite a table of verbs. It is about consequences, strategy, motives, and resources, and the way these are molded by speculation. Engineering is asking the right questions. It requires intelligence plus wisdom, and applies to a deep fund of knowledge based on experience that others have accrued.

History is subject to many misconceptions—as many, one might suggest, as is engineering to historians. It has much in common with astronomy, which is also a study of history. The further you are away from it (and the more finely tuned your tools of observation), the more you see. Much that is written shortly after an event is grossly distorted. Now, at a distance of more than 50 years, more information is available, though much has been lost in the intervening years through the passing of many who were, as they were called, the back-room boys.

Often the privilege of writing a Foreword falls on one whose name or contribution to the field in question is well known. My qualification, though my background is in aircraft, is simply that I was in on this project from the beginning. It began over a lunch in Pittsburgh, Pennsylvania, where I shared a drink with the author and listened to his story. I looked at photos of aircraft engines he had renovated and rebuilt as others might a classic car, and found that I was in conversation with someone who could talk with equal authority and enthusiasm on the products of GM Allison and Rolls-Royce, Wright and Bristol. I was not surprised to hear that Graham White had been born English but had become American.

White is no armchair historian, and he is certainly not an armchair engineer. His curiosity and quest for information took him many thousands of miles, to many libraries, factories, museums, and homes. His energy never seemed to wane. Every morning of the week he spent under my roof in North Kent, under the very skies in which the Battle of Britain had been fought, he was off at the crack of winter's dawn for a two-mile run amid the marshland farms. Each day was filled with the frenetic search for information, anecdotes, and pictures, from sources ranging from London's Science Museum to such treasures as might turn up in a rural Kentish barn. I was witness to much of this, and have little doubt that he carried this enthusiasm wherever he went in England or America.

The result, and every historian must come to this realization, tells part of the story. It pulls back the curtains of time to reveal just a little more of one theater of war in which the part played by engineers was more than significant—it was vital to the freedom that we enjoy today.

Don Goodsell
Faversham, U.K., 1994

Acknowledgments

Describing the complex inner workings of military aircraft engines is not the easiest of endeavors! Gathering the information has required the invaluable help of many people to whom I am deeply grateful.

In the United States:

Aviation historian extraordinaire Dan Whitney has provided not only priceless technical assistance, but Dan also took the time to review the manuscript chapter by chapter. The General Electric turbo-supercharger information was supplied by Dan along with many other anecdotes and pieces of long-buried, technical information.

Kevin Cameron, technical editor of *Cycle World* magazine, lit the original fire under me to write this book. Kevin has always been a source of inspiration with his encyclopedic knowledge of the internal combustion engine and his enthusiasm for anything mechanical. He was kind enough to loan me his valuable High Speed Internal Combustion Engine, 1968 edition by Sir Harry Ricardo and his copy of Robert Schlaifer's and S. D. Heron's Development of Aircraft Engines and Development of Aviation Fuels.

Retired Pratt & Whitney archivist Harvey Lippincott reviewed the Pratt & Whitney chapter. In addition to his review, Harvey related to me many anecdotes concerning Pratt & Whitney engines.

Dr. Max Bentele subjected himself to my questions for an afternoon that I found to be totally enlightening. Dr. Bentele shared many pieces of technical information with me that have never been published before, such as German ingenuity in salvaging shot-down Allied aircraft engines and using components from them.

Despite suffering horrendous health problems, the late Gerry Abbamont supplied invaluable information on Wright engines. Sadly, Gerry passed away in June 1994, just a scant two and a half months after our interview.

I first met Jack Wetzler at an SAE seminar on World War II aircraft engines that I presented in 1992. Afterward Jack shared with me his experiences as an engineer with Allison and gave me a copy of his SAE paper, written in 1946, on the turbocompounded V-1710. Several of the V-1710 photographs are from Jack's collection. Jack later headed up the design team that produced the Allison 250, one of the most successful small aviation gas turbines.

Jack Hovey, Merlin magician and a hive of information on Rolls-Royce's finest, was always willing to take time out of his schedule to be subjected to my constant queries.

The staff at the National Air and Space Museum patiently dug out numerous manuals and files for review.

Others who provided help were: Frank Hill, owner of Hill Air; Willie Walter, who has probably rebuilt more Pratt & Whitney R-1830s and R-2800s than any other man alive; The New England Air Museum staff, including Norm Mullings for providing access to the museum's extensive collection of aircraft manuals; Al Marcucci, owner of Savage Magneto Services; John Morgan, who is restoring the ultra-rare P-51G; Irv Rosenblum, who kindly loaned me his large collection of Jane's; Bob Scott, owner of AeroTropic; Carlos Arana, owner of Florida Airline Services; and many others who supplied moral and technical support.

In England:

Thank goodness Rolls-Royce has such a profound interest in its history; it made my job a lot easier! Dave Birch, editor of the *Rolls-Royce Archive* magazine, was kind enough not only to review the Rolls-Royce chapter but got me into the holy grail at Rolls-Royce, the company archives. Mike Evans, founder of the Rolls-Royce Heritage Trust, opened up his office and supplied many photographs of engines and aircraft. Both Dave and Mike continually went "above and beyond" to assist me in my endeavors.

My good friend Keith Gough, author of The Vital Spark, has always been an inspiration and valued friend. Keith's hospitality during a visit to England in December 1993 was invaluable. He took time out to help me go through the Fleet Air Arm Museum archives in Yeovilton.

Don Goodsell, a distinguished author in his own right, was kind enough to extend his hospitality to me in December 1993. He greased the skids in numerous ways by gaining access to various archives and collections. Don also critiqued my work and added several interesting and little-known anecdotes that added immeasurably to the interest of the book.

Another company dedicated to preserving their history is Napier. The Napier Power Heritage, and in particular Alan Vessey, Hon. Secretary of the NPH, always came through for me with definitive answers to my constant requests for information.

Andrew Nahum, Curator of Aeronautics of the Science Museum in South Kensington, provided priceless information on the often overlooked and misunderstood Napier Sabre.

During the preparation of this book, I was dating my future wife. To Diane, I owe a sincere debt of gratitude for her understanding and forbearance while I pursued this project.

For those I have not mentioned who have contributed in some way, my most sincere apologies.

For any errors which may be contained in the text, I take full responsibility.

On a final note, it is heartwarming to see people like Mike Evans, Dave Birch, Harvey Lippincott, Alan Vessey and the late Gerry Abbamont preserving their respective company's history and heritage. Despite the efforts of these gentlemen, a depressing amount of technical information and hardware has been systematically destroyed. This is knowledge and hardware lost to historians and future generations forever.

Graham White
August 1994

Preface

Development of technology is not a steady and predictable endeavor. Likewise, having an advancement in technology without an apparent application is practically meaningless. Furthermore, practical people do not want to squander their time and tangible resources inventing and developing better "mousetraps." At least this is the ardent fervor often found in Chief Executive and Government offices. It is all the more satisfying, then, when we find individuals and teams with the intuition, knowledge, and foresight to look over the horizon and do what needs to be done. This is the atmosphere that energized many in the pioneering days of aviation.

While it took the demands of two World Wars to bring aviation into acceptance by the general public, it was a relative handful of engineers, entrepreneurs, and pilots who positioned the technology and resources necessary to make aviation practical and the deciding factor in ending World War II.

This book attempts to illuminate some of the historically significant technical developments and achievements that directly contributed to the execution and tactics of the war. Many writers have focused on technical incidents that impacted particular aircraft or events—for example, that early Merlin-powered Spitfires and Hurricanes would "cut-out" during negative g maneuvers, giving the Luftwaffe a critical advantage. We have all heard that a British woman engineer came up with an elegantly simple and expedient fix, and now you can find out how it worked and how she did it!

Tactics are dictated as much by the capabilities of the combatants and their equipment as they are by the tactical situation. It was no accident that when the United States chose to fly high-altitude daylight bombing raids over "Festung Europa," they had turbosupercharged engines and the Norden bombsight.

The World War I lesson, beware of the "Hun-in-the-Sun," was not lost on planners in the 1930s; having the altitude advantage was significant to surviving combat in the air. Flight into the stratosphere required development of many new and highly advanced technologies. The specific differences between aircraft and engines, which in turn dictated their tactical order, are described and explained in the following text.

Much has been written about the organization of the production capability of the Allied nations to produce and equip their armies and navies with the necessary machines of war. Interestingly, little of a comprehensive nature has been compiled about the technological development that was incorporated into the engines that powered the aerial armadas of the war.

The following text is specific to the British- and American-developed engines. Collecting material for a book such as this has been difficult, for much of it was "secret" during the war, and after the war everyone was "tired" of the old technology, anxious to get into "jets," and simply weary of anything to do with "the War." Sources of information, to a similar level of detail, on the engines used by the Axis belligerents of World War II are far from comprehensive and superficial at best. Still, the belligerents countered practically every Allied technical advance and introduced many themselves. The story of their engine developments has yet to be told.

Although first-class engines were developed by other British manufacturers—such as de Havilland, with their range of Gipsy engines; Armstrong Siddeley, who produced the Cheetah; and Blackburn, who produced their range of Cirrus engines—these secondary-role engines are not covered in this book.

Likewise, in the United States, excellent engines were produced by Jacobs, Ranger, and Kinner but are not covered, and only the hyper- and/or large-engine developments of Lycoming and Continental are covered, since the focus of this book is on front-line combat engines.

Examples are given of the applications of the engines covered. By no stretch of the imagination are all applications covered. As an example, so many aircraft were powered by the Rolls-Royce Merlin that it would be impossible to cover all applications with any degree of detail. In the same vein, not all variations or dash numbers of a particular engine are covered. For example, Pratt & Whitney produced a dizzying array of variations and permutations on the R-2800; indeed there were several examples of the Pratt & Whitney R-2800 that they did not even manufacture but instead were built by licensees.

Although numerous excellent books have been published on all of the more common World War II aircraft and several books have been published on engines, rarely have the two been brought together.

Contents

Chapter 1

Introduction

World War II was one of the most profound events in the history of mankind. It now seems like ancient history, and yet in the relatively brief time span of 1939 to 1945 technology in all aspects of warfare advanced in leaps and bounds—none more so than in piston engine development.

Virtually the entire world was embroiled in a struggle of good against evil. Aviation played a major part in this monumental endeavor; indeed many major battles were fought solely in the air. Who can forget the inspiring words spoken by Winston Churchill: "Never in the field of human conflict was so much owed by so many to so few." The "few," of course, were the brave Royal Air Force (RAF) pilots, flying Supermarine Spitfires and Hawker Hurricanes, who, outnumbered, fought against Messerschmitt Bf 109s and Bf 110s as well as hordes of bombers, predominantly Heinkel He 111s and Junkers Ju87s. Victory in the Battle of Britain saved Britain from invasion by Germany, although it was an incredibly close-run thing. Halfway across the world two years later in 1942, another pivotal battle took place in the Pacific—the Battle of Midway—which again was fought entirely by aircraft, although this time all the aircraft that took part were based on aircraft carriers instead of on land. Interestingly, the ships involved never saw the opposing side, such was the scale of the battle. Historians are still arguing about who was really the victor in the Battle of Midway. In terms of losses it was probably a stalemate; however, the fact that the Japanese had been stopped in their tracks represented a major psychological victory for the United States.

Air battles often involved huge formations of overloaded bombers struggling and fighting their way to the target. As the war progressed, it was not unusual for the U.S. Eighth Air Force and British Royal Air Force (RAF) to attack a target with 1000 bombers, giving rise to the phrase "aluminum overcast" to describe an event surely never to be repeated. Even transport aircraft hauling much-needed equipment to battle fronts were subjected to constant harassment and attack by the opposing side. The resupply effort undertaken by the Fourteenth Air Force flew some of the most dangerous missions of World War II, flying over such incredibly inhospitable territory as the Himalayas in overloaded Curtiss C-46 Commandos and Douglas C-47 Dakotas in poor weather, constantly exposed to attack by Japanese fighters.

Such was the pace of the war that it was imperative to get the finest equipment with best performance into service as quickly as possible. This led to some of the shortest development times ever achieved for complex military hardware. On occasion this abbreviated development and testing cost dearly, as in the case of the Boeing B-29, which suffered numerous problems during its introduction to combat service, as did the Avro Manchester with its failure-prone Rolls-Royce Vulture engines. Germany compromised its long-range bombing capability because of the insurmountable problems with the Daimler Benz DB 610 and DB 613 engines installed in the Heinkel He 177. Japan forced many underdeveloped aircraft, particularly those with poor engines, into combat during the later stages of the war when they realized that the Zero, as fine an airplane as it was, just was not competitive after 1942.

The struggle for air superiority by all sides focused on squeezing the most performance out of the available technology as well as Herculean efforts to advance technology. Although there were many instances of aircraft with inferior performance coming out victorious, the odds were obviously stacked against this occurrence. Throughout the conflict a seesaw battle of technology was waged. Part of this technological battle was in the area of engine development, as this is the most influential aspect of the performance of an aircraft, although it could be argued that an aircraft featuring old-technology aerodynamics but with a superior power plant will not outperform an aircraft with state-of-the-art aerodynamics and a mediocre engine. For example, the P-40F powered by the single-stage Rolls-Royce Merlin was still a mediocre performer. Conversely, the P-51A, powered by the Allison V-1710, was still a good performer; however, when the P-51 was redesigned to take the two-stage Rolls-Royce Merlin, the aircraft came alive and was arguably the finest fighter aircraft built in World War II.

This book attempts to document the remarkable development that took place with these mechanical masterpieces produced during the conflict and that often shaped the tactics and strategy of the battles.

Chapter 2

Requirements

The performance parameters of an aircraft can be put into several categories, such as maximum speed, service ceiling, rate of climb, that is, altitude gained per minute, time required to reach 10,000 ft, maximum diving speed, and so forth.

Most of these parameters depend on horsepower for enhanced performance. Clearly, other factors come into play, such as overall weight of the aircraft, propeller efficiency, and aerodynamics for example.

As the sophistication of engines, propellers, and airframes improved, aircraft were optimized for certain performance aspects such as speed at high altitude or, conversely, high performance at low altitude. This process was controlled by optimizing the engine/airframe combination at the desired altitude. For instance, high-altitude performance could be gained primarily through supercharger design such as multiple stages of supercharge and/or increasing the speed of rotation of the supercharger by means of two-speed or three-speed gearing or variable-speed drive to the supercharger impeller(s). These supercharger enhancements introduced their own set of problems. As the boost pressure (manifold pressure) increased, the resultant increase in the temperature of the charge (fuel/air mixture or air) due to compression heating would lead to detonation. This could be controlled in a number of ways. Fuel octane rating/performance number has a strong bearing on how much boost pressure an engine can withstand before destructive detonation occurs.

Fuels

Fuel quality and supercharger technology went hand-in-hand with contributing to power increases. The first hints that fuel quality had a strong bearing on power output occurred during World War I. Britain and France started receiving fuel from the United States with an octane value of 50 or less, although the octane scale had not yet been introduced. Problems with preignition and knocking resulted. Prior to the supply of U.S. fuel, supplies originated from Borneo, Java, or Sumatra with a highly aromatic "straight cut" with what was later shown to have an octane value of 70 (Ref. 2.1).

Several key players investigated fuels and their impact on engine performance in the 1920s. Harry, later Sir Harry, Ricardo developed the single-cylinder E-35 research engine that featured an infinitely variable compression ratio (Ref. 2.2). By increasing the compression ratio until the onset of knocking, accurate comparison of fuels was possible (Ref. 2.3). Thomas Midgley and Charles Kettering in the United States investigated the fuel quality issue when the coil ignition developed by Kettering for automobiles was wrongly blamed for preignition problems. Their research led them to the advantages of adding tetraethyl lead (TEL) to fuels and the resulting dramatic improvement in knock resistance. Tests conducted in 1922 by the U.S. Army at McCook field confirmed the advantages of adding TEL to fuel; consequently, the Navy started using it as an additive in 1922.

In 1931 Sam Heron (Fig. 2.1), head of research at Wright Field, added 8 cm³ of TEL per gallon to a batch of California straight run gasoline resulting in an octane value of 98. This fuel was used in a Pratt & Whitney R-1340 engine for performance testing. The R-1340 was normally rated at 450 horsepower at that time. With 98-octane fuel, power was doubled to 900 hp by allowing higher manifold pressures to be used (see Ref. 2.1). The higher manifold pressure was obtained by increasing the supercharger gear ratio.

As a result of the considerable improvements in the quality of fuel used by the Allies in World War II, particularly the fuel from the United States, engine performance was significantly improved. Having started out in 1939 with 87-octane fuel, the British RAF received 100-octane fuel from the United States just in time for the start of the Battle of Britain (Ref. 2.4). As the war progressed, 100/130 performance number (PN) fuel was developed, and later 115/145 PN fuel became available. It should be noted that the octane scale ends at 100; fuels with a higher performance than 100 octane were designated with a "performance number," which corresponds to a percentage of the octane scale; for example, 140 PN fuel has a 40% higher rating than 100 octane. The dual numbers indicated the lean and rich performance numbers. It was realized in the 1920s that an engine running a

Fig. 2.1 Sam Heron, born in England, where he made major contributions to engine development during World War I. He then emigrated to the United States where he continued his work on engine development, including the sodium-cooled valve, air-cooled cylinder design, and fuel development. He also enjoyed shocking Americans with his risqué jokes! (Courtesy of the National Air and Space Museum, Smithsonian Institution, Photo No. 2B-12187.)

rich mixture showed greater resistance to knocking than the same engine running at the same power setting on a lean mixture. Finally, fuel development peaked at 150 PN (see Ref. 2.1). This fuel was used in special situations that required high performance when Germany started attacking Britain with V-1 flying bombs, commonly referred to as "buzz bombs." This ingenious device was the forerunner of the modern-day cruise missile. Usually launched from "ski" ramps from the Continent or air-launched from Heinkel He 111s, the V-1s, powered by primitive but effective pulse jets, would cruise at 2000 to 5000 ft traveling at 350 to 400 mph. Piston engine fighters of the time needed all the performance they could muster in order to catch and shoot down these devices. The introduction of high-performance-number fuels made a major contribution to neutralizing this menace by allowing manifold pressures of 80 in Hg and higher in conjunction with water/methanol injection.

Charge Heating

As manifold pressures increased with the introduction of high-performance-number fuels and higher-performance superchargers, methods of cooling the charge due to compression heating had to be devised.

Cooling the charge with aftercoolers and intercoolers was one method of solving charge heating. The compressed air or fuel/air mixture was routed through a radiator matrix, through which air or coolant in the form of a water/ethylene glycol mixture was circulated, or in some cases routed directly to the ambient air stream.

By 1944 anti-detonation injection (ADI) was used quite extensively by all sides (Ref. 2.5). With anti-detonation injection, a 50/50 mixture of atomized distilled water and methanol was injected into the supercharger, usually at the eye of the impeller. Rapid evaporation of the injected ADI mixture cooled the charge, the resultant steam reducing detonation by slowing the combustion process. The methanol was used primarily as an antifreeze because of the extremely low temperatures experienced at high altitudes. When a fuel with a performance number of 115/145 was used in conjunction with ADI, the effective performance number jumped to 175. ADI was needed only at elevated manifold pressures; aircraft would therefore carry a 10- to 15-min supply, typically burning 0.5 to 1.0 lb per pound of fuel. Above the critical altitude ADI had minimal or no effect, and therefore it was more effective at lower altitudes.

The use of ADI by the Allies was restricted to fighter aircraft during World War II, although it would have been of inestimable value during take-off for some of the heavy bombers, which often took off on missions overloaded well beyond the design specification. Boeing B-29s in particular would have benefited from the addition of water/methanol injection (Ref. 2.6). Many suffered take-off accidents on missions to bomb Japan due to overheated and overstressed Wright R-3350 engines. Avro Lancasters carrying 22,000-lb Grand Slam bombs would also have reaped the benefits of water/methanol injection during the harrowing, overloaded take-off phase of these missions. Germany made extensive use of ADI, along with nitrous oxide injection, not only for fighters but for medium bombers also (Ref. 2.7).

Radiator Development—Liquid-Cooled Engines

The large size of these engines, both physically and in terms of displacement (typically 2000 to 3000 in^3), and the countering need for low installed drag always presented a challenge to the airframe designer. When it is realized that the cooling load is approximately equal in magnitude to the horsepower being delivered, the enormity of the cooling requirement can be appreciated.

Cowling panels that fitted skintight, minimum size coolant and oil radiators consistent with reliability, and compact engine mounts were other design challenges. The solutions varied.

For example, coolant radiators were mounted in different parts of the airframe with varying degrees of success. Some aircraft, such as the Curtiss P-40, Hawker Typhoon, and Hawker Tempest when fitted with the Napier Sabre engine, featured all the radiators, both coolant and oil, under the engine. Supermarine Spitfires and Messerschmitt Bf 109s featured underwing radiators; the de Havilland Mosquito and Westland Whirlwind chose the novel location of the wing leading edge for the cooling requirements; and the masterpiece of airframe design, the North American P-51 Mustang had all the cooling radiators mounted in an aerodynamic duct in the belly of the fuselage. The Hawker Hurricane, Fiat G.55, Caproni-Reggiane Re 2005, and Kawasaki Ki-61, among others, also shared this design feature.

Radiator design also continued unabated in order to obtain the greatest amount of heat rejection from the smallest frontal area. Two advances in the 1930s assisted in this quest. The first was the introduction of ethylene glycol coolant, which with its higher boiling point (and higher coolant temperature) allowed a smaller radiator, thus contributing to reduced cooling drag. Initially 100% glycol was employed; however, this introduced new problems such as leakage and the flammability of the glycol. By World War II most liquid-cooled engines used a mixture of water and glycol, typically 30 to 50% glycol. This permitted coolant temperatures of up to 250°F when the system was pressurized to 25 psi (40 psia).

The mechanical design of radiator cores also made dramatic strides during the late 1930s. Construction of early radiators typically consisted of a honeycomb matrix of tubes. Originally this comprised a number of brass or copper tubes of 5-mm diameter stacked together and swaged and soldered at their ends for a distance of approximately 12 mm. The open ends of the tubes faced the airflow, and the coolant or oil then flowed around the outer circumference. This resulted in the same areas being exposed to the coolant and air. By 1937 Rolls-Royce realized that far greater heat rejection could be achieved if a larger area was exposed to the air than to the coolant. In fact, it was found that the area exposed to the coolant needed to be only one-fifth the area of the air side. Therefore, a radiator with 5 to 10 times the surface area exposed to the air side was needed. From this investigation it was found that a secondary surface radiator or fin-and-tube would fit the bill. This style of radiator had been used for many years by automobile companies. It consisted of vertical, oval tubes through which the coolant flowed and cooling fins attached to the outside, making contact with neighboring tubes. This then gave the optimal 5-to-1 air-to-coolant surface ratio needed for the unsurpassed cooling associated with minimum drag and weight.

From experiments conducted by Rolls-Royce, a 10% reduction in drag and a 38% reduction in weight resulted. Fin-and-tube radiators were not only more efficient from a heat rejection aspect but were also cheaper to manufacture.

Aircraft radiator manufacturers of the late 1930s did not have the manufacturing capability to build fin-and-tube radiators, and the automotive radiator suppliers had their hands full supplying the automotive market. In addition, the small quantities required by peacetime military aviation did not justify getting involved with this small market segment. Therefore, it was not until the outbreak of World War II that the automotive radiator manufacturers, who saw their traditional market dry up almost overnight, got into high gear to supply the aviation industry (see Ref. 2.5).

F. W. Meredith of the Royal Aircraft Establishment studied the installation of aircraft radiators in the 1930s. Realizing that a tremendous amount of heat energy was being rejected, he devised radiator installations that would turn the rejected heat into useful thrust. Prior to Meredith's work, aircraft radiators were typically hung out in the breeze with minimal attempts at ducting. Working with wind tunnel models, Meredith designed a duct that slowed the velocity of the incoming cooling air; as it made contact with the radiator core, the resultant rise in temperature of the cooling air and its release into a divergent duct resulted in positive thrust, like a simple jet engine. The North American P-51 Mustang was probably the most effective application of this system with tests showing the thrust equaled the drag of the installation under ideal conditions.

Air-Cooled Radial Engine Installation

Providing optimal cooling of the air-cooled radial engine while keeping drag and weight to a minimum presented design challenges that were just as great as those faced in liquid-cooled engine design. Early radial engine installations resulted in a large amount of installed drag as no attempt was made to cowl the engine.

Two parallel efforts in 1927 resulted in dramatically reduced installed drag. The National Advisory Committee for Aeronautics (NACA) in the United States developed the NACA cowl, which consisted of an airfoil shape wrapped around the engine (Figs. 2.2, 2.3).

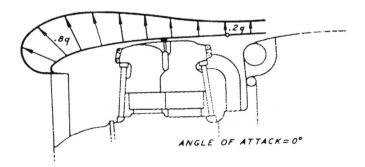

ANGLE OF ATTACK = 0°

Fig. 2.2 Section through a typical NACA cowl showing pressure distribution on the outside of the cowl. When properly designed and installed, this device could reduce the cooling drag of the radial engine. (Pratt & Whitney. Courtesy of the New England Air Museum.)

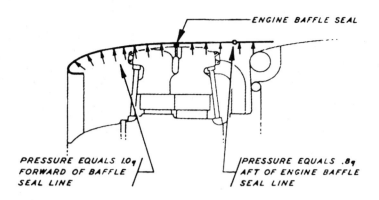

ENGINE BAFFLE SEAL

PRESSURE EQUALS 1.0q
FORWARD OF BAFFLE
SEAL LINE

PRESSURE EQUALS .8q
AFT OF ENGINE BAFFLE
SEAL LINE

Fig. 2.3 Pressure distribution on the inside of a typical NACA cowl. (Pratt & Whitney. Courtesy of the New England Air Museum.)

The NACA cowl optimized the cooling air entering the cowl, and once the cooling air entered the cowl, baffles wrapped around the cylinders and the cylinder head forced air around the rear of the cylinder and other areas normally inaccessible for the cooling air. This prevented the front of the cylinder from overcooling and the rear of the cylinder from overheating. The end result was that maximum use was made of the available cooling air. After the cooling air had passed through the cooling fins, the heated air escaped through adjustable flaps, usually hydraulically operated or occasionally electric servomotor operated. As the flaps, or gills as the British call them, opened, a low pressure was created that accelerated air through the cowling. This was intended to maintain the ideal cylinder head temperature of 350 to 450°F, although these temperatures were often exceeded during combat or climbing to altitude. As the cooling air picked up the rejected heat by passing over the cylinders and exhaust system, expansion took place that under ideal circumstances could reduce the overall drag of the cooling system due to the expanded air accelerating out of the cowling.

To assist the air out of the cowling, a curved profile sheet of stainless steel, known as the fireseal or the dishpan, offered a low restriction path for the now heated and expanded cooling air. Ejector-type exhaust systems could also accelerate cooling air through the cowling.

The National Physical Laboratory in England developed a similar drag-reducing cowl (Ref. 2.5) invented by H. Townend, and consequently known as the Townend-ring. NACA- and Townend-type cowls were used in World War I for rotary-powered aircraft; however, their drag-reducing properties were not realized or appreciated at the time as their only function was to protect the pilot from the exhaust, mainly castor oil. At the conclusion of World War I, rotary engines quickly fell from grace, replaced by radials.

Mounting

Aircraft engines have many internal components producing reciprocating loads that transmit considerable vibration to the airframe resulting in the ever present menace of fatigue failure. Attenuating these loads has always been a major design challenge.

Many conflicting requirements had to be met: ensuring ease of maintenance, that is, accessibility; feeding the loads of the engine mount into the airframe structure; isolating engine vibration from the aircraft structure; isolating engine fires from the structure; and ensuring that the necessary structural integrity existed not only to support the weight of the engine/propeller combination but also the horrendous gyroscopic and *g* loads imposed by turbulent air and during violent maneuvers, as well as by the intended thrust and torque loads.

After meeting these and other structural requirements, the mount had to share the same requirement as every other component on the aircraft; it had to be as light as possible consistent with a reasonable safety margin. Design philosophies varied greatly as to the best way to achieve these goals.

For radial engines, trapezoidal mounts manufactured from thin-wall chrome molybdenum alloy steel tubing was the most common design concept. A ring of circular cross-section supported the engine vibration isolators. These loads were then fed into the trapezoidal mount, which typically attached at four points on the aircraft firewall (Fig. 2.4).

There were some innovative departures from this type of mount, such as those in the Douglas A-26 and Boeing B-29.

If the aircraft fuselage, or engine nacelle in the case of multiengine aircraft, featured monocoque or semimonocoque construction, the loads were distributed through the airframe through four longerons and then through the remainder of the airframe. In the case of aircraft that featured space frame construction, the main load-bearing components were chrome molybdenum steel alloy tubes. An example of this construction would be the Hawker Hurricane.

The engine mount would tie into the four main longeron tubes, again distributing the engine-mounting loads throughout the airframe. In the case of some single-engine fighters, such as the Supermarine Spitfire and the Messerschmitt Bf 109, the lower mounting points would tie into the main wing spar, which then not only distributed these heavy loads through the airframe but integrated the engine mount into the main wing spar, which is typically the strongest part of the aircraft.

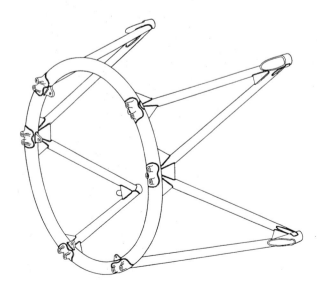

Fig. 2.4 Typical mounting ring for a radial engine. This example shows six mounts for the engine and four-point mounting for attachment to the firewall. (Pratt and Whitney Aircraft-Installation Handbook, Apr. 1947. Courtesy of Harvey Lippincott.)

The Shakes!

Isolating engine vibration varied from very sophisticated solutions to very simple ones. The dynamics of piston engine vibration attenuation is a very complex and involved subject that is beyond the scope of this book. However, Pratt & Whitney probably led the world in piston engine mounting that incorporated shock absorption and damping with the dynafocal principle (Ref. 2.8).

Dynafocal simply means the mounts are angled in such a way that if an imaginary line were drawn through the center of all the mounts, these imaginary lines would converge at the center of gravity of the engine/propeller combination. The Pratt & Whitney mounts took care of the shock-absorption chores through a number of rubber disks laminated together. The damping requirements were handled by a clutch plate loaded with a diaphragm spring, a very simple, ingenious, light, and innovative design (Ref. 2.9).

In-line engine mounting was no less difficult, and various innovative solutions were developed during World War II. Like their radial engine counterparts, many liquid-cooled in-lines used chrome molybdenum steel alloy tubular mounts designed from the same principles as a cantilever bridge terminating in four mounting points attached to the firewall, which then distributed the loads through the airframe structure (Fig. 2.5).

Variations on this concept existed in the form of the fabricated aluminum mount used by the North American P-51 Mustang; this idea was later adapted by Supermarine Aviation Works with the Rolls-Royce Griffon powered Spitfire. Perhaps the definitive in-line mounting systems were the designs used by Germany to mount the Daimler Benz and Junkers inverted V-12 engines.

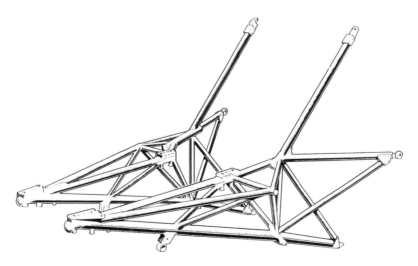

Fig. 2.5 Typical engine mount for a V-12 aircraft engine. This example is for a Rolls-Royce Merlin. (Courtesy of Rolls-Royce plc.)

The main structural member was a lightweight (9-lb) magnesium forging with a chrome molybdenum steel alloy tube supporting the main forging. The four-point mounting terminated with a spherical ball joint at the firewall.

Engine Vibration

Engine vibration could be disastrous if it was not contained. To give an idea of some of the loads concerned, the center main bearing on a typical, high-performance aircraft V-12 had to withstand radial loads of up to ten tons that reversed direction as many as 3000 times a minute and had to be able to do this for up to 1000 h!

Again, conflicting requirements existed; on the one hand weight reduction was essential, and on the other reliability and the capability to withstand enormous loads were prime requisites. As is usually the case in aircraft engine design, ingenious and innovative design solved these dilemmas.

From the early days of aircraft engine design, second-order vibratory modes created havoc, particularly with crankshafts, resulting in frequent failures. The situation was often aggravated by the use of reduction gearing. The severity of the problem was so profound that in certain models of the World War I Hispano Suiza water-cooled V-8 that incorporated reduction gearing, crankshaft failure was inevitable after as few as 10 h of operation.

During the years leading up to World War II, much research was done and a good understanding of the problem was established. Several creative ideas were incorporated into crankshaft design, primarily the dynamic balancer for attenuating second- and higher-order vibration (Ref. 2.10).

The execution of this device varied widely between engine manufacturers; however, the basic principle remained the same. The crank web incorporated a floating member that adjusted its position relative to the crankshaft according to the angular velocity of the crankshaft. It is easy to realize that when ignition occurs in the cylinder of a high-performance engine the crankshaft is "jolted" into a momentary acceleration. An 18-cylinder radial, for instance, running at 2800 rpm, is thus "excited" 25,200 times a minute, resulting in a potential harmonic vibration that can "excite" the crankshaft into unusually high loads leading to fatigue failure. The most famous example of this phenomenon was the ABC Dragonfly, a British nine-cylinder radial designed at the end of World War I when the dynamics of crankshaft design were little understood. The Dragonfly was inadvertently designed to run at its natural frequency, resulting in crankshaft failure within a few hours of running. Fortunately, World War I ended before this disastrous engine entered service. The British Government had pinned all its hopes on this engine to the point of shutting down production lines of existing engines. If World War I had continued into 1919, the British would have been in serious trouble because of the Dragonfly episode (see Ref. 2.5).

Introduction of the dynamic counterweighted crankshaft detuned this vibration to keep it out of the harmonic range by lagging behind the momentary acceleration of the crank then "catching up" with the crank. The dynamic counterweight relied solely on acceleration and centrifugal forces to determine its position. In the case of a long crankshaft, such as would be employed by a V-12, the problem was compounded by the fact that the crank had all the characteristics of a rubber band. The crank literally wound up and unwound. If this torsional vibration was kept out of its harmonic range and the twisting was within the mechanical limits of crankshaft material, all was well.

However, with all this torsional vibration from the crankshaft twisting back and forth, additional loads were focused on the accessory drives such as generators, magnetos, fuel pumps, propeller governors, vacuum pumps, and so forth. To solve these potential problems, quill shafts or hydraulic couplings in the case of the later Allison V-1710 engines and some of the Daimler Benz 600 series engines were often employed to protect these accessories from undue stress.

The two components that suffered the most from crankshaft-induced torsional vibration were the supercharger drive and the propeller reduction gearing. For the supercharger drive, several solutions to this difficult problem surfaced in time for World War II, most of which centered around the use of a torsionally resilient quill shaft that was allowed to "twist" within its elastic limit. The winding up and unwinding of the quill thus protected the supercharger drive gears from the shock loads emanating from the crankshaft. Alternatively, cushion springs, similar to the springs found in an automotive clutch plate, were used, usually in radials.

Several reasons existed for the severity of the problem. One was the amount of power needed to drive the supercharger, upward of several hundred horsepower in a 1500-hp engine; another was the sharp increase in gearing necessary to obtain the desired boost pressure. In many cases this could be as high as ten to one, that is, the supercharger could be spinning ten times faster than the crank. It is easy to realize that when the pilot made a power adjustment that resulted in an increase in engine rpm, the supercharger was accelerated up to an order of magnitude faster than the crank. Therefore, supercharger drives were critical from an operational and manufacturing aspect due to the heavy and high-speed tooth loadings involved.

Propeller reduction gears were by far the most heavily loaded gear trains incorporated in the engine design, as they transmitted the entire output of the engine to the propeller, although the unit-bearing stresses remained the same as other gear trains in the engine. Again, design trends dictated that most in-lines featured simple spur reduction gearing and radials utilized planetary gearing for strength and streamlining.

These trends were usually followed to accommodate the smallest and most aerodynamic cowl form. The design challenge of the in-line with spur gearing (usually straight cut) was greater because of heavier tooth loading compared with that in planetary gearing, which shared the load over several gear teeth. One of the design mistakes made by the early World War I engine designers was to attach the pinion gear directly to the crankshaft, usually overhung from the No. 1 main bearing. As can be imagined, this pinion then took all the torsional vibration of the crankshaft with no protection. The inevitable result was frequent crankshaft or pinion failure.

The solution was to isolate the pinion from the crank and to mount it in its own set of bearings. The isolation feature was usually accomplished by a short, stiff quill shaft. Even with good design, manufacturing quality needed to be of the highest order. This included gear design, tooth profile, material surface treatment, extremely tight manufacturing tolerances, and the highest surface finish.

Lubrication

Lubrication systems, analogous to the lifeblood of the engine, had a number of innovative design features. All the combat aircraft used in World War II used the dry sump system. This meant the oil reservoir, typically contained in an oil pan or sump in an automobile, was contained in a remote and separate oil tank. An oil line conveyed the oil through a flexible rubber hose from the tank, which could hold as much as 45 gal in the case of some of the large long-range strategic bombers, to the engine "oil in" connection. This was routed to the pressure pump through galleries. The pressure pump, usually of the gear type, then pumped the oil through a filter and onto the oil pressure control valve (Fig. 2.6).

Most lubrication requirements needed 50 to 90 psi, and occasionally a lower pressure was used for duties such as the tooth-engagement point for propeller reduction gears, camshafts, and so forth. Excess pressure was relieved through the relief valve, typically a coil-spring-loaded disk with a screw adjustment. Due to the critical nature of the adjustment of this relief valve, a lead seal was used to give tamperproof evidence of nonauthorized adjustment of this essential component.

The regulated oil was then routed to the crankshaft main bearings through galleries or holes drilled in the crankcase. Oil was also routed to other essential components such as cam gears, cams, rockers, supercharger bearings, supercharger step-up gears, propeller reduction gears, etc. Oil ejected from the bearings then performed secondary lubrication and cooling duties such as piston lubrication, piston crown cooling, wrist pin lubrication, and so forth. After the oil had fulfilled its lubrication and cooling duties, it drained into sumps in the case of a radial, usually one at the front and one at the rear, into the lower crankcase in the case of an upright in-line or into the cam covers of an inverted in-line.

The oil was then pumped out of the engine by a gear pump, called the scavenge pump, which was of higher capacity than the pressure pump. This ensured the engine did not load up with oil. After leaving the engine, again through flexible rubber hoses, the oil was routed through a cooler. Typically manufactured from brass, coolers were usually of the honeycomb type. Although a fin-and-tube cooler would potentially have been more efficient, the high pressures experienced, particularly in cold operations, dictated this style of cooler. Even so, bombers flying over Europe during the cold winter months at high altitudes where temperatures could dip to a frigid –60°F, would occasionally suffer burst oil coolers due to the oil congealing in the cooler.

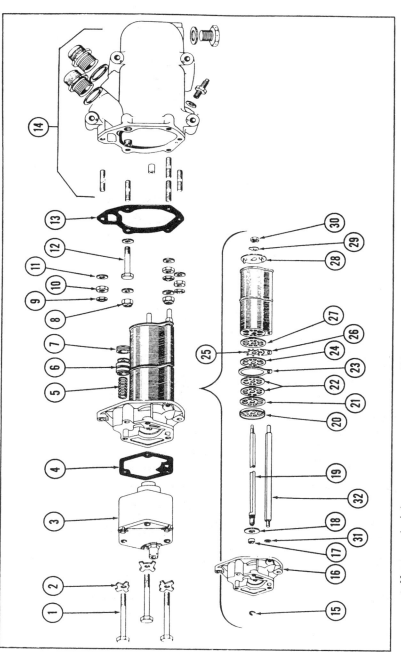

1. Motor mounting bolt
2. Tab washer
3. Hydraulic motor assembly
4. Motor gasket
5. Relief valve spring
6. Relief valve
7. Relief valve seat
8. Elastic stop nut
9. Palnut
10. Stud nut
11. Plain washer

12. Bolt
13. Sump gasket
14. Housing assembly
15. Thrust collar
16. Adaptor
17. Spindle bushing
18. Thrust washer
19. Spindle
20. Inner closer
21. Reinforcing disc (.050-in.)
22. Closer disc

23. Locking plate
24. Reinforcing disc (.031-in.)
25. Spacer
26. Cleaner blade
27. Filter disc
28. Outer closer assembly
29. Tab washer
30. Spindle nut
31. Plain washer
32. Cleaner blade rod

Fig. 2.6 The Cuno company supplied most of the oil filters for U.S. aircraft engines in World War II. The filter shown is self-cleaning. Disks, rotated by a hydraulic motor that ran off engine oil pressure, trapped contaminants. A blade scraped the contaminants from the disks. Example shown is for a Packard-built Rolls-Royce Merlin V-1650-1. (Maintenance Manual for the Cuno Oil Filter, AN 03-1-32. Author's collection.)

From the cooler, oil was routed back to the oil tank, where it would then go through a de-aerator. One essential with a high-performance engine was the requirement for "solid" oil, that is, oil that did not contain air bubbles. If the aircraft went through acrobatic maneuvers, as fighters do during combat, oil needed to be supplied to the engine under all conditions, even when the aircraft was flying inverted.

To accomplish this, a "flop" tube was employed in the oil tank. This was essentially an articulated arm, free to swing in the direction that *g* forces demanded. Dry sump lubrication offered many advantages, among them increased engine performance due to lower "windage" losses, which were losses due to rotating and reciprocating components thrashing around in oil, at high speeds, losses which could be considerable. Additional losses were attributable to pumping losses, that is, gears acting as gear pumps; therefore, it was essential to get the oil out of the engine as quickly as possible as soon as the lubrication and cooling duties had been performed, and return it to the tank via the cooler.

Various design features were incorporated to assist in this requirement, such as "windage" trays, typically used in in-line engines. The windage tray consisted of a formed piece of sheet metal extending the length of the crankcase and set under the crankshaft. As oil spilled out of the main and connecting rod bearings, it was scooped up by the windage tray and routed to the scavenge pumps.

During cold-weather operations, it was essential that a combat aircraft be capable of being sent aloft at a moment's notice. This placed large demands on the lubrication system as the oil most used during World War II was 50 weight. This resulted in the oil turning to the consistency of molasses in cold weather.

To overcome this problem, oil-dilution systems were incorporated in many aircraft, particularly fighters that often needed to be combat-ready at short notice. If cold weather was forecast for the next foreseeable flight, the pilot had the option of injecting gasoline into the oil system prior to shutting the engine down from a just-completed flight. This dilution would then allow the engine to be cranked considerably more easily as the oil would flow far more freely. As the engine warmed up, following a cold start, the gasoline would boil off. This procedure, however, was not without its pitfalls. One of the major side effects with oil dilution was the de-sludging effect on the engine. Gasoline was an excellent solvent for the sludges that inevitably built up inside an aircraft engine. Therefore, oil dilution sometimes gave mechanics fits as the sludge broken loose by the dilution process would block oil galleries and oil lines with resultant maintenance woes.

Design features were incorporated in some engines to keep the sludging problem under control. One of the more common was a centrifuge, which was a small cylinder, gear driven at high speed, that had the effect of centrifuging any sludge built up to the periphery, and the clean oil would then be pumped through the center. At regular maintenance intervals, the sludge would require removal from the centrifuge (Fig. 2.7).

Various features in the engine would also act as sludge traps, such as the interior of hollow crankshaft journals, particularly the connecting rod journals. Pitch change mechanism domes for hydraulically operated propellers were another source of this maintenance headache.

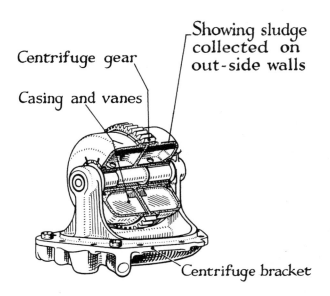

Centrifuge gear

Showing sludge collected on out-side walls

Casing and vanes

Centrifuge bracket

Fig. 2-7 Sectional view of a centrifuge unit. This illustration is from a Bristol Hercules, but all engines fitted with centrifuge units operated on a similar principle. ("Bristol Hercules XI & VI Engines, Operating Instructions," Issue No. 1, Jan. 1943. Author's collection.)

Exhaust Systems

Exhaust system development continued at a frantic pace during World War II. Many requirements were asked of the exhaust. The primary one was to safely expel the white hot, toxic, and highly corrosive products of combustion overboard. Other requirements from the exhaust system were flame damping, performance enhancement through taking advantage of the residual jet thrust, and a low restriction design in order to reduce engine back pressure to a minimum.

In addition to the above-mentioned performance-related requirements, the materials had to withstand a high-temperature, high-vibration/high-fatigue, highly corrosive environment at the lowest weight. Manufacturing these complicated exhaust systems required expertise and workmanship of the highest order.

Night operations were fraught with hazards at the best of times. During combat conditions, these hazards were multiplied. Avoiding detection by enemy aircraft was always a prime concern by flight crews, and unfortunately the characteristic stoichiometric blue flame issuing from the exhaust system was always a giveaway. Numerous solutions were tried with varying degrees of success for an exhaust that would offer good flame-damping characteristics without compromising the performance of the engine or aircraft.

Early aircraft engines had what can only be described as primitive exhaust systems, but by the end of World War I airframe and engine designers realized the importance of well-designed exhausts.

Leading up to World War II, extensive research had been done and by careful design of the exhaust could make an appreciable contribution to the performance of the aircraft through reduced drag, residual jet thrust, and engine performance enhancing features that allowed improved breathing for the engine.

In-line engines commonly featured individual ejector stacks; this offered good breathing character-istics and utilized the jet thrust from the energy in the exhaust in high-speed aircraft (Fig. 2.8). Bombers, if they were used for night operation, had flame damping as the prime requisite. Numerous methods were incorporated for this requirement, such as shrouds, siamesed stacks, manifold systems, and fishtail systems (Fig. 2.9).

For radial engines, collector rings were customarily employed. A collector ring was a circular pipe with the exhaust from each cylinder manifolded into the collector ring (Fig. 2.10). The exhaust was then fed overboard, or routed to the exhaust-driven turbosupercharger if one was fitted. Germany broke away from this design theme with the excellent BMW 801, as did Japan in later versions of the famous Zero. Instead of a collector ring, BMW implemented individual stacks for this 14-cylinder radial. It came as quite a shock for the British when they started encountering Focke-Wulf 190s in 1941. This aircraft advanced the state of the art for radial engine installations in fighters.

Like the in-line engine, performance of the aircraft could be appreciably improved by careful design of the exhaust. Cooling a large high-performance air-cooled radial was always a major design chal-lenge. To assist in this task, the exhaust energy could be used to eject (i.e., "pump") the cooling air through the cowling, thus increasing the mass cooling airflow over the engine.

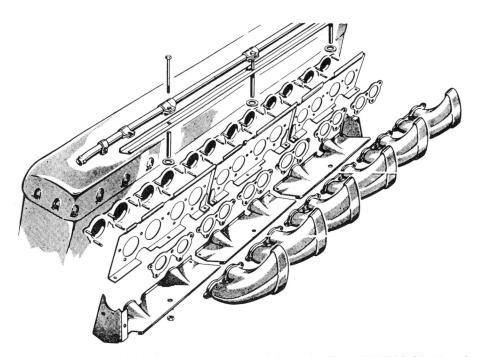

Fig. 2.8 Exhaust stack assembly for North American P-51A with Allison V-1710-81. Note how each pair of exhaust ports was siamesed into a single ejector stack. Each stack served one cylinder. (North American A-36 Erection and Maintenance Manual, 8 May 1944. Courtesy of the National Air and Space Museum.)

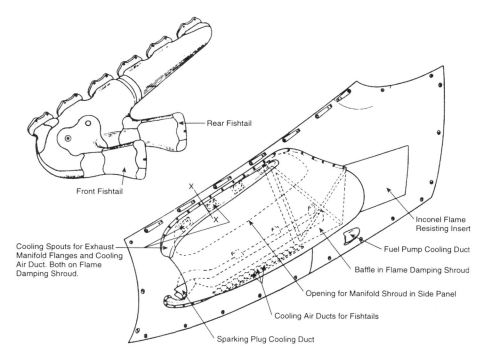

Rear Fishtail

Front Fishtail

Inconel Flame
Resisting Insert

Cooling Spouts for Exhaust
Manifold Flanges and Cooling
Air Duct. Both on Flame
Damping Shroud.

Fuel Pump Cooling Duct

Baffle in Flame Damping Shroud

Opening for Manifold Shroud in Side Panel

Cooling Air Ducts for Fishtails

Sparking Plug Cooling Duct

Fig. 2.9 Example of a fishtail exhaust system. The one illustrated is from a de Havilland Mosquito F Mk. II. A shroud covered the pair of fishtails for additional flame damping. (The Mosquito NF Mk. XVII Aeroplane, Air Publication 2019 B. British Crown Copyright/Ministry of Defense. Reproduced with the permission of the Controller of Her Britannic Majesty's Stationery Office.)

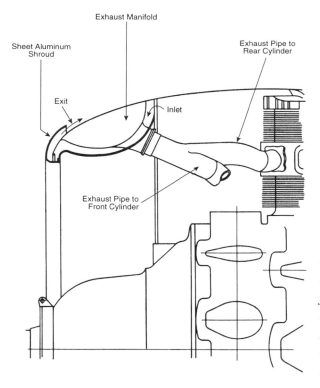

Exhaust Manifold

Sheet Aluminum
Shroud

Exhaust Pipe to
Rear Cylinder

Exit

Inlet

Exhaust Pipe to
Front Cylinder

Fig. 2.10 Typical Bristol exhaust system. Exhaust gases were routed to the front of the cowl. The leading edge of the cowl doubled as the collector ring. For clarity, plane of front cylinders is not shown. Only one rear cylinder is illustrated. ("Instructions for the Maintenance of the Bristol Hercules III Air-Cooled Radial Engines," Issue No. 1, Nov. 1940. Author's collection.)

Diagnosing engine problems could be difficult at the best of times for the ground crew; however, for an engine with individual exhaust stacks, problem diagnosis could be considerably simplified by "reading" the exhaust flame. Nighttime was obviously the ideal time for this type of fault determination. Some of the characteristics a mechanic would look for would be defective spark plugs, oil burning, rich mixture, lean mixture, overpriming, and so forth. Each of these maladies would have its own unique color and shape of flame. The ideal flame, indicating that everything was healthy with a particular cylinder, would be a short, snappy stoichiometric blue flame. Construction of exhaust system components usually consisted of an Inconel (trademark of International Nickel Corporation) high-nickel-content stainless steel alloy, mild steel, or stainless steel fabrication welded from sheet and tubular stock. Considerable effort was expended to provide for thermal expansion and retraction within the exhaust components. Solutions required slip joints, ball joints, and pressure-sealing gaskets.

Ignition Systems

From time immemorial, with few exceptions, aircraft engines employed magneto ignition. Several reasons were responsible for this trend. First was the safety aspect; magnetos did not require an external electrical power source as they generated their own power due to the rotation of the magneto. Therefore, even if the entire electrical system of an aircraft was disabled, the ignition system continued to function.

At cranking speed, the magneto generally did not generate enough power to produce a spark. At these times a booster coil, basically a Tesla coil, was often used. As the engine started and ran under its own power, the boost coil was deactivated.

The magneto ignition system could be relied on to give a fat, healthy spark for thousands of hours. One idiosyncrasy that the conventional magneto ignition system could not deal with, however, was the changed conditions at high altitude. Due to the reduced dielectric strength of the atmosphere at high altitudes, serious misfiring and cross firing inside the distributor took place. Various solutions were tried with limited success; pressurizing the magneto was probably the most effective. Pressurization methods included tapping off the discharge from the supercharger or using a small compressor driven off the accessory case. The definitive solution was low-tension ignition, which was under development but did not quite get into service during World War II.

A low-tension ignition system generated a relatively low voltage, on the order of 100 V instead of the 20,000 V needed to fire the plug. The distributor then sent this low-tension voltage to the appropriate cylinder, where it was boosted to the necessary 20,000+ V required to fire the plug with a high-tension coil. This eliminated the potential for high-tension cross firing inside the distributor and across spark plug wires.

All World War II aircraft engines employed two spark plugs per cylinder for the following reasons:

1. Due to the size of the cylinder bore, typically over 5 inches, two ignition sources were required. With one ignition source much earlier ignition timing would be required because of the distance the flame front had to travel. With two ignition sources two flame fronts are established; conse-

quently later ignition timing was possible with less likelihood of detonation. Often the plugs were timed to fire at different times, optimizing the combustion characteristics of the engine design.

2. Two independent ignition sources offered improved dependability; if one failed, the engine would continue to run, although at considerably reduced power.

Several methods were employed to fire the dual ignition systems:

• Two separate magnetos with integral distributors—for example, Merlins, R-1830s, R-1820s, the General Electric System used on R-2800s, etc.
• A single magneto which supplied high-tension voltage to dual distributors—for example, the V-1710, R-3350, etc.
• A single dual magneto and distributor in one housing—for example, Griffons.

Turbosupercharging

When the exhaust valve opens, a considerable amount of pressure and thermal energy is retained by the still-expanding exhaust gases. The engine designer may choose to take advantage of this energy using an ejector-type exhaust system, or the still-expanding, hot exhaust gases could be piped to a turbosupercharger, which consists of a gas turbine and centrifugal air compressor. The discharge from this compressor then feeds the engine with pressurized air by way of an intercooler.

At low altitudes, the turbosupercharger could potentially overboost the engine leading to catastrophic detonation. To avoid this condition, a sophisticated control system was employed that monitored manifold pressure, and at a predetermined level, some of the exhaust gas was bypassed around the turbine unit. This was accomplished by a waste gate, that is, a butterfly valve, which opened as the boost pressure reached the predetermined level. When the waste gate opened, exhaust gases were allowed to flood out, thereby reducing the amount of power the turbine delivered to the compressor. As the aircraft gained altitude, the waste gate automatically closed to compensate for the lower atmospheric pressure to the compressor, thus maintaining sea-level power until the waste gate was completely closed. This defined the critical altitude; consequently, as the aircraft climbed above this altitude sea-level power could not be maintained.

Excessive speed of the turbo could be catastrophic, therefore it was common to incorporate a tachometer reading turbo rpm. As can be imagined, if a turbine wheel, running red-hot at 20,000 rpm, failed, the flying debris could cause serious damage to the airframe.

The United States was the only nation to make extensive use of turbosupercharging in World War II, although Germany had a limited number of BMW 801s, Junkers 205 diesels, and Daimler Benzes in production with turbos. Toward the end of the war Japan also started incorporating turbosupercharging for its fighters in order to reach high-flying B-29s.

Dr. Sanford Moss of the General Electric Company (Lynn, Mass.) was one of the driving forces behind turbosupercharger development in the United States. Moss started his investigations during World War I using a Liberty V-12 fitted with one of his turbos. His testing took him to the top of 14,000-ft Pikes Peak with the Liberty mounted on the back of a truck to ascertain performance at altitude. Moss was awarded the Collier Trophy in 1940 for pioneering work on turbosuperchargers (Ref. 2.11).

Many problems were experienced during these early days of turbosupercharger development; the most challenging was to find a material that could withstand the highly corrosive, hot (1500°F+) environment produced by the exhaust gases. Turbine blades in particular were prone to failure.

The material that saved the day was Haynes-Stellite No. 21 (H-S 21). Interestingly, this material is similar to vitallium, which is used in dentures (Ref. 2.1). Initially the blades were manufactured by forging and machining. Owing to the excellent casting characteristics of H-S 21, the lost wax casting process took over in 1940. The late Sam Heron is credited with introducing the casting process when he persuaded the manufacturing engineers that a high degree of accuracy was possible from the casting process by pulling out his dentures during a meeting to discuss this problem!

Germany had similar problems finding a high-temperature alloy; however, they took a different tack to solve the material issue. Instead of developing a new high-temperature alloy, they developed air-cooled turbine blades; this was to be of inestimable value for the later German gas turbine developments. As the Germans could not obtain strategic high-temperature alloy elements such as nickel, chromium, and cobalt, they were forced into using more innovative methods to overcome the problems of high-temperature operating environments.

Specifics

Quoting the horsepower of an engine without giving any other information can be misleading. For example, if an engine was quoted as producing 1000 hp, how long could the engine maintain that power? How heavy was the engine? How much fuel was being consumed to produce that power? What was the frontal area? What was the horsepower per unit area of the piston? What was the displacement? Perhaps most important of all was the average pressure in the cylinder during the firing stroke, or brake mean effective pressure (BMEP). Determining these and other specifics was essential in order to understand how good (or bad) an engine was.

Let's look at a hypothetical 1000-hp engine. If this engine displaced 1000 in^3, then clearly it develops 1 hp/in^3. At the start of World War II no production engines came close to developing 1 hp/in^3; by the end of hostilities, this specific power was quite common, and at the upper end of the performance spectrum, 1.6 hp/in^3 was being approached.

Along the same lines, specific weight influenced the rating of an engine. One horsepower per pound of weight was the goal most designers strove for and in some cases exceeded handsomely, at the cost of reduced time between overhauls and in some cases reliability.

Specific fuel consumption and fuel tank capacity dictated the range of an aircraft. Unfortunately, good fuel economy was usually in conflict with high specific power. Specific fuel consumption, typically called out as pounds of fuel burnt for each horsepower developed per hour was highly dependent on the conditions the engine is operated under, for example, take-off, maximum military, or lean cruise. It usually varied from 0.4 to 0.6 lb of fuel per horsepower per hour for high-performance engines, although many examples existed of greater and lower figures than these. Good specific fuel consumption was essential for fighters, particularly in pre-radar days as good duration on standing patrols was vital. As an example, the Messerschmitt Bf 109 was severely limited in range, consequently during the Battle of Britain it had a combat duration of only 15 min over the south of England. Many planes were lost returning to France because they ran out of gas. Many B-29 fight engineers sweated out the last miles returning to base after a harrowing mission to Japan, eking out the best mileage from their temperamental Wright R-3350 engines.

Several horsepower ratings were used depending on the situation in which the engine operated. War emergency was the absolute maximum power the engine could deliver and typically had a limit of 1 to 5 min, although one could not imagine a fighter pilot with an enemy aircraft on his tail timing his one minute! War emergency power often involved the use of a power-augmentation system such as ADI, nitrous oxide injection, or extra fuel enrichment and a high manifold absolute pressure (MAP) limit.

Anti-detonation injection was used quite extensively by all combatants with the exception of the Russians. Nitrous oxide or laughing gas, first used by Germany, was not exploited by anyone else with the sole exception of one squadron of de Havilland Mosquitos flown by the RAF (Ref. 2.12). If war emergency power was used, the engine would need additional maintenance such as valve clearance checks, spark plug change, compression check, and checking of filters and screens for contaminants such as metal particles. Take-off power would naturally be the power used for take-off and would normally be limited to 5 min. Maximum except take-off (METO) had a typical 15-min limit. Finally, cruise power would be the power setting giving the best fuel economy.

Output per unit piston area is also a good indicator of the performance potential of a high-output engine. For example, 6 hp/in² would be a good benchmark figure; although outputs approaching 7.5 hp/in² were achieved, this would represent a phenomenal power output.

The speed of an engine is not solely dependent on rpm; in fact, this is not a reliable method due to factors such as the dimension of the stroke. One measurement that is a good indicator of the speed of an engine, regardless of its size or displacement, is piston speed. Piston speed is the best comparator as it tends to remain constant regardless of the size and displacement of the engine. A benchmark figure of 3000 ft/min differentiates medium-speed engines from high-speed engines. This holds true for high-performance auto engines and for the multiple-thousand cubic-inch engines used to power front-line military aircraft in World War II. Most of the engines used during this conflict were limited to 3000 ft/min with temporary overspeeds allowed during emergencies. A failed connecting rod was usually the penalty for exceeding the safe limit speed of the engine.

The Air-Cooled Radial Versus In-Line Controversy

During World War I, the radial engine was still under development and saw relatively little service. The rotary engine quickly faded out after World War I, leaving the water-cooled in-line engine to reign supreme until the arrival of the first radial engines. After World War I, radial engine development took off in leaps and bounds and quickly found many applications in military and civilian aircraft. Thus the scene was set for the controversy that raged through the 1920s, 1930s, and 1940s regarding the better approach: air-cooled radial or liquid-cooled in-line. A study of the various attributes of each configuration is in order.

Air-Cooled Radial Engines

Radial engines could be shorter and more compact than liquid-cooled in-line engines for equal displacement and also tended to be lighter for the same displacement, but not necessarily lighter for the same horsepower.

Cooling systems were considerably simpler because an active cooling system was eliminated; this was probably the dominant advantage over its liquid-cooled counterpart. This was particularly advantageous in cases of battle damage, as there were by definition one vital system fewer to be damaged. The oil cooler was the most vulnerable system. Certain maintenance chores could be simplified. For example, an individual cylinder could be changed rather than a complete cylinder bank as in the case of a liquid-cooled in-line engine.

Radial engines tended to have more installed drag, although investigations done by NACA in the 1930s helped to negate some of this disadvantage. When Focke-Wulf introduced the Fw 190 in 1941, it showed that a radial engine could feature a low-drag, efficient installation because of a then innovative individual ejector exhaust system, beautifully designed oil cooler installation, and ram air for the supercharger. The cowling was tightly wrapped around the 14-cylinder BMW 801 radial, which featured cooling augmented by a twelve-blade fan running at 1.72 times crankshaft speed (Refs. 2.7, 2.13).

Specific power for radials, that is, power per cubic inch, tended to be lower because higher cylinder head temperatures existed that led to detonation at lower manifold pressures than in liquid-cooled cylinders. Several rationales accounted for this characteristic. Cooling was limited by the air flowing through the cowling and picking up the rejected heat of combustion from the cooling fins cast or machined into the cylinder head and the fins machined into the cylinder barrel or, alternatively, an aluminum heat muff shrunk onto the barrel. Under war emergency or high-power conditions, thermal overload could quickly result as the cylinder had little "thermal inertia."

Several developments reduced the drawbacks associated with air cooling. The Bristol Aeroplane Company pioneered the forging process for manufacturing cylinder heads. Starting with a solid aluminum forging, cooling fins were machined-in with ganged slitting saws. This process allowed deeper, closer-pitched finning than would be possible by casting; consequently, a far greater surface area was exposed for improved cooling. In addition, the forging process offered greater mechanical strength (Ref. 2.14).

As manufacturing techniques and materials improved, it was possible for engine designers to increase the total cooling area. The following table illustrates the trend toward increased cooling fin area and the higher horsepower per cylinder for Pratt & Whitney engines (Ref. 2.15).

	1927	**1932**	**1940**	**1946**
Displacement	149 in³	131 in³	155 in³	155 in³
Horsepower	45 hp/cylinder	67 hp/cylinder	100 hp/cylinder	125 hp/cylinder
Total Cooling Fin Area	1200 in²	1500 in²	3100 in²	4300 in²
Cooling Fin Area per Horsepower	26 in²/hp	22 in²/hp	31 in²/hp	34 in²/hp

Wright Aeronautical pioneered the heat muff cooling system for the cylinder barrel. Instead of machining-in the cooling fins from a solid steel forging, an aluminum muff with Wright Aeronautical's patented W-type finning was heat shrunk onto the forged steel barrel.

A master connecting rod bearing journal was typically required to withstand the load of seven or nine cylinders. This placed high loads on this critical bearing. Liquid-cooled V-12 engines normally used blade-and-fork connecting rods. Therefore, each connecting rod journal took the load of two cylinders, only one of which was on the power stroke at any given time. This greatly reduced the total load on this highly stressed bearing compared with the radial master rod bearing.

Liquid-Cooled In-Line Engines

Although they were longer, in-line engines tended to have less frontal area than radial engines for the same displacement.

High power and war emergency power settings could be tolerated for longer periods due to the higher built-in thermal reserve of the liquid-cooling system.

Liquid-cooling systems were more vulnerable to battle damage. A single bullet hole in the radiator would result in loss of coolant, which would precipitate rapid overheating, although it has been reported that the effects of loss of coolant could sometimes be delayed by running the engine full rich and operating the primer. An air-cooled radial could sustain considerable damage and continue to produce power. Many examples occurred when complete cylinders were shot off an engine and it continued to function for hours.

Specific power of the liquid-cooled in-line tended to be higher because of the improved cooling characteristics that would allow higher boost pressures to be used prior to the onset of detonation.

As can be seen from the above, the radial/liquid-cooled in-line controversy was a complex one, and during World War II there were excellent examples of both types of engines powering aircraft for the same mission. For example, the liquid-cooled, in-line powered North American P-51 Mustang and the air-cooled, radial powered Focke-Wulf 190 were two examples of contemporary fighters. The Boeing B-17 (with air-cooled radials) and the Avro Lancaster (with liquid-cooled engines) were bombers designed for similar missions.

Most of the period arguments for/against one type or the other were resolved when the cooling drag of both types was fully developed. The piston engine/propeller air speed record set by the liquid-cooled in-line Messerschmitt Bf109R in 1939 was broken by the radial-engine-powered Grumman F8F Bearcat in 1969, only to be retaken in 1979 by the hybrid, liquid-cooled Red Baron RB-51, a highly modified P-51D from Ed Browning team. The record is currently held by an air-cooled radial in the form of the Wright R-3350 powered F8F Bearcat, "Rare Bear," which has reigned supreme at the Reno Air Races for many years.

Manufacturing

The demands for performance and for ease of manufacture for these mechanical masterpieces were invariably difficult to reconcile. Massive manufacturing efforts were necessary in order to meet production demands yet the highest order of quality, fits, clearances, and precision was a prerequisite. All highly stressed components needed a high degree of surface finish to achieve good fatigue qualities. Therefore it was normal practice for crankshafts, connecting rods, gears, and other heavily loaded components to be machined and polished all over. This was naturally very labor intensive but unavoidable if the performance potential of an engine was to be achieved.

Castings had to be of the highest quality, typically of aluminum or magnesium, featuring the thinnest possible wall section commensurate with the load to be imposed on them. Forgings also required the highest degree of quality and often required numerous machining operations. As an example, the Rolls-Royce Merlin crankshaft was made from a chrome molybdenum steel alloy forging weighing 500 lb. After completion of all machining and manufacturing operations, the completed crankshaft weighed 120 lb.

Inspection was of major importance, indeed some engine components were literally "tattooed" with numerous inspection stamps as each stage of manufacture was carefully examined. It was normal practice to test-run each engine for 4 to 10 hours as it came off the manufacturing line.

Various methods were used to simulate a load on the engine; test clubs and dynamometers were the most common. Power recovery was utilized in some installations by way of driving electric generators used to power the manufacturing plant producing the engine. In order to head off potential problems during production, it was common practice to remove one out of ten engines after successful completion of a test run and tear it down to check for trends that would indicate a degradation of quality control (Fig. 2.11).

After a successful test run, an engine would be prepared for shipping by draining oil and coolant and replacing spark plugs with plastic plugs filled with desiccant. Corrosion preventative compound was sprayed inside the cylinders; all orifices such as exhaust ports, carburetor openings, oil connections, and fuel fittings would be plugged. The engine would then be wrapped in plastic or waterproof paper and placed in a wooden shipping crate or a steel can for shipment to the airframe manufacturer or to a maintenance depot.

Fig. 2.11 Two views inside a typical test cell used in the United States during World War II. The window is manufactured from bullet-proof glass to protect the operator in case of engine failure. The three levers in the center console operate the throttle, the propeller, and the mixture controls. The gauges indicate fuel flow and oil flow, both scavenge and pressure. All temperatures are monitored including coolant (if liquid cooled), cylinder head temperature (for radial engines), charge temperature, oil in, and oil out. Pressures monitored include main oil, scavenge oil, fuel, and the all-important manifold pressure. All engines were run about 10 h, much of it at high power, before a final teardown, inspection, and preparation for delivery. (Courtesy of Bill Gillette and Continental Motors.)

A thin line was often walked between reliability and catastrophic failure from the pressure of ever increasing power demands made by pilots and airframe manufacturers. The seesaw technology battle continued unabated by all combatants during this monumental conflict.

References

2.1   Heron, S. D., <u>The History of The Aircraft Piston Engine</u>, Ethyl Corp., Detroit, 1961.

2.2   Ricardo, Sir Harry R., <u>The Ricardo Story</u>, 2nd ed., Society of Automotive Engineers, Warrendale, Pa., 1992.

2.3   Ricardo, Sir Harry R., <u>The High Speed Internal Combustion Engine</u>, 5th ed., Blackie and Son, Ltd., London, 1968.

2.4   Banks, Air Commodore F. R. (Rod), "I Kept No Diary," *Airlife,* 1978.

2.5   Schlaifer, Robert, and S. D. Heron, <u>Development of Aircraft Engines and Development of Aviation Fuels</u>, Harvard University, Boston, 1950.

2.6   Johnson, Robert E., "Why the Boeing B-29 Bomber and Why the Wright R-3350 Engine?" *J. American Aviation Historical Society,* Fall 1988.

2.7   <u>Jane's All The World's Aircraft</u>, McGraw-Hill, New York, 1945/1946.

2.8   Yates, T. L., "Dynafocal Suspension for Radial Aircraft Engines," SAE Paper, Society of Automotive Engineers, Warrendale, Pa., 15 Dec. 1939.

2.9   Overhaul Instructions with Parts Catalog for Vibration Isolators for R-1830, R-2000, R-2800, and R-4360 Aircraft Engines, Pratt & Whitney, 6 Nov. 1945, East Hartford, Conn.

2.10 Don Hartog, J. P., <u>Mechanical Vibrations</u>, 4th ed., McGraw-Hill, New York, 1956.

2.11 Moss, Sanford A., <u>Superchargers for Aviation</u>, National Aeronautics Council, 1944.

2.12 Harvey-Bailey, Alec, "The Merlin in Perspective—The Combat Years," Rolls-Royce Heritage Trust Historical Series, No. 2, 1983, Derby, England.

2.13 <u>Fw 190A-8 Aircraft Handbook</u>, Part 0 General, D.(Luft)T.2190 A-8, effective July 1944, issued Sept. 1944.

2.14 Nelson, Wing Commander H., <u>Aero Engineering</u>, Vol. 1, Pt. 2, George Newnes Ltd., London.

2.15 Ryder, Earle A., "Recent Developments in the R-4360 Engine," SAE Paper No. 500197, Society of Automotive Engineers, Warrendale, Pa., June 1950.

SECTION I

Chapter 3

The British Contribution

Three British companies supplied engines for front-line RAF aircraft during World War II: Rolls-Royce, Bristol, and Napier. Although Armstrong Siddeley was still manufacturing the Tiger at the outbreak of war, this outdated design was soon dropped. Armstrong Siddeley spent most of the war manufacturing different models of the Cheetah. Fairey Aviation also had some interesting projects, such as the Prince, but none saw production. It has been suggested that Fairey Aviation fell from grace with the Ministry of Aircraft Production (MAP) after it installed a U.S. Curtiss D-12 engine in the Fairey Fox in the 1920s.

England, under attack and expecting invasion, built numerous "shadow" factories as a means of dispersing their production capability. The automobile industry figured heavily in this effort, with companies like Rover and Ford becoming major producers of combat engines designed by the aircraft engine companies. Ford built a major share of the Merlins, which powered the famous Lancaster bomber.

Charismatic leaders such as E. W. Hives of Rolls-Royce (Fig. 3.1) and Roy Fedden at Bristol left their impression on these companies. Despite his idiosyncracies, there was no doubting Fedden's drive, engineering ability, and foresight, particularly with the emerging sleeve valve technology. Hives was a hard-driving taskmaster and also well connected with the Ministry of Aviation Production. The personalities of these men were indelibly cast into their companies' cultures and products.

The intricacy of a Rolls-Royce product cannot fail to impress. As an example, the Merlin supercharger volute housing is held together by closely pitched 2BA bolts (No. 2, British Association), roughly equivalent to SAE No. 10-32. A Pratt & Whitney R-2800 supercharger, by comparison, uses widely spaced $5/16$-24 studs. Just as effective, but not as elegant.

Hives has been quoted as stating, upon the occasion of Rolls-Royce undertaking the manufacture of the early Whittle jet engine with its one major moving part, "Give it to us and we'll soon design the simplicity out of it!" Those words were to ring true as the gas turbine developed.

Fig. 3.1 E. W. Hives, Works Director of Rolls-Royce during World War II. Hives was a man of vision with the great leadership qualities that were critical during those trying times. (Courtesy of Rolls-Royce plc.)

British industry had been based upon the apprenticeship system and the mystique of the craftsmen. A 15- or 16-year-old schoolboy would be indentured as an apprentice for five years in his chosen craft. This produced a pool of well-educated, skilled craftsmen. As the production demands of World War II increased, less emphasis was placed on skilled craftsmen; they just were not available in the necessary numbers. Mass production methods, with less reliance on the individual skill of the craftsmen, became increasingly necessary to meet the demands of the front.

The outbreak of World War I highlighted Britain's lack of aviation technology, particularly with airframes and engines. In response, the Royal Aircraft Factory at Farnborough was established as a research and development center (Ref. 2.5). In addition, many World War I aircraft were manufactured by the Royal Aircraft Factory. Much of England's engine technology in these early formative years was developed at the RAF, later renamed the Royal Aircraft Establishment (RAE).

Superchargers, air-cooled cylinder design, materials, and manufacturing techniques were some of the more significant contributions to engine technology. As supercharger technology became increasingly important to engine performance in the 1930s, the RAE worked on developing automatic boost controls. These devices subsequently saved many pilots in combat by freeing them of engine-management responsibilities; likewise, it saved many engines from the destructive consequences of overboosting while the pilot's attentions were focused on more important things.

With a less parsimonious outlook than their U.S. counterpart, the Ministry of Aircraft Production gave adequate funding for essential developments during the 1930s when war clouds were ominously forming. Rolls-Royce worked miracles with the Merlin because of the amount of effort put into it.

Likewise with Fedden's sleeve valve projects, enormous expenditures of money and manpower were necessary, not only to resolve the design problems but also to make the engines easier to manufacture without the necessity of hand fitting every sleeve (Refs. 2.5, 3.1).

These efforts bore fruit just in time for the outbreak of World War II.

References

2.5 Schlaifer, Robert, and S. D. Heron, <u>Development of Aircraft Engines and Development of Aviation Fuels</u>, Harvard University, Boston, 1950.

3.1 Gunston, W. T., <u>By Jupiter</u>, R.Ae.S., London, 1978.

Chapter 4

Rolls-Royce

When Rolls-Royce is mentioned, the first image that comes to mind is expensive, beautifully crafted automobiles, and in fact that is how Rolls-Royce was established. The almost fanatical attention to detail and workmanship stood the company in good stead for the arduous requirements of building high-performance aircraft engines.

The company was formed in 1906 by Henry Royce and Charles Rolls for the purpose of manufacturing automobiles. In 1910, Rolls had the unfortunate distinction of being the first aviation fatality in England (Ref. 4.1). During a flying contest held in Bournemouth on the south coast of England, Rolls' Wright aircraft went into a spin from which he could not recover.

Royce was described by Sir Harry Ricardo as the most brilliant mechanical designer of the twentieth century (Ref. 2.3). Royce always had his hand in the design of his company's products and therefore always surrounded himself with his top designers and draftsmen (Fig. 4.1).

Fig. 4.1 Sir Henry Royce, described by Harry Ricardo as the most brilliant mechanical designer of the twentieth century, guided his company through difficult times and passed on a legacy of uncompromised quality. (Courtesy of Rolls-Royce plc.)

Rolls-Royce got its start on aircraft engines in 1914 (Ref. 2.5), at the request of the British Air Ministry. Initially reluctant when asked to manufacture French Renault air-cooled engines of dubious quality, Royce countered by offering to build better engines of his own design.

Establishing a trend that continued through most of the piston engine era, engines were named after birds of prey, with several exceptions.* The first engine was the Eagle, a water-cooled V-12 with Mercedes-style steel-fabricated separate cylinders (Fig. 4.2). This approach was a result of the limitations of the manufacturing methods and the need for uniform cooling. This design concept was continued for all the World War I engines. After the Eagle, Rolls-Royce developed a straight six, the Hawk, loosely based on the Silver Ghost car engine (Fig. 4.3). (It has been suggested that all the World War I aircraft engines owed something to the design philosophy of the Ghost.) The Falcon was the last engine designed in World War I to see service (Fig. 4.4). It was another V-12 similar to but smaller than the Eagle and was used primarily for the Bristol Fighter. Another V-12, the Condor, introduced the use of four valves per cylinder, a new concept for Rolls-Royce (Fig. 4.5) (Ref. 4.2). However, this engine did not get into service during World War I.

Fig. 4.2 Rolls-Royce Eagle, first of a long line of successful aircraft engines. Naturally aspirated, this particular example has four Claudel Hobson carburetors, two at the front, which can be seen in the photo, and two at the rear. (Courtesy of Rolls-Royce plc.)

Fig. 4.3 Rolls-Royce Hawk, which featured Silver Ghost automobile engine technology. Used mainly for powering airships. (Courtesy of Rolls-Royce plc.)

---

*Although Rolls-Royce named most of its liquid/water-cooled engines after birds of prey, the air-cooled sleeve valve projects were named after British mountain ranges and two-strokes were named after famous battles.

Fig. 4.4 Rolls-Royce Falcon. Conceptually similar to the Eagle. (Courtesy of Rolls-Royce plc.)

Fig. 4.5 Rolls-Royce Condor, first of their four-valves-per-cylinder engines. (Courtesy of Rolls-Royce plc.)

The improved breathing capability of this arrangement is now well understood; however, one of the primary purposes of it for early aircraft engines was not the upgraded breathing capability but better valve cooling inherent with comparatively smaller valves. During the early stages of aircraft engine development, high-temperature steel alloys or sodium-cooled valves had not been developed; consequently, other means were required to protect the exhaust valve from the harsh conditions they operated under. The primary path for the heat to escape from the exhaust valve is through the valve seat. Naturally, if the seat surface area can be increased, then the exhaust valve has a greater heat rejection path. The best way to achieve this goal is to direct the heat through four smaller valves rather than through two large valves.

After World War I and into the early 1920s, Rolls-Royce almost abandoned the aircraft engine business due to several factors: the glut of World War I surplus aircraft engines flooding the market, little demand for new military aircraft, and, most significantly, the booming demand for Rolls-Royce automobiles. However, there was just enough work overhauling Eagles and development work on the Condor to keep a foot in the aviation door. The civilian market took advantage of the Eagle's reliability and used it extensively in converted Vimy bombers and de Havilland commercial planes.

The aviation world was shocked when the United States won the 1923 Schneider Trophy Race with ease. What really woke people up, however, was the new technology incorporated in the engine of the race-winning Curtiss R3C; technology which, in improved form, would continue on through to World War II. The technological innovations were use of surface cooling, which replaced conventional radiators, and replacement of the laminated wood propeller with the far more efficient forged aluminum propeller. This engine challenged all aircraft engine design thinking in one fell swoop. The Curtiss D-12 engine, a water-cooled V-12, displacing 1145 in³ (18.8 L), featured monoblock, cast aluminum, cylinder construction with wet, steel forged liners and developed 400 hp. This was accomplished with a smaller displacement compared with existing 400-hp engines, such as the 1650-in³ (27-L) Liberty. This engine then set the standard for all subsequent water-cooled and later liquid-cooled V-12s.* The Fairey Aviation Company was so enamored with the D-12 that Sir Richard Fairey made a trip to the United States to purchase one. Returning in February 1924 aboard the luxury ocean liner *Leviathan,* with his prized D-12 in his cabin as luggage (Ref. 4.3), Sir Richard had planned on manufacturing D-12s under license. Less than a year later the Fairey Fox, a single-engine bomber, was flying powered by the D-12. It easily outperformed all other RAF aircraft. The British Air Ministry, their pride hurt by the fact that an RAF aircraft was powered by an American engine, arranged to have two D-12s delivered to Derby, the home base for Rolls-Royce. Surprisingly, Napier was the first choice of the Air Ministry, but that company rather shortsightedly turned down the offer. Rolls-Royce reverse-engineered the D-12, incorporating improvements such as open-end cylinder liners replacing the D-12's inferior closed-end design, resulting in the F type, or Kestrel as it was later known. The Kestrel (with a displacement of 1296 in³ [21.25 L] from 5-in bores and 5.5-in stroke) established Rolls-Royce's liquid-cooled V-12 poppet valve design philosophy that lasted to the end of the piston engine era.

Early engines featured natural aspiration using two downdraft carburetors (Fig. 4.6); later Kestrels featured supercharging (Fig. 4.7), a first for a Rolls-Royce production engine. Early superchargers suffered from poor efficiency; this was remedied much later by the Royal Aircraft Establishment, based in Farnborough. The RAE engineers had performed extensive research work on supercharger

Fig. 4.6 Rolls-Royce Kestrel. This example is naturally aspirated. The two oval-shaped objects above the valve covers are the air intakes for the carburetors. Later models were supercharged. (Courtesy of Rolls-Royce plc.)

---

*The terms liquid-cooled and water-cooled are often confused. Water-cooled means the cooling medium is plain water. Liquid-cooled means the cooling medium is a mixture of water and a high-boiling-point liquid such as ethylene glycol.

Fig. 4.7 Supercharged Kestrel. This engine gave Rolls-Royce valuable experience in improving the efficiency of superchargers. (Courtesy of Rolls-Royce plc.)

development starting during World War I. In an effort to improve on the 64% efficiency of the early Kestrel superchargers, J. E. Ellor, the resident supercharger expert of the RAE, worked on the problem. The result was a supercharger with a 70% efficiency and a resultant improvement in power and fuel economy. Ellor subsequently became a Rolls-Royce employee. He later made substantial contributions to the company's supercharger and engine developments.

Supercharger development was to be a cornerstone of Rolls-Royce engine development during the ensuing years, particularly as fuel development also progressed at a fast pace allowing ever increasing manifold pressures and therefore demanding even more from the supercharger.

The 1929 Schneider Trophy Race was another significant event for Rolls-Royce aircraft engine development. England had won the 1927 event (it was now held every 2 years) with a Napier Lion powered Supermarine S5 designed by the legendary R. J. Mitchell of subsequent Spitfire fame. As the Lion was an engine of World War I vintage, the Air Ministry felt its racing days were over, although as an aside it is interesting to note that the world land-speed record was broken in September 1947 by John Cobb driving the Napier Railton Special. This car was powered by two surplus Napier Lion Schneider Trophy engines from the 1929 effort! The Railton Special was also the first car to exceed 400 mph, and its two-way average was 394 mph.

The Air Ministry "leaned" on Rolls-Royce to produce an engine for the 1929 Schneider Trophy race. Initially, Henry Royce was reluctant to participate in a racing event, fearing bad publicity in case of failure. However, when the decision was made to develop an engine, Rolls-Royce pursued the objective with typical thoroughness, vigor, attention to detail, and just plain dogged determination to overcome all adversities.

Rather than develop a totally new engine, it was decided, owing to the shortage of development time, to modify an existing engine. Complying with the hot-rodders premise, "there ain't no replacement for displacement," Rolls-Royce based the Schneider Trophy engine, called the R (one of the few times Rolls-Royce deviated from birds of prey names), on the Buzzard (Fig. 4.8). This engine, which

Fig. 4.8 Rolls-Royce Buzzard. Forerunner of the famous R engine. The later Griffon shared the same bore and stroke with the Buzzard. (Courtesy of Rolls-Royce plc.)

was in production for large flying boats, had all the design features of the Kestrel but with almost twice the displacement, at 2239 in³ (36.7 L), derived from twelve cylinders of 6.0-in bores and 6.6-in stroke. Perhaps the greatest contribution the R engine made was gearing up Rolls-Royce into a rapid development mode with a very real deadline to meet (Fig. 4.9). This rapid development and troubleshooting experience was to be of inestimable value during World War II and became one of the hallmarks of Rolls-Royce.

Development of the R engine took less than one year and was installed in the winning Supermarine S6, again designed by R. J. Mitchell (Fig. 4.10). Rated at 1900 hp at 2900 rpm, this engine created the engineering equivalent of culture shock with its unheard of manifold pressure of 55 in Hg. The supercharger that developed this stratospheric, for those times, manifold pressure was a departure from the usual blower design in that it featured a two-sided impeller with dual intakes. This was done in an effort to keep the diameter to a minimum and increase the mass airflow through the super-

Fig. 4.9 Rolls-Royce R engine for the 1929 Supermarine S6 Schneider Trophy Racer. (Courtesy of Rolls-Royce plc.)

Fig. 4.10 Head-on view of the Supermarine S6. The clean lines and closely cowled Rolls-Royce R engine are evident in this shot. (Courtesy of Rolls-Royce plc.)

charger. The diameter of the S6 fuselage was dictated by the diameter of the supercharger housing. Interestingly, one of the spin-offs from the two-sided impeller design was the compressor of the early Whittle and Rolls-Royce gas turbines, which also featured a two-sided centrifugal impeller as a way to double the volume of air flowing through the engine.

As expected, the 1929 race was won with relative ease despite a challenge from the Italian team. Average race speed was 328 mph, and later a successful attempt was made on the world air-speed record, raising it to 357.7 mph.

Another contributing factor to the success of the 1929 race effort, which later had a profound influence on World War II engines, was the importance of using a detonation-resistant fuel. The race fuel was a concoction formulated by Rodwell Banks, later Air Commodore Rodwell Banks, and consisted of 78% benzole and 22% Romanian petrol plus 2 cm³ per gallon of tetraethyl lead, which had recently been developed in the United States by Thomas Midgley and the Ethyl Corporation (Ref. 2.4). Another contributing factor was the use of ram air for the supercharger intake. This deceptively simple idea was patented by Rolls-Royce in 1927, and in the Schneider trophy S6 ram air induction contributed as much as 10% additional horsepower. All front-line aircraft engines used in World War II used some form of ram air induction to great effect.

The final Schneider Trophy Race, held in 1931, was again won by the British using an updated R engine in a revised version of the Supermarine S6, the S6B. A new aircraft and engine were not developed because of the economic climate. By this time a worldwide, devastating economic depression had set in. For some time it appeared that Britain would not compete due to the tight money situation. As it turned out, Lady Houston came to the rescue by guaranteeing a sum of 100,000 pounds. It has never been revealed how much of this money was actually used in the 1931 Schneider Trophy effort.

Again, Rolls-Royce was under the gun to produce an engine that would maintain the required 2300 hp for 1 h. Although it was not realized or appreciated at the time, Rolls-Royce was in its element, that is, a situation where it had to meet an extremely aggressive development schedule as well as pioneer much new ground. As in the 1929 effort, many problems surfaced during testing of the R engine, including failed connecting rods and crankshafts. Correcting the connecting rod problem required the abandonment of the preferred blade-and-fork design for the simpler bearing design and increased loading surface available from using a master rod and articulated rod on each crankshaft throw. Other problems that challenged the design team included an incredibly high oil consumption, which at one time amounted to a rate of 112 gal/h. This led to an improved piston ring design incorporating tighter oil control in order to control blow-by, the culprit for the 112-gal/h oil consumption. Exhaust valves, which had proven adequate in 1929, were simply not up to the task for the power requirements of 1931. As a result, sodium-cooled valves, which had been developed by an ex-Royal Aircraft Factory, later the Royal Aircraft Establishment, employee, Sam Heron, were used. Sam Heron, who made many significant contributions to aircraft engine design and fuel development, had emigrated to the United States in the 1920s but continued to consult with Rolls-Royce.

Problems continued right up to the last minute prior to the race. However, despite many setbacks, such as a failed crankshaft at 58 min into a 1-hour (Ref. 2.4) test run one month prior to the race, the engine was ready by race day. Installing the engine in the S6B airframe introduced a whole new set of problems insofar as running an engine in a test house on a dynamometer is a different proposition from running the same engine installed in an aircraft. Coolant leaks, oil leaks, and other installation problems plagued the aircraft, but they were all overcome through perseverance and hard work.

Race day turned out to be almost an anticlimax due to the absence of the much respected team from Italy, the only other nation competing by this time. As it turned out, the Italians had a potentially far more competitive aircraft than the S6B (Fig. 4.11), the Macchi Castoldi MC.72, an aircraft somewhat similar to the S6B and powered by a Fiat AS.6, which was essentially two AS.5 V-12s in tandem. This V-24 had a number of novel features including one of the first applications of contra-rotating propellers* (Fig. 4.12). By this stage of Schneider Trophy development, aircraft had become increasingly difficult to handle for a number of reasons such as high wing loading and particularly the effects of torque reaction. Several interim solutions for the torque reaction problem had been introduced, for example, making the left float larger than the right and loading the right float with additional fuel, but these fixes offered only partial relief.

---

*"Contra-rotating" means two shafts or two propellers that rotate in opposite directions on the SAME axis. For example, the propeller drive for a Rolls-Royce Griffon 85 is contra-rotating. "Counter-rotating" means two shafts or two propellers that rotate in opposite directions on DIFFERENT axes. For example, the propellers on a Lockheed P-38 are counter-rotating. To put things in perspective, the two output shafts of the Allison V-3420-23 are counter-rotating, but they drive a contra-rotating propeller.

Fig. 4.11 Supermarine S6B being prepared for the 1931 Schneider Trophy Race. The pickup truck in the foreground is a modified Rolls-Royce Phantom II. Note the R engine in the bed of the truck covered with a tarp. The Phantom II transported the engines from Derby to Calshot. With a life of less than 5 h, engine changes were commonplace. (Courtesy of Rolls-Royce plc.)

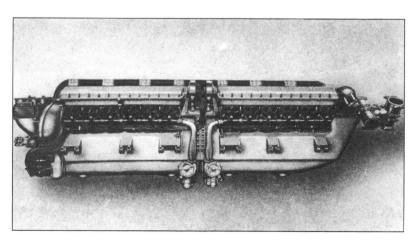

Fig. 4.12 Machii MC.72 Schneider Trophy racer. It could have given the British a run for the money in the 1931 race if the ram air induction system had been properly developed. Lower photograph shows the Fiat AS.6 24-cylinder engine used to power this aircraft to its subsequent, post-Schneider Trophy, world air-speed records. (Courtesy of the National Air and Space Museum, Smithsonian Institution, Photo No. 1B-17665.)

The absence of the Italian team was the result of several insurmountable problems, primarily severe misfiring and backfires through the carburetor at high speed due to the ram air induction utilized by the MC.72. It was later found that as the aircraft gained speed, the mixture leaned out due to the additional mass airflow through the carburetor. The ensuing severe backfires blew off pieces of the cowling. As Rolls-Royce owned the original patent, its engineers were very aware of the pitfalls of a ramming intake and consequently performed many hours of testing by simulating the aircraft air speed in the engine test house. In the case of the R engine, a Kestrel was used to drive a blower to simulate a 400 mph airflow through the ram air trunking, an essential piece of work. Italy on the other hand neglected this vital piece of testing, with the result that several aircraft and pilots were lost during testing. This forced the team to withdraw from the 1931 race.

By race day the only aircraft competing was a single S6B flown by Flight Lieutenant John Boothman. It would have been quite legitimate for Boothman to cruise around the course; however, he ran the S6B as hard as it would go and in fact had to back off on the power partway through the race due to high water and oil temperatures. He averaged 340 mph. England now held the Schneider Trophy permanently, with this, its third consecutive victory.

Again, one of the valuable lessons demonstrated in the 1931 Schneider race was the value of using a high-performance fuel, which this time consisted of 70% benzole, 20% Californian petrol and 10% methanol plus tetraethyl lead (Ref. 2.4). Rod Banks was again responsible for fuel development.

As in the 1929 race, an attempt was made on the world air-speed record after the successful completion of the race. This was accomplished with a speed of 379 mph. Rolls-Royce, not satisfied with 379 mph, wanted to be the manufacturer of the first engine to exceed 400 mph. The 1931 R engine was further boosted to 70 in Hg (20 psig boost) manifold pressure running a fuel consisting of 60% methanol, 30% benzole, and 10% acetone plus lead. At this stage, the R was stressed to its limit, even to the point of stretching the cylinder hold-down bolts. The "sprint" engine, as it was known, powered the S6B to another world air-speed record of 407.5 mph, thus breaking the 400-mph barrier. This was not the end of the line for the R, as it went on to power two world land-speed record cars, Malcolm Campbell's *Bluebird* and George Eyston's *Thunderbolt*.

Bluebird (Fig. 4.13) had the R mounted in the front of the car driving the rear wheels with gearing of 100 mph per 1000 rpm, thus the car was theoretically capable of 340 mph. This never occurred due to a number of factors that frustrated Campbell for several years. The primary problem was traction; the car was simply incapable of delivering the awesome power of the R to the ground. Wheel spin was the Achilles heel of this car despite many attempts to overcome it. When the car was run initially on Daytona Beach, the hard-packed sand just created a massive amount of wheel spin plus some hair-raising slides. At this point Campbell was tipped off that a stretch of flat smooth salt flats in Bonneville, Utah, would be far more suitable, and so it was. Campbell became the first to exceed 300 mph in a car in 1935 and the first person to use the Bonneville salt flats for this activity.

George Eyston's car, *Thunderbolt*, was more sophisticated and advanced than Campbell's *Bluebird*. This three-axle, eight-wheel car was powered by two R engines and featured four-wheel drive and air brakes actuated by hydraulic rams at the rear. Suffering the same travails as Campbell with wheel

Fig. 4.13 Sir Malcolm Campbell with Bluebird *(powered by the Rolls-Royce R engine), the world's first car to exceed 300 mph. This versatile engine held all three absolute world speed records. Photo taken in Daytona Beach, Florida, 1935. (Courtesy of Robin Richardson, Speed Record Club.)*

spin despite the four-wheel drive, Eyston upped the world land-speed record to 357 mph in 1938, but the true potential of this magnificent car was hardly realized. Unfortunately this imposing car was destroyed in a fire in New Zealand during World War II.

Sir Henry Segrave's *Miss England* boat, powered by two R engines, established a new world water-speed record in 1930 at 98.76 mph. *Miss England* went on to break the record several more times, piloted by Kaye Don. The last hurrah for the R was Campbell's boat, again named *Bluebird,* powered by one R. This hydrodynamically advanced design broke the water-speed record on several occasions, the final one at 142 mph in 1939, just prior to the outbreak of World War II.

One of the unique aspects of all these record-breaking efforts was the fact that the R was the only engine ever to power the world's fastest boat, car, and airplane (Table 4.1). It is very doubtful that all three absolute speed records will ever again be held by the same power plant, an astonishing achievement. Even more interesting is the fact Campbell came close to setting another record, for he used the S6B record-breaking engine in his car. He used the same R in his Bluebird boat until it was damaged by overheating on the final run before breaking the water-speed record; otherwise he would have used the same engine for all three records.

The Schneider Trophy experience thus established Rolls-Royce as a premier builder of high-performance aircraft engines. The influences from the R were profound. The British ran their aircraft engines at typically higher manifold pressures and consequently extracted higher specific powers from their front-line World War II aircraft engines than any of the other combatant nations. British aircraft engines typically had displacements of only 70% of the displacements of their counterpart engines from all other combatants (Ref. 2.3). This design philosophy was not without its drawbacks, however. Due to the higher stresses and loads, a weight penalty resulted from the requirement for stronger internal components. Maintenance difficulties and a shorter time between overhauls also resulted, though with typical Rolls-Royce thoroughness, each of these criticisms was satisfactorily resolved.

TABLE 4.1—SUMMARY OF R-POWERED WORLD RECORDS

WATER SPEED RECORDS

Year	Driver	Boat	mph
1930	Sir Henry Segrave	*Miss England II*	98.76
1931	Kaye Don	*Miss England II*	103.49
1931	Kaye Don	*Miss England II*	110.22
1932	Kaye Don	*Miss England III*	119.81
1937	Malcolm Campbell	*Bluebird*	129.50
1938	Malcolm Campbell	*Bluebird*	130.86
1939	Malcolm Campbell	*Bluebird II*	141.74

LAND SPEED RECORDS

Year	Driver	Car	mph
1933	Malcolm Campbell	*Bluebird*	272.108
1935	Malcolm Campbell	*Bluebird*	276.82
1935	Malcolm Campbell	*Bluebird*	301.1
1937	George Eyston	*Thunderbolt*	311.42
1938	George Eyston	*Thunderbolt*	345.49
1938	George Eyston	*Thunderbolt*	357.5

AIR SPEED RECORDS

Year	Pilot	Aircraft	mph
1929	Sqn. Ldr. A. H. Orlebar	Supermarine S6	357.7
1931	Flt. Lt. G. H. Stainforth	Supermarine S6B	379.05
1931	Flt. Lt. G. H. Stainforth	Supermarine S6B	407.5

Source: Ref. 4.4.

Merlin

By the early 1930s Sir Henry Royce's (he was knighted in 1931) health, never good, deteriorated, and in 1933 he died. Prior to his death he laid out the most significant aircraft piston engine in history. It is doubtful if even Royce had any perception how profound his immortal Merlin would be.

As good an engine as the Kestrel was, by the early 1930s, it was starting to reach the end of its potential, so at Royce's instigation a new engine was designed as a replacement. It was initially referred to as the PV-12, for Private Venture twelve-cylinder, because government funding had not been assured during the austere years of the depression. When government funding came through, the PV-12 became known as the Merlin, named after a small hawklike bird of prey. By this stage, many years of intense development were required not only to get a reasonable degree of reliability, but also to obtain the best specifics. The days of the World War I Eagle, when the engine ran remarkably well and trouble-free straight off the drawing board, were long gone. This was due to the higher demands and specific powers now being extracted from aircraft engines. In the case of the Merlin, years of difficult development followed, and even at the start of World War II many problems still required resolution.

Conceptually, the Merlin was similar to the Kestrel configuration, being a 60°, liquid-cooled mono-block V-12; it displaced 1649 in³ (27 L) derived from a 5.4-in bore and 6.0-in stroke. It had originally been proposed by Rolls-Royce as an inverted V-12, but this configuration was rejected by the airframe manufacturers (Ref. 2.5). Each cylinder bank featured a single-shaft-driven, overhead camshaft actuating four valves per cylinder, with sodium-cooled exhausts, using the lessons learned from the R. Single-stage, single-speed supercharging was employed, using lessons learned from the Kestrel. The propeller reduction gearing deviated from previous practice in that instead of straight-cut spur gears, double helical gears were used; however, due to early failures more conventional straight-cut spur gears soon replaced them.

Early engines were rated at 790 hp at 3000 rpm during the type tests in July 1934. Evaporative steam cooling was initially employed in early engines but this later gave way to glycol cooling using pure glycol. All production engines, however, used the conventional mix of water and ethylene glycol in conjunction with a radiator, rather than evaporative steam cooling.

The novel crankcase design featured integral cylinder banks with removable cylinder heads. This was done in an effort to increase the beam strength of the engine structure. The size and complexity of this casting led to difficulties such as porosity. This led to a Kestrel-type detachable cylinder bank/crankcase arrangement with the cylinder head integral with the cylinder bank. At the same time the combustion chamber design was revised from the Kestrel cylindrical style to the so-called "ramp head," which promised shortened flame travel and increased turbulence. It was based on the Phantom II car engine combustion chamber, which had worked admirably in the Phantom II, featuring two valves per cylinder. In the case of the Merlin, things did not work out so well due in part to the four-valve arrangement and the far higher specific power extracted from the Merlin (Fig. 4.14). The significant problems that surfaced with this design, which was essentially a pent-roof chamber tilted over to one side, were with exhaust valve burning from localized detonation and exhaust port erosion (Fig. 4-15). However, there were even more severe problems with coolant leakage at the cylinder liner/cylinder head joint, evidenced by white smoke issuing from the exhaust stack of the leaking head joint.

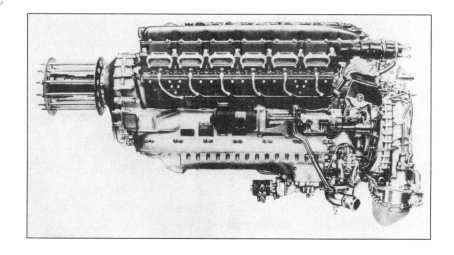

Fig. 4.14 Early ramp head for a Rolls-Royce Merlin. (Courtesy of Rolls-Royce plc.)

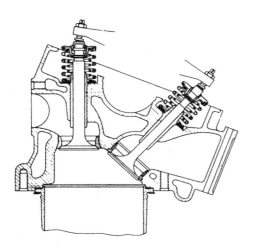

Fig. 4.15 Cross section through the ramp head for a Rolls-Royce Merlin I. Although successful in single-cylinder test engines, severe problems were experienced with the multicylinder design. Cam follower wear was excessive, and more seriously, detonation caused severe erosion of the exhaust port. Subsequent Merlins reverted to the Kestrel-style combustion chamber. Compare to Fig. 4.29. (Courtesy of Rolls-Royce plc.)

Due to the extensive redesign of the combustion chamber, crankcase, and reduction gearing, the engine received the designation Merlin B, rated at 950 hp. The Merlin B retained the ramp head as did subsequent engines through the Merlin F, which was the first production Merlin (also known as the Merlin Mk. I). Although the PV-12 was built in 1933, it did not fly until 1935, and that honor fell to a Hawker Hart single-engine biplane light bomber, one of Sydney Camm's earlier successes, modified to accommodate the bigger PV-12 in place of its standard R-R Kestrel. Much of the development flying was accomplished with a Hawker Horsely, a similar fabric-covered biplane. A second Horsely was used by the RAE for further development flying.

At this stage, in the mid to late 1930s, it seemed as though the Merlin would never be a successful engine because of all the development problems. In fact, an attempt in 1935 to pass a 50-h civilian type test by the Merlin C, rated at 1045 hp, failed due mainly to the problems associated with the ramp head. The Merlin E finally managed to pass the 50-h civilian type test in December 1935 but failed the more stringent 100-h military type test in March 1936. By this time Rolls-Royce was under pressure from the airframe manufacturers for Merlins. Even by the mid 1930s war clouds were ominously appearing, and the British government was relying on the Merlin for fighters. As a result, the type testing requirements were relaxed to allow replacement of exhaust valves during the 100-h test. Even with a relaxation of the requirements difficulties persisted, and it was not until November 1936 that the relaxed type test was passed. This probably represented the nadir of Merlin development, although it would be another four long years before the worst of the problems were overcome. By now it was apparent the ramp head had to go, and in its place a Kestrel-style cylindrical combustion chamber was incorporated. This alleviated the detonation and exhaust port erosion problems, although leakage at the liner/head joint persisted. This was not resolved until a detachable cylinder head was developed and, as we will see later, Packard manufactured the detachable cylinder head before Rolls-Royce, primarily due to Rolls-Royce's pressing production commitments.

By early 1940, Merlin development had reached the Merlin Mk. III level alongside the two-speed Merlin Mk. X (Fig. 4.16). It still retained the one-piece cylinder bank and cylinder head and was rated at 1030 hp at 16,250 ft burning 87-octane fuel. From 1937 to 1939, some limited development work had been done using 100-octane fuel, but at the time it was felt to be only of academic value.

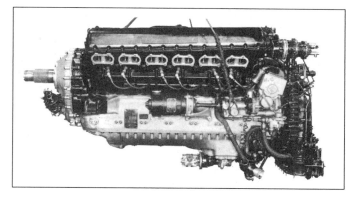

Fig. 4.16 Rolls-Royce Merlin III. Many of the Hawker Hurricanes and Supermarine Spitfires flown in the Battle of Britain were powered by this engine. Top photograph shows right (starboard) side of engine; bottom photograph shows left (port) side. (Courtesy of Rolls-Royce plc.)

The British incorrectly believed that large-scale production of 100-octane fuel was a long way in the future. Fortunately, this turned out not to be the case as 100-octane fuel was being refined in the United States. A shipment of this fuel aboard the Esso tanker *Beaconhill* arrived in the nick of time for the Battle of Britain, with a profound effect (Ref. 2.4). The main adversary of the RAF Supermarine Spitfire and Hawker Hurricane was the Messerschmitt Bf 109E, which possessed a very similar performance capability to the Spitfire I/II used in the Battle. With the introduction of 100-octane fuel, the manifold pressure of the Merlin III was increased from 42.6 to 48.2 in Hg. This 5.6-inch increase in manifold pressure improved power from 1030 to 1160 hp. Later, in mid 1940 a further increase in manifold pressure to 54.3 in Hg was authorized, yielding a power of 1310 hp at 3000 rpm. These power increases proved vital in the victory of the Battle of Britain; even so it was an incredibly close call for England. By now the worst of the development problems had been overcome, and it was a question of building and repairing them fast enough. To this end, some elaborate schemes were devised to salvage what would normally be considered damaged-beyond-repair engines. Bullet holes, for example, were patched and repaired (Ref. 4.5), cracked crankcases damaged from gear-up landings had steel braces attached in order to re-establish the structural integrity of this highly stressed component (Ref. 2.12), and other major components were salvaged whenever possible to keep the supply of Merlins meeting the ever growing demand from the airframe manufacturers and repair depots. Even parts deemed not airworthy were used in the manufacture of the Meteor engine for the Cromwell tank. Later, Rolls-Royce exchanged their Meteor tank engine business with the Rover car company for their gas turbine development under the leadership of Frank (later Sir Frank) Whittle.

Stanley (later Sir Stanley) Hooker heard about the work of Whittle and realized immediately the potential of this new form of aircraft power plant. He persuaded Hives to pay a visit to Whittle and his work. Under Hooker's persuasion, he was sold on the concept. Hives arranged a meeting with his counterpart at Rover and consummated a deal with a handshake; the result of the deal was Rover would get the tank engine business in exchange for the gas turbine contract. Consequently in 1943, Rolls-Royce was among the first aircraft engine manufacturers to be involved in gas turbine development and manufacture.

Stanley Hooker, a brilliant Oxford graduate, had joined Rolls-Royce in 1938. Although trained as a mathematician, he had done postgraduate work on fluid dynamics. Hooker soon realized that all the calculations being used for determining supercharger parameters were incorrect. Previous supercharger calculations were derived by the Royal Aircraft Establishment and were based on empirical formulas that Hooker found to be either suspect or incorrect (Ref. 4.6). The first result of these discoveries was a redesign of the supercharger to be used in the Merlin XX powering the Hurricanes and in the Merlin 45 intended for the Spitfire (Fig. 4.17). This engine featured a single-stage, two-speed supercharger. Two-speed supercharging had been experimented with in the 1930s using a Kestrel, but had not been developed. Two-stage step-up spur gearing was employed with multiplate clutches used in the second-stage gear train. Due to the higher loadings required for the high blower ratio, or full supercharge (FS) as Rolls-Royce referred to it, two gear trains were required. One set of gears was used for low blower ratio, or moderate supercharge (MS) (Fig. 4.18). Gear shifting was effected by cams that would disengage one set of clutches and at the same time engage the other set. Scavenge oil, pumped through a direction control valve, acted as a servo to actuate the cams. Henri Farman, a Frenchman, patented this supercharger drive along with many other aviation-related drives, such as the Farman planetary gears used extensively by Bristol and Pratt & Whitney for propeller reduction gearing.

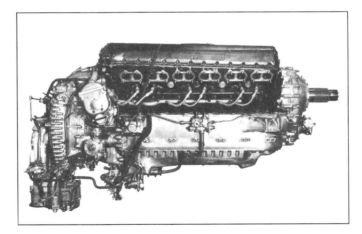

Fig. 4.17 Rolls-Royce Merlin XX. This was the first two-speed engine to incorporate Hooker's supercharger design. This was also the first Merlin Packard built under license. Designated V-1650-1, it differed from the Rolls-Royce version by incorporating a Bendix injection carburetor, a Cuno self-cleaning oil filter, and an SAE No. 50 spline for the propeller shaft for U.S. aircraft. All other features were the same as the Merlin XX. Two-stage Packard-built Merlins deviated from the Rolls-Royce blower drive by using an epicyclic system. (Courtesy of Rolls-Royce plc.)

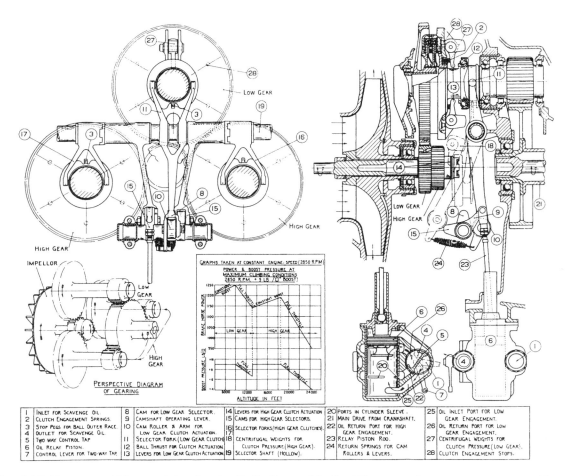

1	INLET FOR SCAVENGE OIL.	8	CAM FOR LOW GEAR SELECTOR.	14	LEVERS FOR HIGH GEAR CLUTCH ACTUATION	20	PORTS IN CYLINDER SLEEVE.	25	OIL INLET PORT FOR LOW
2	CLUTCH ENGAGEMENT SPRINGS.	9	CAMSHAFT OPERATING LEVER.	15	CAMS FOR HIGH GEAR SELECTORS.	21	MAIN DRIVE FROM CRANKSHAFT.	GEAR ENGAGEMENT.
3	STOP PEGS FOR BALL OUTER RACE.	10	CAM ROLLER & ARM FOR	16	SELECTOR FORKS (HIGH GEAR CLUTCHES).	22	OIL RETURN PORT FOR HIGH	26	OIL RETURN PORT FOR LOW
4	OUTLET FOR SCAVENGE OIL.	LOW GEAR CLUTCH ACTUATION.	17		GEAR ENGAGEMENT.	GEAR ENGAGEMENT.
5	TWO WAY CONTROL TAP	11	SELECTOR FORK (LOW GEAR CLUTCH)	18	CENTRIFUGAL WEIGHTS FOR	23	RELAY PISTON ROD.	27	CENTRIFUGAL WEIGHTS FOR
6	OIL RELAY PISTON.	12	BALL THRUST FOR CLUTCH ACTUATION.	CLUTCH PRESSURE (HIGH GEAR).	24	RETURN SPRINGS FOR CAM	CLUTCH PRESSURE (LOW GEAR).
7	CONTROL LEVER FOR TWO-WAY TAP.	13	LEVERS FOR LOW GEAR CLUTCH ACTUATION	19	SELECTOR SHAFT (HOLLOW).	ROLLERS & LEVERS.	28	CLUTCH ENGAGEMENT STOPS.

Fig. 4.18 Two-speed blower drive for the Rolls-Royce Merlin. The operating cam was actuated by engine scavenge oil. Packard retained this system of blower drive for the V-1650-1; however, the -3 and later engines used a Wright-designed epicyclic gear drive that was totally different. ("Merlin XX Aero Engine," Air Publication 1590G, British Crown Copyright/Ministry of Defence. Reproduced with the permission of the Controller of Her Britannic Majesty's Stationery Office. Author's collection.)

During experimentation, Hooker found the intake elbow for the Merlin II to be very restrictive. In an effort to make the engine as short and compact as possible, the intake, which featured updraft carburetion, made a tight 90° turn into the eye of the supercharger. Hooker redesigned this intake elbow with a smoother 90° transition without a significant increase in the length of the engine. This was accomplished by simply turning the carburetor 180° on its axis.

The supercharger impeller, diffuser, and volute housing also benefited from Hooker's scrutiny. The result was a dramatic improvement in power at all altitudes, improving to 1480 hp at 6000 ft in moderate supercharge (low blower ratio) and 1480 hp at 12,250 ft in full supercharge (high blower ratio). It was these features that turned the Merlin III into the Merlin 45. Requirements for a low-altitude Spitfire V resulted in a modified Merlin 45. Three-quarters of an inch was machined off the overall diameter of the supercharger impeller. In addition to engine modifications, the airframe was also modified by simply removing the wing tips. Because these modified aircraft were somewhat "war weary" and the modified Merlins were not new production engines, these modified Spitfire Vs were given the nickname "clipped, cropped, and clapped"!

The requirement for a high-altitude engine to be installed in a Vickers Wellington twin-engine bomber resulted in the definitive Merlin, the two-stage, two-speed, intercooled, and aftercooled 60 series. This high-altitude version of the Wellington was intended to bomb from 40,000 ft. As it turned out the aircraft was not put into production, but the 60-series Merlin and its variants powered many significant aircraft (Figs. 4.19, 4.20).

The first appearance of the German Focke-Wulf 190 came as a rude shock for the British in 1941. This very advanced fighter easily outperformed the Merlin 45 powered Spitfire Mk. V, the best of the British aircraft at the time. One of the answers to this menace lay in the 60-series Merlin. When installed in the Spitfire, the tables reversed in favor of the two-stage powered Spitfire. Due to the additional length of this engine to accommodate the second supercharge stage compared with a single-stage engine, an increase in length of 8 in forward of the firewall was required for the first of the two-stage Spitfires, the Mk. IX.

It had been realized for some time that as manifold pressures were increased, charge heating due to the compression of the fuel/air mixture became a limiting factor to the potential power output of an engine. Rolls-Royce had earlier experimented with an air-cooled aftercooler; however, the results were mixed, owing to the size and weight of the aftercooler. Hooker revisited the problem and, using research material from the RAE, designed a very compact liquid-cooled aftercooler consisting of a fin-and-tube radiator matrix mounted on the discharge side of the second stage of the blower. The intercooler simply consisted of a cooling jacket surrounding the space between the first and second supercharger stages. This required an additional cooling system, which was incorporated into the engine and consisted of a centrifugal circulating pump driven from the generator drive mounted on the left side of the engine. Coolant, the same as engine coolant (30% ethylene glycol and 70% water), was discharged from the pump and was circulated through the intercooler. From there, the coolant flowed into the radiator matrix of the aftercooler removing intake charge heat, through a coolant radiator, and finally returned to the suction side of the pump. The requirement of an addi-

Fig. 4.19 Rolls-Royce Merlin 60 series. First of the two-stage, intercooled, and aftercooled engines. Aftercooler is the ribbed, rectangular component above the wheelcase. (Courtesy of Rolls-Royce plc.)

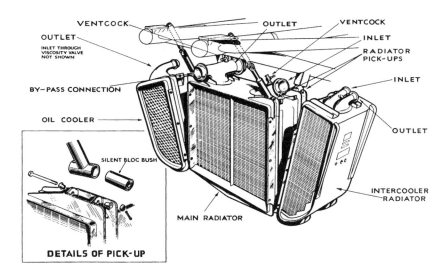

Fig. 4.20 Cooling system for the high-altitude Vickers Wellington fitted with a 60-series Rolls-Royce Merlin. Although developed for the Wellington, the 60-series Merlin was hastily installed into the Spitfire in order to combat the formidable Fw 190A, thus creating the immortal Spitfire Mk. VIII. (Courtesy of Rolls-Royce plc.)

tional coolant radiator now meant the Spitfire lost its asymmetric look, now featuring equal size radiators under both wings; each wing had a main coolant radiator with either the oil cooler or the intercooler/aftercooler radiator alongside. The intercooling/aftercooling system was designed to remove 50% of the supercharger heat of compression, dropping potential charge temperatures of 240°C to a more manageable 120°C.

In an effort to reduce design time and get the engine into production as rapidly as possible, considerable design and testing time was saved by the simple expedient of using the supercharger impeller from the abandoned X-24 cylinder Vulture engine for the first stage and a Griffon II impeller for the second stage. It turned out that this combination worked admirably during flow testing! Consequently, the production supercharger impellers bore a strong resemblance to their Griffon and Vulture counterparts.

The effects of this now very sophisticated two-speed, two-stage, intercooled, and aftercooled supercharger was dramatic: power improved to 1560 hp at 12,250 ft in moderate supercharge (low blower ratio) and 1390 hp at 23,500 ft in full supercharge (high blower ratio). Up to this phase of development the Merlin could withstand all the loads imposed on it; however with the introduction of the two-stage engines, failures started to occur, most significantly in the main bearings. The cure to this potentially alarming problem was a beautifully simple and effective one.

In a conventional in-line engine lubrication system, the oil is conveyed to the main bearings through galleries, which are holes drilled in the crankcase joining up with the main bearings. A groove machined in the main bearing transfers the oil to the connecting-rod journals through holes drilled in the crankshaft. The later 100-series, two-stage Merlins deviated from this practice by using what was known as "end-to-end" lubrication. Instead of each main bearing being fed with pressurized oil from a gallery, the oil was fed into the crankshaft from both ends. This arrangement offered several advantages. First, the requirement for an oil distribution groove in the main bearing was eliminated. Second, centrifugal force aided the oil pressure instead of the oil pump having to fight centrifugal force when pumping the oil into the main bearing.

At the same time end-to-end lubrication was introduced, another design "tweak" was introduced. The hollow crankshaft throws acted as ideal sludge traps due to the high centrifugal forces that tended to trap the sludge as it was pumped through the bearings. To avoid this condition, small pipes were press fitted into the journals; this allowed the sludge to be centrifuged to the inside walls of the journals but kept it away from the bearings.

By this stage of development, the Merlin was going from strength to strength, burning 115/150 grade fuel, horsepowers were reaching over 2200 bhp, almost three times the original design goal. The Merlin exemplified the Rolls-Royce heritage of dogged determination in the face of adversity, as well as clever engineering.

Manufacturing

Initially, all Merlins were manufactured by Rolls-Royce; however, as World War II got into full stride, it was very apparent that even with rapid expansion Rolls-Royce's manufacturing capability would be incapable of keeping up with demand.

To meet this challenge, Ford Motor Company in England was approached to build Merlins under license, and, rather surprisingly, Ford built Merlins to closer tolerances than Rolls-Royce did! The reasoning for this apparent anomaly was the fact that Ford was geared to produce inexpensive cars at a high volume, and therefore all parts needed to be interchangeable, whereas Rolls-Royce relied on highly skilled craftsmen to hand fit all assemblies. Obviously, this approach would not work in the crisis environment of World War II. Ground was broken for a new plant in Trafford Park, a suburb of Manchester located in the grim industrial northwest of England, and by 1941 the new facility was turning out complete Merlins. All Ford-built engines were single-stage, two-speed, 20-series engines mainly for bombers. Between June 1941 and March 1946, a remarkable 30,400 Merlins were produced at Trafford Park.

At the same time negotiations were taking place for Ford production in England, similar negotiations took place in Detroit with Henry Ford. These negotiations fell through, but the Ford company got their hands on all the engineering drawings for the Merlin. It is interesting to note that when Henry Ford rejected the request to build the Merlin, he set out to build his own aircraft V-12 engine. Although the Merlin cylinder dimensions and configuration were used, automotive practice replaced aircraft design practice in several key areas. Side-by-side connecting rods replaced the blade-fork rods, and a cast crankshaft was used. After spending $2 million and a year, Ford (Detroit) gave up on this design. Never one to pass up a business opportunity, Henry Ford found out that the Army was looking for a 450-hp engine for its new tanks. Ford (Detroit) kept the 60° cylinder bank angle and made a V-8 engine out of the V-12 aircraft engine by removing the middle four cylinders and reworking it for natural aspiration. Ford (Detroit) manufactured 25,741 of these tank V-8 engines, the majority of which ended up in Shermans. A final, 750-hp tank engine that reverted to the V-12 configuration was manufactured in small quantities.

In 1938 and 1939 negotiations were initiated with Ford of France for Merlin production. The plan was for Ford to manufacture Merlins in partnership with Matra. Negotiations were still ongoing when the situation in France deteriorated, and it obviously became futile to continue. The French Merlins were intended for Armée de l'Air (French Air Force) aircraft.

Packard Car Company, also located in Detroit, was approached. This time things fared a lot better than they had with Ford. Packard turned out to be a fortuitous choice due to their high standard of workmanship and experience with building aircraft V-12 engines in the 1920s and 1930s. Work started in 1940, and Packard test-ran their first engine in 1941. However, many major obstacles needed to be overcome to reach this milestone, such as redrawing all the British drawings in order to convert them from first-angle projection to the third-angle projection used in the United States and to include manufacturing specifications in American terminology. Several significant improvements were incorporated in the Packard engines, such as the replacement of the g-sensitive SU* carburetor by the far superior Bendix injection carburetor. Because of the tremendous production pressures Rolls-Royce was under, particularly in 1940 and 1941, it had been unable to introduce a two-piece cylinder bank into production; thus, Packard was first to manufacture the two-piece cylinder head and bank assemblies. U.S.-manufactured magnetos were used; the AC Delco units were similar in design to and interchangeable with their British BTH counterparts. Perhaps the most significant change made by Packard was the redesign of the supercharger drive for the two-stage engines. Rather than use the Farman drive used by Rolls-Royce, Packard preferred an epicyclic drive patented by Wright Aeronautical. The Wright Aeronautical blower drive was used only on the two-stage engines; the single-stage engines followed and were interchangeable with the Rolls-Royce design. Crankshaft bearing material also changed; Rolls-Royce used a lead bronze with a lead-indium flash, whereas Packard used silver with a lead-indium flash. This was a common design practice in the United States, particularly for manufacturers of large radials. Engines supplied by Packard to North American Aviation and Curtiss featured SAE No. 50 propeller shaft splines, and engines supplied to Canada for Mosquito, Lancaster, and Hurricane production used the standard British propeller shaft spline, the SBAC (Society of British Aircraft Constructors).

Packards delivered to or procured by the U.S. Army were designated V-1650, using the standard Army nomenclature where the "V" signified the configuration of the cylinders and the "1650" denoted the displacement in cubic inches rounded out to the nearest 5 in³. The dash number designated the development stage. A V-1650-1 was equivalent to a Merlin 28 or 29 with single-stage, two-speed supercharger (Fig. 4.21). The V-1650-3, -7, -9, -22, -23, and -24 were two-stage, two-speed engines. Merlin-224 and Merlin-225 single-stage, single-speed engines were equivalent to Rolls-Royce Merlin 24s and 25s that were being supplied to Canadian airframe manufacturers. The Merlin-266 was equivalent to the Rolls-Royce Merlin 66 for Spitfire production.

---

*Skinner's Union, Carburetor Division of Morris Group.

Fig. 4.21 Packard-built V-1650-1. This engine was probably built for a Canadian-license-built British aircraft. If the engine was intended for U.S. production, a standard SAE No. 50 spline would be used on the propeller shaft rather than the British SBAC spline shown. (Courtesy of Rolls-Royce plc.)

Continental Motors built a new manufacturing facility in Muskegon, Michigan, in 1942 initially to build Pratt & Whitney R-1340s for North American T-6 advanced trainers. When this contract was complete, Continental tooled up for Merlin production using some of Packard's subcontractors for major castings such as head, cylinder bank, and crankcase (Fig. 4.22). Interestingly, one of the primary suppliers of castings was the Maytag Washing Machine Company. Maytag qualified for this work due to their broad experience with large intricate aluminum castings, which were used extensively in prewar washing machines. This explains the nickname the P-51 received during World War II of "Maytag Messerschmitt"! Continental's production amounted to 897 engines (Ref. 4.7).

Exhaust systems were continually under development to optimize the various requirements. For the night bombing offensive over Germany, flame damping was of paramount importance. German night fighters were always on the lookout for the giveaway stoichiometric blue flame issuing from the glowing red-hot exhaust stacks.

Fig. 4.22 Three-quarter rear view of a Rolls-Royce Merlin built under license by Continental. The engine shown in the photograph is a V-1650-7. (Courtesy of Bill Gillette and Continental Motors.)

The Handley Page Halifax, a four-engine bomber, used a manifold system with a single "fishtail" outlet on each side of the engine for flame quenching. The Avro Lancaster, another four-engine bomber, retained individual ejector stacks with a shroud covering the individual jet stacks.

Considerable development also took place for fighter exhaust systems where the prime requirement was to take advantage of the exhaust energy to propel the aircraft to a higher speed. Rolls-Royce had performed early investigations and determined that simple ejector stacks were preferable to the weight and complexity of turbosupercharging; consequently, the Merlin was never developed with a turbo (Refs. 2.5, 4.8) (Fig. 4.23).

Early designs consisted of siamesed ejector manifolds with three outlets per cylinder bank; this later gave way to various designs based on individual stacks. The resulting thrust horsepower could be considerable; in a well-designed installation over 200-thrust horsepower could be recovered at 24,000 ft and 400 mph. The higher the altitude and the higher the speed, the greater the effect (Ref. 4.9).

Exhaust system materials could be mild steel, stainless steel, or Inconel.

Construction

The Merlin was a classic 60° V-12 with a 120° crankshaft, that is, the crank, supported in seven main bearings, used six crank pins, and each crank pin had the blade-and-fork connecting rods from both cylinder banks running on it. Numbers 1 and 6 crankpin journals were located at 0°, No. 2 and 5

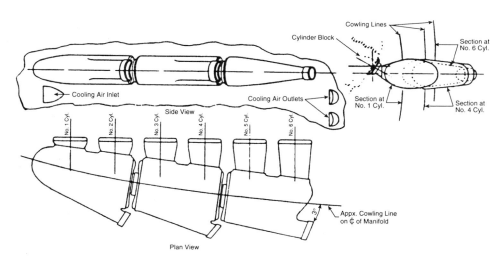

Fig. 4.23 Ejector-type exhaust system developed by Rolls-Royce for early Merlin applications. (Courtesy of SAE International.)

were located at 120°, and No. 3 and 4 were located at 240°. This is typical V-12 design practice that offers even firing every 60°. Merlin crankshafts started life as 500-lb chrome molybdenum steel alloy forgings, and after all the manufacturing processes were complete weighed in at a featherweight 120 lb, a remarkably low figure for such a large and highly stressed component (Ref. 4.10). The entire surface was machined for high finish all over. This ensured good resistance to fatigue, but this necessary manufacturing operation was time consuming and expensive. All journals were bored internally to reduce weight and plugged with plates attached with through bolts. Four first-order counterweights were designed in, two situated at the extremities of the crank at the No. 1 and 7 main bearing locations and two in the middle straddling the No. 4 center main bearing. All bearing journals were nitrided.

Crankshaft main bearing support is critical in a high-performance engine. In the case of the Merlin this was accomplished by "cross bolting." The forged aluminum main bearing caps were press fit into the crankcase. Two long bolts went through the crankcase at each main bearing location, through the main bearing cap, thus "locking" the sides of the crankcase onto the main bearing caps. This gave the necessary rigidity to the crankshaft support.

Connecting rods consisted of the classic blade-and-fork design manufactured from nickel-steel forgings machined and polished all over. The forked rod featured a detachable bearing block with an integral journal for the blade rod. The bearing block was attached with four bolts that also attached the bearing cap. The blade rod was a conventional design, using the forked rod for its journal, and in addition obtaining its oil supply from the forked rod. Each rod had the ubiquitous floating phosphor-bronze bushing for the wrist pin end. Rods were relatively trouble-free in service; however, rod bolt failures were likely to occur at engine speeds in excess of 4200 rpm, which could be reached during dive-bomber operations. Early forked rods had a stress riser in the form of a step as the rod blended into the foot of the bolt head locater. After a number of rod failures due to this design, the profile of the rod was modified to eliminate this feature with a dramatic increase in fatigue strength (Ref. 2.12).

Pistons were conventional aluminum forgings with three compression and two oil control rings. Several redesigns of the pistons were necessary; the most noticeable was a dramatic reduction in skirt length. Much of the piston ring development came from the Schneider Trophy R engine.

The crankcase was made up of two aluminum castings. The upper crankcase provided support for the seven main crankshaft bearings, with the main bearing caps attached by two bolts. For additional rigidity for this heavily loaded component, cross bolts, two per main bearing, ran right through the engine; this feature was used first on the Buzzard and put to good use in the R engine. Twenty-eight long studs, 14 per side, were screwed into the top face of the upper crankcase. Integral with the upper crankcase was the rear half of the nose case incorporating the propeller reduction gear. The generator was mounted on the left side, as was the aftercooler/intercooler pump in the two-stage Merlin. The oil pressure relief valve, and in some Navy applications the mount for a Coffman starter, was situated on the right.

The nose case, which attached to the upper crankcase, housed the propeller reduction gear in addition to the V drive. The V drive, also known as the dual drive, was driven by a floating quill shaft that powered the propeller governor and vacuum pump by means of right-angle bevel gears. In order to protect the propeller reduction gear pinion from the tremendous torsional vibration that was transmitted, it was isolated from the crankshaft, mounted on two substantial roller bearings. A short, stiff quill shaft coupled the crankshaft to the pinion. The propeller reduction gear support was provided by two massive roller bearings that took care of radial loads and a thrust bearing for handling the propeller thrust loads (Fig. 4.24).

A. Reduction Gear Pinion
B. Propeller Shaft and Gear
C. Coupling
D. Crankshaft Driving Flange with Timing Marks
E. Pinion Splines
1. Constant Speed Governor Adaptor
2. Vacuum Pump Adaptor
5. Oil Seal – Front
6. Oil Seal – Rear
8. Thrust Bearing
9. Bearing Retaining Nut
10. Bevel Pinion
11. Dual Drive Coupling Shaft
12. Constant Speed Governor Driving Shaft
13. Vacuum Pump Driving Shaft

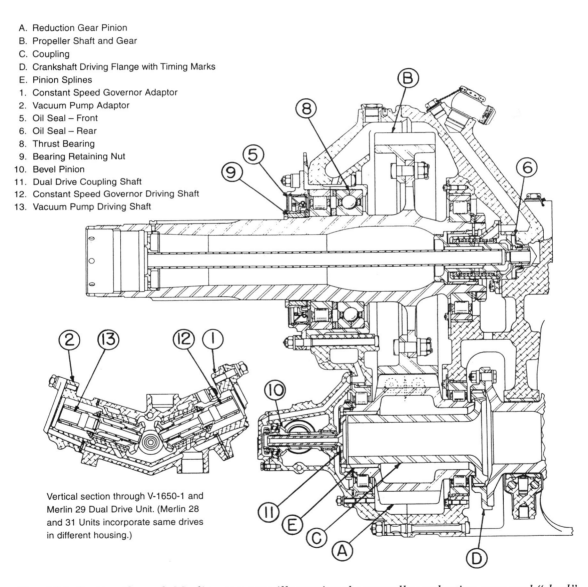

Vertical section through V-1650-1 and Merlin 29 Dual Drive Unit. (Merlin 28 and 31 Units incorporate same drives in different housing.)

Fig. 4.24 Section through Merlin nose case illustrating the propeller reduction gear and "dual" drive. (Handbook of Service Instructions, V-1650-1 and Merlin 28-29-31 Aircraft Engines, Technical Order No. AN 02-55AA-2. Author's collection.)

The wheelcase was the housing at the rear of the engine that contained the drive gears and clutch packs for the supercharger. In the case of the two-stage Merlin, up to 400 hp was required to drive the supercharger. Therefore, supercharger drive for high-performance aircraft engines has traditionally been a difficult issue to resolve with the required dependability, lightness, and compactness—all conflicting requirements! A torsionally flexible quill shaft driven from splines machined inside the No. 7 main bearing journal supplied the drive to the supercharger drive gears (Fig. 4.25). The quality of the Merlin supercharger gears was not lost on the Germans. When German engineers needed a gear unit to test turbosupercharger compressors for Daimler Benz and Junkers engines, Merlin wheel case assemblies removed from shot-down aircraft were used. They were driven by 3000 rpm electric motors (Ref. 4.11).

The upper and lower vertical driveshafts and starter motor reduction gearing were also contained in the wheelcase (Fig. 4.26). The upper vertical driveshaft transmitted drive to the inclined driveshafts that drove the camshafts. Approximately halfway up the upper vertical driveshaft, a bronze skew gear drove the magnetos, which were mounted on the wheelcase. As it turned out, this was a mistake;

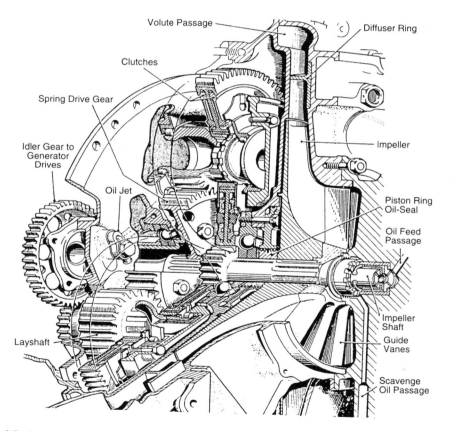

Fig. 4.25 Supercharger drive gears and clutches for a single-stage, two-speed Merlin. ("Merlin XX Aero Engine," Air Publication 1590G, British Crown Copyright/Ministry of Defence. Reproduced with the permission of the Controller of Her Britannic Majesty's Stationery Office. Author's collection.)

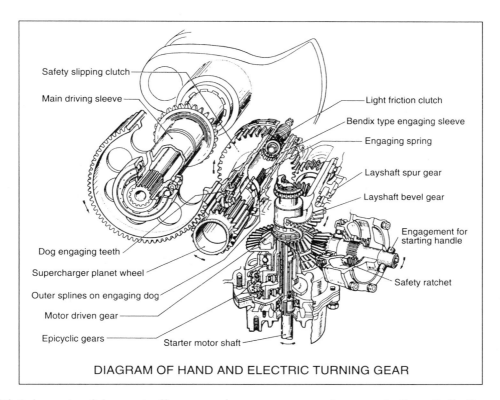

Safety slipping clutch

Main driving sleeve

Light friction clutch

Bendix type engaging sleeve

Engaging spring

Layshaft spur gear

Layshaft bevel gear

Engagement for starting handle

Dog engaging teeth

Supercharger planet wheel

Outer splines on engaging dog

Motor driven gear

Epicyclic gears

Starter motor shaft

Safety ratchet

DIAGRAM OF HAND AND ELECTRIC TURNING GEAR

Fig. 4.26 Schematic of the vertically mounted starter motor and gear train for a Rolls-Royce Merlin. ("Merlin XX Aero Engine," Air Publication 1590G, British Crown Copyright/Ministry of Defence. Reproduced with the permission of the Controller of Her Britannic Majesty's Stationery Office. Author's collection.)

many failures of this skew gear occurred with a consequent total loss of the ignition system and therefore a total and instant loss of power (Ref. 2.12). Even though the gear appeared to be substantial enough for the load it transmitted, in reality the skew gear suffered from the severe torsional reversals and vibration resulting from the cam drive. As the cam lobes came over top center on the rocker arm pad, the cam shaft "drove" the driving mechanism, resulting in a severe torsional vibration particularly if the backlash in the gear train was not set correctly (Ref. 4.12). Although this problem never received a definitive "bulletproof" fix, the situation could be kept under control by careful attention to backlash adjustment (Fig. 4.27).

The lower vertical driveshaft powered the oil pumps (both scavenge and pressure), the fuel pump, and the coolant pump, which was driven from the top of the lower vertical driveshaft with a long quill shaft terminating at the coolant pump flexible coupling (Fig. 4.28 on page 63). The coolant pump gear drove the hydraulic pump gear.

The direction control valve for the supercharger speed change mechanism was housed at the bottom of the wheelcase. This valve was lever operated by cables or rods from the cockpit; later, an aneroid valve sensed altitude and shifted blower speeds at the appropriate time. To ensure that the blower did

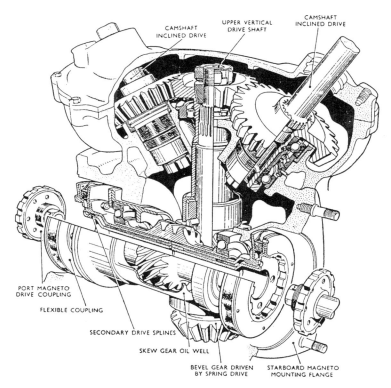

Fig. 4.27 Detail view of the upper vertical drive for a Rolls-Royce Merlin. The skew gear for the magnetos, which caused Rolls-Royce problems, is illustrated. ("Merlin XX Aero Engine," Air Publication 1590G, British Crown Copyright/Ministry of Defence. Reproduced with the permission of the Controller of Her Britannic Majesty's Stationery Office. Author's collection.)

not "bounce" between high and low blower speeds (FS and MS, respectively) if the aircraft was being flown at its critical altitude in low blower speed (MS), a buffer was built in requiring a descent of 1500 ft before a speed change would occur (Ref. 4.13).

Cylinder heads were manufactured from aluminum castings with screwed-and-shrunk steel valve seats, cast iron inlet valve guides, and bronze exhaust valve guides (Fig. 4.29). Valves were manufactured from K.E. 965* forgings with the exhaust having a protective coating of "Brightray," an alloy of 80% nickel and 20% chrome, applied with an oxyacetylene torch (Ref. 2.4). For further protection in the highly corrosive, high-temperature environment in which exhaust valves operated, they were sodium cooled. The cylinder head also mounted the single overhead camshaft, which ran in plain bearings. The cam actuated the valves by means of rocker arms pivoted at one end, and the opposite end opened and closed the valves. The cam lobe ran on a hardened pad approximately centered on the rocker. This arrangement was part of the Achilles heel of the Merlin, as it was prone to excessive wear due to the tremendous bearing loads imposed on it. Although the rocker pad had a

*K.E. 965 is an alloy steel manufactured by Kayser Ellison & Co., Ltd., Sheffield, England. Its composition is 0.4% C, 13% Cr, 13% Ni, 3% W, and 1.5% Si.

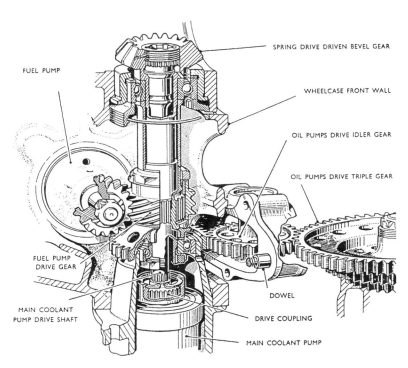

FUEL PUMP

SPRING DRIVE DRIVEN BEVEL GEAR

WHEELCASE FRONT WALL

OIL PUMPS DRIVE IDLER GEAR

OIL PUMPS DRIVE TRIPLE GEAR

FUEL PUMP
DRIVE GEAR

MAIN COOLANT
PUMP DRIVE SHAFT

DOWEL

DRIVE COUPLING

MAIN COOLANT PUMP

Fig. 4.28 Detail view of the lower vertical drive for a Rolls-Royce Merlin. ("Merlin XX Aero Engine," Air Publication 1590G, British Crown Copyright/Ministry of Defence. Reproduced with the permission of the Controller of Her Britannic Majesty's Stationery Office. Author's collection.)

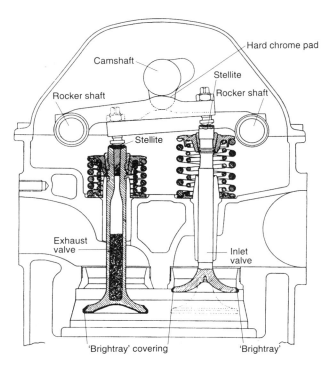

Hard chrome pad

Camshaft

Stellite

Rocker shaft

Stellite

Rocker shaft

Stellite

Exhaust
valve

Inlet
valve

'Brightray' covering

'Brightray'

Fig. 4.29 After a brief fling with the ramp head, Rolls-Royce reverted to the tried and tested Kestrel-style combustion chamber for the Merlin. This style of combustion chamber was also used for the later Griffon. It must have been effective, for racers have been able to pull over 3000 hp from the Merlin without detonation. The engine was originally designed for 1000 hp. (Courtesy of Rolls-Royce plc.)

hard chrome surface, unless the grinding operation was closely monitored the chrome would flake off. At the supercharger end of the head, a plain bearing was incorporated for the bevel gear driving the camshaft. Accommodation was made for two spark plugs per cylinder, one on the intake side of the head and one on the exhaust side. In service, the intake plugs were very difficult to access; therefore, it was common for ground crews to change only the exhaust plugs prior to every combat mission.

Cylinder banks, machined from aluminum castings, had wet cylinder liners pressed in at their tops. The wet liners were manufactured from high-carbon steel, nitrided, and in a few cases, chrome plated in the upper half.

The lower crankcase, also made from an aluminum casting, contained the oil pumps, both pressure and scavenge. In an effort to reduce windage losses, an aluminum windage tray was strategically placed to catch oil flung from the crankshaft and connecting rods and divert it to the pickup for the scavenge pump.

The cooling system was fairly conventional, consisting of a centrifugal pump gear driven from the wheelcase. Two discharges from the pump volute housing directed coolant to distribution manifolds mounted on the outer sides of the cylinder banks. This ensured a parallel flow of coolant through the engine rather than a serial flow, which would result in widely varying temperatures. The coolant flowed through the cylinder banks to the heads and into a discharge manifold or coolant rail. The coolant rails discharged into the header tank, typically mounted on the engine nose case and usually of a horse-collar shape to conform with the shape of the cowling. Some applications, such as the Hawker Hurricane, positioned the header tank behind the engine. From the header tank, coolant flowed to the radiator, which may have been mounted in a number of locations: under the engine in the classic "chin" configuration, under the wings, in the leading edge of the wing, or under the fuselage. After the coolant exited the radiator, it was routed back to the suction side of the pump to start the cycle over again.

Interestingly, the de Havilland Mosquito's coolant flow was reversed, that is, the coolant pump discharged into the radiator instead of the cylinder banks. Because of the relatively high position of the radiator compared with the pump, coolant flowed from the header tank to the suction side of the pump and then discharged through the radiator where the now cooled coolant was routed through the engine to the cylinder banks and returned to the header tank.

For British-manufactured engines, carburetion consisted of a two-barrel SU carburetor with automatic boost control. As was the case with all World War II combat aircraft engines, overboosting was a constant threat at low altitudes, that is, the supercharger could deliver a higher boost pressure to the engine than was desirable, possibly causing detonation or thermal or mechanical stress. A fighter pilot in particular had more things to worry about than monitoring manifold pressure during the heat of battle. To eliminate this chore, Rolls-Royce developed, in conjunction with the Royal Aircraft Establishment, an automatic boost control that allowed the pilot to "firewall" the throttle without concern for overboosting (Fig. 4.30). This task was accomplished by a servo system that read manifold pressure and opened the throttle butterflies far enough to give the maximum-rated boost and no more. As the aircraft climbed, the automatic boost control allowed the throttle to open until the critical altitude was reached, that is, the point at which the throttle would be wide open.

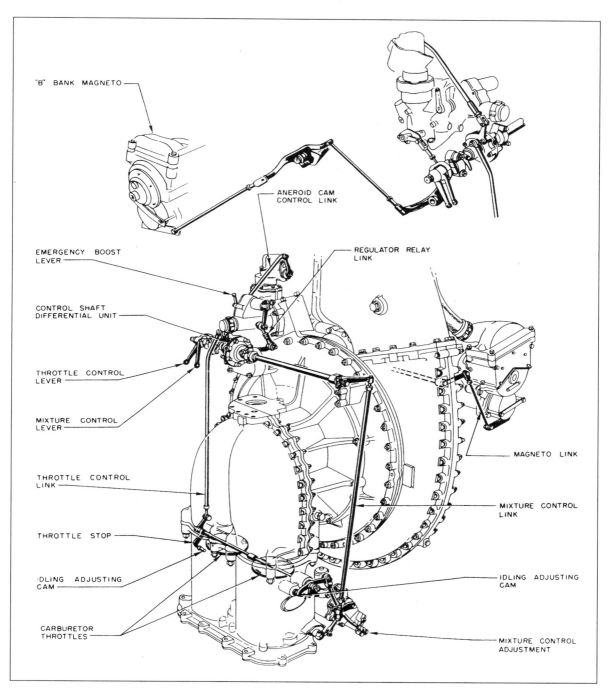

Fig. 4.30 Throttle linkage for a two-stage Rolls-Royce Merlin. Automatic boost control determines the position of the carburetor throttles. As the aircraft climbed, the automatic boost control allowed the carburetor throttles to gradually open. When the critical altitude was reached and the throttle butterfly valves were wide open, the supercharger shifted into full supercharge. The throttle opening was then reduced until the critical altitude for full supercharge was reached, at which point they would be wide open again. (North American P-51D Erection and Maintenance Manual, AN 01-60JE-2. Author's collection.)

An idiosyncrasy of the original SU carburetor was a condition known as rich "cutout" caused by negative *g*. In fact, the negative *g* cutout was a two-stage event. At the onset of negative *g,* fuel was forced to the top of the float chamber, which exposed the main jets to air. This caused the first, momentary, lean cutout (Fig. 4.31). If a negative *g* condition continued, the floats reacted to the reverse of normal conditions and floated the wrong way, that is, they floated to the bottom of the float chamber. The needle valve opened wide, allowing full fuel pressure from the engine-driven pump to flood the carburetor. An excessively rich mixture was then admitted into the supercharger, causing the more serious rich cutout (Ref. 4.14).

For a fighter pilot this could pose a severe limitation; if the stick was pushed forward a momentary loss of power or complete cutout would result. To work around this anomaly, pilots had to ensure that the aircraft was always flown with positive *g*. The solution turned out to be disarmingly simple. Miss Beatrice "Tilly" Shilling, a young physicist working at the Royal Aircraft Establishment, was assigned to work out a solution, which turned out to be a simple flow restrictor somewhat similar to a plain flat washer. The orifice was sized to allow to flow only the amount of fuel needed to satisfy maximum engine output and no more. Two restrictors were developed, one for 12-psi boost (54-in Hg. manifold pressure) and one for 16-psi boost (62-in Hg manifold pressure) (Ref. 4.14). Along with the flow restrictor, other improvements were incorporated to overcome negative *g* sensitivity. A

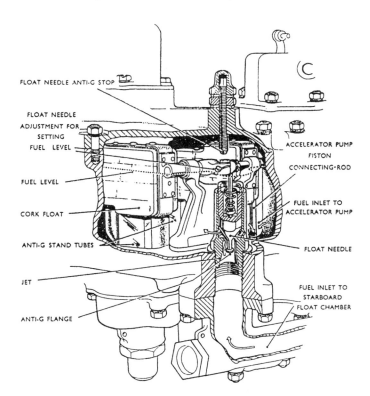

Fig. 4.31 RAE anti-g carburetor developed for the Rolls-Royce Merlin. Note the flange machined into the end of the needle valve and the stand tubes. Both of these features were incorporated to negate the effects of negative g. The Shilling orifice (not shown) was installed in the fuel inlet fitting. (Air Publication 1590V, Vol. 1, Sect. 4, Chap. 2, British Crown Copyright/Ministry of Defence. Reproduced with the permission of the Controller of Her Britannic Majesty's Stationery Office.)

flange was incorporated at the tapered end of the needle valve that also created a flow restriction if it was exposed to negative *g*. For bomber applications the negative *g* issue was not a serious problem; however, the definitive solution was single-point fuel injection of the Bendix or later Rolls-Royce type.

The intake system followed the Kestrel design, that is, the supercharger discharged into an intake trunk that was essentially a large diameter pipe tapering slightly toward the front of the engine. From this intake trunk the intake runners were tapped off, siamesed in pairs. This intake system was elegantly simple but very effective, giving excellent flow characteristics (Fig. 4.32).

The essential flame traps were sandwiched between the intake manifold and the cylinder head. The flame traps were based on the theory of the Davy safety lamp; they consisted of a stainless steel mesh. This arrangement quenched any backfires into the induction system, which if uncontrolled would cause catastrophic damage to the engine due to the explosion of a highly compressed and volatile fuel/air mixture in the intake system. Backfires could be caused by any number of factors, among them excessive manifold pressure, leaky intake valve(s), bad plugs, incorrect ignition timing, incorrect valve timing, etc.

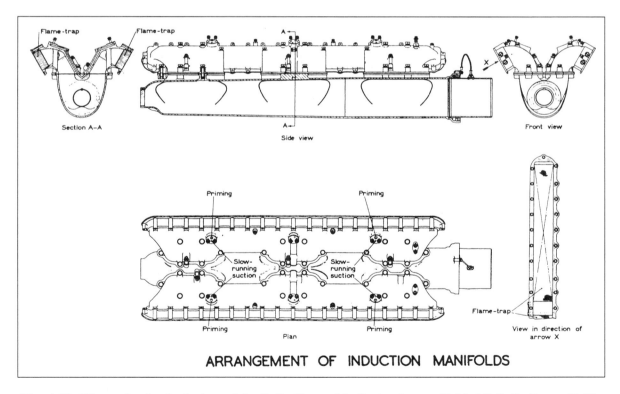

ARRANGEMENT OF INDUCTION MANIFOLDS

Fig. 4.32 Elegantly simple design of the Rolls-Royce Merlin intake manifold. All Rolls-Royce V-12 poppet valve engines, after the supercharged Kestrel, used this design. As a Rolls-Royce drawing, this is a first angle projection, i.e., the reverse of conventional third angle projection. ("Merlin XX Aero Engine," Air Publication 1590G, British Crown Copyright/Ministry of Defence. Reproduced with the permission of the Controller of Her Britannic Majesty's Stationery Office. Author's collection.)

Applications

Because the Merlin was one of the most significant military aircraft engines in history, it was installed in a wide variety of aircraft including fighters, bombers, transports, and numerous Navy aircraft. Table 4.2 summarizes the Merlin's performance and applications.

TABLE 4.2—ROLLS-ROYCE MERLIN PERFORMANCE AND APPLICATION SUMMARY

Dash Number	Applications	hp/rpm/alt	Comments
I	Battle I	1030/3000/16,250	Two-piece head/cylinder bank. Ramp head
II and III	Spitfire I Defiant I Sea/Hurricane I Battle I	1440/3000/5500	
VIII	Fulmar I	1035/3000/7750	1275 hp available with 100-octane fuel. Navy engine fitted with Coffman starter
X	Halifax I Wellington II Whitley V/VII	1130/3000/5250 1010/3000/17,750	First Merlin fitted with two-speed supercharger
XII	Spitfire II	1150/3000/14,900	Coffman starter
XX	Beaufighter II Defiant II Halifax I/V Hurricane II/IV Lancaster I/III	1480/3000/6000 1480/3000/12,250	First engine to incorporate Hooker-designed supercharger. Two-speed
21	Mosquito I/II/IV Mosquito VI	1480/3000/6000 1480/3000/12,250	Same as XX but reverse-flow cooling
22	Lancaster I/III York I	1480/3000/6000 1480/3000/12,250	
23	Mosquito I/II/IV Mosquito XII/XIII	1480/3000/6000 1480/3000/12,250	Reverse-flow cooling
24	Lancaster I/III York I	1640/3000/2000 1500/3000/9500	Fitted with RAE anti-*g* carburetor, i.e., Schilling orifice and other improvements
25	Mosquito VI/XIX	1640/3000/2000 1500/3000/9500	Same as 24 but reverse-flow cooling

(continued)

TABLE 4.2, continued

Dash Number	Applications	hp/rpm/alt	Comments
28 V-1650-1	Lancaster I/III Kittyhawk II P-40F	1300/3000/SL 1260/3000/8750	First of the Packard-built Merlins. Designated V-1650-1. Featured separate head/bank assemblies
29 V-1650-1	Canadian Hurricane Kittyhawk II P-40F	1300/3000/SL 1260/3000/8750	Built by Packard
30	Barracuda I Fulmar II	1300/3000/SL 1260/3000/8750	Navy engine, single-stage, single-speed. Coffman starter
31 V-1650-1	Canadian Mosquito XX Australian Mosquito 40 P-40F/L	1300/3000/SL 1260/3000/8750	Built by Packard. Reverse-flow cooling
32	Barracuda II Seafire II	1645/3000/2500	Single-stage, single-speed. Coffman starter
33 V-1650-1	Canadian Mosquito XX Australian Mosquito 40	1480/3000/6000 1480/3000/12,250	Built by Packard. Same as Merlin 23
38 V-1650-1	Lancaster I/III	1480/3000/6000 1480/3000/12,250	Built by Packard. Same as Merlin 22
45	Spitfire V/P.R. IV Spitfire VII Seafire II	1470/3000/9250 1480/3000/12,250	
45M	Spitfire L.F. V	1585/3000/2750	The "clipped, cropped, and clapped" Merlin. Supercharger impeller reduced in diameter for improved low-altitude performance
46	Spitfire V/P.R. IV Seafire I	1415/3000/14,000	
47	Spitfire VI	1415/3000/14,000	
50	Spitfire V	1470/3000/9250	
50M	Spitfire L.F. V	1585/3000/2750	Cropped supercharger impeller
55	Spitfire V Seafire III	1470/3000/9250	Modified Merlin 50
55M	Spitfire L.F. V Seafire L.F. II	1585/3000/9250	Cropped supercharger impeller

(continued)

TABLE 4.2, continued

Dash Number	Applications	hp/rpm/alt	Comments
60	Wellington VI		First of the two-speed, two-stage engines. Still retained one-piece head/bank assembly. All 60 series were two-stage, two-speed
61	Spitfire VII/VIII Spitfire IX/P.R. XI	1565/3000/12,250 1390/3000/23,500	Improved altitude perfor-mance due to the two-stage blower
62	Wellington VI		
63	Spitfire VII/VIII Spitfire IX/P.R. XI	1280/3000/SL 1710/3000/8500 1505/3000/21,000	Two-piece head/bank assembly. Strengthened supercharger quill shaft
64	Spitfire VII	Same as above	Spitfire VII fitted with cabin supercharger
66	Spitfire L.F. VIII Spitfire L.F. IX	Same as above	
68 V-1650-3	Mustang III, P-51B P-51C	1670/3000/SL 1700/3000/6400 1490/3000/19,400	Built by Packard, designated V-1650-3. First of the Packard two-stage, two-speed engines
69 V-1650-7	Mustang III/IV P-51C/D/F/K	Same as above	Built by Packard, designated V-1650-7
70	Spitfire H.F. VIII Spitfire H.F. IX Spitfire P.R. XI	1240/3000/SL 1710/3000/11,000 1475/3000/23,250	Similar to -66 but with different blower ratios
71	Spitfire H.F. VII	Same as above	H.F. VII fitted with cabin supercharger
72	Mosquito P.R. IX/B Mosquito IX/XVI, 30 Welkin I	Same as -63	Reverse-flow cooling
73	Mosquito XVI Welkin I	Same as -63	Reverse-flow cooling and cabin supercharger
85	Lancaster VI Lincoln I	1635/3000/SL	Lancaster VI was proto-type for Lincoln
224	Lancaster I/III	Same as -24	Built by Packard. Same as Merlin 24
225	Canadian Mosquito 25 and 26	Same as -25	Built by Packard. Same as Merlin 25
266	Spitfire L.F. XVI	Same as -66	Built by Packard. Same as Merlin 66

Note: V-1650 designations above are Packard engines.

(continued)

TABLE 4.2, continued: ADDITIONAL PACKARD-BUILT MERLINS

Dash Number	Applications	hp/rpm/alt	Comments
V-1650-5		1400/3000/SL 1490/3000/13,750 1210/3000/25,800	Similar to -3 except equipped with extension shaft and Allison reduction gear assemby. Intended for Merlin-powered P-39
V-1650-9	P-51D/H/K/C	1380/3000/SL 1500/3000/16,100 1230/3000/21,400	End-to-end crank lubrication. Fitted with ADI and Simmonds speed and boost control. Also built by Continental
V-1650-11	P-51L P-82B	1380/3000/SL 1500/3000/16,100 1240/2700/30,700	Similar to -9 except speed density pump replaces carburetor giving improved altitude performance
V-1650-13		1380/3000/SL 1490/3000/13,750 1210/3000/25,800	Similar to -3 except Simmonds SA-5 boost control
V-1650-15		1490/3000/SL 1490/3000/13,750 1210/3000/25,800	Similar to -5 except Simmonds SA-5 boost control
V-1650-17		1490/3000/SL 1590/3000/8500 1370/3000/21,400	Similar to -7 except Simmonds SA-5 boost control
V-1650-19		1700/3000/SL 1430/3000/25,000	Similar to -11 except variable-speed blower drive
V-1650-21	P(F)-82B	1380/3000/SL 1495/3000/1530 1230/3000/28,700	Similar to -9 except Aeroproducts propeller and left-hand rotation
V-1650-23	XP-82/P-82/B	1520/3000/SL 1600/3000/24,000	Similar to -11 except fitted with PD (Bendix injection) carburetor in place of SD (speed density) carburetor
V-1650-25	P-82B/XP-82	1490/3000/SL 1600/3000/24,000 1470/3000/23,000	Similar to -21 except fitted with PD carburetor in place of SD carburetor

Source: Refs. 2.5, 2.7, 4.15–4.18.

Supermarine Spitfire and Seafire

The Supermarine Spitfire perhaps personified the ideal Merlin application as it went through all the development stages of the Merlin from the early ramp head Merlin Cs with single-stage, single-speed supercharging, to the two-stage, two-speed, intercooled, aftercooled, 60-series Merlins. Finally, the last production Spitfires sported the R-size Rolls-Royce Griffon, which was almost 40% larger in displacement and horsepower.

R. J. Mitchell of Schneider Trophy Supermarine S6B fame, designed the Supermarine Type 300, as the prototype Spitfire was known, in 1934 (in accordance with Air Ministry Specification F.37/34). Construction began in 1935. By March 1936 the prototype was ready for its maiden flight, piloted by the famous Vickers (Aviation) chief test pilot, "Mutt" Summers (by this time Vickers [Aviation] owned Supermarine). The prototype was powered by a Merlin C engine, which featured a ramp head combustion chamber and two-piece head and cylinder bank.

Flight testing went remarkably smoothly for such a radically new design, and by 1937 Spitfires in Mk. I form, powered by Merlin Mk. IIs, were entering squadron service.

War in Europe was declared in 1939 when Germany invaded Poland. This put additional demands on the already stretched-to-the limit production capabilities of Supermarine. Consequently, large numbers of subcontractors from all types of industries were enlisted in a mad scramble to manufacture parts for Spitfires. In particular, the British automobile companies were contracted as "shadow" factories. The Nuffield organization, a major British prewar car manufacturer, quickly came up to speed building Spitfires.

The fuselage was of aluminum monocoque construction with the Merlin mounted on a chrome molybdenum steel alloy tubular mount with no shock or vibration mounts. The mount terminated at four points at the firewall. Mount loads were transferred through the fuselage monocoque by means of two upper longerons; the two lower mounts were located on the wing spar, thus transferring the loads though the wing (Ref. 4.8). Spitfires were often recognized and remembered for the classic elliptical wing planform, although some Marks deviated from this graceful shape. The wing construction was based on a tubular, tapered spar with a relatively thick skin forming the leading edge resulting in a D spar of high torsional stiffness. Aft of the main spar, thinner skin was incorporated. Coolant and oil radiators were mounted under the wings at mid span. From a frontal view the radiators were asymmetric, that is, the larger, rectangular, engine coolant radiator was mounted under the right wing and the smaller, circular oil cooler was mounted under the left wing. With a counter-clockwise-turning propeller, torque reaction tended to pull an aircraft to the left; therefore, the larger and more drag-producing coolant radiator was mounted under the right wing. The 8-gal oil tank was mounted under the engine with the lower surface of the tank forming the lower cowling; this exposure to the slipstream provided additional cooling (Fig. 4.33).

Powered by most variations of the Merlin during its production life, the Spitfire could be broken down into two basic types: those with the single-stage and those with two-stage engines. The Spitfire began production with the Merlin II or III, which still had the one-piece head and cylinder bank assembly (Fig. 4.34). The next major production variant was the Mk. V series, which represented the most-produced version of the Spitfire. The Spitfire V, powered by the Merlin 45, was the first Spitfire to benefit from Sir Stanley Hooker's supercharger work. With the development of the Merlin 60 series, two-stage, two-speed engines, the Spitfire VIII was produced, which offered a significant increase in speed and performance. With the introduction of the Spitfire XII, Griffon power was phased into production; the last Merlin Spitfire was the Mk. XVI.

Fig. 4.33 The exposed Supermarine Spitfire oil tank is evident in this view. The circular oil cooler, a characteristic of the single-stage-powered aircraft, is also evident under the left wing. (Courtesy of the National Air and Space Museum, Smithsonian Institution, Photo No. 2A-42984.)

Fig. 4.34 Supermarine Spitfire I powered by a Rolls-Royce Merlin III. This model and power plant combination, along with the similarly powered Hawker Hurricane, bore the brunt of the 1940 Battle of Britain. (Courtesy of the National Air and Space Museum, Smithsonian Institution, Photo No. 2A-27528.)

The Fleet Air Arm (FAA), the British branch of naval aviation, took advantage of the fighter qualities of the Spitfire. The Navy version was known as Seafire. Pilot skill was required when operating the Seafire from the confines of a carrier deck. The narrow landing gear contributed to the difficulty of these conditions. The primary changes to the Spitfire that created the Seafire were the addition of wing folding, arrester gear, and catapult spools (Fig. 4.35).

Service

Victory in the Battle of Britain was crucial to the survival of England; consequently, the Spitfire bore the brunt of the best the Luftwaffe could throw against the RAF. Because of the higher performance of the Spitfire compared with the Hurricane, tactics soon evolved for the Spitfires to engage the German fighters, primarily Messerschmitt Bf 109Es and Bf 110s, and for the Hurricanes to engage the more vulnerable bombers. The battle was waged through the summer of 1940, and by September the Luftwaffe changed tactics by attacking cities, primarily London, and thus relieved the strained RAF, which had suffered unrelenting attacks on their fighter bases.

With the Battle of Britain over, tactics shifted to hit-and-run attacks over France. With the introduction of the Focke-Wulf 190, the Spitfire Is and IIs were at a severe disadvantage until the 60-series-powered Spitfire IXs were introduced in 1942.

Fig. 4.35 Mk. III Supermarine Seafire taking off from HMS Hunter. *The narrow landing gear that made carrier operations hazardous is apparent in this shot. Note early style siamesed ejector exhaust stacks. (Courtesy of the Fleet Air Arm Museum.)*

Elsewhere, the Spitfire was employed in all theaters of the war, including North Africa, where purpose built air filters gave it a deeper nose profile, the China-Burma-India (CBI) theater, and Italy (Ref. 2.7).

Until later purpose-built U.S.-manufactured aircraft such as the Vought Corsair became available, the Seafire was the best fighter the Fleet Air Arm had at its disposal. Seafires were used operationally for the first time in support of the U.S. Army's invasion of North Africa, known as operation Torch.

The Salerno landings in Italy proved to be an expensive operation for Seafires. Losses due to accidents were prohibitive; 60 aircraft were lost in five days, a testament to the difficulty of operating Seafires from carrier decks (Ref. 4.19).

Hawker Hurricane

The Hawker Hurricane, designed by Sydney, later Sir Sydney, Camm to Air Ministry Specification F.36/34, looked superficially similar to the Spitfire in that it also was a low-wing monoplane; however, the type of construction differed totally (Fig. 4.36). It was an evolutionary design based on the famous Fury biplane, which featured chrome molybdenum steel alloy tube construction for the fuselage and fabric covering aft of the cockpit. Forward of the cockpit, easily removable metal panels gave access for maintenance. Wing construction was of the two-spar type featuring stressed skin outer panels; the remainder was fabric covered. The oil tank was mounted on the wing leading edge (Fig. 4.37) (Refs. 2.7, 4.20).

Fig. 4.36 Hawker Hurricane I powered by a Merlin III. This combination, along with the similarly powered Spitfire I, was the RAF mainstay during the Battle of Britain. The engine was initially rated at 1030 hp with 87-octane fuel; the arrival of a shipment of 100-octane fuel allowed a manifold pressure increase of 12 in Hg and increased power to 1310 hp. This proved vital in the Battle of Britain. (Courtesy of Rolls-Royce plc.)

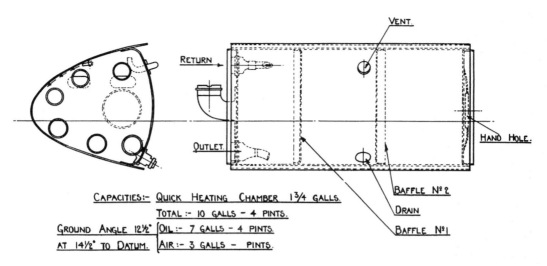

Fig. 4.37 Hawker Hurricane oil tank, which formed part of the leading edge of the left wing. (Rolls-Royce Aero Instruction School, 1942, Technical Notes. Author's collection.)

In this first monoplane project by Camm, the wing was conservatively designed with a thick section that offered ample room for internal bracing and mounting the armament of eight (later twelve) 303 (0.303-in caliber) machine guns. This was the same caliber as the standard Lee Enfield rifle used by the British Army at the time. Alternatively, four 20-mm cannon were later employed. The first flight occurred on 6 November 1935; this was also the first flight of a Merlin, as all previous test flying in the Hawker Hart was done with the PV-12 engine, the Merlin prototype.

Unlike its contemporary, the Supermarine Spitfire, the Hurricane went through few engine model changes. Hurricane Is were powered by Merlin IIs or IIIs, and all subsequent aircraft were powered by Merlin XXs. The possibility of installing a two-stage 60-series Merlin was investigated but not executed. A Griffon-powered Hurricane was also designed and a prototype partly built before the project was cancelled.

Service

After the early military successes of Germany in 1939, England sent several squadrons of Hurricanes to France as part of the British Expeditionary Force to defend that country, along with a squadron of Fairey Battles and Boulton Paul Defiants, also powered by Merlins. At this time the crucial decision was made to send over a minimum number of the precious Spitfires. They represented the best fighter aircraft the RAF had at this time, and Winston Churchill could see already at this early date the possibility that a "Battle of Britain" may become an eventuality. As events turned out, Churchill was quite correct when the Battle of France was lost and the Battle of Britain was fought during the summer of 1940; it was also the first military battle fought by aircraft alone.

Although other aircraft were involved, the brunt of the battle was fought by Hurricanes and Spitfires. The other deciding factor was radar, which, although in its infancy, turned out to be as critical as the Spitfires and Hurricanes as it alleviated the need for constant standing patrols. Hurricanes racked up a far higher score than the Spitfires, a fact often overlooked by historians studying the Battle of Britain. Part of this was attributable to the tactics employed; that is, the Hurricanes attacked the more vulnerable bombers and the Spitfires concentrated on the fighters, Messerschmitt Bf 109s and Bf110s, which were far more formidable foes. Additional factors contributing to the Hurricanes' success were that more of them were in service and that they had a simpler design, making repairs easier.

Allied shipping losses due to German U-boats almost brought England to its knees. So serious was the problem that modified merchant ships known as catapult-equipped merchantmen (C.A.M.) ships were built. Modified Hurricanes designated Sea Hurricane I were rapidly brought into service. A purpose-built catapult was mounted on C.A.M. ships with the Sea Hurricane I mounted on it. If a German aircraft such as a Focke-Wulf Condor or a U-boat was sighted, the Sea Hurricane was launched. Most operations were in the North Atlantic; consequently, if the pilot was out of range of land, he had no choice but to splash down near a ship and hope he would be picked up. When powered by Merlin IIs or Merlin IIIs, the Hurricane's boost pressure was increased from the normal maximum of 12 psi (54 in Hg) to 16 psi (62 in Hg).

North African operations required the use of a Vokes air filter built into the ram air induction system, which altered the Hurricane's nose profile.

North American P-51 Mustang

The North American P-51 Mustang offered ample evidence of the superiority of the Merlin over its contemporaries. Initially fitted with an Allison V-1710 60° V-12 of very similar size, displacement, and configuration to the Merlin, the Allison lacked the altitude performance of the Merlin.

The Mustang was procured by the British Purchasing Commission in 1940. Initially they wanted the Curtiss P-40, even though it was realized that by 1940 it was essentially obsolete. North American Aviation, when approached on becoming a second source for the Curtiss P-40, wisely talked the British into letting them design a better aircraft based on new NACA laminar flow data. Because of the extensive work North American Aviation had done in studying laminar flow aerodynamics at the California Institute of Technology, spectacular performance was attained by the Mustang (Ref. 4.7). Because of the urgency of the British requirements, the aircraft was designed in a startlingly brief 100 days, with the first flight occurring in October 1940. When the Mustang, as it was called by the RAF, entered service it became apparent that the aircraft possessed good low-level performance, but this performance deteriorated as the critical altitude of the Allison engine was approached. This was due to a lack of altitude performance compared to the two-stage Merlin. It was soon used by the RAF as a low-level reconnaissance fighter and fitted with an oblique camera in the port backward vision panel behind the pilot (Ref. 2.7).

The performance of the Mustang was not lost on the U.S. Army Air Corps (USAAC), which retained the 5th and 10th production examples for their own evaluation at Wright Field and designated it P-51.

Five early RAF Mustang 1s were delivered to the Rolls-Royce engine installation facility at Hucknall in 1942. The Allison engines were replaced with Merlin 65s from Spitfire Mk. IXs (Ref. 4.21). In many respects the installation was a proof-of-concept lash-up, but after the inevitable initial problems had been ironed out the performance proved to be nothing short of spectacular (Fig. 4.38). Seven weeks after Rolls-Royce flew its first Merlin Mustang, North American Aviation test-flew its version powered by a Packard-built two-stage engine. The P-51B, or Mustang II in RAF parlance, was the first production Merlin-powered Mustang (Fig. 4.39). The effects were far-reaching and profound. With the improved fuel economy (miles per gallon) of the Merlin compared with that of the Pratt & Whitney R-2800 powered P-47 (the R-2800 had a slightly better specific fuel consumption compared with that of the two-stage Merlin), it was now possible to have fighter escort by the Eighth

Fig. 4.38 One of the early RAF Mustang 1 test beds modified by Rolls-Royce for Merlin installation. Many of the quick engine change (QEC) components were from a Spitfire IX (Merlin 66). (Courtesy of Rolls-Royce plc.)

Fig. 4.39 Factory-fresh North American P-51B powered by a Packard V-1650-3 on test flight. (Courtesy of Roll-Royce plc.)

Air Force to Berlin. When Herman Goering saw B-17s and B-24s escorted by Merlin-powered P-51s bomb Berlin, he realized the war was lost for Germany. North American Aviation obtained their engines from Packard, who also supplied the Canadians with engines for Hurricane, Mosquito, and Lancaster production. They also provided the British with engines for various aircraft.

Unlike previous schemes for mounting the Merlin, North American Aviation deviated from the usual chrome molybdenum steel alloy tubular structure. Instead, a fabricated aluminum box section mount made of deep vertical members that sandwiched aluminum extrusions was used, making a light and strong assembly (Ref. 4.22) (Fig. 4.40). Interestingly, several British manufacturers copied this concept for mounting Merlins or Griffons. Perhaps the crowning glory of the magnificent P-51 design was its beautifully designed cooling system (Fig. 4.41). Hot coolant discharging from the header tank, mounted on the Merlin's nose case, was then piped to the main coolant radiator mounted under the belly of the aircraft, where the oil cooler and intercooler/aftercooler radiators also resided. Endless hours were spent in wind tunnel testing to arrive at the optimal shape for the duct housing the coolers and radiators. The results were well worth the effort as the P-51s, particularly the Merlin-powered P-51s, exhibited remarkably low cooling drag. North American Aviation engineers were aware of Meredith's work in the 1930s on heat-recovery cooling systems; consequently, the P-51 design followed his theories. Air, at ambient temperature, entered the cooling duct. When the air made contact with the 220°F (or higher) radiator matrix, a rapid rise in temperature caused the air to expand; consequently, it was discharged from the duct at a higher velocity than when it entered. Although it is doubtful whether positive thrust ever resulted from this arrangement, some of the drag due to the radiator was recovered.

Ram air for the supercharger was obtained through an opening just behind the spinner. Ductwork routed the air into the updraft carburetor (Fig. 4.42).

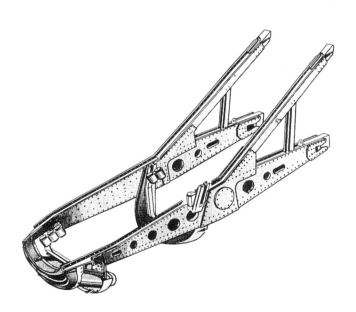

Fig. 4.40 Engine mount for the Packard-built Rolls-Royce Merlin installed in the North American P-51B/C/D. This style of mount differed from its British counterpart fitted to contemporary Spitfires, for example. The primary load-bearing members were fabricated from sheet aluminum formed into box sections. This gave a light, strong, and rigid mount. British airframe manufacturers later used this style of mount for Rolls-Royce Griffon powered aircraft. (North American P-51D Erection and Maintenance Manual, AN 01-60JE-2. Author's collection.)

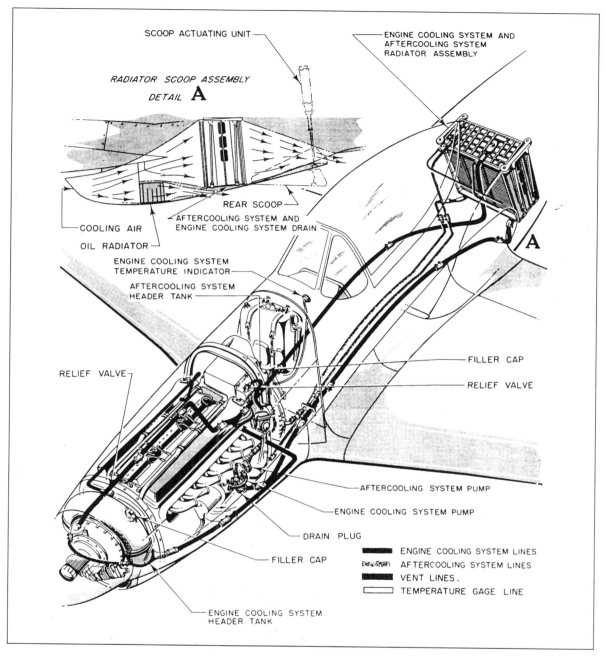

Fig. 4.41 *Magnificently designed cooling system for the North American P-51B/C/D Mustang. Detail A shows a cross section through the radiator ductwork. Cooling air entered the scoop at ambient temperature. As the cooling air passed through the radiator matrix, it picked up considerable heat energy, thus experiencing considerable expansion. The heated air was ejected through the rear of the duct at a higher velocity than when it entered, thus offering some energy recovery. During design conditions the installation produced net positive thrust over the accompanying drag of the installation. (North American P-51D Erection and Maintenance Manual, AN 01-60JE-2. Author's collection.)*

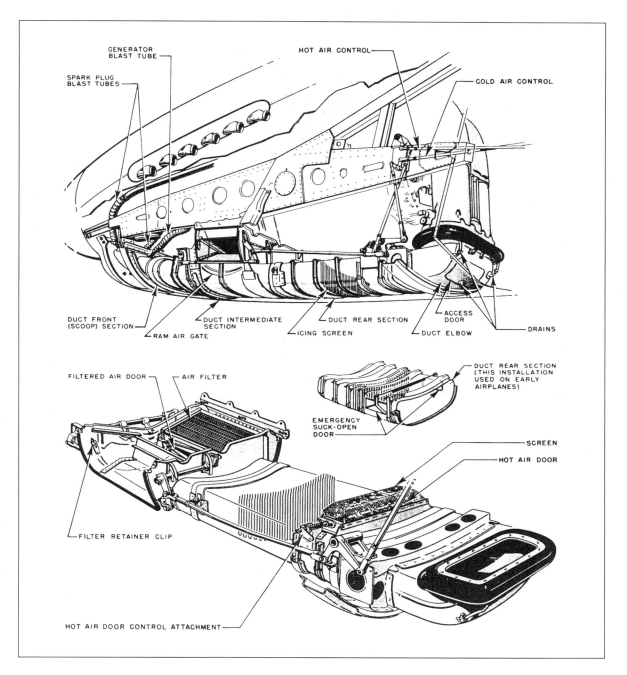

Fig. 4.42 Air induction system for the North American P-51D powered by a Packard-built Rolls-Royce Merlin V-1650-3 or -7. Three options were available to the pilot: 1) ram air, 2) filtered air, or 3) hot air. P-51Bs and P-51Cs had only the options of ram or filtered air. If ice formed on the icing screen, an automatic door opened, admitting heated air. (North American P-51D Erection and Maintenance Manual, AN 01-60JE-2. Author's collection.)

Once the Merlin transition had taken place, the P-51 proved a formidable fighter in all theaters including the Pacific, where it escorted B-29s on long missions to Japan flying out of Iwo Jima. Although the P-51 had excellent flying characteristics, the early part of the long-range Pacific escort missions were fraught with hazard as the aircraft took off with fuel in the fuselage tank resulting in an aft center-of-gravity situation, making the aircraft very unstable until some of the fuel was burned off.

Although manufactured in various models, the most common P-51s were the B, C, and D models. The B and C models were essentially the same but were manufactured at different facilities. The D introduced the bubble canopy (Fig. 4.43). Because the area of the fuselage was reduced after the turtle deck was replaced by the bubble canopy, it was possible for a pilot to get into an unrecoverable spin. The quick fix for this problem was the addition of a dorsal fillet on the vertical stabilizer (Fig. 4.44).

Fig. 4.43 North American P-51D powered by a Packard-built V-1650-3 or -7 Merlin. (Courtesy of Rolls-Royce plc.)

Fig. 4.44 Early production model of the North American P-51D. A small dorsal fillet was added to the vertical stabilizer on later aircraft. Several P-51Ds were lost in accidents due to unrecoverable spins prior to the addition of the dorsal fin. (Courtesy of Rolls-Royce plc.)

The H model, the next variant to be manufactured in quantity, did not quite get in service prior to the end of hostilities. Although it looked very similar to the D model, in fact it was an entirely new light-weight design built to British Spitfire factors and standards, featuring much thinner skins and redesigned landing gear among other improvements. The result was an aircraft that was considerably lighter and that easily outperformed the D model. Part of the performance enhancement was provided by the V-1650-9 or -11 engine, which offered ADI and a potential 2200 hp burning 115/150 grade fuel and 81 in Hg manifold pressure (Fig. 4.45). Another variation on the P-51 theme that did not quite get into service prior to the end of World War II was the P-82 twin Mustang. Superficially it looked like a pair of P-51 fuselages mounted on a common wing; however, it was, again, a totally new design. As it was based on the lessons learned with the H model, the P-82 could have been a formidable weapon if it had been introduced earlier.

Avro Lancaster

Out of the ashes of catastrophe came one of the finest strategic bombers of World War II. The origins of the Avro Lancaster went back to Air Ministry Specification F.13/36 issued in 1936 for a large twin-engine bomber. Avro responded to this specification with the Manchester, powered by two Rolls-Royce X-24 Vulture engines. As will be related in the Vulture section, this engine was beset with problems that could not be resolved in the short term. By mid 1940 the situation with the Vulture had become intolerable. Consequently Ernest Hives, Works Director of Rolls-Royce, suggested to Roy Chadwick, chief designer at Avro, that four Merlins should be installed in place of the two Vultures, resulting in the new designation of Lancaster (Fig. 4.46).

Fuselage construction for the Lancaster remained essentially the same as for the Manchester; however, as may be expected, the wing required extensive redesign. A new, larger span center section was incorporated to accommodate the two additional engines. Because of the critical nature of the Lancaster program, top priority was placed upon getting the design complete and into production in

Fig. 4.45 North American P-51H "lightweight" Mustang, the last and the fastest of the production Mustangs. Although the H model was superficially similar to the D model, in fact the H was a totally new design with very few components interchangeable with the D. (Courtesy of the National Air and Space Museum, Smithsonian Institution, Photo No. 1B-27372.)

Fig. 4.46 Head-on view of Avro Lancaster powered by four 20-series Merlins. It was possible for a Lancaster to be powered by Merlins from three different manufacturers: Rolls-Royce, Ford, and Packard! (Courtesy of Rolls-Royce plc.)

the shortest possible time. This was completed and the prototype flown in the remarkably short time of eight months. One of the factors that expedited the process was the incorporation of the Bristol Beaufighter power plant, or quick engine change (QEC) in U.S. terminology, which Rolls-Royce had designed for the Merlin-powered version of this formidable heavy twin-engine fighter (Fig. 4.47). All Merlin Lancasters (Lancaster IIs were powered by Bristol Hercules VI air-cooled radials) were powered by single-stage, two-speed engines, primarily Merlin 20 series, or Merlin 38s. A small number of Mk. VI Lancasters were powered by Merlin 85s. Packard provided the Merlin 224 for Canadian-built Lancasters, the 224 being comparable to a Rolls-Royce Merlin 24 (after the XX, Rolls-Royce used Arabic numerals for Merlin designation). Many of the British-manufactured Lancasters were powered by Ford engines built at Trafford Park and were completely interchangeable with their Rolls-Royce counterparts. It was not unusual for a Lancaster to have a mix of Ford, Rolls-Royce, and possibly Packard engines on the same aircraft (Ref. 4.14).

Fig. 4.47 Bristol Beaufighter II powered by two Merlin XXs. This QEC was later used, in slightly modified form, for the Avro Lancaster. (Courtesy of Rolls-Royce plc.)

Construction was semi-monocoque stressed skin; however, unlike U.S. aircraft, British aircraft tended to use thinner gauge skin and to compensate with additional internal stiffening. The Lancaster was a typical example of this design philosophy. A feature of the Lancaster that was to be of tremendous value during its combat career was the massive size of the unrestricted bomb bay, which measured a cavernous 33 ft long. This made the Lancaster ideally suited to the special missions that were flown primarily by 617 squadron, which became famous for the dam raids in the Ruhr Valley.

Maintenance is a major chore for any piece of military equipment, particularly something as complex as a four-engine heavy bomber. Several innovative features were incorporated into the Lancaster design to make life a little easier for the overworked "erks," as RAF ground crew were known. Engine changes were a constant requirement with overhaul lives of 400 hours but usually as brief as 100 hours. Avro built in "hard" points on the upper surface of the wing located at the front and rear spars. An A-frame was assembled with lifting tackle to remove the engines; consequently, a crane was not required for this major maintenance chore (Ref. 4.23).

Service

The squadron that personified the Lancaster was 617, which gained fame in May 1943 when they made a daring moonlit raid on the major dams in the Ruhr Valley. In order to breach the dams, an ingenious rotating bomb, shaped like a 55-gal oil drum, was suspended from the modified bomb bay on a trapeze. A hydraulic motor spun the bomb prior to release. After release, the bomb skipped across the surface of the water until it hit the face of the dam, where it drove itself down to the base of the dam with the force of its rotation imparted by the hydraulic motor and detonated. This innovative weapon was developed by Barnes (later Sir Barnes) Wallis, the designer of the Vickers Wellington. Although referred to as a bomb, it was actually a mine. Subsequently, 617 squadron gained fame for dropping another of Barnes Wallis' inventions, the 12,000 lb Tallboy. This was the weapon used for the sinking of the German pocket battleship *Tirpitz* in a Norwegian fjord. The largest bomb dropped during World War II was yet another Barnes Wallis innovation, the massive 22,000-lb Grand Slam. In order for 617 squadron Lancasters hauling the 22,000-pounder to get airborne with this gross overload, numerous modifications were necessary, including the deletion of the nose and dorsal gun turrets, strengthening of the landing gear, removal of the bomb bay doors, and so forth. Where 5000-lb blockbusters had barely chipped the concrete, the Tallboys and Grand Slams wreaked havoc against the heavily fortified U-boat pens, penetrating through as much as 35 ft of reinforced concrete and creating significant local "earthquakes."

De Havilland D.H.98 Mosquito

An unarmed bomber relying on speed alone for defense was a radical concept in the late 1930s; however, that was the theory behind what was arguably the most versatile twin-engine aircraft of World War II. The roots of the Mosquito went back to the early 1930s when de Havilland was approached to build a purpose-built aircraft for the upcoming race from England to Melbourne. Three D.H.88 Comets were built for the race, which was won by the entry fielded by C. W. A. Scott and T. Campbell Black. This aircraft gave de Havilland invaluable experience with high-performance wooden aircraft. De Havilland's wood construction techniques were further refined with the Albatross, an innovative, four-engine transport of the late 1930s.

The Mosquito was conceived in 1938 as a small bomber that would rely on speed for protection (Fig. 4.48). Although it was initially resisted by the British Air Ministry, its one savior was Air Marshal Sir Wilfrid Freeman, who had faith in de Havilland's radical new aircraft. Known as Freeman's Folly, it came close to cancellation on several occasions. Luckily common sense prevailed, and the prototype was ready for its maiden flight on 25 November 1940, after an eight-month design period.

After completing de Havilland's initial three-month trial period, the prototype was handed over to the RAF for service evaluation. The only complaint levied against this remarkable new aircraft was the fact that they were not available in sufficient quantities. Showing the diversified nature of the original design, fighter and photo reconnaissance versions were quickly developed.

Power for the prototype was supplied by Merlin XXs, which were single-stage, two-speed engines modified with a reversed cooling flow (Ref. 4.14). All early production examples were powered by 20-series engines, which were also single-stage, two-speed engines. With the introduction of two-speed, two-stage engines, a dramatic increase in performance was demonstrated, particularly at high altitude where the two-stage engines came into their element. A photo reconnaissance (P.R.) Mk. VIII was the first recipient of the two-stage engines, which were Merlin 61s intended for Spitfire Mk. IXs. The 9-in-longer two-stage engines necessitated a slightly longer nacelle; this additional length also allowed the installation of individual exhaust stacks. The single-stage-powered aircraft had individual stacks for the front four cylinders; the rear two cylinders were siamesed to avoid interference with the radiator intake. Because of lack of space in the existing radiator housing, the intercooler radiator was housed under the nacelle, fed by a leading-edge duct. Most of the subsequent two-stage engines were the 70 series, some of which were fitted with a cabin supercharger for cabin pressurization at high altitude. Single-stage engine production was allocated to the fighter versions (Fig. 4.49), and two-stage engines were used for bombers because of the typically higher altitudes they flew.

Fig. 4.48 Bomber version of the de Havilland Mosquito. The bombers were usually powered by two-stage, 70-series Merlins. This shot shows shrouds in place for some degree of exhaust flame damping. Due to the extra length of the two-speed engines, it was not necessary to siamese the rear two exhaust stacks as in the case of the single-stage-powered aircraft. (Courtesy of Rolls-Royce plc.)

Fig. 4.49 Fighter version of the de Havilland Mosquito identifiable by the solid nose and flat windshield. Most fighters were powered by single-stage, two-speed 20-series Merlins. (Courtesy of Rolls-Royce plc.)

The construction techniques were highly unusual; the Mosquito had one of the original composite structures used for aircraft, much of it based on experience from the Albatross. Although wooden aircraft were nothing new, the Mosquito advanced the state-of-the-art for this construction material by creating a monocoque fuselage from a sandwich of two outer skins of thin, 0.035- to 0.080-in ply loaded in tension. The two outer skins sandwiched a balsa core typically 0.75 to 1.25 in thick. The grain of the balsa ran between the outer skins thus taking advantage of the high compressive strength of this remarkable material. Wing construction was no less impressive, featuring double skins of birch ply sandwiching spruce stringers. The skins contained two spars, thus making a massive and strong torsion box.

Engine mounts were chrome molybdenum steel alloy tubular assemblies attached to the front and rear spars. The main landing gear was also attached to the engine mounts.

Cooling the pair of Merlins with the minimum of drag was a major challenge, which de Havilland solved beautifully. A 22-in extension added to the leading edge of the wing between the fuselage, and the nacelle housed the oil and coolant radiators. A unique idiosyncrasy of the Merlin installation in the Mosquito was the so-called "reverse flow." Because of the high relative position of the radiator, coolant flowed from the pump discharge (on the bottom of the engine) to the radiator, where it was routed to the cylinder banks, discharged into the header tank and back to the pump (Ref. 4.24).

Operationally the Mosquito was a major factor in the Allied victory in Europe because of its remarkable versatility and performance. The missions that personify the Mosquito mystique were the precision bombing raids carried out against the Amiens jail in France. Captured French resistance workers were facing torture and certain death at the hands of the Nazi SS; consequently bombing accuracy was vital. The raid was successful in allowing 250 prisoners to escape.

Bombing accuracy, particularly at night, was difficult at the best of times; therefore, the RAF developed new tactics for their four-engine heavy bombers. They aimed for carefully placed colored incendiaries dropped by fast, low-flying Mosquitos. This gave the Mosquito the critical mission of pathfinder, which dramatically improved RAF bombing accuracy.

With a modified bomb bay and the bomb doors bulged, it was possible for a Mosquito to haul a specially modified 4000-lb bomb aloft (Fig. 4.50).

Curtiss P-40F

The Curtiss P-40, although an excellent aircraft when first introduced in the 1930s as a P-36 variant, was a dated design by the start of hostilities (somewhat analogous to the Hawker Hurricane). However, it was in production when more advanced designs were still on the drawing board or still in prototype form. The vast majority were powered by various models of the Allison V-1710 (see chapter 10 on Allison engines). The F model of the P-40 was powered by a Packard-built Merlin V-1650-1, equivalent to the Rolls-Royce Merlin 20-series, single-stage, two-speed engine. Because of the updraft induction (the Allisons all had downdraft induction) a deeper chin plenum was designed, not only to handle the induction requirements but also to house a larger, rectangular radiator, as opposed to a pair of circular radiators (Fig. 4.51).

Fairey Barracuda

As the first of the Fleet Air Arm's monoplane torpedo bombers to have a retractable undercarriage, the Fairey Barracuda represented a vast improvement in technology compared with the contemporary Fairey Swordfish (Fig. 4.52).

Fig. 4.50 The load-carrying capability of the de Havilland Mosquito was used to its full advantage carrying these 4000-lb loads. Known as "cookies," they were modified to fit the bomb bay of the Mosquito, which needed bulged bomb doors to accommodate this outsized load. (Courtesy of Rolls-Royce plc.)

Fig. 4.51 Curtiss P-40F powered by a single-stage, two-speed Packard-built V-1650-1, similar to a 20-series Rolls-Royce Merlin. (Courtesy of Rolls-Royce plc.)

Fig. 4.52 Fairey Barracuda II powered by a Rolls-Royce Merlin 32, a single-stage, two-speed engine. (Courtesy of Rolls-Royce plc.)

The Barracuda project was delayed when it became obvious that serious problems existed with the original engine, the Rolls-Royce Exe. The Merlin replaced the Exe, which led to a major redesign of the Barracuda. The prototype flew in early 1941, powered by a single-stage, two-speed Merlin 30 rated at 1300 hp. Subsequent aircraft were powered by the Merlin 32, rated at 1645 hp.

A feature that remained with the follow-on to the Barracuda, the Firefly, was the use of Youngman flaps. The flaps were attached behind the trailing edge and below the wing and could be set at different angles for take-off, landing, and dive-bombing. Other construction features were conventional. An all-metal, monocoque fuselage housed the two crew members. The main landing gear was pivoted at the base of the fuselage and retracted outwardly into the wings.

One of the more significant missions flown by the Barracuda was the 3 April 1944 attack on the German pocket battleship, *Tirpitz,* which was holed up in a Norwegian fjord. Barracudas were also used extensively in the Pacific against the Japanese (Ref. 2.7).

Armstrong Whitworth Whitley

Another old soldier that performed satisfactorily during World War II, the Armstrong Whitworth Whitley was designed to Air Ministry Specification B.3/34 (third bomber specification for 1934), which called for a twin-engine medium bomber (Fig. 4.53). It was totally obsolete by the start of hostilities, but it was the best the RAF had at the time. The prototype first flew in 1936 powered by a pair of Armstrong Siddeley Tigers, which were 14-cylinder, two-row air-cooled radials. The Tiger was the world's first production engine fitted with a two-speed supercharger (Ref. 2.5).

During the initial stages of World War II, the so-called "phony war" took place, that is, the gloves were not off and both sides were feeling each other out. Leaflet raids were a part of this phony war. The RAF dropped propaganda leaflets on Germany at night in the vain hope Germany would not continue with the war. In retrospect, the only effect these raids had was to give the German population an abundant supply of toilet paper! Whitleys were used extensively during these raids; however, when the war started to get more serious they were quickly withdrawn from front-line duties.

In secondary roles, Whitleys were used extensively for training fight engineers, general reconnaissance, antisubmarine and convoy protection duties, glider towing, Coastal Command, and so forth.

Whitley Vs made up most of the production run, powered by Merlin Xs, which were single-stage, two-speed engines rated at 1130 hp (Fig. 4.54).

Fig. 4.53 Armstrong Whitworth Whitley powered by two Rolls-Royce Merlin Xs. It was used extensively during the early "phony" war stages of World War II by dropping leaflets on the German population. (Courtesy of Rolls-Royce plc.)

Fig. 4.54 Close-up of the Armstrong Whitworth Whitley QEC showing the Merlin X installation. Note the early style Merlin siamesed exhaust system. Scoop on the lower cowl supplies induction air to the two-barrel carburetor. Another, similar air scoop is on the opposite side. (Courtesy of Rolls-Royce plc.)

Boulton Paul Defiant

In the 1930s military strategists felt a single-engine fighter with a powered gun turret would be the wave of the future. Boulton Paul met this challenge by producing the Defiant, built to Air Ministry Specification F.9/35 (the ninth fighter specification of 1935). The prototype first flew on 11 August 1937, powered by a Merlin III.

Mounting the gun turret behind the pilot was a new concept at the time. However, the idea was seriously flawed as the pilot had no forward defensive armament. The first real taste of battle occurred in May 1940 during the retreat of the British Army from France. Luftwaffe pilots were fooled into thinking the Defiant was a Hurricane or Spitfire. Thirty-seven Luftwaffe aircraft were shot down in one day with no losses. This initial success was short-lived. As the Luftwaffe learned of this new aircraft, they were found to be vulnerable and thereafter suffered unacceptable losses. Consequently, Defiants were soon used for night fighting only and finally relegated to target towing (Fig. 4.55). Later production Defiant IIs and IIIs were powered by the Merlin XX.

Power Augmentation

Rather surprisingly, Rolls-Royce did not employ ADI (water/methanol injection) during World War II, although its advantages were well known. The rationale was that the extra complexity and weight were not worth the additional power. Instead, power was increased primarily through increased boost pressure, requiring enriched fuel/air mixture and charge cooling. Nitrous oxide was the only form of power augmentation used, and that only in one squadron of de Havilland Mosquitos (Ref. 2.12).

Packard, on the other hand, developed ADI on their later engines, including the -9s and -11s, but these engines did not quite get to the front prior to VJ-Day.

Fig. 4.55 Boulton Paul Defiant powered by a Rolls-Royce Merlin III. Not long after its combat debut in France, it was relegated to secondary roles such as night fighting, training and target towing. (Courtesy of the National Air and Space Museum, Smithsonian Institution, Photo No. 2A-11943.)

Would Haves, Could Haves, Should Haves

By 1942 the Merlin had the enviable reputation of being one of the finest aircraft engines available in the world. This led to ever increasing demand for it by aircraft designers and manufacturers.

In 1944 an Eighth Air Force Lockheed P-38 was flown from Bovington to Hucknall for a trial installation of single-stage, two-speed Merlin XXs. Rolls-Royce test-flew the aircraft a number of times, unmodified, until word came down to return the aircraft immediately! It seems that the decision was political in nature due to the fact the orders to stop work came from Washington (Refs. 4.14, 4.25). Considering the problematic service record of the P-38 in the Eighth Air Force, it seems almost criminal that politics should be allowed to interfere with the development of a potentially useful aircraft. Lockheed did an extensive engineering evaluation of the P-38 powered by two-stage Merlins; the resulting aircraft would have been dramatically transformed in a manner similar to the North American P-51 Mustang.

Don Berlin, designer of the Curtiss P-40, recognized the altitude superiority of the two-stage Merlin over the Allison and had a proposal for one of these engines to be installed in the Curtiss P-40. Again this did not happen, probably because of the obsolescence of the P-40 after 1942 (Ref. 2.5). Installing a state-of-the-art engine that was in great demand for other aircraft did not make sense.

A feasibility study was made of installing the Merlin in the Bell P-39,* and preliminary work was done to develop the Packard Merlin V-1650-5 for the installation of a remote propeller reduction gearbox. Yet again this ended up only a paper airplane.

Curtiss built a version of the P-60, designated XP-60D, powered by a Packard V-1650-3. The prototype crashed in May 1943.

---

*Some sources say P-63.

Other Interesting Applications

Merlins saw service in a number of nonaircraft applications, primarily the Cromwell tank, used extensively during World War II. Designated Meteor, it was based on the Merlin, although several design changes were made including substitution of cast iron for the aluminum lower crankcase, repositioning of the coolant pump, elimination of the supercharger, and so forth. Meteor engines ran in the opposite direction to the Merlin in order to accommodate the Cromwell's five-speed transmission. It also featured Kestrel valve timing. As a point of interest, many restored World War II aircraft powered by Merlins have Meteor tank engine components in them (Ref. 4.26)!

The RAF took advantage of the Merlin's power-to-weight ratio and installed them in motor torpedo boats (MTB) (Fig. 4.56). Three "marinized" Merlins were installed, although few MTBs were manufactured with the Merlin; most were powered by a marine version of the World War I vintage Napier Lion known as the Sea Lion.

Perhaps the wildest Merlin application was the torpedo. A Merlin-powered torpedo was designed and tested, intended for use in the Pacific, but the ceasing of hostilities halted this effort. Induction air for the Merlin was obtained via a Schnorkel mast (Ref. 2.12).

A V-8 version of the Merlin, known as the Meteorite, was built to be used as the engine for a tank transporter; however, relatively few were manufactured.

Fig. 4.56 Marine version of the Rolls-Royce Merlin. They were installed in motor torpedo (MTB) boats (equivalent to PT boats). Due to urgent aircraft requirements for Merlins, relatively few saw this service. A marine version of the Napier Lion, known as the Sea Lion, was substituted. (Courtesy of Rolls-Royce plc.)

Griffon

The Griffon was initially developed at the request of the Fleet Air Arm. Navy aircraft tend to be larger and heavier than their land-based counterparts. This obviously puts greater demands on the engine if performance is to be maintained. To meet this demand, Rolls-Royce went back to the concept of the Schneider Trophy R engine. The Griffon, essentially a modernized Merlin, was a 60° V-12 with 6.0-in bores and 6.6-in stroke giving a 2239 in³ displacement (the same parameters as the R and 36% greater than the Merlin) (Fig. 4.57). However, this was a totally new engine featuring many design updates and improvements over the Merlin.

Development started in 1939 and, compared with the early Merlin, went quite smoothly. Several deviations were made from previous Rolls-Royce V-12 practice. The camshaft and magneto drives were taken from the front, offering two advantages. First, the length of the engine was reduced, thus satisfying one of the main requirements of the Griffon, that it be retrofitted in existing Merlin-powered aircraft. Second, the critical timing function of the valves and the ignition were not left to the mercy of the torsional excursions of the crankshaft. The magneto and camshaft drive gears tapped off the propeller reduction gear for their drive requirements, along with the starter. Early development and production Griffons also drove the supercharger from the front by means of a long quill shaft that ran under the crankshaft, driven off a gear on the front of the crankshaft. Because of various manufacturing problems, this promising idea was quickly dropped (Fig. 4.58). In later engines, the supercharger took its drive in a similar way to the Merlin, by a quill shaft splined into the No. 7 rear main journal of the crankshaft. Early engines featured single-stage, two-speed supercharging, again copying Merlin practice, but beefed up to take the heavier loads imposed upon it. The crankshaft, also like the Merlin, was a 120°, nitrided, forged chrome molybdenum steel alloy unit supported in seven cross-bolted main bearings. However, the firing order was different from the Merlin. A 60° V-12 with a 120 crank and paired throws had a number of permutations on ideal firing order, not one superior to another provided the intake system was "tuned" for the firing order chosen. However, the exhaust note varied. This gave the Griffon its classic "Griffon Growl" exhaust sound,

Fig. 4.57 Rolls-Royce Griffon IIB. This is an early production version of this long-lived engine. The oil feed for the end-to-end crankshaft lubrication is shown in the circular plate at the front of the engine. Camshaft and magneto drives were taken from the front of the engine. (Courtesy of Rolls-Royce plc.)

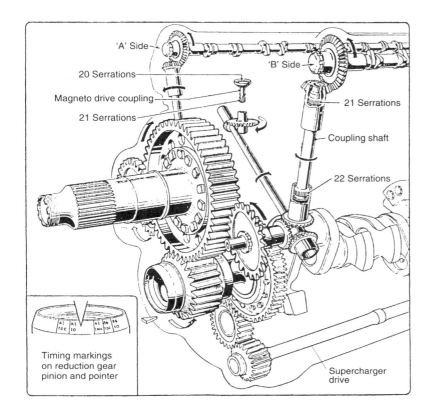

'A' Side
20 Serrations
Magneto drive coupling
21 Serrations
'B' Side
21 Serrations
Coupling shaft
22 Serrations
Timing markings
on reduction gear
pinion and pointer
Supercharger
drive

Fig. 4.58 One of the deviations Rolls-Royce made when developing the Griffon was the drive arrangement for the magneto and cams. The Merlin drove the camshafts and magnetos from the rear of the engine; consequently, these critical timing functions were at the mercy of the torsional twist of the crankshaft and spring drive. Cam and magneto drive on the Griffon came from the front of the engine, thus eliminating any torsional windup in the system. Note the early supercharger drive using a quill shaft driven off the front of the crankshaft. (Courtesy of the Fleet Air Arm Museum.)

not as sweet as the Merlin, but still impressive! Different valve timing also contributed to the difference in exhaust note. The Griffon had a relatively modest 28° of overlap and 248° of cam duration compared with the Merlin's more radical 43° of overlap and 263° of duration. Later Merlins had 70° of overlap and 288° of duration. The crankshaft rotated in the opposite direction to that in the Merlin. In the late 1930s, the Society of British Aircraft Constructors (SBAC) established standardization guidelines, including the direction of propeller rotation, which was clockwise when viewed from the front. Consequently, with a simple spur reduction gear, the Griffon crankshaft rotated in the opposite direction from most previous Rolls-Royce aircraft engines.

A further refinement was made to the propeller reduction gear pinion drive by incorporating a floating ring at the crankshaft end featuring male and female splines. This was an effort to further isolate the pinion gear from the torsional vibration of the crankshaft. After the debacle with the ramp head on the Merlin, the Griffon featured the by now ubiquitous and well-proven Kestrel-based combustion chamber, which traced its heritage back to the Curtiss D-12. Another lesson learned from Merlin experience was the incorporation of end-to-end crankshaft lubrication; indeed, this feature proved so successful that all subsequent Rolls-Royce piston engines employed it after its introduction in the 100-series Merlin. One of the design peculiarities of the Merlin that dated to the early 1930s was the extensive use of external oil lines rather than the more modern internal oil galleries. These external oil lines tended to be maintenance headaches, and at times were major contributors to oil leaks and the occasional fracture, resulting in serious engine damage. By comparison the Griffon was a clean design with few external oil lines. Accessories required for aircraft systems such as electric generators, hydraulic pumps, vacuum pumps, and so forth, took their drive from a remotely mounted gear box driven from a power take-off from the wheelcase. The Merlin on the other hand had accessories cluttering the exterior of the engine with the vacuum pump and propeller governor mounted on the front, and the tachometer generator or tachometer drive, air compressor, and hydraulic pump were mounted on the cylinder heads driven off the camshafts. The lower crankcase also offered a drive take-off for a hydraulic pump, overall a somewhat disorganized arrangement.

Shoehorning the Griffon into a relatively small, light, single-engine aircraft such as the Spitfire created some handling difficulties primarily due to the enormous torque reaction. This could amount to a very significant 4700 lb-ft at take-off power. Designing a gear reduction unit for a contra-rotating propeller turned out to be the definitive answer after various aerodynamic attempts such as enlarged vertical stabilizer area presented only partial solutions. Eighty-series Griffons were the first to receive dual-rotating propeller drives and were introduced just prior to the end of World War II. This was accomplished by having two pinions and two reduction gears. The front pinion and driven gear were of a smaller diameter than those in the rear. An additional idler gear in the front reduction gear resulted in opposite rotation. The reduction gears drove coaxial, contra-rotating propeller shafts (Fig. 4.59). Contra-rotating propellers were essential for the Navy version of the Griffon Spitfire, known

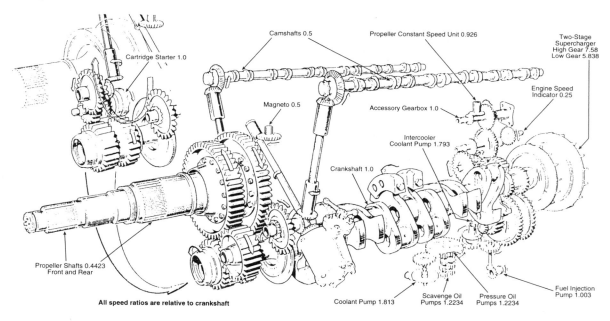

Fig. 4.59 Gear trains for the Rolls-Royce Griffon 80 series. Note the contra-rotating propeller drive and elimination of the front quill drive for the supercharger. (Courtesy of the Fleet Air Arm Museum.)

as the Seafire, because of the extremely hazardous nature of carrier landings, particularly during a go-around when maximum power needed to be applied at low altitude and low air speed. Torque reaction pulled a Griffon Spitfire with a single propeller to the right, toward the carrier island, obviously a very precarious situation. Other internal features of the engine followed Merlin practice.

Early Griffons entered service with two-speed, single-stage superchargers, rated at 1735 hp at 16,000 ft, which soon gave way to two-speed, two-stage superchargers with intercooling and aftercooling, similar in design to the Merlin, rated at 2350 hp. This was achieved with the extremely high manifold pressure of 25 psig or 80 in Hg. This manifold pressure required ADI and 150 PN fuel to control detonation.

The two-speed supercharger shifting was automatic, relying on an aneroid switch controlled by atmospheric pressure to shift to the appropriate blower speed. Centrifugal bob weights mounted on the blower clutches added to the drive capability of the clutches—the faster it spun, the harder the clutch grabbed. When the blower shifted, a small degree of clutch slip was built in, otherwise the accelerating forces would damage and possibly strip the blower drive gears (Fig. 4.60). The clutches also absorbed some of the torsional vibration emanating from the crankshaft; this design feature may help explain why no Rolls-Royce piston engines—except for the Eagle 22, the last of their piston engines—required any dynamic crankshaft counterweights.

A few examples of the 100-series Griffon were built with three-speed, two-stage supercharging. The only application was the Supermarine Spiteful and its Navy counterpart the Seafang, which was a development of the Spitfire featuring laminar flow wings.

Two-stage, two-speed Griffons, the 60 series, were typically rated at 2045 hp at sea level in moderate supercharge and 2245 hp at 9250 ft in full supercharge. All horsepower ratings were at 2750 rpm (Figs. 4.61, 4.62).

Carburetion could be accomplished by a three-barrel injection carburetor, built by Rolls-Royce and based on the Bendix injection unit. Alternatively, carburetion was accomplished by a single-point Rolls-Royce injection unit (Ref. 2.7), which, like the Bendix unit, sprayed atomized fuel into the first-stage supercharger impeller eye but operated on the speed density principle.

Applications

Table 4.3 summarizes the performance and applications of the Griffon engine.

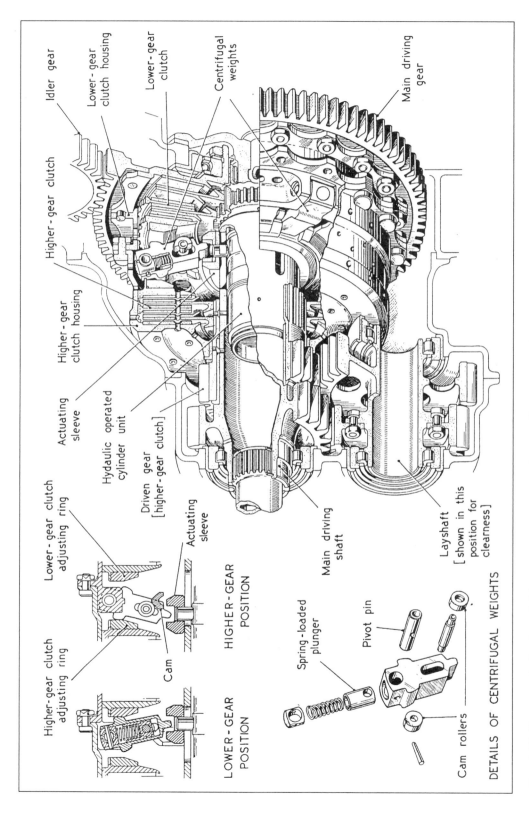

Fig. 4.60 Two-speed clutch and drive gear arrangement for a Rolls-Royce Griffon two-stage supercharger. (Courtesy of the Fleet Air Arm Museum.)

98

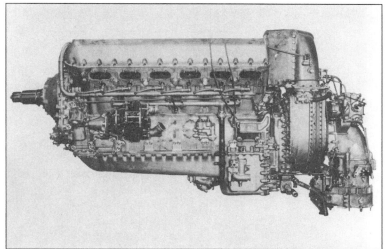

Fig. 4.61 Side view of two-stage Rolls-Royce Griffon, illustrating the massive size of the supercharger. (Courtesy of Rolls-Royce plc.)

Fig. 4.62 Bottom view of a Rolls-Royce Griffon 60 series. The coolant pump is shown to good advantage along with the two-barrel carburetor. Similar in operation to a Bendix injection carburetor. Some Griffons were fitted with a single-point fuel-injection system designed by Rolls-Royce. (Courtesy of Rolls-Royce plc.)

TABLE 4.3—ROLLS-ROYCE GRIFFON PERFORMANCE AND APPLICATION SUMMARY

Dash Number	Applications	hp/rpm/alt	Comments
II	Firefly I/II	1730/2750/750 1490/2750/14,000	Single-stage, two-speed
III	Spitfire XII	1730/2750/750 1490/2750/14,000	Similar to Griffon II
IV	Spitfire XII	1730/2750/750 1490/2750/14,000	Similar to Griffon II, different propeller reduction gear ratio
VI	Seafire XV/XVII	1850/2750/2000 1635/2750/10,500	Similar to Griffon IV but higher boost pressure of 60 in Hg

(continued)

TABLE 4.3, continued

Dash Number	Applications	hp/rpm/alt	Comments
XII	Firefly I/II	1765/2750/SL 1665/2750/11,000	Similar to Griffon VI but lower supercharger gear ratios
61	Spitfire 21/22 Seafire 45/46	2035/2750/7000 1820/2750/21,000	First of the two-stage, two-speed Griffons. Blower conceptually similar to Merlin 60 series. Note dramatically improved altitude performance compared to single-stage engines
65	Spitfire XIV Spitfire F.R. XVIII Spitfire P.R. XIX Spiteful F. Mk. XIV	2035/2750/7000 1820/2750/21,000	Similar to Griffon 61 except different propeller reduction ratio
66	Spitfire P.R. XIX	2035/2750/7000 1820/2750/21,000	Same as Griffon 65 except provision made for cabin supercharger drive
72	Firefly IV	2045/2750/SL[a] 2245/2750/9250[b]	Modification of Griffon 65 for Navy requirements. Rolls-Royce Bendix-Stromberg carburetor
74	Firefly IV	2045/2750/SL 2245/2750/9250	Same as Griffon 72 except 74 is fitted with Rolls-Royce speed density fuel injection
83	Seafire MB.5	2035/2750/7000 1820/2750/21,000	Similar to Griffon 65 except fitted with contra-rotating propeller drive
85	Spitfire 21/22 Spiteful F. Mk. XV	1935/2750/SL 2350/2750/1250 2120/2750/15,750	Fitted with Bendix Stromberg 9T-40-1 injection carburetor. Contradrive
101/121 130	Spiteful Seafang	2420/2750/5000[c] 2050/2750/21,000	Griffon 101/121/130 series featured two-stage, three-speed superchargers. 121 and 130 used contra-rotating propeller drive. Griffon 101 used single propeller shaft

(a) 67 in Hg. (b) 80.8 in Hg with 150-PN fuel. (c) Power obtained with 150-PN fuel and 80.8 in Hg. Source: Refs. 2.5, 2.7, 4.15–4.18.

Fairey Firefly

The first recipient of the Griffon was the Fairey Firefly, a carrier-based Fleet Air Arm torpedo bomber. It was initially fitted with single-stage, two-speed Griffon IIs rated at 1730 hp; later Fireflys were upgraded with two-stage, two-speed engines. No new ground was broken in the design of the Firefly, which was a low-wing stressed-skin design featuring manual wing folding. Early Fireflys fitted with single-stage Griffon IIs used a "chin"-type radiator mounted under the engine (Fig. 4.63). With the introduction of the two-stage-powered aircraft, the radiators and oil coolers were relocated to the wing leading edge (Fig. 4.64). One of the first missions flown by Fireflys was the attack in November 1944 on the *Tirpitz*.

Griffon-powered Supermarine Spitfire and Supermarine Seafire

In early 1941, the Focke-Wulf 190 menace appeared over England for the first time, creating havoc with its then superior performance over anything the British could throw against it at the time. Immediately, plans were put in place to shoehorn the Griffon into the Spitfire, not an easy task. The finished product was a masterpiece of engineering, representing the state-of-the-art technology for engine installation at that time. From the firewall forward, everything was new. The oil tank was relocated from its previous position under the engine to the firewall. A fabricated sheet aluminum mount, similar in concept to the North American P-51, replaced the previous chrome molybdenum steel alloy tubular mount. Three bumps at the front of the cowl accommodated the valve covers and the single large magneto. Because of the much greater heat rejection requirements of the Griffon, the familiar underwing radiators now grew, having far greater depth for additional radiator capacity (Fig. 4.65).

Fig. 4.63 Early Fairey Firefly T1 used for training. Later Fireflys had the radiators and coolers relocated to the leading edge of the wing. (Courtesy of the Fleet Air Arm Museum.)

Fig. 4.64 Fairey Firefly being prepared for a catapult take-off. Note the extended Youngman wing flaps. (Courtesy of the Fleet Air Arm Museum.)

Fig. 4.65 Supermarine Spitfire Mk. XIV powered by a Rolls-Royce Griffon 65 two-stage engine rated at 2000 hp. (Courtesy of the National Air and Space Museum, Smithsonian Institution, Photo No. 1B-42639.)

Spitfire XIIs were the first recipient of the Griffon powered by the Mk. III or IV variants with single-stage, two-speed supercharging. A number of subsequent Spitfires retained Merlin power, but toward the end of Spitfire production all were powered by Griffons. Starting with the Spitfire XIV, two-stage, two-speed intercooled and aftercooled superchargers became standard.

As can be imagined, the Griffon-powered Seafire was initially a dangerous handful when operated from a carrier (Fig. 4.66). The solution was to fit contra-rotating propellers on the Seafire F.R. 47. This modification did not see service in World War II (Fig. 4.67).

Fig. 4.66 Arrested landing for a Supermarine Seafire Mk. XV. The Griffon-powered Seafires were almost unmanageable when fitted with a single four-blade propeller as shown in this shot. Various fixes were tried with limited success, including widening the landing gear. The definitive fix was the fitting of contra-rotating propellers, thereby eliminating the effects of torque reaction. (Courtesy of the Fleet Air Arm Museum.)

Fig. 4.67 Supermarine F.R. 47 Seafire. Torque reaction from the mighty Griffon could make the aircraft a handful, but the six-blade contra-rotating propeller eliminated this torque reaction. The F.R. 47 also featured a 1-ft wider undercarriage track for improved deck handling. (Courtesy of the National Air and Space Museum, Smithsonian Institution, Photo No. 1B-42653.)

Supermarine Spiteful and Seafang

Under development throughout most of World War II, the final and ultimate Spitfire variation, the Spiteful (designed to Air Ministry Specification F.1/43), along with the Navy derivative, the Seafang (Navy specification N.5/45), did not see action during the war (Fig. 4.68). Essentially a brand-new design with a lot of Spitfire influence, it was the first Supermarine aircraft to feature laminar flow flying surfaces. Other design refinements included less-drag-producing, wide slim radiators mounted under the wings, and wide-track, inwardly retracting landing gear that corrected one of the Spitfire's few faults, that of poor ground handling. First flown on 30 June 1944, the prototype looked promis-

Fig. 4.68 The ultimate Supermarine Spitfire variant was the Spiteful and its Navy counterpart, the Seafang (shown). Powered by a variety of two-stage Griffons, most had Griffon 85s installed. Rolls-Royce developed the 100-series Griffon for this aircraft, featuring two-stage supercharging with three speeds. (Courtesy of the Fleet Air Arm Museum.)

ing, although shortly afterward it was destroyed in an accident, killing the test pilot. This set the program back, and eventually the Spiteful/Seafang faded away into history with only a small handful of aircraft built, none of which entered squadron service.

Initially powered by a Griffon 65, later versions used a Griffon 85, which was essentially the same engine but drove a six-blade contra-rotating propeller. Finally, the ultimate Griffon variant was fitted, the 100 series, which featured three-speed, two-stage supercharging.

An interesting footnote is the fact that Spiteful flying surfaces were used as the basis for Supermarine's first jet powered aircraft, the Attacker.

Martin-Baker MB.5

Another near miss was the Martin-Baker (of ejection seat fame) MB.5 single-engine fighter (Fig. 4.69). Superficially, it looked similar to the North American P-51, but it was larger and featured totally different construction methods. A chrome molybdenum steel alloy tube fuselage was covered with quickly detachable metal panels, and a classic D spar wing had a laminated steel spar, a design feature of Martin-Baker aircraft (Ref. 2.7). It was powered by a Griffon 83 with two-stage, two-speed supercharging driving contra-rotating propellers rated at 2035 hp. This combination gave the MB.5 a formidable top speed of over 450 mph.

This promising project, built only in prototype form, was canceled at the end of the war. In the meantime, Martin-Baker went on to develop its famous line of ejection seats.

Fig. 4.69 Martin Baker M.B.5 powered by a Rolls-Royce Griffon 83 two-stage, two-speed engine driving a Rotol contra-rotating propeller. Superficially similar to the P-51, the M.B.5 was considerably larger and heavier and was built using different construction methods. (Courtesy of the National Air and Space Museum, Smithsonian Institution, Photo No. 2A-23529.)

Paper Airplanes

If a little is good then more must be better, right? This was the philosophy behind a scheme to install the Griffon into the P-51. Unlike the Griffon conversion of the Spitfire, the Griffon-powered P-51 entailed a totally new design incorporating only the flying surfaces from the P-51. An all-new fuselage featuring a mid-engine layout with the pilot sitting in front of the engine, à la P-39, driving a six-blade Rotol contra-rotating propeller would have made it a new aircraft.

Transfer gears mounted at the front of the engine provided drive to the propeller. The driveshaft ran under the cockpit and terminated at the propeller reduction gears mounted in the nose. A torque tube mounted on the propeller reduction gear case at the front, and on the engine at the rear, enclosed the driveshaft, thus alleviating the nose structure of the aircraft from the considerable torque reaction loads, which were instead transmitted back to the engine (Fig. 4.70). Splines on both ends of the torque tube allowed longitudinal float. Three early Allison-powered RAF Mustang Is, equivalent to USAAC Mustang As (North American P-51As), were obtained to supply parts for the project.

Since the Griffon P-51 was intended to be a flying test bed, there was never any intention of placing it into production. Substantial work had been completed when the project was cancelled for the usual reason during this time frame—gas turbine development (Refs. 4.14, 4.21).

Peregrine

The Peregrine was one of the lesser-known Rolls-Royce engines from World War II, based on the Kestrel with the same bore and stroke in V-12, 60° configuration (Fig. 4.71). Updates from the Kestrel included downdraft carburetion. This enabled a smaller frontal area compared to the updraft set-up

Fig. 4.70 Specially modified Rolls-Royce Griffon intended for the Griffon-powered Mustang. Note the transfer gear case at the front of the engine. (Courtesy of Rolls-Royce plc.)

used in most previous Rolls-Royce engines (Fig. 4.72). Downdraft carburetion appeared on some of the later Merlins for frontal area reduction. Although the Peregrine was a promising engine, by World War II 1296 in³ (21.25 L) was simply insufficient. It was often described as a "Merlinized" Kestrel because of the many Merlin features incorporated into the design, such as the cylinder head/cylinder bank design, drive systems for accessories, and the familiar dual V drive at the front. Rated at a respectable 885 hp at 3000 rpm, even this high specific power was inadequate for the demands of aerial combat in World War II (Ref. 4.2).

Application

The only aircraft produced in significant numbers to receive the Peregrine was the Westland Whirlwind. A light, twin-engine fighter, the Whirlwind had many advanced features, such as a "T" tail, leading-edge radiators, and a bubble canopy—a world's first when introduced on the Whirlwind (Fig. 4.73).

In order to eliminate the serious effects of torque, particularly on take-off, it was planned to make the engines handed, that is, turn in opposite directions. Logistically, this would have led to problems in servicing the engines, so the idea was dropped. In the case of the Merlin 130 and 131 for the de Havilland Hornet, the elegantly simple solution of adding an idler gear in the propeller reduction gear gave the required opposite rotation, leaving the rest of the engine interchangeable.

Fig. 4.71 Rolls-Royce Peregrine. Based on the Kestrel, it incorporated many Merlin features. (Courtesy of Rolls-Royce plc.)

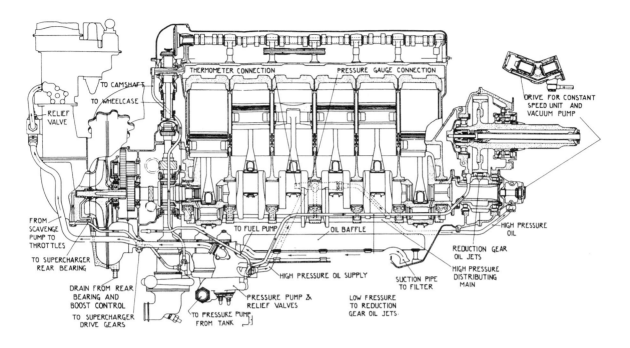

Fig. 4.72 *Often described as a "Merlinized" Kestrel, the Peregrine saw very little service; the only application was the Westland Whirlwind. Note the downdraft carburetion, which was featured on the last military Merlins to great effect. One of the less desirable Merlin features was the extensive use of external oil lines. ("Peregrine Aero Engine," Air Publication 1761A, British Crown Copyright/Ministry of Defence. Reproduced with the permission of the Controller of Her Britannic Majesty's Stationery Office. Courtesy of Dave Payne,* The Fighter Collection, *Duxford.)*

Fig. 4.73 *Westland Whirlwind powered by two Rolls-Royce Peregrines of 885 hp each. Innovations abounded in the Whirlwind, such as the wing leading-edge radiators, "T" tail, and bubble cockpit canopy. (Courtesy of the National Air and Space Museum, Smithsonian Institution, Photo No. 1B-49885.)*

Numerous problems during its brief service life gave it the unflattering nickname the "Pesky Peregrine." Overheating seemed to have been the major problem; however, that was not the fault of the engine but rather a quirk of the installation. The Whirlwind featured leading-edge radiators, similar to those on the Mosquito. In certain flap configurations, airflow through the radiator was reduced thus inducing overheating. The Whirlwind was introduced in 1940 and most had been withdrawn from service by 1941.

Vulture

It seems that at one time or another, every major corporation manages to produce a "lemon." Everyone is familiar with the Ford Edsel debacle, the embarrassing Chevrolet Vega, or the IBM PC Jr. Rolls-Royce also had its "lemon" in the form of the Vulture. Often described as a doubled-up Kestrel or Peregrine, in fact the Vulture was a totally new design.

It was a liquid-cooled X-configuration engine with four banks of six cylinders at 90° spacing for even firing, driving a common crankshaft (Fig. 4.74). Design work started in 1935.

The only Kestrel features used were the 5.0-in bores and the 5.5-in stroke. Merlin cylinder spacing of 6.1 in offered the opportunity to increase the displacement by enlarging the bore dimension to 5.4 in, same as in the Merlin. As it turned out, due to the development difficulties no Vultures were manufactured with the larger cylinder bore.

Single-stage, two-speed supercharging with downdraft induction was implemented. Two discharges from the supercharger fed the intake manifolds in the upper and lower Vs. Exhaust manifolds were mounted on the sides of the Vs.

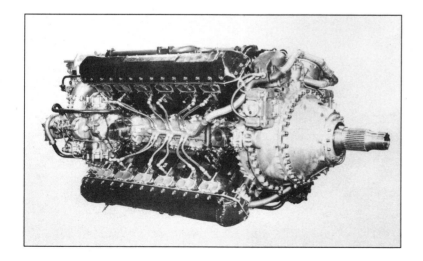

Fig. 4.74 Rolls-Royce Vulture. (Courtesy of Rolls-Royce plc.)

Reduction gearing featured a two-stage "back gear" set-up. Heavily loaded gear trains with multiple drive pinions offered the challenge of ensuring equal tooth loading. The Vulture dealt with this engineering issue by mounting the gears on a flange with a ring of bolts. At final assembly a preload was applied on the gear train, and the final reaming operation for the bolts was performed (Fig. 4.75). This was a typical example of the workmanship required to build a Rolls-Royce aircraft engine. Had the engine remained in production, plans were in place to use an epicyclic reduction gear, thus yielding an appreciable weight reduction. The first stage of the reduction gears, of which there were four, incorporated a bevel gear for each of the four tower shaft drives to the camshafts. This feature, shared by the Griffon, ensured that the torsional oscillations of the crankshaft would not affect valve timing. A contra-rotating propeller drive was developed for use in the Hawker Tornado.

Connecting rods, which contributed to the Vulture's woes, were of the master rod, link rod arrangement. Although this offered the advantage of mounting all four cylinders on the same centerline with a consequent minimal length, the rods were plagued with problems throughout the short and dismal

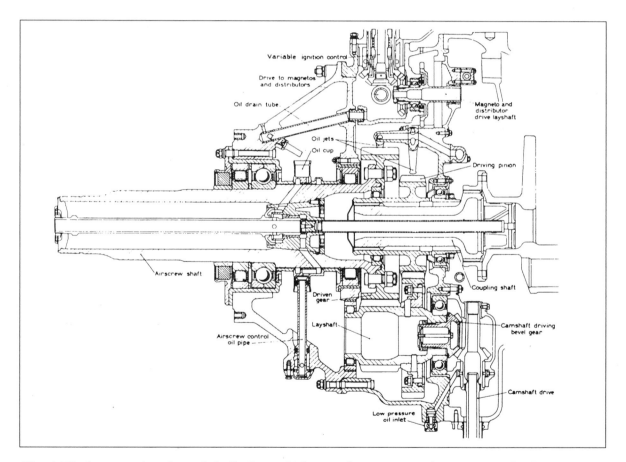

Fig. 4.75 Cross section through Rolls-Royce Vulture reduction gear. This two-stage back-gear design was to have been replaced with a more compact and lighter epicyclic gear if the Vulture had remained in production. (Courtesy of Rolls-Royce plc.)

life of the Vulture. In retrospect, it has been stated by several Rolls-Royce personnel that a preferable arrangement would have been pairs of blade-and-fork rods side by side. This design feature was in fact used successfully on the Eagle XVI, a 16-cylinder X engine designed shortly after World War I. Due to the shortage of space for cap bolts, early master rods featured a pivoted cap with a pair of bolts on the opposite side of the pivot. After several iterations of this pivoted rod design, a method was devised to use a conventional removable cap held in place with four bolts. Even this did not eliminate the problems as fretting at the face of the cap and rod would occur, resulting in master rod bearing failure. Pratt & Whitney got around this problem on their two-piece master connecting rods by incorporating a silver-plated shim at this critical intersection, thus avoiding the fretting problems that plagued the Vulture (Fig. 4.76).

Main bearing failures also attributable to fretting between the two crankcase halves were corrected by installing steel dowels in the crankcase faces. The dowels were drilled for the crankcase cross bolts to pass through them; this eliminated further main bearing problems.

A number of aircraft were lost because of fires due to overheating. One of the causes of the overheating was determined to be cavitation in one of the dual coolant pumps. A single outlet pipe from the radiator joined into a Y connection, which fed into the suction side of the coolant pumps. It was found, when using transparent pipes, that one pump would starve the other resulting in cavitation of the starved pump. The simple solution was a balance pipe between the two suction sides of the pumps, which balanced the load on them and eliminated any tendency toward cavitation (Ref. 4.14).

If the foregoing sounds like a disaster story, it was. Vultures were flown into combat with many of these problems unresolved, resulting in many losses from mechanical failure. In retrospect it could be argued that it should never have entered service until all the development problems had been

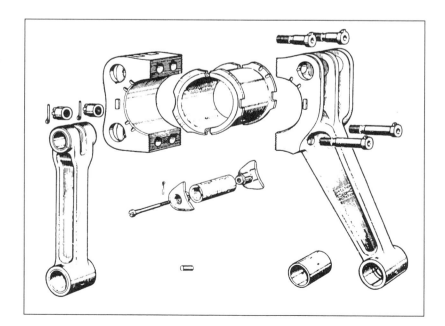

Fig. 4.76 Rolls-Royce Vulture connecting rod. Fretting at the face of the cap and rod could lead to rod failure, a ruptured crankcase, and a nasty oil fire. (Courtesy of Rolls-Royce plc.)

resolved. Unfortunately, war is not that simple. England had her back against the wall in 1940 when the Vulture entered service; anything that could be done to harm the enemy, was done. By 1941 the problems with the Vulture were becoming insurmountable and were absorbing huge amounts of resources that were desperately needed on other projects, so to no one's regret the engine was discontinued in April 1942. The primary reason for this was that the Avro Manchester heavy bomber, the only aircraft in large-scale production powered by the Vulture, was redesigned to take four Merlins in place of the two Vultures, thus evolving into the Avro Lancaster. The performance of the Lancaster surprised everyone including Roy Chadwick, the designer of both aircraft.

The Vulture was initially rated at 1845 hp at 3200 rpm at 5000 ft and 1710 hp at 15,000 ft; this power was later downgraded because of the reduction in maximum rpm to 3000 caused by the connecting rod woes (Refs. 4.2, 4.14).

Applications

Avro Manchester

In the 1930s, heavy bomber theory held that superior performance could be obtained from two large engines rather than from four smaller ones. This led Rolls-Royce to develop the Vulture for the Avro Manchester twin-engine bomber, which was designed in competition with the Handley Page HP 56 to specification P.13/36 (Fig. 4.77). This specification called out for a 12,000-lb bomb load to be carried internally, or a single 8000-lb bomb or a pair of torpedoes. Avro won the contract, and the prototype Manchester took to the air for the first time on 25 July 1939. Even this maiden flight was a harbinger of things to come, with overheating of the engines and heavy controls making things difficult for the test pilot.

Fig. 4.77 Avro Manchester powered by the problematic Rolls-Royce Vulture. Note the servo spade on the elevator and the hangar camouflaged as a house in the background. (Courtesy of Rolls-Royce plc.)

207 squadron was the only one to receive the Manchester, taking it into action for the first time in February 1941 on an attack of a German cruiser in Brest harbor (Ref. 4.27). As can be imagined, the squadron was plagued by mechanical problems, and on several occasions the Manchester was grounded until solutions for the more serious issues, such as the engine overheating and crankshaft main bearing problems, could be resolved.

Marginal performance limited the ceiling of the Manchester to 10,000 ft when loaded. Altitude could not be maintained on one engine, again aggravating an already bad situation. This left the aircraft especially vulnerable to the deadly medium-altitude German 88-mm flack batteries.

When the four-Merlin solution was initially suggested for the Manchester in 1940, the idea was scorned upon by Lord Beaverbrook, Minister of Aircraft Production. His concerns were well founded. After all, it was during the Battle of Britain and the situation was desperate. Every available Merlin was critical to the success of the battle. Ernest Hives, Works Director of Rolls-Royce, realized the Vulture was a lost cause and assured Roy Chadwick that Merlins would be made available for the Manchester III, as it was initially known and later renamed Lancaster I. In order to save on engineering time, Hives suggested the use of the Bristol Beaufighter power plants or quick engine change (QEC), which had been developed by Rolls-Royce. The QEC included engine, radiator, oil cooler, engine mount, all associated fuel, coolant and oil lines, and cowlings. This greatly expedited the redesign and development effort.

Blackburn B.20

Flying boats often compromised aerodynamic efficiency for the capability of operating from water. Propellers had to remain clear of water spray; otherwise excessive erosion, particularly on the leading edge and the tips, would take place. This resulted in very deep hulls, reversed gull wing, or parasol designs. The hull design of flying boats again had conflicting requirements, hydrodynamic and aerodynamic. The ideal hydrodynamic design placed the wing at a high angle of incidence in order to get the aircraft "on the step" during the take-off phase. In flight, a penalty was paid in the form of increased parasitic drag from the hull.

Blackburn Aircraft addressed these issues and more in the B.20 Experimental Flying Boat, powered by two Rolls-Royce Vultures (Fig. 4.78). Their innovative solution to these challenges was a retractable hull. In the extended position, adequate propeller clearance was offered plus the optimal angle of incidence. The hydraulic retraction system placed the hull at the ideal angle for take-off and in flight the hull retracted into the upper fuselage (Ref. 2.7).

The prototype was tested in 1940 and proved the advantages of the retractable hull concept. Unfortunately, this aircraft was lost in an accident thought to have been caused by aileron flutter (Ref. 4.28). Although a follow-on aircraft had been started, the project was dropped. This was due to Blackburn's more pressing needs for wartime production.

Fig. 4.78 Unusual Blackburn B.20 experimental flying boat powered by two Roll-Royce Vultures. When in flight, the wing tip floats retracted and the lower fuselage retracted into the main fuselage. (Courtesy of the National Air and Space Museum, Smithsonian Institution.)

Other Applications

The Vulture was considered for a number of other aircraft and flew in several prototypes, including the Hawker Henley, which was the first aircraft powered by a Vulture. The Hawker Tornado fighter, built to the same specification as the Typhoon, featured a six-blade, contra-rotating propeller for the Vulture. The Vickers Warwick, powered by the Bristol Centaurus in production form, was also designed with Vulture power. The Handley Page bomber, designed to the same specification (P.13/36) as the Manchester, was also planned to be powered by Vultures; however, none were built. Production versions of the Handley Page bomber, known as Halifax, were powered by four Merlins.

The Fairey Barracuda was another aircraft designed around the Vulture. Again, due to the problems Rolls-Royce was experiencing, no Vulture-powered Barracudas were built. Production models were powered by the Merlin. The last production Barracudas were powered by Griffons.

The Ones That Never Made It

Prior to and during World War II, Rolls-Royce embarked on a number of experimental engine projects.

The Exe was a 24-cylinder X-configuration and, unusually for Rolls-Royce, was air-cooled (Fig. 4.79). Another unusual feature for Rolls-Royce was the use of sleeve valves (see Chapter 5 on the Bristol engine for further details on sleeve design). By this time Harry (later Sir Harry) Ricardo was becoming more involved with Rolls-Royce, and it was his influence that persuaded Rolls-Royce to look at sleeve valve technology.

Fig. 4.79 Rolls-Royce Exe, first of the air-cooled sleeve valve engines. (Courtesy of Rolls-Royce plc.)

The Exe shared several features with the Vulture, such as the 24-cylinder, 90° X configuration and the same master rod/link rod connecting rod configuration. Unusually, coil ignition was used, consisting of four coils and contact breaker assemblies. This was a feature shared with the early Vultures, although it was soon dropped in the latter instance because of unreliability of the contact breaker assemblies. Even with 24 cylinders, the Exe was lacking in displacement at 1348 in^3 (21.7 L), barely greater than the Kestrel's displacement. This displacement was derived from minuscule 4.2-in bores and 4.0-in strokes. Supercharging consisted of a single-stage, two-speed unit with separate discharges feeding the upper and lower Vs in similar fashion to the Vulture. Reduction gearing consisted of simple spur gearing giving a high thrust line. Early reduction gear design concepts called for an annulus gear driven by an internal gear resulting in a lower thrust line; however, difficulties in manufacturing this reduction gear caused its abandonment.

Cooling air was introduced into a plenum below the engine, discharged into the upper and lower Vs, then routed through the cylinders to be discharged to the side Vs exiting the sides of the cowling at a higher velocity and temperature than when it entered, thus gaining energy recovery from the cooling air.

Built to a Fleet Air Arm request for a 1000-hp air-cooled engine, the first Exe ran in the late 1930s rated at 920 hp at 3800 rpm. Later development versions were rated at 1150 hp at 4200 rpm with a potential for 1500 hp, a very respectable specific horsepower for an air-cooled engine.

The Exe was test-flown in a Fairey Battle where it gave a good account of itself; however, the program was abandoned in 1941. The Battle, with its Exe, soldiered on for several years as a Rolls-Royce transport (Ref. 4.2).

Pennine

The Pennine was conceptually the same as the Exe, that is, a 24-cylinder air-cooled sleeve valve **X** engine. However, the Pennine was considerably larger at 2685 in^3 (44 L) derived from 5.4-in bores by 5.0-in strokes (Fig. 4.80). Employment of epicyclic reduction gearing gave a central thrust line, an improvement over the Exe. Potentially a 3000-hp engine, it was another casualty of the intense manufacturing and development efforts occurring during World War II with engines already in production. Gas turbine development killed off this promising program (Ref. 4.2).

Crecy

Without a doubt, the most radical and promising of all the Rolls-Royce aircraft piston engines was the Crecy (Fig. 4.81), a 90°, sleeve valve two-stroke V-12 displacing 1593 in^3 (26.1 L) from 5.1-in bores and 6.5-in stroke. Ninety degrees sounds wrong for a V-12, which is true in the case of a four-stroke engine, due to uneven firing. However, a 90° two-stroke V-12 is fine, giving the required even firing. Although engines have been produced with uneven firing, for example the 90° V-6s and 45° V-12s, it is undesirable due to the uneven first, and higher, modes of vibration generated.

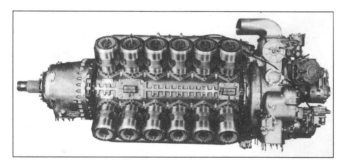

Fig. 4.80 Rolls-Royce Pennine. (Courtesy of Rolls-Royce plc.)

Fig. 4.81 Rolls-Royce Crecy. The ultimate two-stroke engine. (Courtesy of Rolls-Royce plc.)

At the mention of a two-stroke, thoughts of simple, primitive, weed-whacker and lawnmower engines running on the loop scavenged principle come to mind. With the Crecy, nothing could be further from the truth; it was a very complex, advanced engine featuring direct fuel injection into the stratified charge combustion chamber and scavenged by means of sleeve valves and high blower pressures. Again, Sir Harry Ricardo became involved, doing much of the development work on the stratified charge combustion chamber and the sleeve valves (Fig. 4.82) (Ref. 2.3). Although the Crecy was under development for much of World War II, Rolls-Royce abandoned it in December 1945 due to the overwhelming superiority of gas turbines, even at this early stage of this new technology. Undaunted, Ricardo was infatuated with the Crecy and at his own expense continued its development and testing in single-cylinder form at his laboratory in Shoreham. With nothing to lose, Ricardo ran the test units to their limits and beyond (Fig. 4.83).

The results were nothing short of phenomenal: A BMEP of 325×2 psi (the "$\times 2$" is because the Crecy was a two-stroke, and consequently had twice the power strokes of a four-stroke) and 219 hp/L (3.6 hp/in^3), running at 37-psi boost pressure (104-in Hg manifold pressure) augmented with ADI was finally achieved. The lack of fuel-injection pump displacement was the main factor inhibiting achievement of even more remarkable performance figures. Not surprisingly, sleeve failures were occurring at these extreme power ratings (Ref. 2.3).

Rolls-Royce built several full-size, twelve-cylinder Crecy engines with two basic families in mind: a fighter version and a transport version for multiengine applications. Open exhaust stacks featured on the fighter promised considerable exhaust thrust horsepower. The transport version was planned to take advantage of the exhaust energy (approximately twice that of a similar-size Merlin) through a power recovery turbine that fed power back to the crankshaft by driving the supercharger, thus relieving the crankshaft of this requirement.

Fig. 4.82 Sir Harry Ricardo, consultant to all the major British aircraft engine manufacturers. Ricardo convinced Roy Fedden at Bristol of the superiority of sleeve valve technology. (Courtesy of the Ricardo Consulting Engineers.)

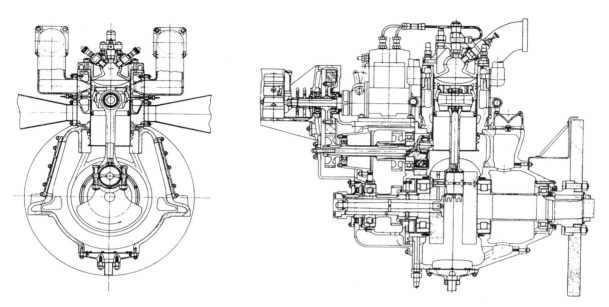

Fig. 4.83 Two cross-sections of the Ricardo E.65 development engine. This single-cylinder unit was used for the development of the Rolls-Royce Crecy. (Courtesy of Ricardo Consulting Engineers.)

The Crecy was not trouble-free, suffering from high crankshaft torsional vibration, which played havoc with the supercharger drive. This necessitated a freewheel in the drive train to dampen out the worst of the torsional vibration. As is the case with most high-performance two strokes, piston cooling became a major concern, with several remedies tried, including various schemes for spraying oil on the underside of the pistons. Because of development difficulties, it is doubtful whether Rolls-Royce ever obtained more than 1700 hp from the full-size, twelve-cylinder engine (Refs. 4.2, 4.29).

Eagle 22

The last hurrah for Rolls-Royce piston engines was the Eagle 22. Conceptually, it was influenced by the Napier Sabre, a 24-cylinder sleeve valve H engine or two flat twelve-cylinder engines pancaked on top of each other (Fig. 4.84). Unlike the Sabre, the Eagle 22 crankshafts rotated in opposite directions.

The Eagle 22, which was larger than the 2238 in³ Sabre, used 5.4-in bores and 5.125-in stroke giving a displacement of 2807 in³ (46 L). With the engine's rating of 3500 hp at 3500 rpm, the specific power was quite good, at well over 1 hp/in³; however, specific weight was poor due to the engine being considerably overweight at 3900 lb (Ref. 4.17). The supercharger was a two-stage, two-speed, intercooled, and aftercooled affair. Each bank of cylinders had its own aftercooler, for a total of four (Ref. 4.2).

Fig. 4.84 Rolls-Royce Eagle 22. Napier Sabre influence is very apparent. (Courtesy of Rolls-Royce plc.)

Most of the problems encountered revolved around the sleeve drive, which consisted of a shaft running the length of the engine with skew gears placed along its length for the sleeve drives, six in all (Fig. 4.85).

Under development throughout World War II, the Eagle 22 finally flew after the War in the early prototypes of the Westland Wyvern, driving a massive six- or eight-blade Rotol contra-rotating propeller (Fig. 4.86).

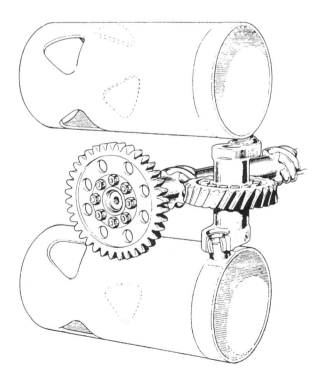

Fig. 4.85 Rolls-Royce Eagle 22 sleeve drive detail. Two sleeve driveshafts were employed; each one drove twelve sleeves. (Courtesy of Rolls-Royce plc.)

Fig. 4.86 Under development during World War II, the Westland Wyvern initially flew with a Rolls-Royce Eagle 22. Six-blade or eight-blade contra-rotating propellers were fitted. Production aircraft were powered by a gas turbine. (Courtesy of Rolls-Royce plc.)

References

2.3   Ricardo, Sir Harry R., The High Speed Internal Combustion Engine, 5th ed., Blackie and Son, Ltd., London, 1968.

2.4   Banks, Air Commodore F. R. (Rod)., "I Kept No Diary," *Airlife,* 1978.

2.5   Schlaifer, Robert, and S. D. Heron, Development of Aircraft Engines and Development of Aviation Fuels, Harvard University, Boston, 1950.

2.7   Jane's All The World's Aircraft, McGraw-Hill, New York, 1945/1946.

2.12 Harvey-Bailey, Alec, "The Merlin in Perspective—The Combat Years," Rolls-Royce Heritage Trust Historical Series No. 2, 1983, Derby, England.

4.1   Bruce, Gordon, "Charlie Rolls—Pioneer Aviator," Rolls-Royce Heritage Trust Historical Series No. 17, Derby, England, 1990.

4.2   Rubbra, A. A., "Rolls-Royce Piston Aero Engines—A Designer Remembers," Rolls-Royce Heritage Trust Historical Series No. 16, Derby, England, 1990.

4.3   Foxworth, Thomas G., The Speed Seekers, Doubleday & Co., New York.

4.4   *Archive,* Rolls-Royce Heritage Trust, Derby, England.

4.5   "V-1650 and Merlin 28, 29, and 31," Handbook of Overhaul Instruction, 20 July 1942.

4.6   Hooker, Sir Stanley, "Not Much of an Engineer," *Airlife,* 1984.

4.7   Gruenhagen, Robert W., Mustang, The Story of The P-51 Fighter, Arco Publishing, New York, 1980.

4.8   The Spitfire V Manual, Air Publication 1565E, Ministry of Defence, U.K., July 1943.

4.9   Pinkel, Benjamin, "Utilization of Exhaust Gas of Aircraft Engines," SAE Paper No. 460259, Society of Automotive Engineers, Warrendale, Pa., 5 Apr. 1946.

4.10 *Contribution to Victory,* Public relations movie, Rolls-Royce, 1946.

4.11 Bentele, Dr. Max, interview with author, Mar. 1994.

4.12 McFarland, Forest R., "Aircraft Engine Gears," SAE Paper No. 450213, Society of Automotive Engineers, Warrendale, Pa., 7 May 1945.

4.13 F-51D Mustang Handbook, 20 Jan. 1954.

4.14 Birch, Dave, Rolls-Royce Co. Archivist and Editor of *Archive,* interview and correspondence with author, 1992–1994.

4.15 Wilkinson, Paul H., Aircraft Engines of The World 1946, Paul H. Wilkinson, New York, 1946.

4.16 Wilkinson, Paul H., Aircraft Engines of The World 1947, Paul H. Wilkinson, New York, 1947.

4.17 Wilkinson, Paul H., Aircraft Engines of The World 1948, Paul H. Wilkinson, New York, 1948.

4.18 Wilkinson, Paul H., Aircraft Engines of The World 1949, Paul H. Wilkinson, New York, 1949.

4.19 Bowyer, Chaz, Supermarine Spitfire, Chartwell Books, 1980.

4.20 Tuffen, Harold J., MBE, CEng, MRAeS, and Albert E. Tagg, CEng, MRAeS, The Hawker Hurricane: Design, Development and Production, Royal Aeronautical Society, London, 1985.

4.21 Birch, David, "Rolls-Royce and the Mustang," Rolls-Royce Heritage Trust, Historical Series No. 9, 1987, Derby, England.

4.22 "Erection and Maintenance Instructions for Army Models P-51D Series and P-51K Series," British Model Mustang IV Airplanes, 20 Dec. 1944.

4.23 Air Publication 2062A and C, Vol. I, Ministry of Defence, U.K., Apr. 1943.

4.24 Air Publication 2019B, G, and K, Vol. I, Ministry of Defence, U.K., Apr. 1944.

4.25 Colman, P. A., "P-38 Performance Comparison Allison And Rolls-Royce Engines," Lockheed Aircraft Corp., Burbank, Calif., 9 Feb. 1944.

4.26 Lecture, Rolls-Royce Heritage Trust, Derby, England.

4.27 Sweetman, Bill, The Great Book of World War II Airplanes, Bonanza Books, 1984.

4.28 *Archive,* Rolls-Royce Heritage Trust, Derby, England.

4.29 Hiett, G. F., and J. V. B. Robson, "A Description of the Development of the Two-Cycle Petrol-Injection Units Built and Tested in the Laboratory of Messrs. Ricardo & Co. Ltd.," *Aircraft Engineering,* Jan. and Feb. 1950.

Chapter 5

Bristol

Poppet Valve Engines

The origins of the Bristol Aeroplane Company go back to 1910 when, as the Brazil Straker Company, it manufactured automobiles. Aircraft engine experience was gained during World War I by manufacturing Rolls-Royce Hawks and Eagles under license. This experience had profound effects on Bristol for the rest of the piston engine era. Rolls-Royce forbade Roy Fedden, the chief engineer and driving force behind Bristol piston aircraft engines, to manufacture water-cooled engines of his own design. This restriction on Fedden turned out to be a blessing in disguise and resulted in the design of some of the finest and most innovative air-cooled radial engines (Ref. 3.1).

In 1918 Brazil Straker was purchased by a new owner and renamed Cosmos Engineering Company. The Jupiter, a nine-cylinder radial engine, was the first product of this new company (Fig. 5.1). It immediately set the high standards of workmanship that Cosmos, and later Bristol, were to establish. As good as it was, the Jupiter was not enough to save the fledgling company from filing for bankruptcy in 1920, despite the fact that it made a very good showing in the abortive 1919 Schneider Trophy Race powering the Sopwith 107 Schneider (Ref. 4.3). Realizing the significance of the Jupiter, and more importantly the genius of Roy Fedden, the British Government persuaded the Bristol Aeroplane Company to purchase the assets of Cosmos. Fedden was immediately set up as the Chief Engineer of the Bristol Aero Engine Department with a small department of 35 men. This set the scene for an exceptionally difficult relationship with the Bristol Board of Directors that was never resolved until Fedden, under fire, departed from Bristol at a very crucial stage of World War II when his services were needed more than ever!

The Jupiter was developed into the Jupiter II, which produced 400 hp, in 1921 (Ref. 2.5). At this stage it represented the state of the art for radial engine development, incorporating such advanced features as four valves per cylinder and an ingenious compensating device to accommodate expansion and contraction of the cylinders while maintaining valve clearances.

4009

Fig. 5.1 Bristol Jupiter. This engine influenced all subsequent Bristol poppet valve engines. Two compensating devices for consistent valve clearance as the engine warmed up can be seen on either side of each pushrod tube. Advanced features included the use of four valves per cylinder in a pent-roof combustion chamber. Not bad for 1920s technology! (Courtesy of Rolls-Royce plc.)

Fatigue failure of highly stressed parts, such as connecting rods and crankshafts, always plagued high-performance engines. In World War I this phenomenon was little understood, and when fatigue failures occurred it was blamed on "crystallization." In the early 1920s professor Leslie Aitchison, who had studied this phenomenon and worked with the British Aeronautical Research Council, shared the results of this important work with Fedden. Bristol engines henceforth were designed with high fatigue strength in mind; it was possibly the first case of scientific component design to provide fatigue resistance. Corner fillets, generous radii, good surface finish, gradual transition of cross section, and elimination of even the smallest surface flaw or blemish were just a few of the requirements and resulted in Bristol not only gaining an early, well-deserved reputation for first-class workmanship but also resulted in unequaled reliability.

Because of Bristol's superb attention to detail, their engines were the first British engines to pass the rigorous 100-h military type test.

Up until 1923, Jupiters incorporated a two-piece master connecting rod held together by bolts. Fedden was convinced that a one-piece master rod, with a two-piece, bolted-together crankshaft, would be superior (Ref. 5.1). At this time it was a radical departure from accepted radial engine design, even though World War I rotary engines used this feature to advantage. One-piece master rods then became a feature for all subsequent Bristol piston engines. The reputation of the Jupiter was enhanced by breaking several world records including the height record in 1929 with a Jupiter VII, the first Jupiter with a gear-driven supercharger. It also held the distinction of powering the first aircraft to fly over Mount Everest, an open cockpit biplane, in April 1933.

Follow-on engines based on the Jupiter concept, that is, nine-cylinder, air-cooled, four-valve radials, were the Pegasus and Mercury, which were used extensively in World War II. New technologies incorporated in the designs kept Bristol engines at the forefront during the 1930s when advances in manufacturing, materials, and engine design were occurring at a breathtaking pace. As horsepower ratings approached, then exceeded, 100 hp per cylinder, new materials and manufacturing techniques were demanded. Cylinder bore wear was kept under control by the use of nitrided chrome molybdenum steel alloy barrels; however, keeping cylinder head temperatures under control was a more difficult challenge.

Early radials had what was known as the "poultice" head, which was a very inefficient design that featured a closed-end cylinder incorporating the valve seats and spark plug opening. The cylinder head, typically an aluminum casting, was clamped to the closed end with through bolts or studs. This resulted in poor heat rejection due to the requirement for a perfect face-to-face seal between the head and the closed end of the cylinder. Sam Heron realized the shortcomings of the poultice design when he worked at the Royal Aircraft Factory (later Royal Aircraft Establishment) during World War I. He initiated development of the screwed-and-shrunk cylinder assembly, which featured an open-end cylinder with a large diameter male thread equal to the outside diameter of the cylinder. The cylinder head, usually an aluminum casting, had an internal thread to match the thread on the cylinder. Interference was designed into the thread requiring heating of the head and freezing of the cylinder barrel. "Timing" of the thread ensured that the threads tightened at the correct location. This cylinder design revolutionized engine performance, allowing greater power outputs because of the improved heat transfer and thus heat rejection (Ref. 2.1).

Engine designers historically take full advantage of new technologies and then go one step beyond, which demands another leap in technology! Such was the case with radial engine cylinder design. Casting techniques in the 1930s limited the depth and pitch of cooling fins.

Again, cooling became the limiting factor for air-cooled radials as powers reached and exceeded 100 hp per cylinder. Consequently, Bristol developed new manufacturing methods for producing cylinder heads. They were made from aluminum forgings instead of from castings; this allowed unrestricted depth and pitch of the cooling fins, a critical breakthrough picked up by other manufacturers of large, high-power radials. From a raw forging, all the necessary features of the head were machined in, with cooling fins created from ganged slitting saws.

In the four-valve engines, the two intake valves were located at the rear of the cylinder and the two exhausts at the front. Nine intake pipes came off the supercharger housing, with a Y split just prior to joining the cylinder head. Each inlet port was fed by a pipe from the Y junction. Exhaust valves, situated at the front, allowed the exhaust gases to discharge to the front where they merged into a collector ring that usually formed the leading edge of the cowl. A tail pipe discharged the gases to atmosphere from the cowl leading-edge collector ring. As can be imagined, at night the whole leading edge of the cowl lit up with an incandescent glow.

A design feature that dated all the Bristol poppet valve engines, particularly by World War II, was the use of exposed valve gear. Popular in the 1920s because of the additional cooling offered, it was a totally obsolete and unnecessary concept by the late 1930s because of improved valve spring materials and manufacturing methods along with improved exhaust valve design incorporating features such as sodium or salt cooling. The trend toward pressure lubrication also demanded enclosed valve gear.

Mercury

The Mercury, the first of the Jupiter follow-ons, had many of its predecessor's features; the primary difference was a shorter stroke of 6.5 in, which gave a smaller overall diameter of 51.5 in (Fig. 5.2). With the Mercury's bore of 5.75 in, the resulting displacement became 1520 in^3 (24.9 L), which limited its usefulness as a front-line aircraft engine for World War II.

In 1927 Bristol had another shot at the Schneider trophy with a Mercury installed in the Short Crusader. Through no fault of the engine, the attempt was not a success and was finally terminated when the aircraft crashed due to crossed controls for the ailerons (Ref. 4.3). The experience did offer useful information to Bristol on running the Mercury at higher boost and rpm.

Fig. 5.2 Front view of a Bristol Mercury. Two pushrods are housed in a single tube. Each pushrod actuated two valves. Bristol pioneered the use of the forging process for cylinder head construction, evident in this shot by the close pitch and depth of the cooling fins. (Courtesy of the National Air and Space Museum, Smithsonian Institution, Photo No. BB-040590-20.)

By World War II the Mercury was developing 965 hp at 2650 rpm with an overspeed rating of 2750 rpm. Construction was typical Bristol poppet valve technology that consisted of a two-piece, aluminum-forged crankcase split vertically and held together by nine through bolts passing between the cylinders. The crankcase supported a two-piece crankshaft that ran in two roller bearings. This construction allowed the use of a one-piece master rod. Farman, epicyclic bevel reduction gears in the nose case transmitted the power with a 0.57:1 ratio.

Supercharging was single-stage, single-speed. In fact Bristol never produced a two-stage engine (Fig. 5.3). Turbosupercharging was investigated in 1923 with good results, but the program ran out of funds.

Cylinder construction was the conventional forged chrome molybdenum steel alloy, nitrided barrel with a forged aluminum head screwed and shrunk onto the barrel. Four valves per cylinder were mounted in a pent-roof combustion chamber; the exhausts were sodium-cooled. A feature that dated the engine and was a throwback to its Jupiter heritage was the use of semi-exposed valve gear. The pushrods were housed in a streamlined tube, the rocker pivots were housed in a cover, and the outer extremities, along with the valve stems and valve springs, were exposed (Refs. 2.7, 4.15–4.17).

Applications

Table 5.1 summarizes the Mercury's performance and applications.

TABLE 5.1—BRISTOL MERCURY PERFORMANCE AND APPLICATION SUMMARY

Dash Number	Applications	hp/rpm/alt	Comments
VIII	Blenheim I/IV	840/2650/SL	Max. boost 5psi., 40 in Hg
XV and 25	Blenheim IV	725/2650/SL	Rating on 87-octane fuel
	Lysander I	905/2650/SL	Rating on 100-octane fuel
XX and 30	Miles M-25	870/2650/SL	Rating on 87-octane fuel
	Miles M-19		
	Sea Otter		
	Westland Lysander III		
	Lysander IIIA		

Source: Refs. 2.7, 4.15–4.17.

Westland Lysander

One of the better-known Mercury applications during World War II was the Westland Lysander (Fig. 5.4 on page 128). It was a single-engine, tube-and-fabric monoplane and was used primarily for covert operations, for dropping supplies to French resistance workers, and for dropping agents in by parachute or dropping them off on clandestine landing strips. This could be accomplished because of its good short take-off and landing (STOL) capabilities.

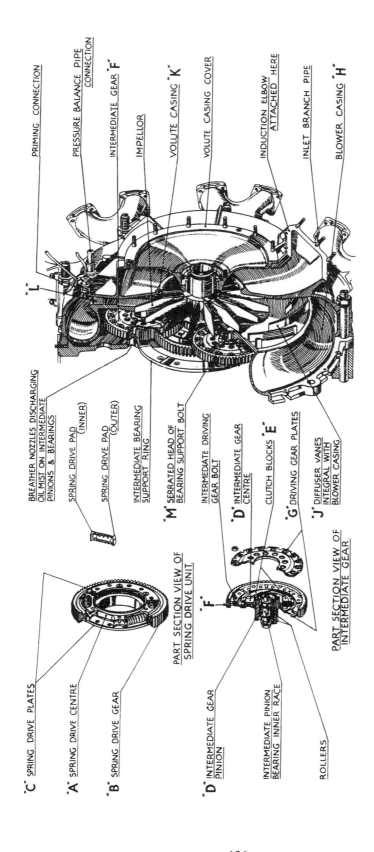

SECTIONAL PERSPECTIVE VIEW OF SUPERCHARGER UNIT

PRIMING CONNECTION

PRESSURE BALANCE PIPE CONNECTION

INTERMEDIATE GEAR "F"

IMPELLOR

VOLUTE CASING "K"

VOLUTE CASING COVER

INDUCTION ELBOW ATTACHED HERE

INLET BRANCH PIPE

BLOWER CASING "H"

"L"

BREATHER NOZZLES DISCHARGING OIL MIST ON INTERMEDIATE PINIONS & BEARINGS

SPRING DRIVE PAD (INNER)

SPRING DRIVE PAD (OUTER)

INTERMEDIATE BEARING SUPPORT RING

"M" SERRATED HEAD OF BEARING SUPPORT BOLT

INTERMEDIATE DRIVING GEAR BOLT

"D" INTERMEDIATE GEAR CENTRE

CLUTCH BLOCKS "E"

"G" DRIVING GEAR PLATES

"J" DIFFUSER VANES INTEGRAL WITH BLOWER CASING

PART SECTION VIEW OF INTERMEDIATE GEAR

"F"

PART SECTION VIEW OF SPRING DRIVE UNIT.

"C" SPRING DRIVE PLATES

"A" SPRING DRIVE CENTRE

"B" SPRING DRIVE GEAR

"D" INTERMEDIATE GEAR PINION

INTERMEDIATE PINION BEARING INNER RACE

ROLLERS

THE BRISTOL AEROPLANE CO. LTD. SERVICE. (ENGINES) MAY 1941.

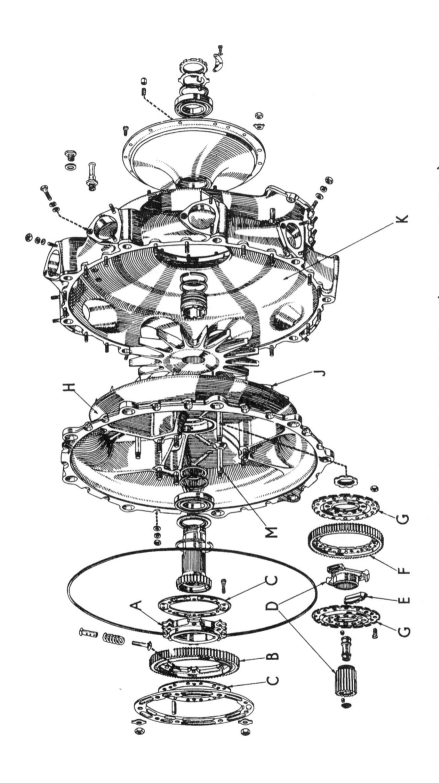

K

H

J

M

C

A

D

C

B

C

G

F

G

E

G

THE BRISTOL AEROPLANE CO. LTD. SERVICE (ENGINES) MAY 1941

EXPLODED VIEW OF SUPERCHARGER......(9·4 : 1 RATIO)

Fig. 5-3 Section showing Bristol Mercury supercharger assembly: Note open design of impeller machined from a steel forging. Drive shock loads were absorbed by compression springs incorporated into the spring drive gear. (Bristol Aeroplane Co., Ltd., Lecture on Superchargers, issued May 1941. Author's collection.)

Fig. 5.4 Westland Lysander powered by Bristol Mercury. (Courtesy of the National Air and Space Museum, Smithsonian Institution, Photo No. 2A-28946, and the Fleet Air Arm Museum.)

Lysanders were also used for target towing and air sea rescue. For the latter missions, they were fitted with inflatable dinghies and food supplies attached to the landing gear (Ref. 5.2).

Miles M-25 Martinet and M-19 Master

The Miles M-25 Martinet was used primarily for target-towing duties; it was a tandem two-seat monoplane with a top speed of 232 mph at sea level (Fig. 5.5).

Other target-towing, Mercury-powered aircraft from the Miles company were the M-19 Master II and III; they were similar to the Martinet but of wooden construction. The Master I was powered by the Rolls-Royce Kestrel.

Fig. 5.5 Miles M-25 target-towing aircraft powered by Bristol Mercury. (Courtesy of the National Air and Space Museum, Smithsonian Institution, Photo No. 1B-22989.)

Airspeed Limited A.S. 45

The Airspeed A.S. 45 was an attempt by Airspeed Limited to provide the RAF with an advanced trainer. It was similar in appearance, performance, and mission to the North American T-6 advanced trainer. Only two prototypes were built to Air Ministry specification T.4/39 (Ref. 2.7).

Supermarine Sea Otter

Supermarine, normally associated with high-performance fighter aircraft, also designed more mundane aircraft such as the Sea Otter (Fig. 5.6), a follow-on design of the Walrus (see the discussion under Pegasus engine applications below). The tractor configuration of the Sea Otter, rather than the pusher configuration of the Walrus, was the primary difference between the two aircraft.

The fundamental mission for the Sea Otter was spotting and air sea rescue. It was also often carried on battleships and cruisers, catapulted into the air and retrieved with a crane.

The Sea Otter was introduced in 1940 with the intention of replacing the Walrus. However, even by 1940 standards, this biplane design featuring fabric-covered wings and mixed wood and metal construction for the fuselage was obsolete. The engine nacelle was carried on the center section of the upper wing, supported on four compression struts and bracing wires (Ref. 2.7).

Bristol Blenheim

On 3 September 1939 the first British operational sortie of World War II against Germany was flown by a Bristol Blenheim (Fig. 5.7). The twin-engine, light bomber powered by Mercurys first flew in 1935 and caused a sensation with its remarkable performance by outperforming contemporary biplane fighters of the time.

The Mk. I was powered by a Mercury VIII engine rated at 840 hp, and the last production Blenheim, the Mk. V, was powered by Mercury XXVs rated at 950 hp and 2750 rpm.

Fig. 5.6 Supermarine Sea Otter being hoisted aboard ship. (Courtesy of the Fleet Air Arm Museum.)

Fig. 5.7 Bristol Blenheim Mk. IV powered by a pair of 905-hp Bristol Mercury XV engines. (Courtesy of the National Air and Space Museum, Smithsonian Institution, Photo No. 1A-16207.)

Blenheims were used in all theaters of World War II, including Europe and North Africa. Following a disastrous attempt at daylight operations, they were used primarily for night bombing raids. The night-operated Blenheims could be identified by the two massive flame-damping exhaust systems. For desert operations, a large Vokes air filter was fitted under the engine nacelle for the updraft induction system.

As later types with higher performance became available, Blenheims were withdrawn from front-line duties and before the end of hostilities were removed from production.

Pegasus

The only other Bristol poppet valve engine to see extensive use during World War II was the Pegasus, another derivative of the ubiquitous Jupiter (Fig. 5.8).

Essentially a longer-stroke version of the Mercury, the Pegasus had bore and stroke dimensions of 5.75 in and 7.50 in, respectively. At 1753 in^3 (28.7 L), specific power was inferior to most of its contemporaries. Typically rated at 1065 hp at 2600 rpm, this engine had a surprisingly high piston speed of 3250 ft/min. All other mechanical design features were similar to the Mercury, although some Pegasus engines featured two-speed supercharging (Ref. 2.7).

Applications

Table 5.2 summarizes the Pegasus engine's performance and applications.

Fig. 5.8 Three-quarter front view of a Bristol Pegasus. Very similar to the Mercury, primary difference was the cylinder stroke, which was 1 in shorter in the case of the Mercury. (Courtesy of the National Air and Space Museum, Smithsonian Institution, Photo No. BB-040640.)

TABLE 5.2—BRISTOL PEGASUS PERFORMANCE AND APPLICATION SUMMARY

Dash Number	Applications	hp/rpm/alt	Comments
VI XC	Walrus	775/2475/SL 920/2475/SL 830/2600/5250	Two-speed blower used three clutches actuated by main oil pressure
22	Sunderland I	1010/2600/SL 865/2600/6500	
XVIII	Sunderland II/III Wellington I Wellington VIII	1000/2600/3000 885/2600/15,500	Two-speed blower
30	Swordfish	1050/2600/SL[a] 750/2600/14,750	Two-speed blower

(a) 1050 hp obtained at 43.6 in Hg manifold pressure. Source: Refs. 2.7, 4.15–4.17.

Fairey Swordfish

The Fairey Swordfish must rank as the most amazing aircraft powered by the Pegasus (Fig. 5.9). By World War II this carrier-based, fabric-covered biplane designed as a torpedo bomber was obsolete, and yet it outlived its successor! Although several torpedo bombers were on the drawing boards for the Fleet Air Arm at the start of World War II, none were ready for combat.

Fig. 5.9 Fairey Swordfish. One of the most amazing torpedo bombers of World War II. Even though it was thought to be antiquated at the outbreak of World War II, it racked up an incredible combat record, including the destruction of the Italian fleet at Taranto and sinking up to 98,000 tons of shipping a month in the Mediterranean. (Courtesy of the Fleet Air Arm Museum.)

Despite the Swordfish's slow top speed of 128 mph, amazing feats were performed by this venerable aircraft. The most well-known operation carried out by the Swordfish was the attack on Taranto harbor on 11 November 1940, which disabled the Italian fleet. It is hard to believe that such total havoc and destruction could be wreaked by twelve obsolete tube-and-fabric biplanes. The effect of this raid was profound; the day after the attack the survivors pulled up anchor and sailed north to safer waters, thus yielding the Mediterranean to the British Royal Navy. (Halfway across the world, the Japanese Navy took note of the occurrences of the night of 11 November, and a little over one year later— 7 December 1941, a day that will live in infamy—created similar havoc with the U.S. Navy anchored in Pearl Harbor.)

A number of Fleet Air Arm Swordfish were fitted with airborne interception (AI) radar and were surely the oldest design of aircraft to be fitted with this sophisticated equipment (Ref. 5.2).

Supermarine Walrus

The Supermarine Walrus (Fig. 5.10), a ponderous single-engine amphibious biplane typical of early 1930s design concepts, was the predecessor of the Sea Otter (see the discussion under Mercury engine applications above). The single Pegasus engine was carried between the wings in a pusher configuration. Despite its slow speed, invaluable work was carried out by the Walrus, particularly in air sea rescue.

Its mixed construction featuring an aluminum hull, later redesigned in wood, with fabric-covered wings, was conceptually similar to Supermarine's early biplane Schneider Trophy aircraft (Ref. 5.2).

Short Sunderland

Antisubmarine warfare became critical for the British war effort, particularly during the heyday of the U-boat scourge. The Short Sunderland played a crucial part in the hazardous job of keeping the North Atlantic sea lanes open (Fig. 5.11).

Fig. 5.10 Supermarine Walrus II about to be lowered into the water. (Courtesy of the Fleet Air Arm Museum.)

Fig. 5.11 Short Sunderland powered by four Bristol Pegasus engines. This was the first flying boat equipped with powered gun turrets. (Courtesy of the Fleet Air Arm Museum.)

Based on the prewar "Empire Class" flying boats, the Sunderland was designed to Air Ministry Specification R.2/33; the prototype first flew in 1937. It was the first flying boat fitted with power-operated gun turrets.

This heavily armed four-engine aircraft, nicknamed the "flying porcupine" by the Germans, relied on Pegasus XXIIs (22s) for power in Mk. I form. Mk. IIs used Pegasus XVIIIs, which were similar to the Pegasus XXIIs except for two-speed supercharging.

Sunderland Vs were powered by Pratt & Whitney R-1830-92 engines (Ref. 2.7).

Sleeve Valve Engines

In a conventional four-stroke engine, it is usually taken for granted that the fuel/air mixture and the exhaust gases are allowed ingress/egress through poppet valves. In actuality, the engine does not care how the mixture gets into the cylinder or how the products of combustion are removed, provided these events take place at the correct time and the cylinder is completely sealed during the compression and power strokes. Understanding these requirements makes it easier to comprehend the rationale behind the sleeve valve engine (Fig. 5.12).

Two different concepts of sleeve valve engine were developed. The first was the Knight, Silent Knight, or Willys Knight, which featured two reciprocating sleeves. Although quiet and smooth, its poor volumetric efficiency and excessive oil consumption disqualified it from aircraft use. When the engine was forced to operate at high specific powers, sleeve wear became excessive because the oil was not distributed around the sleeves (Ref. 2.3).

The Burt-McCollum single-sleeve valve was a very different concept from the Knight, consisting of a single reciprocating and rotating sleeve running in a cylinder. It was invented independently in 1909 by Peter Burt of the Argyll Company in Scotland and James McCollum in Canada, and an agreement was made between McCollum and the Argyll Company. Since then it was known as the Burt-McCollum single-sleeve cylinder. One of the first attempts at an aircraft sleeve engine for the Royal Navy, made by the Argyll Company, suffered crankshaft failures during testing.

Harry (later Sir Harry) Ricardo picked up development of the Burt-McCollum concept. Needing to satisfy his curiosity as to the superior approach, poppet or sleeve valve, he built two similar single-cylinder research engines, one with a sleeve valve, the other with poppet valves. Extensive testing was done by Ricardo to ascertain which valve arrangement held the advantage. In all parameters, Ricardo found the sleeve valve to be superior as it had higher specific power, lower specific fuel consumption, and lower specific weight. The lack of red-hot exhaust valves (which plagued the early poppet valve engine with failures) allowed a higher compression ratio, and the unrestricted combustion chamber design plus excellent volumetric efficiency also contributed to the superiority of the sleeve valve (Ref. 2.3).

Roy Fedden started investigative work on the sleeve concept in 1926 with an inverted air-cooled V-twin of 5.75-in bore and 6.0-in stroke. The intention was to build an inverted air-cooled V-12; however, that project never got beyond the V-twin prototype stage. His findings mirrored Ricardo's and encouraged him to concentrate all future piston engine development on sleeve valves (Ref. 5.3).

The first commercial sleeve valve engine was the Perseus, designed in 1932 as a nine-cylinder air-cooled radial (Fig. 5.13). The advantages of this sleeve valve engine, which had the same bore and stroke as the Mercury (5.75-in bore and 6.50-in stroke), were immediately apparent! Although the engine was officially rated at the same power as the Mercury, no doubt to avoid hurting sales, it was capable of more power.

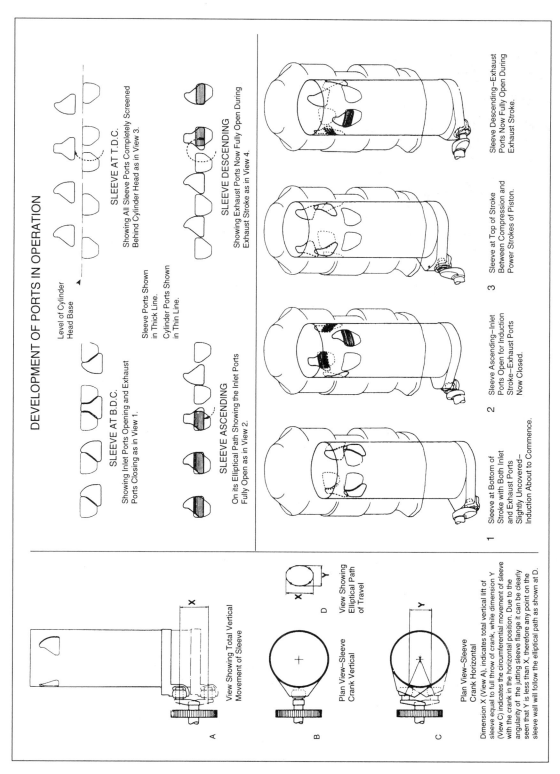

Fig. 5.12 Bristol illustration of sleeve valve theory. ("Bristol Hercules XI & VI Engines, Operating Instructions," Issue No. 1, Jan. 1943. Author's collection.)

Fig. 5.13 Bristol Perseus. The sequence of exhaust port opening can be seen in this shot. Cylinder dimensions were the same as the Hercules. (Courtesy of the National Air and Space Museum, Smithsonian Institution, Photo No. BB-040650-20.)

Many lessons had been learned from the experimental V-twin, among them cooling and sleeve material. Because of the reciprocating motion of the sleeve, a deep cylinder head was necessary, making the cooling job more difficult, particularly when air is the cooling medium. Directing the cooling air into the depths of the "junk" head initially caused problems leading to high head temperatures. The cure was in the form of careful baffling, particularly around the junk head. Radial finning on the top of the head directed cooling down to the top of the combustion chamber where the two spark plugs resided, which also had cooling fins machined onto their bodies in order to dissipate the heat. Cooling air was then ejected past the rear of the head. Cylinder barrel construction consisted of an aluminum forging with cooling fins, mounting flange, and ports machined in (Fig. 5.14).

The V-twin work had exposed the problem of sleeve material. The solution to this serious issue was another of Fedden's breakthroughs. The first engines had nickel-iron sleeves that proved to be unsatisfactory, and the answer proved to be forged KE965 austenitic steel. The fact that KE965 has a similar coefficient of expansion to aluminum was a major factor in its favor. Initially, tests were made with nitrided sleeves and compared with the same material that had not been nitrided. Not surprisingly, the tests concluded that nitriding was essential for the longevity of the engine.

Sleeves were driven from a miniature crankshaft rotating at half engine crankshaft speed by a train of spur gears emanating from the crankshaft. The crankpin of the sleeve drive crank mated with a spherical ball joint mounted at the base of the cylinder sleeve. As the sleeve drive crank rotated, it imparted a reciprocating and rotary motion to the sleeve, which opened and closed the appropriate inlet and exhaust ports at the correct time. This motion also had the benefit of distributing the lubricant evenly around the sleeve, thus sidestepping the major problem of the Knight system. The alu-

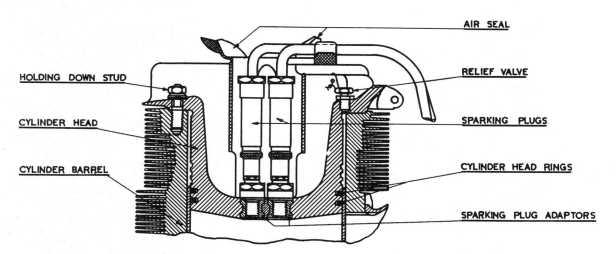

Fig. 5.14 Section through a Bristol sleeve valve cylinder head. The two "head rings" served the same function as piston rings and a cylinder head gasket, that is, they sealed the rotating and reciprocating cylinder sleeve against combustion gases. The relief valve allowed the escape of entrapped oil as the sleeve rose, thus preventing a hydraulic lock and consequent failure of the sleeve drive. ("Instructions for the Maintenance of the Bristol Taurus II & IIA Air-Cooled Radial Engines," Issue No. 1, Nov. 1940. Author's collection.)

minum cylinder barrel had three intake ports and two exhaust ports, with the inlets situated at the rear and the exhausts placed at the front. The cylinder sleeve had two inlet ports, one exhaust port, and one port alternately inlet and exhaust, equivalent to a five-valve poppet valve engine, very clever.

The Perseus was used extensively in the commercial environment, but had relatively few military applications.

Hercules

Developed from the Perseus design, the Hercules used 14 Perseus cylinders in two-row form. The Hercules was the most significant Bristol engine of World War II; approximately 65,000 were manufactured (Fig. 5.15). With 14 Perseus-size cylinders, displacement came out to 2360 in^3 (38.7 L) from which a power output of 1375 hp at 2400 rpm was achieved for its first type test in 1936. In typical Bristol fashion, this power output was to almost double during the development life of the engine.

A drawback of sleeve valve technology in the 1930s was the requirement for individual fitting of each sleeve to its mating cylinder barrel. During the economically depressed 1930s, and with production limited at the time, this limiting factor did not gain the priority it deserved. By the late 1930s, with war obviously imminent, this issue became increasingly important to resolve, that is, to have complete interchangeability between cylinders and sleeves.

Fig. 5.15 Three-quarter front view of a Bristol Hercules. Front-mounted exhaust ports are visible in this shot. (Courtesy of the National Air and Space Museum, Smithsonian Institution, Photo No. BB-40560-20.)

Several breakthroughs in manufacturing and materials contributed to the solution; one of the more interesting was the use of a dull, undressed grinding wheel for the final grinding operation of the sleeve outside diameter. This solution was discovered by accident when an operator used the wrong grinding wheel by mistake.

As in the Perseus, all the sleeve drives came off the crankshaft via spur gears that were housed in the nose case. The sleeve drive cranks for the rear cylinders had extended shafts that were routed between the front cylinders (Figs. 5.16, 5.17). The whole arrangement (Fig. 5.18) was exquisite, somewhat reminiscent of a mechanical Swiss watch!

Propeller reduction gearing was again the Farman bevel epicyclic gearing (Fig. 5.19). Supercharging was typically single-stage, two-speed with automatic boost control (Fig. 5.20).

Crankcase construction consisted of a three-piece aluminum forging split vertically on the cylinder centerlines. Seven studs tied the crankcase sections together at the cylinder centerlines. Three massive roller bearings supported the three-piece crankshaft, which used dynamic counterweights mounted in the crank cheeks (Fig. 5.21). Master rod bearings could be either fully floating or fixed and, interestingly, were made of white metal instead of the usual (by this stage of radial engine development) copper-lead or silver (Fig. 5.22). Two-speed supercharger drive was provided by multiplate clutches, oil-operated with compression springs for torsional shock load protection (Fig. 5.23). Early Hercules engines used single-speed supercharging.

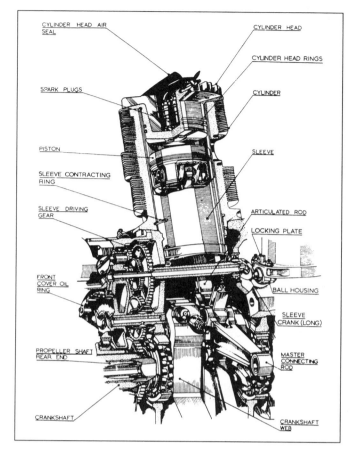

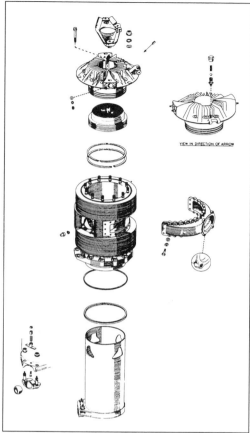

Fig. 5.16 Detail of a front cylinder from a Bristol Hercules showing rolling-element main bearings and sleeve drive. ("Bristol Hercules XI & VI Engines, Operating Instructions," Issue No. 1, Jan. 1943. Author's collection.)

Fig. 5.17 Bristol Hercules sleeve valve cylinder assembly. ("Bristol Hercules XI & VI Engines, Operating Instructions," Issue No. 1, Jan. 1943. Author's collection.)

Carburetion was provided by a Claudel Hobson downdraft unit with automatic mixture and boost control. When the advantages of the single-point Bendix-type injection carburetor became apparent, the Claudel Hobson carburetor was replaced by a Hobson-RAE injection unit in 1942.

A feature of Hercules installations, and all subsequent Bristol engines, was the use of a remote gearbox to drive accessories such as hydraulic pumps, vacuum pumps, generators, and so forth. A jack shaft driven off the rear of the engine drove the Rotol accessory gearbox. Among the many advantages of this arrangement were easier maintenance, fewer parts to swap and remove during an engine change, and a reduction in the overall length of the engine (Fig. 5.24).

Valuable lessons were learned from captured German aircraft, particularly from their engine installations methods. This information led to fan cooling and individual ejector exhaust stacks in later

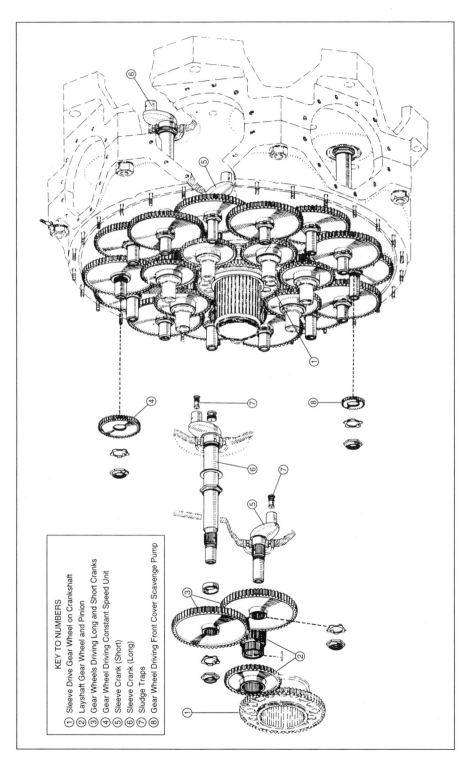

KEY TO NUMBERS
① Sleeve Drive Gear Wheel on Crankshaft
② Layshaft Gear Wheel and Pinion
③ Gear Wheels Driving Long and Short Cranks
④ Gear Wheel Driving Constant Speed Unit
⑤ Sleeve Crank (Short)
⑥ Sleeve Crank (Long)
⑦ Sludge Traps
⑧ Gear Wheel Driving Front Cover Scavenge Pump

Fig. 5.18 Bristol Hercules sleeve drive arrangement. As can be seen from the illustration, it looks like an old style Swiss watch! ("Bristol Hercules XI & VI Engines, Operating Instructions," Issue No. 1, Jan. 1943. Author's collection.)

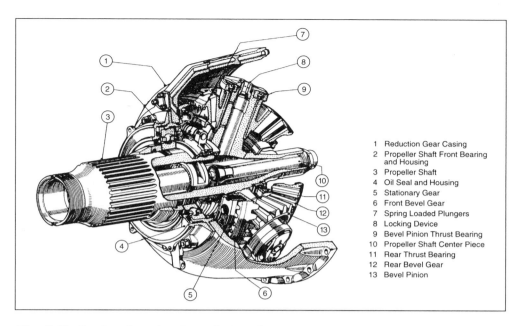

1	Reduction Gear Casing
2	Propeller Shaft Front Bearing and Housing
3	Propeller Shaft
4	Oil Seal and Housing
5	Stationary Gear
6	Front Bevel Gear
7	Spring Loaded Plungers
8	Locking Device
9	Bevel Pinion Thrust Bearing
10	Propeller Shaft Center Piece
11	Rear Thrust Bearing
12	Rear Bevel Gear
13	Bevel Pinion

Fig. 5.19 Section though a Bristol Hercules nose case illustrating the Farman reduction gear. ("Instructions for the Maintenance of the Bristol Hercules III Air-Cooled Radial Engines," Issue No. 1, Nov. 1940. Author's collection.)

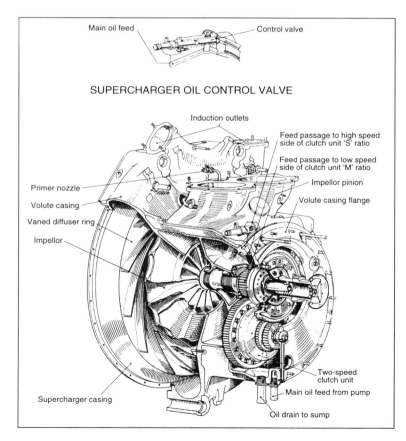

Fig. 5.20 Bristol Hercules supercharger assembly. The fully shrouded impeller was manufactured from an aluminum casting. ("Bristol Hercules XI & VI Engines, Operating Instructions," Issue No. 1, Jan. 1943. Author's collection.)

141

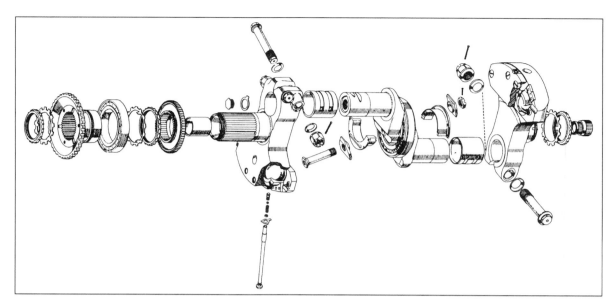

Fig. 5.21 Bristol Hercules crankshaft assembly showing three-piece construction, which allowed the use of one-piece master connecting rods. Of note is the reverse of the bearing gender for the rod bearings, that is, the bearing is the male component and the journal, formed by the inside diameter of the master rod (not shown) is the female, reverse of normal practice. Also noteworthy is the use of solid steel balls housed in the crank cheeks which served as dynamic counterweights. ("Instructions for the Maintenance of the Bristol Hercules III Air-Cooled Radial Engines," Issue No. 1, Nov. 1940. Author's collection.)

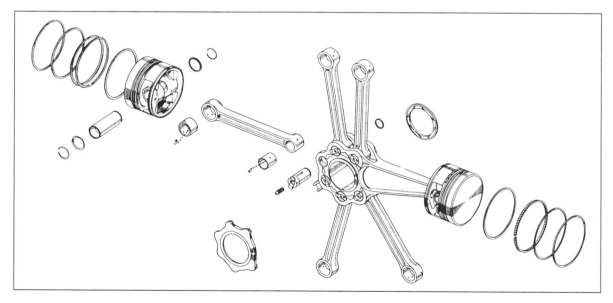

Fig. 5.22 Bristol Hercules master connecting rod assembly. The inside diameter of the master rod forms the journal component of the bearing, the reverse of normal practice. ("Bristol Hercules XI & VI Engines, Operating Instructions," Issue No. 1, Jan. 1943. Author's collection.)

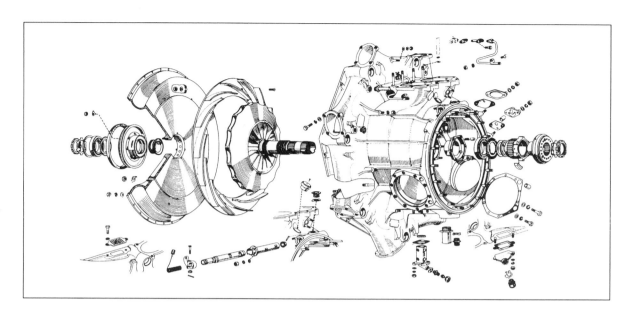

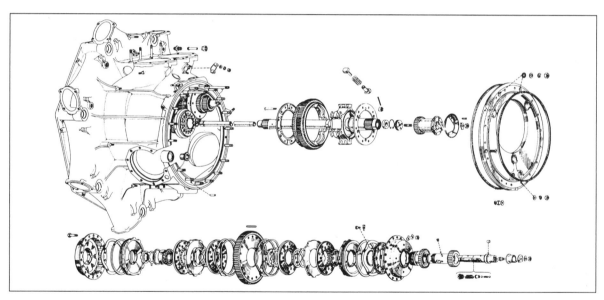

Fig. 5.23 Bristol Hercules supercharger and drive gear clutch assembly. Note the shrouded design of the supercharger impeller as opposed to the open design of the Bristol poppet valve engines. ("Bristol Hercules XI & VI Engines, Operating Instructions," Issue No. 1, Jan. 1943. Author's collection.)

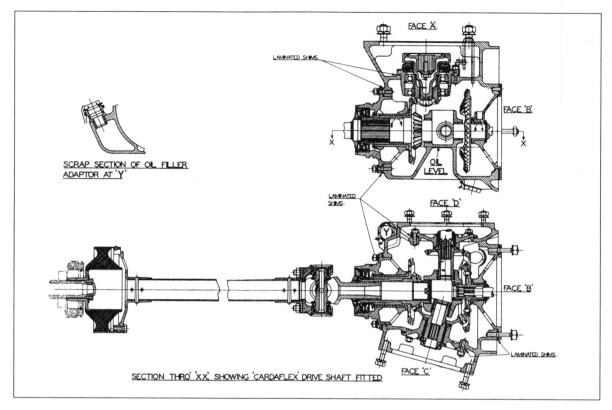

Fig. 5.24 Bristol incorporated remote gearboxes to drive accessories, making engine changes easier. The illustration shows one for a Hercules engine. Most of these gearboxes were manufactured by the Rotol propeller company. ("Instructions for the Maintenance of the Bristol Hercules Air-Cooled Radial Engine," Nov. 1940.)

installations. The later exhaust systems required a total design revision featuring a swept-back configuration and ejection through the cowl flaps instead of the previous system, in which the exhaust system was routed to the front where it was manifolded into a collector ring forming the leading edge of the cowl.

Rear-swept exhaust and fan cooling were incorporated into 100-series and higher engines.

At the start of World War II Hercules production was well in hand with the engine producing 1375 hp and good reliability (Fig. 5.25). By the end of World War II the Hercules HE.20 SM had been type-tested at 2500 hp with ADI and injection carburetion.

Applications

The Hercules was used only in multiengine applications, such as four-engine heavy bombers, twin-engine medium bombers, and heavy twin-engine radar fighters and was well adapted for its assigned roles. Table 5.3 on page 144 summarizes the Hercules engine's performance and applications.

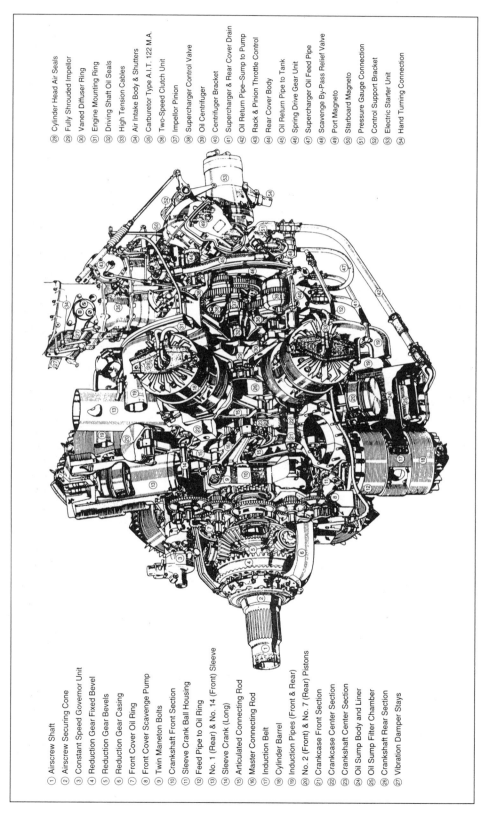

The numbered key to the figure:

1. Airscrew Shaft
2. Airscrew Securing Cone
3. Constant Speed Governor Unit
4. Reduction Gear Fixed Bevel
5. Reduction Gear Bevels
6. Reduction Gear Casing
7. Front Cover Oil Ring
8. Front Cover Scavenge Pump
9. Twin Maneton Bolts
10. Crankshaft Front Section
11. Sleeve Crank Ball Housing
12. Feed Pipe to Oil Ring
13. No. 1 (Rear) & No. 14 (Front) Sleeve
14. Sleeve Crank (Long)
15. Articulated Connecting Rod
16. Master Connecting Rod
17. Induction Belt
18. Cylinder Barrel
19. Induction Pipes (Front & Rear)
20. No. 2 (Front) & No. 7 (Rear) Pistons
21. Crankcase Front Section
22. Crankcase Center Section
23. Crankshaft Center Section
24. Oil Sump Body and Liner
25. Oil Sump Filter Chamber
26. Crankshaft Rear Section
27. Vibration Damper Stays
28. Cylinder Head Air Seals
29. Fully Shrouded Impellor
30. Vaned Diffuser Ring
31. Engine Mounting Ring
32. Driving Shaft Oil Seals
33. High Tension Cables
34. Air Intake Body & Shutters
35. Carburetor Type A.I.T. 122 M.A.
36. Two-Speed Clutch Unit
37. Impellor Pinion
38. Supercharger Control Valve
39. Oil Centrifuger
40. Centrifuger Bracket
41. Supercharger & Rear Cover Drain
42. Oil Return Pipe—Sump to Pump
43. Rack & Pinion Throttle Control
44. Rear Cover Body
45. Oil Return Pipe to Tank
46. Spring Drive Gear Unit
47. Supercharger Oil Feed Pipe
48. Scavenge By-Pass Relief Valve
49. Port Magneto
50. Starboard Magneto
51. Pressure Gauge Connection
52. Control Support Bracket
53. Electric Starter Unit
54. Hand Turning Connection

Fig. 5.25 Sectioned view of Bristol Hercules. Despite Roy Fedden's argument that the sleeve valve engine was simpler than its poppet valve counterpart, it can be clearly seen that in fact they were complex. All sleeve drive requirements came from the front case. The rear row sleeve drive cranks were extended and ran between the front row of cylinders. ("Bristol Hercules XI & VI Engines, Operating Instructions," Issue No. 1, Jan. 1943. Author's collection.)

TABLE 5.3—BRISTOL HERCULES PERFORMANCE AND APPLICATION SUMMARY

Dash Number	Applications	hp/rpm/alt	Comments
XI	Beaufighter I/III Albermarle I Beaufighter VI Stirling I/III	1315/2800/SL 1460/2800/9500	Two-speed blower
VI and XVI	Lancaster II Halifax III/V/VII Stirling III Wellington X/XII Wellington XVII/XVIII	1675/2900/4500 1445/2900/12,000	Two-speed blower. Only difference between VI and XVI is propeller reduction ratio
VII and XVII	Beaufighter VIII Beaufighter X/XI Beaufighter 21 Wellington XIII/XIV	1735/2900/500	Beaufighter 21 built in Australia. Similar to VI and XVI except supercharger impeller cropped for improved take-off and low-altitude performance. Only difference between VII and XVII is propeller reduction ratio
VIII	Beaufighter VII Wellington V		Experimental engine for turbosupercharging. None built
XVIII	Wellington XVII Beaufighter 21	1735/2900/500	

Short Stirling

The Short Stirling (built to specification B.12/36), first of the "modern" four-engine bombers for the RAF, was one of the early recipients of the Hercules. Never a stellar performer, Stirlings suffered a number of shortcomings, the main one being the inadequate wing span of only 99 ft, 1 in. Short Brothers Ltd. requested a wing span of 112 ft, but were rejected by the Air Ministry on the grounds that existing RAF hangars could not accommodate wing spans greater than 100 ft. This restriction was to be the Achilles heel of the Stirling through its entire operational life. The Stirling was beset with other design-related problems; for example, the massive, complicated, and fragile landing gear caused endless problems. The prototype aircraft was written off on its maiden flight due to landing gear collapse . . . an inauspicious start to its career (Fig. 5.26).

The aircraft's ceiling was 15,000 ft, making it vulnerable to German flack. To alleviate this situation, up-rated Hercules IIIs developing 1375 hp were installed, replacing the Hercules IIs fitted in the prototype. Later, Mk. 1 Stirlings were fitted with the Hercules XI, rated at 1500 hp, significantly improving the still marginal performance. More importantly, two-speed supercharging was introduced for improved altitude performance; however, all the additional power could not overcome the basic design defect of insufficient wing span.

Fig. 5.26 Short Stirling III heavy bomber powered by four Bristol Hercules VI or XVI engines. A classic example of an aircraft being a victim of its specification. The wing span was dictated by the size of RAF hangars, resulting in a span of 99 ft, 1 in. This was inadequate for acceptable altitude performance. The complex and fragile landing gear is also shown to advantage in this shot. (Courtesy of the National Air and Space Museum, Smithsonian Institution, Photo No. 1B-37322.)

As Handley Page Halifaxes and Avro Lancasters became available in significant numbers, Stirlings were removed from the hazardous bombing operations over Germany and used in lower-priority operations such as glider towing. Many of the gliders used in the Arnhem attack were towed by Stirlings. Due to the additional strain on the engines from towing heavily loaded gliders, fan-assisted cooling was incorporated.

At the end of World War II Stirlings were rapidly withdrawn, and by July 1946 they had all been retired from RAF service.

Vickers Wellington

Brainchild of the brilliant Barnes (later Sir Barnes) Wallis, the Vickers Wellington featured an unusual fabric-covered, geodetic construction that was a trademark of many of Wallis's earlier aircraft. The Wellington, a twin-engine medium bomber, was to be the mainstay of Bomber Command during the early years of the war (Fig. 5.27).

Mk. I and Mk. II Wellingtons were powered by the Pegasus. As is usually the case with military aircraft, additional power was required and was provided for by the Hercules.

Designed to Air Ministry Specification B.9/32, the Wellington first flew in June 1936 with Pegasus power and soon gained the nickname "Wimpy" from the cartoon character J. Wellington Wimpy. This name would stick with the aircraft throughout its career.

Fig. 5.27 Vickers Wellington. Mainstay of the early bombing effort against Germany. This example was powered by Bristol Hercules engines. (Courtesy of the National Air and Space Museum, Smithsonian Institution, Photo No. 1B-46164.)

A total of 11,461 Wellingtons were built with production ending in 1945. It was used in many theaters of the war, primarily in the night bombing offensive against Germany. Coastal Command put the Wimpy to good use spotting German U-boats with radar in conjunction with the Leigh Light, a powerful, steerable searchlight mounted in the bomb bay powered by a generator driven initially by a Ford V-8 automobile engine; later de Havilland Gipsy Queens were substituted. Tactics involved locating the submarine, reducing the radar signal to give the German U-boat crew the impression that the aircraft was going away, and then retransmitting when DR showed they were close, turning on the Leigh light, and bombing if possible on the first pass. In that way the submarine had no time to dive or man its guns. This tactic of "tuning down" was a result of the Germans using a radar detector antenna called the Biscay Cross.

By 1943 Wellingtons were withdrawn from front-line bombing service in Europe but continued on in service in Italy and the far East into late 1944.

Bristol Beaufighter

Design for this heavy twin-engine fighter progressed rapidly as it was based on the Taurus-powered Bristol Beaufort. The engine mounts and the fuselage were the major new components, allowing the prototype to fly only eight months after design work began in 1939 (Fig. 5.28). Beaufighters were powered by almost the whole range of Hercules engines, from the Hercules III for the Beaufighter Is through the Hercules XVIII for the Beaufighter 21. Two versions, the Beaufighter IV and V, were powered by Merlin XXs. Interestingly, the Beaufighter IV and V QECs (Merlins) were used for the Avro Lancaster.

Radar, along with the Supermarine Spitfire and Hawker Hurricane, saved the British from invasion in the summer of 1940. This new technology was soon adapted for installation in aircraft, and the Bristol Beaufighter was the first RAF purpose-built aircraft to use airborne-interception radar.

Fig. 5.28 Bristol Beaufighter X torpedo carrier powered by two Bristol Hercules XVII engines rated at 1735 hp each. (Courtesy of the National Air and Space Museum, Smithsonian Institution, Photo No. 1A-16103.)

Beaufighters saw service in all theaters of World War II as a bomber, a torpedo carrier, and a rocket fighter.

Taurus

A smaller version of the Hercules, the Taurus, had bore and stroke dimensions of 5.0 and 5.625 in, respectively, giving a total displacement of 1550 in³ (25.4 L) from its 14 cylinders (Fig. 5.29). By a quirk of fate, the 5.0-in bore was to have a profound effect on the manufacture of the Napier Sabre, which also had a 5.0-in cylinder bore. The shorter stroke contributed to reducing the diameter of the engine by 6 in compared with the Hercules; otherwise, all design features were the same. It was usually rated at 1050 hp at 3100 rpm and 39.6 in Hg manifold pressure.

Applications

Relatively few aircraft used the Taurus, as can be imagined from the low production figure of 3400 for World War II (Ref. 2.4).

Bristol Beaufort

The Bristol Beaufort, designed to Air Ministry specifications G.24/35 and M.15/35, was a twin-engine general reconnaissance bomber or a land-base torpedo bomber (Fig. 5.30). The Beaufort was soon relegated to training roles, and its main contribution to the British war effort was its use as the basis for the formidable Beaufighter. Overheating woes plagued the Taurus in the Beaufort application. It was planned to fit Pratt & Whitney R-1830s in place of the Taurus, but a German U-Boat torpedoed the ship transporting the R-1830s from the United States to England (Ref. 5.4).

Fig. 5.29 Side view of the Bristol Taurus, which was essentially a scaled-down version of the Hercules. In service this engine suffered from severe overheating. (Courtesy of the National Air and Space Museum, Smithsonian Institution, Photo No. BB-040680-20.)

Fig. 5.30 Bristol Beaufort powered by two Bristol Taurus II or IV engines. (Courtesy of the National Air and Space Museum, Smithsonian Institution, Photo No. 1A-16161.)

Fairey Albacore

The Fairey Albacore was a carrier-based torpedo bomber that was supposed to replace the Fairey Swordfish. As events turned out, production stopped in 1944 on the Albacore, but carried on until 1945 for the Swordfish! Similar in concept to the Swordfish, the Albacore, powered by a Taurus II rated at 1065 hp or Taurus XII rated at 1130 hp, was a biplane with fabric-covered wings and an aluminum monocoque fuselage (Fig. 5.31).

Fig. 5.31 Fairey Albacore powered by a Bristol Taurus. This aircraft was supposed to replace the antiquated Swordfish. As events turned out, the venerable Swordfish was still in service after the Albacore had been removed from service. (Courtesy of the Fleet Air Arm Museum.)

Centaurus

The rate at which aviation technology accelerated during the 1930s put ever greater demands on the engine. Even though the Hercules had just passed its type test, work started on an even larger project, the Centaurus. An Air Ministry development contract was obtained in February 1938. While retaining the same cylinder bore of the Pegasus, Mercury, and Hercules at 5.75 in, the stroke was increased to 7.0 in, which gave a displacement of 3270 in³ (53.6 L) from its 18 air-cooled cylinders (Fig. 5.32). Under development throughout World War II, it made only a minor contribution to the British war effort due to a desperate shortage of engineers and continuing technical problems that were not effectively corrected until after the war. A number of design changes were made from the Hercules concept. The Hercules drove all the sleeves from the front; the rear cylinder sleeve drives used extension shafts running between the front cylinders. With the Centaurus, rear sleeves were driven from the rear thus avoiding the necessity of "threading" the drive between the front cylinders.

Centaurus development took a severe blow when the Bristol board of directors fired Roy Fedden in October 1942. Up until that time he had single-handedly led every Bristol engine project. In retrospect it seems inconceivable that such an action should have occurred right in the middle of World War II. In fact trouble had been brewing for years. Always a hard taskmaster, he never had a good working relationship with the Bristol Board, and by 1942 things had become intolerable (Ref. 3.1). Prior to his leaving, Fedden introduced the use of injection carburetion based on the highly successful Bendix injection carburetor.

Considering it was conceptually similar to the Hercules, it is somewhat surprising that so many problems were experienced in developing the Centaurus. As a result, relatively few were manufactured during World War II, a total of 2800.

Fig. 5.32 Last of the production Bristol sleeve valve engines, the mighty Centaurus. Note the rear-swept exhaust system, a feature that was also used on the last production Hercules. Although 18 exhaust stacks were used, each stack siamesed a front and rear cylinder because of the 36 exhaust ports. (Courtesy of the Fleet Air Arm Museum.)

Applications

Vickers Warwick

An outgrowth of the Wellington, the Vickers Warwick was a larger version of the former. A typical Barnes Wallis design featuring fabric-covered geodetic construction, the Warwick was intended to be a twin-engine bomber (Fig. 5.33). Most aircraft ended up being adapted for a number of other duties, including general reconnaissance, air/sea rescue, and transport (Ref. 2.7).

Hawker Tempest and Fury

Seemingly insurmountable problems with the Napier Sabre led Hawker engineers to investigate the feasibility of installing a Centaurus engine into the Tempest. The Tempest, first flown in June 1943, was intended for service in the far East against the Japanese but did not reach squadron service until 1946.

A follow-on design to the Tempest was the Fury (Fig. 5.34) and the Navy version, the Sea Fury. Again, it was too late to see action in World War II but soldiered on into the 1950s equipping many air forces and Navies.

Bristol Buckingham, Brigand, and Buckmaster

First produced in 1942 as a high-speed bomber, the Bristol Buckingham fell victim to the superlative performance of the de Havilland Mosquito, which was built to the same specification. The few Buckinghams that were built were relegated to military transport roles. Centaurus XII engines, rated at 2500 hp at 2700 rpm and 47.2 in Hg manifold pressure, were installed.

Fig. 5.33 Vickers Warwick powered by two Bristol Centaurus IV or VII engines. (Courtesy of the National Air and Space Museum, Smithsonian Institution, Photo No. 2A-27866.)

Fig. 5.34 Hawker Fury prototype powered by a Bristol Centaurus XVII. (Courtesy of the National Air and Space Museum, Smithsonian Institution, Photo No. 1B-04608.)

Selected as a replacement for the Beaufighter in the Pacific, the Brigand (Fig. 5.35) had its program cut short when hostilities ended. Its flying surfaces were based on the Buckingham; a new fuselage designed to accommodate bombs, a torpedo, or mines was incorporated. Power was provided by Centaurus 57s rated at 2800 hp at 2700 rpm and 53.5 in Hg manifold pressure.

Based on the Buckingham, the Buckmaster was an advanced trainer, although one feels it must have been a very advanced trainer with 5000 hp available to the erstwhile student pilot! (Refs. 2.7, 4.15–4.17).

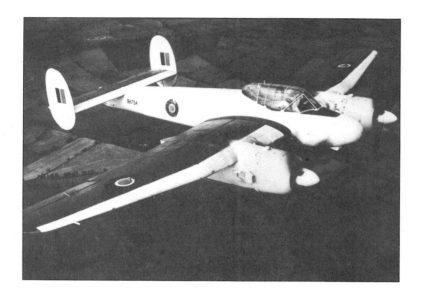

Fig. 5.35 Bristol Brigand powered by Bristol Centaurus 57 engines. (Courtesy of the National Air and Space Museum, Smithsonian Institution, Photo No. 1A-16386.)

References

2.1 Heron, S. D., <u>The History of The Aircraft Piston Engine</u>.

2.3 Ricardo, Sir Harry R., <u>The High Speed Internal Combustion Engine</u>, 5th ed., Blackie & Son, Ltd., London, 1968.

2.4 Banks, Air Commodore F. R. (Rod), "I Kept No Diary," *Airlife,* 1978.

2.5 Schlaifer, Robert, and S. D. Heron, <u>Development of Aircraft Engines and Development of Aviation Fuels</u>, Harvard University, Boston, 1950.

2.7 <u>Jane's All The World's Aircraft</u>, McGraw-Hill, New York, 1945/1946.

3.1 Gunston, W. T., <u>By Jupiter</u>, R.Ae.S., London, 1978.

4.3 Foxworth, Thomas G., <u>The Speed Seekers</u>, Doubleday & Company, New York.

4.15 Wilkinson, Paul H., <u>Aircraft Engines of The World 1946</u>, Paul H. Wilkinson, New York.

4.16 Wilkinson, Paul H., <u>Aircraft Engines of The World 1947</u>, Paul H. Wilkinson, New York.

4.17 Wilkinson, Paul H., <u>Aircraft Engines of The World 1948</u>, Paul H. Wilkinson, New York.

5.1 Ricardo, Sir Harry, <u>Memories and Machines: The Pattern of My Life</u>, Constable, London, 1968.

5.2 <u>Jane's All The Worlds Aircraft</u>, McGraw-Hill, New York, 1942/1943.

5.3 Fedden, A. H. R., "The Single Sleeve as a Valve Mechanism for the Aircraft Engine," Paper 380161, Society of Automotive Engineers, Warrendale, Pa., June 1938.

5.4 Russell, Sir Archibald, "A Span of Wings," *Airlife,* 1994.

Chapter 6

Napier

Napier & Sons Ltd. was one of the premier aircraft engine builders for the RAF in the 1920s, and had a long and illustrious history, having been established in 1808. Like Rolls-Royce, Napier was also a manufacturer of high-performance, luxury cars, giving them excellent experience for the art of manufacturing complex, precision aircraft engines during World War I. Napier initially built Sunbeam Arabs under license, then ventured out to design an in-house engine known as the Lion. At the time, 1917, the Lion revolutionized engine design with its high power-to-weight ratio, smoothness, and reliability. It was a "broad arrow" engine, with three cylinder banks with 60° spacing between banks (120° total between outer banks) and four cylinders per bank; it went into production in 1918 (Fig. 6.1) (Ref. 6.1). Although too late to see action in World War I, it went on to power many RAF aircraft in the 1920s and perhaps more significantly was the primary power plant up to 1927 for the British Schneider Trophy aircraft (Fig. 6.2). The Lion set the tone for all subsequent Napier piston engines, that is, highly sophisticated, high-performance, complex products. Even at this early stage, dual overhead camshafts, six in all, and four valves per cylinder were just two of the advanced features in this remarkable engine, which soldiered on into World War II in Sea Lion form, powering high-speed rescue launches for the RAF.

Fig. 6.1 Direct-drive, naturally aspirated Napier Lion. Blanking plate on the center cylinder bank exhaust ports was a protective plate used for shipping and storage. This dual overhead camshaft, four valve per cylinder engine was ahead of its time when introduced in 1918. (Courtesy of the National Air and Space Museum, Smithsonian Institution, Photo No. BN-300120-20.)

Fig. 6.2 Supermarine S5 built for the 1927 Schneider Trophy race held in Venice, Italy. The three-cowled cylinder banks of the Napier Lion are clearly visible in this head-on view. The S5 won this prestigious race, but it was the last airborne competition hurrah for the Lion. (Courtesy of the National Air and Space Museum, Smithsonian Institution, Photo No. 2A-43197.)

Demonstrating its high-performance heritage, the Lion was used extensively by builders of land-speed-record cars; in fact, the Napier Railton Special was the first car to exceed 400 mph in one direction in 1947, driven by John Cobb. Interestingly, the two engines used in the Railton Special were from the 1929 Schneider Trophy effort. The land-speed record established in 1947 held until 1964, mute testimony to the correctness of this 1917 design.

A. J. Rowledge, the driving force and engineering expertise behind the Lion, resigned in 1920 after a disagreement with Napier management. Rowledge moved on to Rolls-Royce, where he made major contributions to that company's aircraft engine efforts. One of the contributing factors to Rowledge's departure was the "head-in-the-sand" attitude of the Napier management, who felt no replacement for the Lion was necessary and so continued its production even when it became technologically obsolete compared with the competition.

Things did not improve after Rowledge's departure. Napier was offered a government contract to build an Anglicized Curtiss D-12. Amazingly, Napier management declined the offer, feeling that a monoblock V-12 was not a good design concept. Consequently, the British government turned to Rolls-Royce, who in turn produced the excellent Kestrel which formed the basis for all their subsequent poppet valve engines (Ref. 2.5). Napier then made a retrograde step and developed a separate-cylinder V-12 that was not a success.

Several other nonstarters followed, perhaps the most notable being the Cub, the world's first 1000-hp aircraft engine. Several unusual and noteworthy features were incorporated into this X-16 engine. As can be seen from Figure 6.3, the upper and lower V angles are different. The upper V is 52°30′ and the lower V angle is 127°30′. Consequently, the angle on each side between upper and lower banks is 90°. All master rods were situated in the upper cylinders, and interestingly, the three link rods were not evenly disposed on the master rod. Presumably this was done to ensure even firing in conjunction with the 180° crank. It seems that the Cub was Rowledge's last design effort with Napier prior to his departure for Rolls-Royce, as his name appears on the original patent (Ref. 6.2).

Fig. 6.3 World's first 1000-hp aircraft engine, the Napier Cub. The exposed valves and long stroke were a retrograde step compared with the Lion. (Courtesy of the National Air and Space Museum, Smithsonian Institution, Photo No. BN-300020-20.)

The Cub had a very brief service life powering the Avro Aldershot, not entirely attributable to problems with the engine. The wisdom of a single-engine bomber was quite correctly brought into question, effectively killing the Cub program.

Rapier

Major Frank Halford, an engine consultant who had been partly responsible for the BHP engine of World War I, the Siddeley Puma, and the de Havilland range of Gipsy engines, started to play an ever increasing role in Napier's engine developments. Among his many contributions was the introduction of forged aluminum connecting rods, although no aluminum rods were used in Napier engines (Ref. 6.3). The forging process for pistons is now taken for granted in high-performance engines; however, it was Frank Halford who pioneered this manufacturing process for this critical internal engine component.

Halford's first effort for Napier was the Rapier, an H-configured air-cooled pushrod engine of 539 in^3 (8.8 L) derived from sixteen 3.5-in $\times$ 3.5-in cylinders (Fig. 6.4). The use of a large number of diminutive square or oversquare cylinders running at high rpm became a hallmark of all subsequent Napier Otto cycle engines (Ref. 6.4).

The construction of the Rapier, which was rated at 395 hp, at a screaming 4000 rpm, was quite advanced at its introduction in the early 1930s. Despite the high rotational speed of the crankshafts, its piston speed was still a modest 2333 ft/min. Driving its two crankshafts, which rotated in the same direction, from four banks of four separate air-cooled cylinders, the power was transmitted to the propeller by epicyclic reduction gearing. Connecting rod design consisted of master rod/link rod with the link rod pivoted on the bearing cap of the master rod (Fig. 6.5). This obviously put a tremendous amount of additional load on the master rod bearing cap bolts and perhaps helps explain why the outgrowth of the Rapier, the Dagger, and all subsequent Napier engines used blade-and-fork rods.

Fig. 6.4 Napier Rapier, Frank Halford's first engine design for Napier. (Courtesy of the National Air and Space Museum, Smithsonian Institution, Photo No. BN-300180-20.)

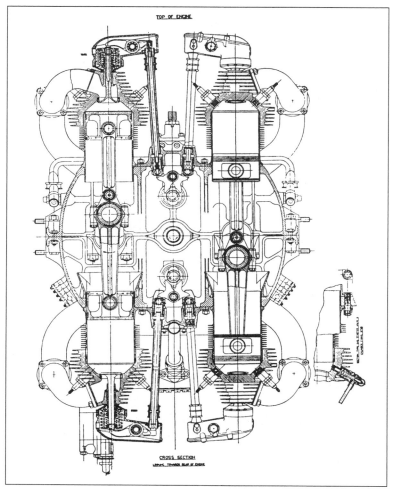

Fig. 6.5 Section through a Napier Rapier. Note the unusual bellcrank arrangement driving the tappets. The master rod/link rod arrangement was changed to a blade-and-fork arrangement on all subsequent Napier H-configured engines. (Courtesy of Alan Vessey and Napier Power Heritage.)

A somewhat dated feature of the engine was the use of pushrod-actuated valves through an unusual bell crank arrangement running off the camshaft lobes (Ref. 6.5).

Cooling was accomplished by two plenums, one above the propeller centerline and one below. The cooling air entered between the banks of cylinders, flowed through baffles through the cooling fins, and finally exited through the sides of the cowling.

Applications

Fairey Seafox

By World War II the Rapier had little to offer because of its relatively small displacement and consequently low power of 395 hp. The only notable application was the Fairey Seafox, a dated biplane design. The pilot and observer were accommodated in the all-aluminum monocoque fuselage. The two-bay, equal-span wings featured two-spar, all-metal construction and fabric covering (Fig. 6.6).

Built to specification S.11/32 as a two-seat light reconnaissance floatplane, the Seafox was usually carried by battleships and cruisers and housed in purpose-built hangers. The Battle of the River Plate gave the Seafox its one moment of glory when one was dispatched from the cruiser H.M.S. *Exeter* and spotted the German pocket battleship, *Graf Spee,* named after the German Admiral of World War I. This open-cockpit, obsolete aircraft was phased out soon after the start of World War II.

Dagger

An outgrowth of the Rapier and another Halford engine, the Dagger was another vertically disposed H-configured engine. Instead of 16 cylinders, the Dagger used 24 cylinders in four banks of six. Following the Napier design philosophy of high specific power at high rpm in a compact package, the Dagger VIII produced 1000 hp at 4200 rpm. Displacement was 1028 in^3 (16.8 L) derived from $3^{13}/_{16}$-in (97-mm) bores and $3\frac{3}{8}$-in (95-mm) strokes (Fig. 6.7).

Fig. 6.6 Fairey Seafox powered by a Napier Rapier. (Courtesy of the Fleet Air Arm Museum.)

Fig. 6.7 Napier Dagger. Note Halford's name on the top cam cover. By the 1930s, Frank Halford was designing all the Napier piston engines. (With permission of the Science Museum, London.)

Construction consisted of 24 individual air-cooled cylinders mounted on a horizontally split, forged aluminum crankcase. Unusually, the cylinders differed from normal air-cooled aircraft engine design practice by having the heads attached to the cylinder barrels by long studs that extended into the crankcase, thus serving to attach the entire cylinder assembly to the crankcase. Although this offered easier maintenance, cylinder head sealing was compromised. Contemporary screwed-and-shrunk cylinder design offered far greater cylinder sealing and cooling capability. A conventional two-valve, hemispherical combustion chamber was used.

Shaft-driven, overhead camshafts replaced the pushrod arrangement of the Rapier. Drive for the tower shafts originated at the front of the engine with a tubular shaft, which ran longitudinally to the rear where bevel gears transmitted the drive to the four tower shafts. The overhead camshafts actuated rocker arms with hydraulic self-adjusting tappets as an integral part of the ingenious design. Blade-and-fork rods replaced the master rod/link rod used on the Rapier. The pair of forged crankshafts were supported in eight lead bronze bearings (Fig. 6.8). Rolls-Royce R engine practice was followed for some variants of the Dagger in that the single-stage, single-speed supercharger featured a double-entry, two-sided impeller (Ref. 6.6).

Cooling design was similar to Dagger practice; that is, two plenums fed pressurized ram air between the upper and lower banks of cylinders. Despite several redesigns to increase cooling fin area, the engine was plagued by overheating primarily because of poor cooling during ground operations. The situation was exacerbated by the propeller roots, which were round and thus offered little, if any, airflow through the ducts when the aircraft was stationary (Ref. 6.2).

Operationally, the Dagger was not a roaring success, even if its exhaust note was!

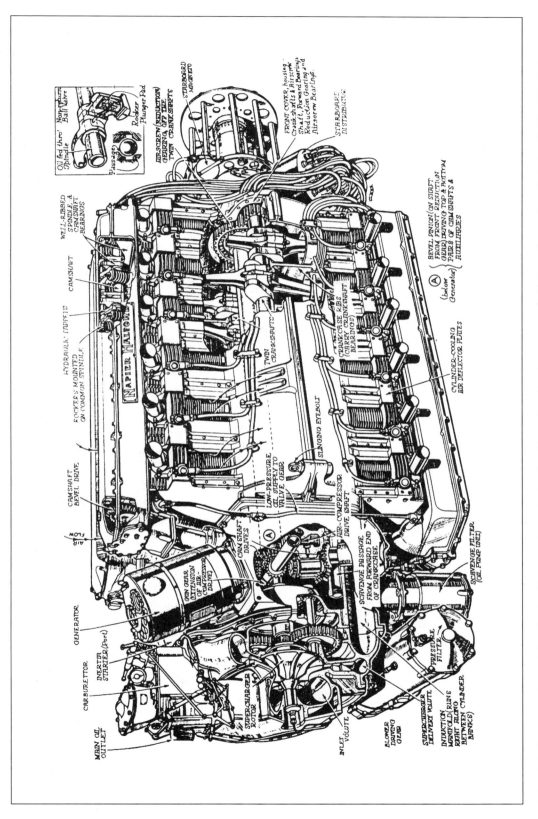

Fig. 6.8 Cutaway view of the Napier Dagger. Note the hydraulic, self-adjusting tappets built into the rocker. (Jane's All The World's Aircraft, 1938.)

161

Applications

Handley Page Hereford

One of the few applications for the Dagger during World War II was the Handley Page Hereford (Fig. 6.9), a derivative of the Handley Page Hampden. The only difference was the power plant, which in the case of the Hampden was the Bristol Mercury. Performance and problems with the Dagger were so disappointing that relatively few were built, and several of those were converted to Mercury power.

Hawker Hector

Another application that again was phased out soon after the start of hostilities and saw little if any combat was the Hawker Hector. Another Sydney Camm design, it was a typical 1930's, open-cockpit, fabric-covered biplane. One squadron was sent to France with the British Expeditionary Force in 1939.

Sabre

The Sabre represented the ultimate in piston engine technology, not only in the 1930s when it was conceived, but even by today's standards (Fig. 6.10). It was a truly remarkable engine, representing the ultimate in complexity, technology, specific power, and unfortunately . . . problems. In retrospect it can be stated that many of the Sabre's woes were due to the pressures in wartime England to get the latest technology into production as rapidly as possible, even though many of the "bugs," both design- and manufacturing-related, had not been worked out (Ref. 2.4).

Yet another Frank Halford engine, brilliantly conceived in the mid 1930s, the Sabre was also based on the H-configuration driving two crankshafts. The Sabre deviated in a number of significant ways from the Rapier and Dagger. The cylinders were oriented horizontally rather than vertically, which offered an even more compact engine package for close, tight cowling. Limitations of air cooling, particularly for a high-performance in-line engine, became very apparent with the Dagger. Consequently, liquid cooling was incorporated into the Sabre design, which not only offered improved control over the considerable heat rejection requirements, but allowed closer cylinder spacing, which in turn resulted in a still more compact engine (Fig. 6.11). Of the many problems suffered by the Sabre, perhaps the primary one was the use of sleeve valve technology (see the section "Manufacture" in this chapter). In order to improve the volumetric efficiency, sleeve valves were employed because of the limitations of poppet valves, even in four-valve form.

Four banks of six cylinders, with a 5.0-in bore and a 4.75-in stroke, resulted in a 2238-in³ displacement, coincidentally almost identical to the Rolls-Royce Griffon's 2239-in³ displacement. As we shall see, however, that was the only similarity between the two engines.

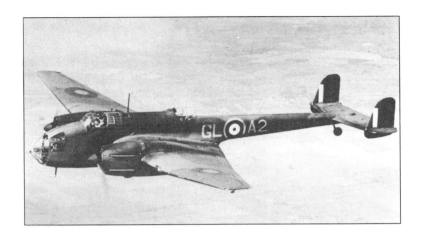

Fig. 6.9 *Handley Page Hereford powered by two Napier Dagger 24-cylinder air-cooled engines. (Courtesy of the National Air and Space Museum, Smithsonian Institution, Photo No. 2A-21387.)*

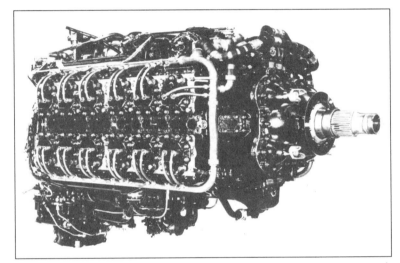

Fig. 6.10 *Three-quarter front view of the Napier Sabre II. Bulges in the nose case are for the four propeller reduction gear pinions. Ignition harness is also visible. (Courtesy of the National Air and Space Museum, Smithsonian Institution, Photo No. BN-300220-20.)*

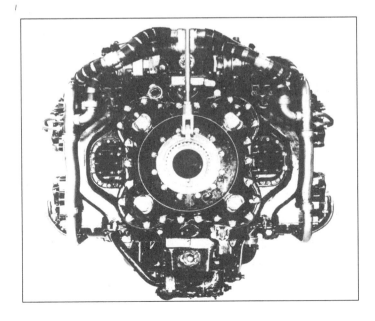

Fig. 6.11 *The compact size of the Napier Sabre is evident in this head-on shot. Clevis and rod on propeller shaft was used to hang the engine for taking the photograph. (Courtesy of the National Air and Space Museum, Smithsonian Institution, Photo No. BN-300220-20.)*

The two-piece, vertically split cast aluminum crankcase supported the two six-throw crankshafts, which, as in previous Halford H engines, rotated in the same direction. Although slightly improved primary balance may have been achieved through counter-rotating crankshafts, the propeller reduction gear design dictated this scheme. As it was, the Sabre was a remarkably smooth running engine. Early engines featured twelve first-order counterweights for each of the two crankshafts. From the Sabre V on, it was found they were not necessary, and therefore they were eliminated, resulting in a significant weight savings for these two components. Seven main lead bronze bearings supported each of the crankshafts.

The Sabre V and all subsequent engines incorporated thin-wall strip bearings manufactured by Vandervell, who in the 1950s designed, built, and sponsored the Vanwall Formula One race cars.

The propeller reduction gearing exemplified the innovative design and engineering that characterized the Sabre. A compounded "back gear" drove the propeller through four pinions. When multiple pinions drive a single reduction gear, the problem of equal tooth loading becomes a major issue, particularly in a heavily loaded, high-speed application with high torsional vibration such as the Sabre reduction gear. The solution Napier devised was nothing short of inspirational. Each crankshaft drove a pair of straight-cut, first-stage pinion gears, which in turn were integral with a second-stage pinion, which drove the propeller reduction gear. The second-stage pinion gears featured a helix angle, which generated an end thrust as power was transmitted. Herein lay the secret to the Sabre's tooth load balancing system. The upper and lower pairs of pinions were connected with a centrally pivoted balance beam. Preloaded volute springs acted on the ends of the beam against the pinions, thus ensuring that the helically cut pinions would float along their longitudinal axis as they transmitted the considerable power of the Sabre and guaranteeing equal tooth loading. Even though the Sabre was beset with numerous problems as will be related, reduction gear problems were non-existent thanks to this very innovative piece of engineering. Propeller shaft radial loads were handled by massive roller and ball thrust bearings mounted back to back, the latter also taking care of propeller thrust loads. In addition, a plain bearing was mounted at the rear of the propeller shaft that also transmitted oil to the de Havilland constant-speed propeller.

The sleeve drive mechanism showed similar ingenuity. Two hollow longitudinal shafts, driven from the front, drove the sleeves of the upper and lower cylinder banks. Each shaft, supported in 14 plain bearings, was split in the center and coupled with a flange. Six skew gears, integral with the case-hardened sleeve drive shafts, drove six ball-bearing-supported bronze wheels with two sleeve drive cranks phased at 180°. These drove the upper and lower sleeves with ball joints. Each sleeve drive assembly was pressure lubricated from the low-pressure side of the lubrication system. Sleeve design followed Roy Fedden's concept at Bristol, featuring a chrome molybdenum steel nitrided forging with two inlet ports, one exhaust only, and a common port for both intake and exhaust.

Cylinder block cores also followed Bristol practice with a three intake and two exhaust port design. In an effort to control high oil consumption, especially when sleeve wear became excessive, helically cut slots were incorporated into the lower sleeves. Each cylinder had a removable head that incorporated the junk head, combustion chamber, coolant passages, and the two centrally located spark plugs. A single piston ring in the junk head sealed against combustion gas pressures. Six ejector-style exhaust stacks fitted on each side of the engine discharged the exhaust, each stack fed from one upper and one lower cylinder. Conventional forged steel blade-and-fork connecting rods, machined and polished all over, were used. Big end bearing technology was again similar to the crankshaft bearings; they were thin-wall lead bronze inserts with a lead flash. A similar bearing surface on the outer central portion of the shell offered a bearing surface for the blade connecting rod, and thus the bore of the rod was the bearing journal.

Supercharger drive, always a major design challenge due to the high rotational speeds, high loads, and torsional vibration, was solved in the Sabre in typical innovative Napier fashion. The hollow sleeve drive shafts contained long, torsionally flexible quill shafts running coaxially with the sleeve drive shafts. Drive originated at the front of the engine and terminated at the rear behind the crankcase. The step-up gears for the two-speed supercharger had their drive transmitted by cone clutches mounted outboard of the supercharger impeller in an arrangement similar to that found on an air-cooled radial rather than on a liquid-cooled in-line (Fig. 6.12). Separate discharge volutes, flowing from the supercharger housing, fed each of the four cylinder banks.

To improve the flow characteristics of the supercharger, a double-entry, two-sided impeller was used, fed by a four-barrel SU carburetor, two barrels feeding each side of the supercharger impeller. Two large accessory drive locations were provided, one on top and the other on the bottom of the engine. The upper location provided drives for the Coffman starter, vacuum pump, hydraulic pump, Heywood air compressor, supercharger oil pump, distributor, magnetos, generator, ignition servo unit, and propeller governor. The lower location provided drives for the oil pumps—pressure and scavenge—and the dual coolant pumps. Coolant flow was a prodigious 367 gal/min with an outlet temperature of 115 to 130°C. Oil flow was 41 gal/min with a maximum outlet temperature of 95°C (Fig. 6.13).

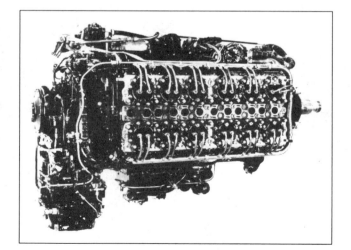

Fig. 6.12 Three-quarter rear view of the Napier Sabre II rated at 2400 hp. The overhung blower clutches and four-barrel updraft carburetor are evident in this view. Sabre Vs used an injection carburetor and moved the blower clutches inboard of the supercharger. (Courtesy of the National Air and Space Museum, Smithsonian Institution, Photo No. BN-300220-20.)

Reprinted from "The Aeroplane," March 24, 1944.

THE NAPIER S

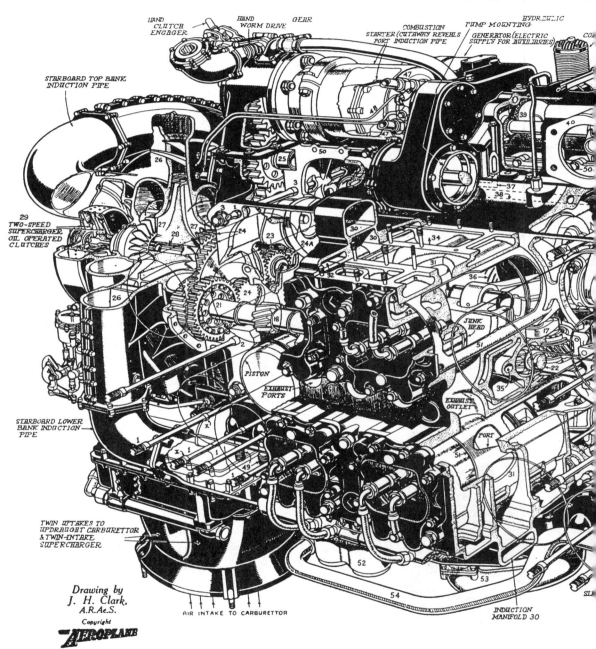

Fig. 6.13 Magnificent Napier Sabre exposed! Innovative engineering features abound in this cutaway view. Note the gear tooth load balancing system for the propeller reduction gear. Supercharger spring drive runs inside sleeve driveshaft. This illustration is of an early Sabre

E AERO-MOTOR

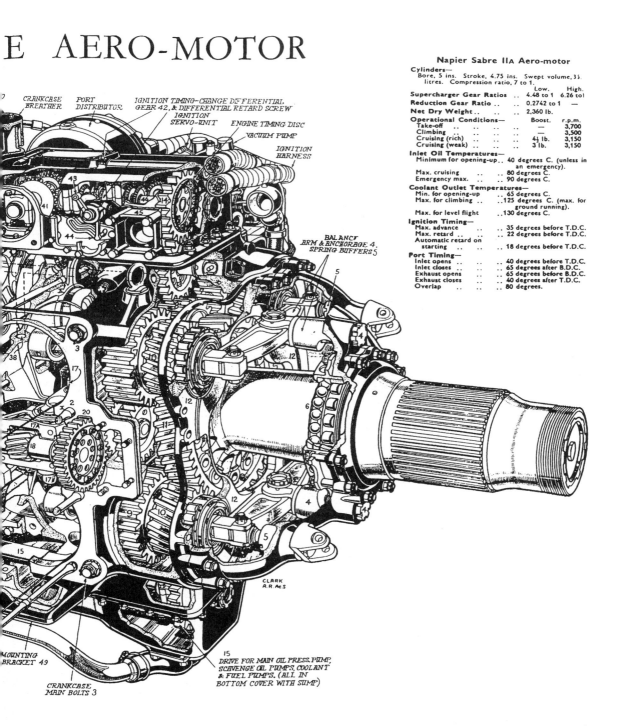

CRANKCASE BREATHER · PORT DISTRIBUTOR · IGNITION TIMING-CHANGE DIFFERENTIAL. GEAR 42, & DIFFERENTIAL RETARD SCREW · IGNITION SERVO-UNIT · ENGINE TIMING DISC · VACUUM PUMP · IGNITION HARNESS

BALANCE ARM & ANCHORAGE 4. SPRING BUFFERS 5

CLARK A.R. Ae.S

MOUNTING BRACKET 49 · CRANKCASE MAIN BOLTS 3

15 · DRIVE FOR MAIN OIL PRESS. PUMP, SCAVENGE OIL PUMPS, COOLANT & FUEL PUMPS. (ALL IN BOTTOM COVER WITH SUMP)

Napier Sabre IIA Aero-motor

Cylinders—
  Bore, 5 ins. Stroke, 4.75 ins. Swept volume, 35. litres. Compression ratio, 7 to 1.

	Low.	High.
Supercharger Gear Ratios ..	4.48 to 1	6.26 to 1
Reduction Gear Ratio	0.2742 to 1	—
Net Dry Weight..	2,360 lb.	

Operational Conditions—	Boost.	r.p.m.
Take-off	—	3,700
Climbing	—	3,500
Cruising (rich)	4½ lb.	3,150
Cruising (weak)	3 lb.	3,150

Inlet Oil Temperatures—
  Minimum for opening-up.. 40 degrees C. (unless in an emergency).
  Max. cruising .. .. 80 degrees C.
  Emergency max. .. 90 degrees C.

Coolant Outlet Temperatures—
  Min. for opening-up .. 65 degrees C.
  Max. for climbing .. 125 degrees C. (max. for ground running).
  Max. for level flight .. 130 degrees C.

Ignition Timing—
  Max. advance .. 35 degrees before T.D.C.
  Max. retard .. .. 22 degrees before T.D.C.
  Automatic retard on starting .. 18 degrees before T.D.C.

Port Timing—
  Inlet opens .. .. 40 degrees before T.D.C.
  Inlet closes .. .. 65 degrees after B.D.C.
  Exhaust opens .. .. 65 degrees before B.D.C.
  Exhaust closes .. .. 40 degrees after T.D.C.
  Overlap .. .. 80 degrees.

with the external blower clutches, four-barrel carburetor and two-sided, double-entry supercharger impeller. (Courtesy of the Science Museum and by permission of Aeroplane Monthly.*)*

Starting was accomplished by a Coffman cartridge starter, which contributed to the Sabre's woes. At the time of its development, an electric starter of sufficient power was not available in England. The Coffman offered several significant advantages, such as lower weight and a smaller battery that yielded additional weight savings. On the down side, the vicious acceleration imposed on the engine when the cartridge was fired could cause considerable damage. During the firing stage, the starter developed a momentary 25 hp (Fig. 6.14). Therefore it was imperative that all engine controls were correctly set when firing the starter. Overpriming was the cause of many problems resulting in sleeve damage and seizure caused by the lubricant being washed off the cylinder walls, and in severe cases hydraulic lock could result. Several schemes were incorporated to alleviate these problems. To ensure adequate lubrication of the sleeves during the critical starting phase, fuel for priming was drawn from a small tank housed in the wheel well of the aircraft. The priming "brew" consisted of 30% lubricating oil and 70% fuel. In cold conditions, the "two-shot" starting system was used. This entailed firing one cartridge with the magnetos turned off but with the primer on. A second cartridge would then be indexed around and fired with the magnetos hot and hopefully a successful start would result. The starter contained five cartridges, and if all five were fired without a successful start the engine required a lengthy maintenance procedure, including the injection of oil in all 24 cylinders through the spark plug holes.

Shock loading from the starter also caused sleeve drive shaft failures until this part was strengthened (Refs. 6.2, 6.7).

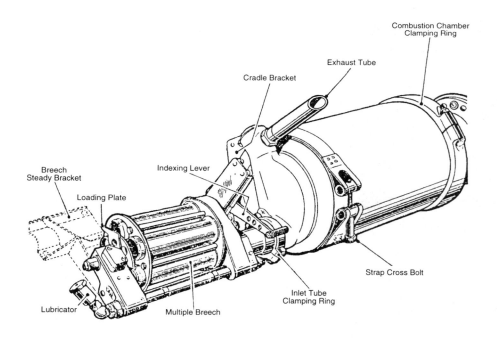

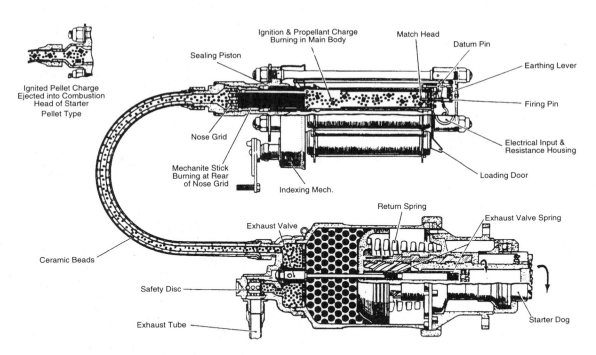

DIAGRAM OF MULTIPLE BREECH & STARTER (STICK TYPE)

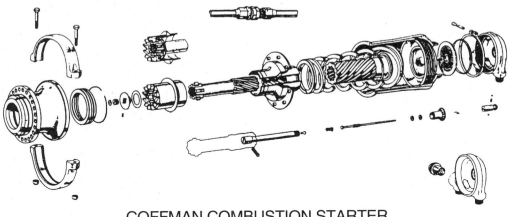

COFFMAN COMBUSTION STARTER

Fig. 6.14 (Facing page and above) Coffman cartridge starter used extensively during World War II. The hot gases of a shotgun shell were harnessed to drive a starter. The advantages were that it was light compared with the weight of an electric starter and did not require battery power to energize the starter. When the cartridge was fired, gas pressure in the breach was piped to the starter unit. The initial surge of pressure forced the piston forward, which caused the starter dog to move forward and engage the engine starter dog. As the piston continued to travel forward, driven by the expanding gases, the starter dog turned due to the helical splines machined into the housing, thus turning the engine over several revolutions. This light, compact package was capable of producing a momentary 25 hp. In some applications the breach was mounted integrally with the starter; in others it was mounted remotely. (Courtesy of Rolls-Royce plc.)

Development

Design was initiated in 1935 based on an earlier study for a compression ignition diesel. British Air Ministry Initial Acceptance tests were completed on 17 January 1938 rated at 1350 hp. This figure rose to 2050 hp by March. By June 1940 it had passed its Air Ministry 100-h type test on its first attempt at 2200 hp and 3700 rpm, making it the world's first 2000-hp production engine (Ref. 6.8).

Napier started negotiations with the Air Ministry in 1938 for full-scale production. At this time Napier was envisioning a delivery rate of 1000 engines per year.

By 31 May 1939 the Sabre was ready for its first flight in the ubiquitous Fairey Battle at RAF Station Northolt.

In an effort to regain the world's absolute air-speed record for the British, a purpose-built aircraft, designed by A. E. Hagg, a member of the Napier design staff, was built. It was constructed from wood and powered by the most powerful engine available, which naturally turned out to be the Sabre. Detail design was performed by George Cornwall of Heston Aircraft Limited. Sponsored by a wealthy British industrialist named Lord Nuffield, the Napier Heston Type 5, as it was known, was ready to fly in June 1940. This date coincided with the successful completion of the 100-h type test and, more ominously, the start of the Battle of Britain. For the record attempt, boost pressure was raised to 9.2 psi and the engine was run at 4000 rpm resulting in a power of 2560 hp. The one and only flight was a disaster and a harbinger of things to come in the development of the Sabre. After the Heston was airborne for 7 min, severe overheating set in, and during the ensuing attempted emergency landing the aircraft stalled 30 ft above the field and was destroyed, fortunately without killing the pilot (Ref. 6.8).

The first design studies incorporating contra-rotating propellers were initiated in 1941. No production Sabre used this concept, possibly because of other more pressing issues with the engine and lack of a suitably developed propeller.

Three-speed, two-stage supercharging, which promised higher boost, was developed in 1942, but again this promising avenue was not pursued and consequently never got into production.

Manufacture

The Sabre was initially manufactured in Acton, a suburb of London, and a shadow factory was later set up in Walton, near Liverpool. Although the engine successfully passed its type test in June 1940, problems started to bubble to the surface as soon as volume production started. At the time, it was not only the world's most powerful aircraft engine, but also the most complicated, and in many areas not only advanced the state of the art for high-performance engine design but in manufacture as well. This established the scene for an unfortunate set of circumstances that were never satisfactorily resolved. The result was Napier's being absorbed, in December 1942, by the English Electric Group.

The engines used for the type test had been hand built, hand fitted, and carefully assembled by top craftsmen. Production engines on the other hand did not have this luxury, resulting in many mechanical problems, particularly as the engines entered squadron service. The majority of the problems centered on the sleeves and sleeve drives. As Bristol had found out to its chagrin, sleeve engines are a very different proposition to manufacture from their poppet valve counterpart. Circularity of the sleeve and the fit of the sleeve to the cylinder were just two of the critical parameters that needed close attention. Sabre sleeves were manufactured from a nitrided chrome molybdenum steel alloy forging. It was found that after final grinding of the exterior and the bore up to 0.010 in, out-of-roundness resulted. This in turn would cause sleeve seizure and/or loss of compression. Several "fixes" were attempted, including—because of its excellent bearing characteristics—silver plating of the sleeve.

The Royal Air Force was committed to this engine; therefore a tremendous effort was expended in getting the engine right. After the English Electric takeover, Rod Banks of Schneider Trophy fame took over the development phase. By sheer coincidence, the Bristol Taurus shared the same cylinder bore of 5.0 in with the Sabre. Banks put plans in place to test the Sabre using Bristol Taurus sleeve material, tools, and manufacturing techniques. The overwhelming success of these tests prompted Banks to have Bristol manufacture Sabre sleeves. Amazingly, the Bristol company objected on the grounds that their sleeve manufacturing methods were confidential and refused to cooperate. Furthermore, Napier thought the idea not worth pursuing (Ref. 2.4). To put things in perspective, it should be noted that at that time, early 1943, the war was far from won, and it is hard to believe that the British could have afforded this kind of corporate infighting. Common sense prevailed, and Sabre sleeves were manufactured from nitrided austenitic forgings using Bristol tooling, making a major contribution to saving the Sabre program.

Because of the critical nature of the Sabre program, some high-level wheeling and dealing took place. When centerless grinders were desperately needed for sleeve production, six Sundstrand grinders were diverted from their intended destination at the new Pratt & Whitney plant in Kansas City, Missouri, for R-2800 C series production and sent to Liverpool instead. Needless to say, Pratt & Whitney was miffed to be the victim of this international maneuvering (Refs. 2.4, 6.9). Again, Rod (later Air Commodore Rod) Banks was responsible for manipulating the Sundstrand grinder deal; the fact that his boss at the time was Lord Beaverbrook, Minister of Aircraft Production, obviously helped.

Even with the improved manufacturing techniques, plus numerous design refinements, the engine was not out of the woods. It has been documented that the Sabre suffered the dual evils of being a very complex product manufactured by a company hard-pressed to deliver under difficult wartime conditions. Cases were cited where poor workmanship contributed to the already bad situation: improperly cleaned castings, broken piston rings, and machine cuttings left inside the engine. When the engine reached squadron service, there were cases of ground maintenance personnel misadjusting the automatic boost control, allowing far too high a manifold pressure at low rpm and resulting in detonation and consequently serious engine damage. Because of the grave consequences of this unauthorized meddling and the sensitive nature of the Sabre program, court-martials resulted from this action.

After the debacle of the early Sabres, the engine became reliable and increasingly powerful. By 1944, in Sabre V form, it became an excellent power plant. Several of the improvements incorporated into the Sabre V were relocating the outboard, overhung supercharger clutches to behind the crankcase, thus reverting to conventional in-line configuration. The double-entry, two-sided supercharger impeller was replaced with a single-sided impeller. Carburetion was improved in 1942 with the introduction of the Series IV, by replacing the four-barrel SU unit with a Hobson-RAE single-point fuel-injection unit spraying atomized fuel into the eye of the now single-sided supercharger impeller.

The Sabre VII was similar to the V; the primary difference was the use of ADI and strengthening of internal components. The VII represented the pinnacle of not only Sabre development, but the development of production aircraft piston engines. From its 2238 in³ (36.7 L) displacement a phenomenal 3500 hp was achieved at 3850 rpm with 70.6 in Hg manifold pressure (Ref. 4.25). Finally, Napier test-ran a Sabre at 4000 hp with ADI. No other production aircraft piston engine has ever equaled these truly impressive numbers.

Discussions were entered into for manufacturing the Sabre in the United States. Although the U.S. manufacturers were impressed with the design, they felt it was so different in construction from what they were used to that it was doubtful it could be manufactured in useful numbers prior to the cease of hostilities (Ref. 6.10).

Applications

Table 6.1 summarizes the performance and applications of the Sabre engine. Although the Sabre was installed in a number of experimental aircraft, it went into only two production aircraft, both of which were fighters built by Hawker.

TABLE 6.1—NAPIER SABRE PERFORMANCE AND APPLICATION SUMMARY

Series Number	Applications	hp/rpm/alt	Comments
Prototype	None	1350	Four-barrel SU carburetor. Two-sided blower impeller. (1938)
Racer "Special"	Nuffield Heston racer	2560/4000/SL[a]	Purpose-built engine for attack on world's air-speed record. Four-barrel SU carburetor. Two-sided blower impeller. (1939)
I	Typhoon	2060/3700/2500[b]	Four-barrel SU carburetor. Two-sided blower impeller. (1940)
II	Tempest I Typhoon F. Mk. 1A MB.3 (2492)	2090/3700/4000[b] 1735/3700/17,000	Four-barrel SU carburetor. Two-sided blower impeller. (1941)

(continued)

TABLE 6.1, continued

Series Number	Applications	hp/rpm/alt	Comments
IIA	Typhoon IA/B	2220/3700/2500[c] 1735/3700/17,000	Four-barrel SU carburetor. Two-sided blower impeller. (1943)
IIB	Tempest V	2420/3850/SL[d] 2045/3850/13,750 1735/3700/17,000	Four-barrel SU carburetor. Two-sided blower impeller. (1944)
IIC	Typhoon	2400/3850/2000[d] 2045/3850/13,750 1735/3700/17,000	Four-barrel SU carburetor. Two-sided blower impeller. (1945)
III	Firebrand F. Mk. 1 Folland Fo. 108 43/37	2305/4000/4250[c] 1735/3700/17,000	Four-barrel SU carburetor. Two-sided blower impeller. (1942)
IV	Tempest I	2240/4000/4250[c]	Hobson RAE single-point injection. Single-sided blower impeller. (1942)
V		2420/3750/6750[c]	Hobson RAE single-point injection. Single-sided blower impeller. (1943)
V	Tempest	2420/3750/4250[e]	Hobson RAE single-point injection. Single-sided blower impeller. (1943)
V	Tempest F. Mk. VI	2600/3850/2500[f] 1970/3650/17,000	Hobson RAE single-point injection. Single-sided blower impeller. (1944)
VA	Tempest F. Mk. VI	2600/3850/2500[f] 1970/3650/17,000	Hobson RAE single-point injection. Single-sided blower impeller. (1945)
VI	Typhoon F. Mk. IB Tempest F. Mk. V Warwick C Mk. III	2600/3850/2500[f] 1970/3650/17,000	Hobson RAE single-point injection. Single-sided blower impeller. (1945). Similar to VA but with gear-driven cooling fan for annular radiator installation
VII	Tempest Fury P.R. Mk. I[g]	3055/3850/2250[h] 2820/3850/12,500	Hobson RAE single-point injection. Single-sided blower impeller. Almost 4000 hp developed on test. (1945)
E.122	Numerous studies, none built	3350/3850/SL	Similar to VII but fitted with two-stage blower. (1946). Contra-rotating propeller drive also developed for this engine.

(a) 48.4 in Hg. (b) 44 in Hg. (c) 48 in Hg. (d) 52 in Hg. (e) 50 in Hg. (f) 60 in Hg. (g) Fastest of the Fury variants. (h) 64 in Hg and ADI. Source: Refs. 2.7, 4.15–4.18, 6.8.

Hawker Typhoon

Hawker designed two similar fighters in the late 1930s, the only difference being the power plant. The Tornado was powered by the Rolls-Royce Vulture and the Typhoon was powered by the Sabre (Fig. 6.15). As has been previously related, the Vulture was not a successful engine; however fewer problems were experienced with the Tornado, possibly because of the improved cooling available in a fighter because of the typically higher air speeds flown compared with a bomber. With the cancellation of the Vulture, the Sabre-powered Typhoon was proceeded with. First flown in February 1940, which was prior to the engine completing its 100-h type test, the aircraft showed great promise. As the Battle of Britain heated up during those crucial days during the summer of 1940, Hawker stopped all experimental and prototype work in order to concentrate on the production of desperately needed Hurricanes. This naturally impacted the Typhoon program. Work recommenced in late 1940, which caused considerable delays while the Typhoon team got back up to speed again. The first production aircraft flew in May 1941 powered by a Sabre II rated at 2200 hp driving a three-blade de Havilland constant-speed propeller. A typical Sydney Camm design, the aircraft featured a thick cantilevered wing mounted to a semimonocoque fuselage with a chrome molybdenum steel alloy space frame structure from the cockpit forward (Fig. 6.16).

Because of its considerable weight and to keep the center of gravity in the correct location, the engine was mounted on top of the front wing spar (Fig. 6.17). A massive "chin" plenum mounted under the engine handled the cooling and supercharger intake duties. The main coolant radiator was oval shaped with the oil cooler mounted in the center of its hollowed-out core. In the center of the oil cooler, a circular opening provided ram air for the supercharger (Fig. 6.18).

Problems with the Typhoon were legion, not all of them engine related. Early aircraft suffered a structural weakness in the rear fuselage resulting in complete failure of the rear monocoque structure. Hawker's chief test pilot suffered a rear fuselage failure during a test flight and through brilliant

Fig. 6.15 Hawker Typhoon IB with the later bubble canopy. Earlier IBs sported a turtle deck and car-type doors. Inset in the upper right side of photograph is a detail shot of the momentum filter that proved invaluable during the early days after the D-Day landings. Courtesy of Alan Vessey and Napier Power Heritage.)

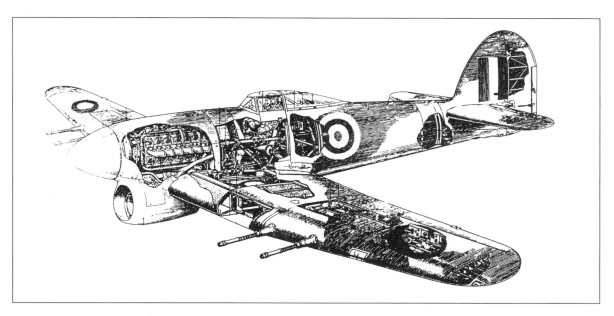

Fig. 6.16 Hawker Typhoon IB powered by a Napier Sabre IIA rated at 2200 hp. Armament consisted of four 20-mm Hispano cannons. Like the Bell P-39 and P-63, the Typhoon IB used car-type doors for access. In an emergency they were jettisoned along with the cockpit roof. ("The Typhoon IB Aeroplane," Air Publication 1804A, British Crown Copyright/Ministry of Defence. Reproduced with the permission of the Controller of Her Britannic Majesty's Stationery Office. Courtesy of the National Air and Space Museum, Smithsonian Institution.)

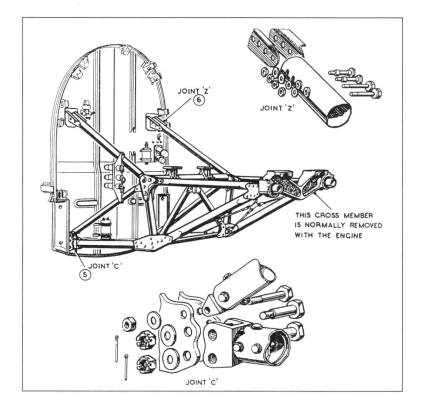

Fig. 6.17 Hawker Typhoon engine mount assembly for Napier Sabre (usually a IIA rated at 2200 hp). ("The Typhoon IB Aeroplane," Air Publication 1804A, British Crown Copyright/Ministry of Defence. Reproduced with the permission of the Controller of Her Britannic Majesty's Stationery Office. Courtesy of the National Air and Space Museum, Smithsonian Institution.)

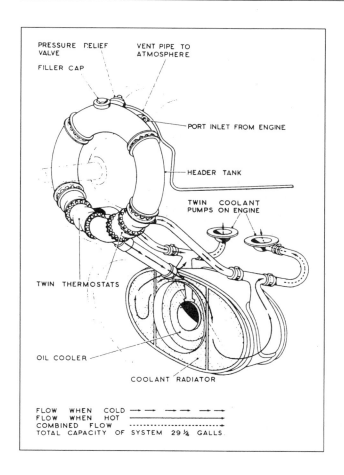

PRESSURE RELIEF VALVE

VENT PIPE TO ATMOSPHERE

FILLER CAP

PORT INLET FROM ENGINE

HEADER TANK

TWIN COOLANT PUMPS ON ENGINE

TWIN THERMOSTATS

OIL COOLER

COOLANT RADIATOR

FLOW WHEN COLD →→ →→ →→
FLOW WHEN HOT ————
COMBINED FLOW ·················
TOTAL CAPACITY OF SYSTEM 29¼ GALLS.

Fig. 6.18 Hawker Typhoon radiator and oil cooler assemblies. Induction air for the Napier Sabre's updraft carburetor was in the middle of the oil cooler. ("The Typhoon 1B Aeroplane," Air Publication 1804A, British Crown Copyright/Ministry of Defence. Reproduced with the permission of the Controller of Her Britannic Majesty's Stationery Office. Courtesy of the National Air and Space Museum, Smithsonian Institution.)

piloting managed to get the aircraft back on the ground, thus allowing evaluation and correction of the problem. Additional rear fuselage failures were caused by fatigue failure of the elevator balance weight, which induced elevator flutter and consequently complete failure of the tail assembly. Numerous fatal crashes were caused by this problem until the fault was discovered and corrected by the addition of fish plates riveted to the exterior of the rear fuselage (Ref. 6.11).

Compressibility effects around the chin plenum also were a problem for the high-speed Typhoon. This little-understood phenomenon, at the time, was caused by localized supersonic airflow. (It should be noted that contrary to some reports, no propeller-driven aircraft ever came close to exceeding the speed of sound during World War II.)

The primary factor that saved the Typhoon and by default the Sabre program from cancellation was the appearance of the Focke-Wulf 190. This very impressive and advanced fighter made its presence felt with "hit-and-run" attacks over England in 1941. The Sabre-powered Typhoon was the only aircraft at the time that had any hope of successfully engaging it until the Griffon Spitfires and two-stage Merlin Spitfires entered squadron service.

At low altitudes the Typhoon was a superb aircraft, so it was only logical that when the first rocket projectiles developed for Allied aircraft during World War II became available, they were installed on the Typhoon. After the Normandy landings, the Typhoon was in its element. With most of the development problems overcome, it created total havoc for the retreating German forces. It has been documented that the whole tortuous Typhoon/Sabre program was worth the trouble based solely on the devastation caused by the Typhoon, specifically in the Falaise Gap on the retreating German Army (Ref. 2.4). One last nasty problem occurred soon after the D-Day landings. As soon as temporary landing strips were prepared in France, fighter squadrons were operating from them. This created huge clouds of highly abrasive dust that was devastating for the Sabre. The quick fix was the installation of rapidly designed, developed, and manufactured Vokes air filters.

The air filter, known as the "Momentum," comprised a dome-shaped aluminum fabrication formed by an aluminum spinning mounted in the induction air intake creating a narrow annular gap. Air was forced inward and forward before entering the engine intake.

The request for a filter was received in the morning, by the afternoon sheet metal was being shaped, and that evening it was test-flown. A week later all Normandy-based aircraft were fitted with the "Momentum" filter (Ref 6.8). (By today's standards, it is amazing how rapidly things got accomplished during World War II.)

Hawker Tempest

A further development of the Typhoon, the Hawker Tempest was similar in concept to a number of major refinements that justified the new designation. The major difference was a totally new wing of much thinner section and featuring laminar flow characteristics (Fig. 6.19). Other changes included a four-blade propeller and a dorsal fin. The prototype, which first flew in September 1942, had the radiators relocated to the wing leading edge. Although offering less drag, it was felt this location would be too vulnerable to enemy fire; therefore all subsequent production Tempests had the same radiator location as the Typhoon, that is, under the nose. From the outset it was planned to have alternative engines for the Tempest and finally three were chosen: Rolls-Royce Griffon, Bristol Centaurus, and Napier Sabre. One prototype was built with the Griffon; a number of aircraft were built with Centaurus power, although most of these were manufactured after World War II. Consequently, the vast majority of Tempests manufactured during World War II were Sabre-powered. Tempests were used for the final drive across the Rhine, operating from bases in Holland, where they created incredible devastation for the Germans in the ground attack role in which the Tempest excelled. Conditions in these forward airstrips could only be described as abysmal. Exacerbating the problem was the fact that the Sabre was a maintenance-intensive, complex engine operating under the worst environment for this high-tech piece of precision machinery.

In June 1944 the first of the V-1 flying bombs ("buzz bombs") appeared over England. At first panic followed the sight of this new type of warfare; however, tactics were quickly put in place to combat this new menace. Flying at relatively low altitudes, rarely over 5000 ft, the Tempest was ideally suited for dealing with the V-1 threat. As the fastest fighter in the world (at the altitudes at which the V-1

Fig. 6.19 Hawker Tempest. (Courtesy of the National Air and Space Museum, Smithsonian Institution, Photo No. 1B-04637.)

flying bombs usually flew), the Tempest had the speed to catch up with them. Shooting them down proved hazardous to the pilot due to the ensuing explosion. When it was found that the V-1s were gyroscopically stabilized, it was soon realized that a skilled pilot could fly alongside the V-1 and raise the wing tip of the Tempest under the wing tip of the V-1. Alternatively, the Tempest pilot could fly in front of the V-1 and the turbulence would again destabilize the gyroscopes, thus sending it out of control (Ref. 6.11).

In an effort to reduce cooling drag, several novel radiator designs were tried, none of which proceeded beyond the prototype stage. The most promising was a radial configuration; that is, the radiator was circular in shape, mounted behind the propeller.

Although the combat career of the Tempest was limited to Europe, plans were in place for it to become a part of the "Tiger Force." To this end, 45 aircraft were being prepared for combat in the Far East when the dropping of the atomic bombs made this effort superfluous.

Projects and Prototypes

With over 2500 hp available in a small, compact package, many interesting projects were designed by airframe manufacturers for the Sabre.

After the success of the Mosquito, de Havilland proposed a twin-Sabre-powered version of this versatile aircraft in 1942. Three design studies known as Projects 2 and 3 (D.H.99) were initiated. The planes were basically Mosquitos with Sabre engines; however, the project was not executed (Ref. 6.8).

In 1942, Blackburn Aircraft powered the preproduction versions of the Firebrand, a Fleet Air Arm strike aircraft, with Sabre series II, III, IV, or V engines. Using the same techniques pioneered by Germany, the engine was mounted in an aluminum forging. Production versions of the Firebrand were powered by the Bristol Centaurus (Ref. 6.8).

Airspeed Limited prepared a design study for a tandem-Sabre, twin-boom, high-speed bomber. Known as the A.S. 47, it never proceeded beyond the design stage. Another Airspeed project, the A.S. 48, fared little better than the A.S. 47. Conceived as a single-engine night interceptor, the prototype was 25% complete when the contract was canceled in 1942 (Ref. 6.8).

Martin-Baker (of subsequent ejection seat fame) embarked on the MB.3, a single-seat interceptor powered by the Series II, in 1942. The use of his unique simplified metal construction, built to Air Ministry Specification F.18/39, resulted in respectable performance with a top speed of 415 mph at 20,000 ft. Following engine failure during a test flight, the single prototype crashed into a tree during the attempted emergency landing, killing Captain Valentine H. Baker, one of the cofounders of the company (Ref. 6.8).

In 1945, a Vickers Warwick was modified by installing Sabre Series VI engines mounted in annular cowlings. Remarkably low installed drag figures were achieved with this installation.

Airspeed Limited prepared a design study based on the Warwick annular radiator installation for a single-seat interceptor. This aircraft, the A.S. 56, was planned to have a top speed of 492 mph (Ref. 6.8).

References

2.4 Banks, Air Commodore F. R. (Rod), "I Kept No Diary," *Airlife,* 1978.

2.5 Schlaifer, Robert, and S. D. Heron, <u>Development of Aircraft Engines and Development of Aviation Fuels</u>, Harvard University, Boston, 1950.

2.7 <u>Jane's All the World's Aircraft</u>, McGraw-Hill, New York, 1945/1946.

4.15 Wilkinson, Paul H., <u>Aircraft Engines of The World 1946</u>, Paul H. Wilkinson, New York.

4.16 Wilkinson, Paul H., <u>Aircraft Engines of The World 1947</u>, Paul H. Wilkinson, New York.

4.17 Wilkinson, Paul H., <u>Aircraft Engines of The World 1948</u>, Paul H. Wilkinson, New York.

4.18 Wilkinson, Paul H., <u>Aircraft Engines of The World 1949</u>, Paul H. Wilkinson, New York.

6.1 Weir, J. G., <u>Napier Lion Aero Engine Instruction Book</u>, Ministry of Munitions, London, Nov. 1918.

6.2 Correspondence by the author with Napier Power Heritage, 1993–1994.

6.3 Brodie, J. L. P., The First Halford Lecture, Frank Bernard Halford 1894–1955, *de Havilland Gazette.*

6.4 Wilkinson, Paul H., Aircraft Engines of The World 1941, Paul H. Wilkinson, New York, 1941.

6.5 Gibson, A. H., and Alan Chorlton, Internal Combustion Engineering, Gresham Publishing Co. Ltd., London, 1937.

6.6 "The Napier Dagger VIII," *Flight and Aircraft Engineer,* Royal Aero Club, London, 12 Jan. 1939.

6.7 *Engineering,* Office for Advertisements and Publications, London, 25 Jan. 1946.

6.8 "The Sabre Breed," Technical Publications Dept., for the National Research Council of Canada's Ottawa Museum, Ottawa, Canada.

6.9 The Pratt & Whitney Aircraft Story, Pratt & Whitney Aircraft Div., United Aircraft Corp., East Hartford, Conn., 1952.

6.10 *Archive,* No. 36, Rolls-Royce Heritage Trust, p. 16, East Hartford, Conn.

6.11 Reed, Arthur, and Roland Beamont, Typhoon and Tempest at War, Ian Allen Ltd., London, 1974.

SECTION 2

Chapter 7

The U.S. Contribution

As in England, three traditional aircraft engine companies supplied engines for U.S. frontline combat aircraft: Allison, Pratt & Whitney, and Wright Aeronautical. Pratt & Whitney and Wright Aeronautical also supplied engines to British manufacturers for their aircraft, for example, the Pratt & Whitney R-1830-92s installed in the Short Sunderland and the Wright R-2600 installed in the Short Stirling.

Again, as in England, the U.S. automobile industry became a production source for combat engines. Packard built the Rolls-Royce Merlin for Commonwealth and English production aircraft, as well as tens of thousands for the U.S. Army Air Corps (USAAC) and U.S. Army Air Force (USAAF) to use in the P-40 and P-51. Buick, Chevrolet, Cadillac, Ford, Dodge, Nash, and Studebaker were some of the major producers of engines and finished components designed by the aircraft engine companies.

As with the British, American cultural and economic factors had a profound influence on engine developments. The United States had been devastated by the economic depression of the 1930s. Lack of funds had a serious delaying effect on many critical engine developments such as the Allison V-1710 and the Wright Field Material Division's "Hyper" program. Consequently, much of the technical achievement was accomplished by a few individuals working privately, or with very restricted corporate and/or military development funds. Their accomplishments were way out of proportion to the costs incurred. Furthermore, the results were there when needed (Ref. 2.5).

World War I brought home the impact of aerial warfare. The Army Air Service initially used British and French designs. After World War I, the U.S. Army General Staff, influenced by the Monroe doctrine, which called for an isolationist policy, determined that an independent air force was not necessary. General Billy Mitchell was court-martialed for his efforts to create an independent air force. Mitchell proved the value of bombers by sinking captured German battleships anchored in Chesapeake bay in 1921 and 1923. His efforts were not totally futile; in 1926 the U.S. Army Air Corps was formed, and on 20 June 1941 the U.S. Army Air Force was created under the leadership of General H. H. (Hap) Arnold (Ref. 7.1).

By the end of World War II, 16 numbered Air Forces under the AAF would be active, as well as a global navy with thousands of aircraft. Four of them were home commands for training and supplying replacement crews for overseas Army Air Forces.

- First Air Force, headquartered at Mitchell Field, Long Island, New York.
- Second Air Force, headquartered at Fort George Wright, Spokane, Washington.
- Third Air Force, headquartered at the National Guard Armory, Tampa, Florida.
- Fourth Air Force, headquartered at Presidio, San Francisco, California.
- Fifth Air Force, initially based in Australia and later Okinawa.
- Sixth Air Force, based in the Caribbean, responsible for the defense of the Panama Canal and the Caribbean area.
- Seventh Air Force, originally based in the Philippines and after the fall of the Philippines became Far East Air Force Okinawa.
- Eighth Air Force, the largest of the Air Forces, based in England until VE (Victory in Europe) Day, then transferred to the Pacific.
- Ninth Air Force, initially based in the Mediterranean and later England, formed the Air Force of occupation in Germany after the surrender.
- Tenth Air Force, originally formed as part of the Allied Southeast Asia Command.
- Eleventh Air Force, a component of the U.S. Navy North Pacific Command, had the unenviable task of fighting the Japanese in the Aleutians.
- Twelfth Air Force, part of the Mediterranean Allied Air Command in Italy.
- Thirteenth Air Force, originally served in the Southern Pacific area, later incorporated into the Far East Air Force.
- Fourteenth Air Force, made up of the former China Air Task Force and the American Volunteer Group (AVG), under General Claire Chenault, later formed part of the China Theater Command.
- Fifteenth Air Force. As Italy was conquered, it was planned to bomb Germany from there, and in 1943 the Fifteenth was formed to bomb Germany in concert with the Eighth flying out of England.
- Twentieth Air Force, formed to bomb Japan, initially from bases in India and as the Pacific campaign liberated more Islands, from the Pacific (Ref. 2.7).

The responsibility of testing new aircraft engines for service use fell to the Materiel Command at Wright Field. They also dictated policy in many cases such as the 300°F coolant requirement for hyper engines in the 1930s (Ref. 2.5).

By the late 1930s U.S. industry was finally coming out of the depression. The British and French realized at the last minute that they were desperately short of much-needed combat aircraft. This shortage created the vital shot in the arm the U.S. aviation industry so desperately needed. Orders placed by the English and French in 1939 got the wheels of industry turning at full speed once more. Both airframe and engine manufacturers benefited from this windfall. The Pearl Harbor attack proved to be the final galvanizing factor for U.S. industry. The entire nation was now focused on one activity: victory against a determined and formidable foe.

As war clouds were forming in the late 1930s and despite the isolationist policies of many politicians, plans were being put in place for the possibility of global warfare. However, years of slow production and miniscule development contracts were to hurt the U.S. war industry for several years after the start of World War II.

Valuable lessons learned in Europe would eventually be incorporated into U.S.-built aircraft. Self-sealing fuel tanks were a prime example. Sometimes referred to as "bulletproof" fuel tanks, in fact they were never intended to be bulletproof. Self-sealing tanks had a coating of self-vulcanizing rubber around them; if they were pierced by a projectile, the leaking fuel would quickly vulcanize the rubber and seal the hole. Even though a considerable weight penalty would result, the value of armor protection for the pilot and critical aircraft systems was again proven in the early stages of the European war. The Japanese failed to learn these lessons until it was too late.

Lack of automatic boost control for most U.S.-designed engines caused many failures due to overboosting, particularly at lower altitudes. Even though the technology was known, the USAAC, USAAF, and the Navy chose not to require this device on their engines. Part of the rationale for this may lie behind the burgeoning and healthy civil aviation scene in the United States during the 1930s. Airline operators could easily dispense with this expensive technology, particularly considering the weight penalty it imposed. Flight engineers could monitor manifold pressures at all times and avoid overboosting. Aerial combat is obviously a very different proposition from routine airline operations; however, the influence of airline operation played a part in the decision not to employ it in military aircraft. This was due partly to the fact that many civil engines were later used in military applications such as the Pratt & Whitney R-1830, Wright R-1820, and Wright R-2600.

All phases of U.S. industry were brought into the manufacture of aircraft engines. The automobile industry in particular played a crucial role in supplying sufficient engines to satisfy the ever growing demand, thus contributing enormously to the eventual victory.

References

2.5 Schlaifer, Robert, and S. D. Heron, <u>Development of Aircraft Engines and Development of Aviation Fuels</u>, Harvard University, Boston, 1950.

2.7 <u>Jane's All The World's Aircraft</u>, McGraw-Hill, New York, 1945/1946.

7.1 Freeman, Roger A., <u>The Mighty Eighth</u>, Arms and Armour Press, London, 1991.

Chapter 8

General Electric Turbosuperchargers

Rather surprisingly, the United States was the only country to employ turbosuperchargers on a series-production scale during World War II, although Japan made some limited progress getting turbo-charged aircraft into combat, primarily to ward off the high-flying B-29s devastating the homeland. As with many of their other endeavors during this time, lack of strategic materials, particularly for turbine blades, hampered progress.

Germany also worked on turbosupercharging, getting a limited number in production. Interestingly, Germany's work on turbosuperchargers had a direct link to their later gas turbine development, particularly in the area of air-cooled turbine blades. However, it was the United States that took the plunge and wholeheartedly used them in bombers and fighters for both air-cooled radials and liquid-cooled in-lines flown by the U.S. Army Air Corps, and later the U.S. Army Air Force.

Dr. Sanford Moss of General Electric took up the challenge of turbosuperchargers at the request of the Army during World War I. Although Moss did not originate the idea of employing turbosuper-charging in aircraft—the French have credit for that accomplishment—he made numerous break-throughs, particularly with materials, and is credited with developing the first practical aircraft turbosuperchargers. The early units were typically only good for a few flights before material failure of the turbine or bearings occurred due to high thermal and mechanical loads. Work continued through the 1920s and 1930s, resulting in reliable units that could be mass produced. It was yet another technology that was refined just in time for World War II.

By far the vast majority of the turbos used by the United States were designated the General Electric Type B and Type C (Fig. 8.1).

General Electric turbosuperchargers were designed to maintain sea-level pressure at the "carburetor deck" up to the rated altitude of the installation. In this fashion, engines were capable of developing their take-off power to an altitude determined by the maximum allowable speed of the turbine, usually 22,000 rpm for the later Type Bs. At the critical altitude, the waste gate would be completely

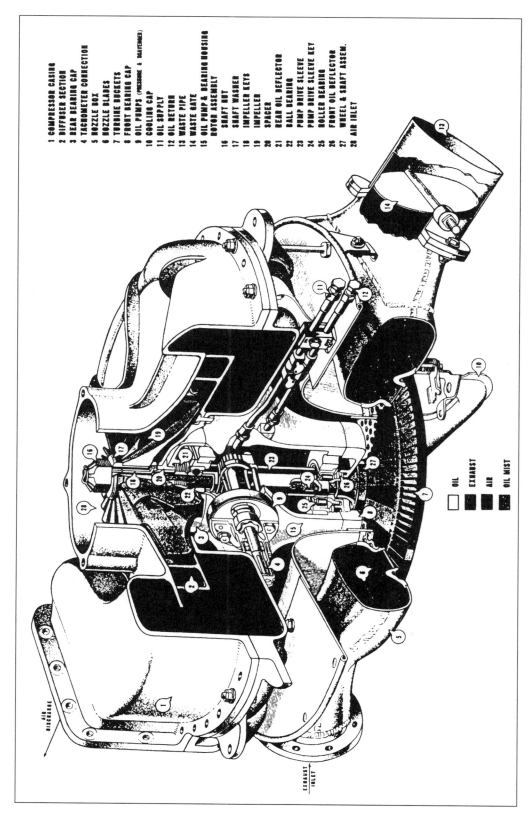

1 COMPRESSOR CASING
2 DIFFUSER SECTION
3 REAR BEARING CAP
4 TACHOMETER CONNECTION
5 NOZZLE BOX
6 NOZZLE BLADES
7 TURBINE BUCKETS
8 FRONT BEARING CAP
9 OIL PUMPS (PRESSURE & SCAVENGE)
10 COOLING CAP
11 OIL SUPPLY
12 OIL RETURN
13 WASTE PIPE
14 WASTE GATE
15 OIL PUMP & BEARING HOUSING
   ROTOR ASSEMBLY
16 SHAFT NUT
17 SHAFT WASHER
18 IMPELLER KEYS
19 IMPELLER
20 SPACER
21 REAR OIL DEFLECTOR
22 BALL BEARING
23 PUMP DRIVE SLEEVE
24 PUMP DRIVE SLEEVE KEY
25 ROLLER BEARING
26 FRONT OIL DEFLECTOR
27 WHEEL & SHAFT ASSEM.
28 AIR INLET

OIL
EXHAUST
AIR
OIL MIST

AIR DISCHARGE

EXHAUST INLET

Fig. 8.1 The component that dictated USAAF bombing strategy during World War II, the General Electric type B turbosupercharger. In combination with an intercooler; conditions at the engine carburetor and in the exhaust manifold were the same as when the engine was operating at sea level. Take-off power was available to over 20,000 ft. (Air Depot Progressive Overhaul Manual, Type B Turbosupercharger, 10 July 1943. Author's collection.)

closed, resulting in maximum back pressure working against the engine. The net effect was not detrimental as it was no more than the back pressure at sea level. Thus, with a turbosupercharger installation the engine did not know it was not operating at other than sea level until the critical altitude was reached, above which point power would fall off as the aircraft continued to climb.

Construction

The unit was made up of three sections, the turbine, the compressor, and the oil pump bearing assembly. The Type Bs and Type Cs used single-stage, centrifugal compressors driven by a single-stage axial-flow turbine. A common shaft supported on two rolling-element bearings, one ball race and one roller bearing, mounted the turbine wheel and the impeller. Lubrication was provided by a dry sump system in which oil was pumped through the bearings by way of a two-section trochoid pump. One section provided pressurized oil to the bearings and the other returned oil to the supply tank. A worm reduction gear drove the oil pump. Integral with the oil pump shaft was the all-important tachometer drive (Ref. 8.1).

Exhaust from the engine was routed to the turbine unit, which was usually mounted flush to the nacelle or fuselage to assist in cooling. The nozzle box directed the exhaust gases through nozzle blades and finally impinged on the turbine blades, or buckets as they were commonly known. Located on the exhaust collector ducting, or the nozzle box, was the waste gate assembly. If all the exhaust energy were allowed to flow through the turbine, excessive boost pressures would result, particularly at lower altitudes. Therefore, a method was required for "bleeding" off some of the considerable exhaust energy. The easiest way to achieve this was by way of a bypass butterfly valve or waste gate. Although the waste gate was a simple mechanism, the method of controlling it was not. Early installations featured manual waste gate control, but this was unsuccessful as it was beset with various problems, particularly with the butterfly valve freezing because of carbon buildup on the valve spindle and the need for constant attention by the pilot or flight engineer whenever altitude was changed. This was especially critical during descent when the danger of overboosting was greater. Later controls were automatic, oil or electric servomotor operated, alleviating some of the problems associated with the earlier manual designs (Fig. 8.2). In an effort to relieve the turbine disk of some of the thermal stresses imposed on it, a cooling cap was incorporated that ducted air over the central portion of the turbine wheel.

Attached at the opposite end of the shaft was a single-stage centrifugal compressor that discharged through a diffuser converting the kinetic energy from the impeller to potential or pressure energy. All USAAF World War II turbosupercharger applications used some form of intercooling to reduce the temperature of the air heated by compression. This was necessary to delay the onset of detonation resulting from the high charge temperature.

Construction of the compressor section consisted of aluminum casting or steel stampings for the casing. The impeller was made from an aluminum forging. Because of this experience in manufacturing supercharger impellers, General Electric manufactured them for gear-driven superchargers, which were required by the major U.S. engine manufacturers. This was particularly true during the early stages of the war.

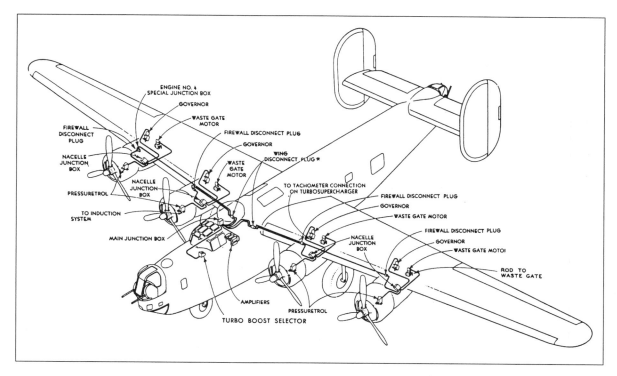

Fig. 8.2 Consolidated B-24 with electronic regulator system for maintaining manifold pressure with the turbosuperchargers. Pilot regulated boost pressure using a turbo boost selector in the cockpit. (Consolidated B-24 Liberator Erection and Maintenance Manual, *AN 01-5E-2, revised 10 Oct. 1945.*)

Because of the high temperatures experienced by the turbine section, extensive use was made of Inconel. The nozzle box was fabricated from Inconel stampings welded together. The turbine blades gave the greatest design challenge because of the high thermal and mechanical loads imposed on them. At operating speeds of up to 24,000 rpm each individual blade would run red-hot and, because of centrifugal loadings, would effectively weigh the equivalent of a small car. Because of the differing mechanical and thermal requirements of the blades and the disk, each blade was individually attached by a bulb-type root attachment until midway through the war when methods for welding the blades to the wheels were developed. Blade material was Haynes Stellite No. 21, which is very similar to vitallium, the material from which dentures are made. Initially forged, this manufacturing method caused production delays until they were made by the lost wax casting process (Ref. 2.1).

All told, more than 303,000 General Electric turbosuperchargers, mainly type Bs, were manufactured during World War II. Ford Motor Company and Allis Chalmers contributed to this truly impressive production figure (Fig. 8.3).

Fig. 8.3 General Electric Type B-22 turbosupercharger about to be installed in the 1000th B-17 built by the Douglas Aircraft Co. This turbo would deliver enough air for the engine to develop take-off power up to 22,000 ft. (Courtesy of the National Air and Space Museum, Smithsonian Institution, Photo No. B3-391050-20.)

Service Difficulties

Although the superchargers were very reliable, as with any other complex, highly stressed aircraft component, problems could arise.

Overspeeding could be a serious issue and was usually caused by a stuck waste gate; the resulting runaway turbine could and often did explode with the force of an artillery piece. Maximum rpm was usually 22,000; consequently, if the flight crew could be exposed to an exploding turbine wheel, a scatter shield would be used; an example was the shield to protect the pilot of the Lockheed P-38 Lightning, which had the turbos mounted on the tail booms adjacent to the pilot.

Waste gate problems were primarily caused by freezing of the moisture in the sense lines leading to the regulator control. This problem was resolved by connecting the exhaust nozzle box to the control rather than to the compressor discharge. Because nozzle box pressure was similar to compressor discharge and given that they only wanted sea-level pressure, there was no problem. This issue was eliminated entirely with the introduction of electronic turbosupercharger regulators.

In general, the reliability was good, most units lasting 400 h between overhaul—the same as the engine in most cases.

Turbosupercharger Strategy

Operationally, General Electric turbosuperchargers gave relatively few problems. The reason it was not used more extensively was the weight, bulk, and complexity it added to an aircraft structure because of all the ducts:

1. Air duct into the compressor
2. Discharge air duct from the compressor
3. Intercooler cooling air duct
4. Exhaust piping routed to the turbine section

In addition to these ducts, additional control mechanisms were required for waste gate and intercooler cooling flap operation. Adding to the bulk and weight was an air-to-air intercooler.

Turbosupercharger development was primarily funded by the Army, although the Navy also showed interest. As events unfolded, the Navy pinned its hopes on gear-driven two-stage, two-speed intercooled superchargers such as those fitted to F4F-3s and various models of the F4U and F6F; consequently, no aircraft mass-produced to Navy specifications were turbosupercharged.

The turbosupercharger's forte was high-altitude operation where the power to drive a gear-driven supercharger increases dramatically. Furthermore, the technology of the day was not able to develop a suitably efficient single-stage supercharger capable of producing the necessary power for combat above 20,000 ft. A two-stage supercharger for a 1000-hp engine at 30,000 ft could easily consume 230 to 280 hp. Because the turbosupercharger obtained its power from the engine exhaust, the power to drive the propeller could remain as if at sea level. The Rolls-Royce Merlin was the most widely used engine with a two-stage gear-driven supercharger, and this is the reason its full power rating is reduced at altitude. Turbosupercharger installations were an effective method of providing a flexible and efficient two-stage engine, at a cost of additional weight, bulk, and complexity.

In retrospect the turbosupercharger was ideally suited to strategic bombers flying at high altitudes on long missions. However, their value was not as great in fighter aircraft because of the weight penalty, providing that either high-altitude combat, that is, over 20,000 ft, was not required (e.g., P-39, P-40, Hawker Typhoon/Tempest, and P-51A) or a suitable two-stage, two-speed supercharger was installed on the engine (e.g., P-51B/C/D/H, F4F-3, F6F, F4U, Spitfire IX, etc.).

It is a little-appreciated fact that the General Electric turbosupercharger was key to the Army Air Corps and Army Air Force long-range, high-altitude strategic bombing strategy for World War II. All four-engine bombers were fitted with them.

With the capability of the turbosupercharged bomber, the USAAC and USAAF carried the War to new heights and seriously damaged the opponent's strategic capacity while imposing a critical requirement on the opponents to develop new and expensive countermeasures or weapons.

Installations

General Electric identified their turbosuperchargers with a "Type" designation, which was intended to describe the horsepower range of the engine to which it was fitted. Types A through I were assigned, though only the Type B and Type C units saw significant production. Type B units were for engines of 801 to 1400 hp. Type C units were for engines of 1801 to 2200 hp. Table 8.1 lists the installations and applications of the turbosuperchargers. Many designated models were never developed or used only for minor testing; consequently, details are unknown. Several examples of dual, parallel installations were developed, such as the Boeing B-29 and Consolidated B-32.

TABLE 8.1—TURBOSUPERCHARGER INSTALLATIONS AND APPLICATIONS

Model	Engine	Application	Comments
Type B-1	V-1710-11	Curtiss XP-37	
	V-1710-11/15	Lockheed XP-38	Early flights
	V-1710-23	Bell YFM-1/1A	
	R-1830-47/57	Republic P-43	
	V-1710-13	Bell XFM-1	
Type B-2	V-1710-11/15	Lockheed XP-38	Later flights
	V-1710-21	Curtiss YP-37	
	V-1710-27/29	Lockheed P-38D/E	
	V-1710-49/53	Lockheed P-38F	
	R-1830-41/43	Consolidated B-24	XB-24B through B-24J
	R-1820-97	Boeing B-17	B-17C through B-17F
Type B-3	R-1820-51	Boeing B-17A/B	
Type B-5	V-1710-17	Bell XP-39	
Type B-6	V-1710-13	Bell YFM-1	
Type B-10	XI-1430-13/21	Lockheed XP-49	First ten flights
Type B-11	R-3350-13/21	Boeing B-29	Two per engine
	R-3350-23	Consolidated B-32	XB/YB/B-32, two per engine
Type B-13	V-1710-51/55	Lockheed P-38F/G	
	V-1710-89/91	Lockheed P-38H	Early models
Type B-14	V-1710-75	Curtiss P-60A	
Type B-22	R-1820-97	Boeing B-17G	Block 25 and later
	R-1830-65	Consolidated B-24J	And all subsequent models
Type B-30	XI-1430-13/15	Lockheed XP-49	Flights 11 through 22
Type B-33	V-1710-111/11	Lockheed P-38H	Block 5 and later
	V-1710-111/11	Lockheed P-38J	
	XI-1430-13/15	Lockheed XP-49	From flight no. 23
Type C-1	R-2800	Republic P-47B/C/D	
Type C-21	R-2800-21	Republic P-47D	Blocks 4, 5, and 6

(continued)

TABLE 8.1, continued

Model	Engine	Application	Comments
Type C-23	R-2800-21	Republic P-47D	Blocks 7 and later
	R-2800-63	Republic P-47D	R-2800-63 same as -21 but with ADI. C-23 turbo has 15 min rpm limit of 22,000
Type CH-5	R-2800-57	Republic P-47M/N	Fitted with C-1 type regulator. -57 engine is a C series
Type CH-5	R-2800-77	Northrop P-61C Northrop XP-61D	

References

2.1   Heron, S. D., The History of The Aircraft Piston Engine.

8.1   Air Depot Progressive Overhaul Manual, Type B Turbosupercharger, Army Air Force, Washington, D.C., 31 May 1943.

8.2   Dan Whitney, aviation historian, correspondence and interviews with author, 1992–1994.

8.3   Moss, Sanford A., Ph.D., Superchargers for Aviation, National Aeronautics Council Inc., New York, 1944.

Chapter 9

Pratt & Whitney

Pratt & Whitney was established in 1925 by 37-year-old Frederick Rentschler, a former president of Wright Aeronautical. Rentschler gained aircraft engine experience during World War I when, as a captain in the Army Air Service, he had responsibility for production and inspection of French Hispano Suiza water-cooled V-8s manufactured under license by the Wright Martin Company. After rising to the presidency of Wright Aeronautical, Rentschler became disenchanted with the board of directors and their lack of support for developing improved air-cooled engines. By September 1924 he had had enough and quit, deciding he would be better off running his own aircraft engine company. Initially he had decided to move to Ohio and return to his family business. As with all fledgling companies, raising capital was a major problem. After Rentschler had discussed his ideas with several family friends, they sent him to Pratt & Whitney with a proposal to build aircraft engines with a start-up capital of $250,000.

Becaue of Pratt & Whitney's lucrative World War I contracts building machine tools, the company had an excess of capital. After some lengthy negotiations, Rentschler got his way and set up shop in one of Pratt & Whitney's unused factories, the former Pope Hartford automobile building in East Hartford, Connecticut. The factory had been rented to a tobacco company prior to Rentschler moving in. It is interesting to note the similarities between the start-up of Pratt & Whitney and that of Bristol; Roy Fedden was in a similar situation to Rentschler in a similar time frame, but with only a fraction of the start-up capital.

During his time at Wright Aeronautical, Rentschler had identified some key personnel to help with the launch of Pratt & Whitney: Andy Wilgoos as chief design engineer; Charles Marks as tooling engineer; John Borrup, production engineer; and finally George Mead, who came aboard (after a stint at McCook Field as chief of the power plant laboratory) as vice president of engineering.

With this nucleus of the finest talent in aircraft engine design, Rentschler set forth on his quest to be the premier engine manufacturer. His first effort was the immortal Wasp, a nine-cylinder air-cooled radial of 1344 in^3 (22 L) (Fig. 9.1). Rentchler's wife originated the Wasp name, which was to last throughout the piston engine era and into the early gas turbines.

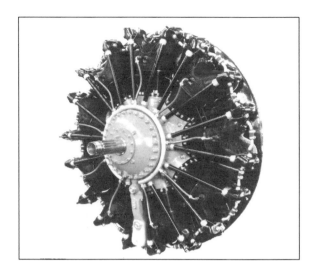

Fig. 9.1 The engine that started Pratt & Whitney onto the road of aircraft engine success, the R-1340. The photograph is a later production version R-1340 AN-1 rated at 600 hp. The AN-1 was installed in many World War II aircraft, most notably the North American AT-6. (Courtesy of the New England Air Museum and Pratt & Whitney Aircraft.)

Andy Wilgoos, with a small team of draftsmen, designed the Wasp, or R-1340 in Army/Navy nomenclature, during the summer of 1925. It was built to a Navy specification for a 400-hp engine weighing less than 650 lb, a formidable challenge for the mid 1920s, particularly for a fledgling upstart manufacturer like Pratt & Whitney. In most respects the design was conventional; however, it perfected one innovation, the use of a forged aluminum crankcase. Radial engine crankcases to this time had been manufactured from aluminum castings, which did not have the strength or other mechanical properties of a forging. The first use of a forged crankcase was by the Bristol Company in the Jupiter engine, yet another innovation from the fertile mind of Roy Fedden. To expedite their manufacture, the first couple of prototypes were built with cast crankcases; all subsequent engine cases were forged.

Although the Wasp was fitted with a supercharger, the boost pressure was very low, as the primary purpose was good fuel/air mixture distribution. By late December 1925, the first Wasp was ready to run. On its first test run the engine developed 380 hp with plenty in reserve. By the third run 425 hp was extracted from the engine. Two contracts, each for six semi-production engines, were completed. The Navy was suitably impressed and purchased 200 engines. Thus Pratt & Whitney was off to a flying start and quickly gained a leading role in military aircraft engine design.

Like many of its contemporaries, Pratt & Whitney became involved in air racing, which provided experience in running engines at high specific powers and high boost pressures at elevated temperatures and loadings. However, the main reason for their involvement with air racing was for public relations. After Wright Aeronautical cornered the civilian market in the early 1930s, particularly with the Douglas DC-2, Pratt & Whitney needed a public relations coup. Racing conditions could be simulated on the test stand; therefore, Pratt & Whitney felt little could be learned from racing.

Eight out of eleven prewar Thompson Trophy Races and eight of nine Bendix races were won with Pratt & Whitney powered aircraft with the company providing support by loaning or renting engines (Ref. 9.1).

In the mid-1930s George Mead took a trip to Europe in order see the latest engine developments there. Sleeve valve technology was starting to show considerable promise, particularly at Bristol and, to a lesser extent, at Napier.

Upon his return to East Hartford, Mead initiated design on a liquid-cooled 24-cylinder H-configured engine displacing 2600 in^3 (42.6 L), similar in general layout to the Napier Sabre. It was designated X-1800, "X" for experimental and "1800" for 1800 hp. Two factors were against this engine: first, it was liquid-cooled, a concept that was out of Pratt & Whitney's area of expertise; second, the use of sleeve valves was a totally new concept for Pratt & Whitney after years of manufacturing poppet valve engines. It took Bristol years to get sleeve valve technology right, and Napier suffered the ignominy of being taken over by English Electric in the middle of World War II because of the problems with the Sabre caused by sleeve failures. In many ways the engine was dated, featuring separate-cylinder construction, a throwback to World War I.

Follow-on developments to the X-1800 were the H-3130 and H-3370, which were similar engines with several refinements such as aftercooling. The H-3130 and H-3370 reverted to the Army method of designation, that is, H-configuration and 3130 in^3 (51.3 L) and 3370 in^3 (55.24 L), respectively. The last of the liquid-cooled sleeve valve engines were built to Navy specifications.

At the time these developments were taking place, Rentschler had removed himself from the day-to-day running of Pratt & Whitney and instead was fully engrossed in United Aircraft and Transport, which was created from a consortium of Boeing, Vought, and Pratt & Whitney. As a result, development programs were getting diversified and disjointed. Other liquid-cooled engine programs in the 1930s were also sapping the strength of Pratt & Whitney. By the late 1930s George Mead's health deteriorated to the point where he was running the H-3370 program from his sickbed; this obviously disturbed Rentschler.

Leonard Hobbs joined the company in 1927 from Bendix, where he had developed that company's line of aircraft carburetors (Fig. 9.2) (Ref. 2.5). Hobbs later went on to win the prestigious Collier Trophy in 1952 for his work on the J-57 engine. Mead respected Hobbs' engineering ability, and the two of them managed to put some sanity in the numerous development programs taking place. As a result several projects were canceled, including the R-2180 twin Hornet, a 14-cylinder radial that powered the Douglas DC-4E, and further development work was stopped on the R-1535, although this engine did make a contribution to the war effort during the first desperate twelve months. By 1939 Hobbs persuaded General Hap Arnold that the future lay with air-cooled engines and consequently started work on the mighty R-4360. Hobbs had also headed up the R-2800 and R-1830 programs in the 1930s. These two engines were by far the most significant Pratt & Whitney engines manufactured during World War II; indeed it could be argued that without them the Allied war effort would have been seriously compromised. By 1940 the disorganization and diversified projects of the 1930s had been consolidated to the R-1830, R-2000, R-2800, and R-4360. The R-985, R-1340, and R-1535 soldiered on in production, but little if any development energy was expended on them.

Fig. 9.2 Luke Hobbs, the driving force behind all Pratt & Whitney two-row engines and the R-4360 with its "corncob" cylinder arrangement. (Courtesy of the New England Air Museum and Pratt & Whitney Aircraft.)

Fortunately, by the time of the Pearl Harbor attack Pratt & Whitney had trimmed down their development projects to the point where they all played significant parts in World War II with the exception of the R-4360. This is in stark contrast to most other major engine manufacturers, particularly in Europe where an almost bewildering number of development projects sapped the strength of organizations like Daimler Benz, BMW, Rolls-Royce, and Junkers.

It was becoming increasingly apparent by the late 1930s that the production facilities at East Hartford would need a dramatic expansion, not only to support domestic demand in the case of the United States being dragged into the quagmire of World War II, but more immediately to satisfy the insatiable demand from Britain and France. A 280,000 ft² extension to the East Hartford facilities was started in October 1939 for French orders, followed in June 1940 by an additional 420,000 ft² extension financed by the British. Thus, the scene was set for Pratt & Whitney to become the largest producer of aircraft engines in World War II.

R-1340 Wasp

As related in the brief history of Pratt & Whitney, the first engine developed was the R-1340, a nine-cylinder air-cooled radial, which played a significant role in World War II, powering many advanced trainers.

At the outset, the R-1340 made significant advances in the area of power-to-weight ratio, due in part to the two-piece forged aluminum crankcase, an uncommon feature at the time of its introduction. The forging process offered far superior mechanical properties and consistency compared to a casting. Other aspects of the design were conventional radial practice, featuring a one-piece master rod riding on a two-piece crankshaft supported on two roller bearings. The master rod bearing in early engines was copper-lead. This was later improved with silver-lead-indium. Pratt & Whitney pioneered and patented this bearing technology in the mid 1930s after a rash of master rod bearing failures in R-1535s and R-1830s. It was found that during aircraft maneuvers, additional loads were placed on the bearings from *g* forces and inertial loadings. Luke Hobbs headed up a team on a crash program to resolve the bearing problem by analyzing failed bearings, which were typically copper-lead or babbitt. Pratt & Whitney was required by the government to release this technology to other manufacturers that supplied engines to the government (Ref. 9.1).

Supercharging was provided by a single-stage, single-speed unit with updraft induction, and the blower ratio was typically 10:1 or 12:1, which would yield the rather modest manifold pressure of 36.5 in Hg (Fig. 9.3). By World War II the R-1340 was rated at 600 take-off hp at 2250 rpm for a weight of 684 lb. The majority of R-1340s had direct propeller drive, though a few production examples were provided with reduction gearing of 0.67:1 (Refs. 4.15, 9.2).

Manufacture

Because of the large demand for this engine, Jacobs, Pratt & Whitney Canada, Continental, and Commonwealth Aircraft (Australia) also built them under license. Continental Motors built a new facility in Muskegon, Michigan, and started production in 1941. After the contract for R-1340s had been completed, the same facilities were used for the production of license-built Rolls-Royce Merlins and Continental's hyper engine, the IV-1430 (Ref. 9.3).

Applications

By the start of World War II, the R-1340 had been relegated to secondary duties, mainly as an advanced trainer where it performed admirably. In many respects, this role was more arduous than its former role of powering front-line fighters such as the Boeing P-26 "Peashooter." The reason for

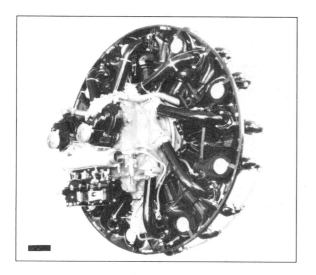

Fig. 9.3 Rear view of the Pratt & Whitney R-1340 AN-1 Wasp. Note dual, rear-mounted magnetos and updraft carburetion. (Courtesy of the New England Air Museum and Pratt & Whitney Aircraft.)

this was that students were not always as considerate to the foibles and sensitivities of a supercharged aircraft engine as an experienced pilot. Even so, the R-1340 did yeoman service as an advanced trainer.

North American AT-6, Harvard, and SNJ

Usually called the T-6 for short, this aircraft was the most famous and well known of the World War II advanced trainers (Fig. 9.4). Student aviators would progress to the AT-6 after successfully completing training in a primary trainer such as the PT-17. Numerous countries' air forces used the AT-6, including the RAF, where it was occasionally used in combat.

The AT-6 started as an evolutionary design based on the North American NA-16 dating back to 1934. The design was perfected into the AT-6 in 1939 and went on to be the most-produced advanced trainer in history with more than 17,000 examples built. With tandem seating for the two pilots, it was ideally suited for its intended role, having the right flying qualities and control response. A carrier version was built for the Navy with a tail hook and designated SNJ.

Structurally, the AT-6 featured a mixture of steel tube space frame and monocoque construction. The fuselage from the firewall back to the rear of the tandem cockpit employed a chrome molybdenum steel alloy tubular space frame with easily removable aluminum panels that gave ground personnel good access to the various systems and flight controls. Semimonocoque construction was used for the rear fuselage. Wing construction was conventional stressed skin with inwardly retracting landing gear. Engine mounting was again of conventional design, a tubular chrome molybdenum steel alloy unit bolted to the firewall.

Performance was adequate for the duties required of it and included a maximum speed of 205 mph, a service ceiling of 21,500 ft, and a range of 750 mi (Refs. 2.7, 9.4, 9.5).

Fig. 9.4 North American AT-6. Most numerous of all the advanced trainers used by the United States during World War II. Most models were powered by Pratt & Whitney R-1340s. (Courtesy of the National Air and Space Museum, Smithsonian Institution, Photo No. 1B-25850.)

R-985 Wasp Jr.

The R-985 was the 1340's smaller sibling with very similar design features. The nine air-cooled cylinders had 5.1875-in bore and stroke (Fig. 9.5). The two-piece forged aluminum crankcase supported the crankshaft in two roller bearings with a ball thrust bearing in the nose section to take care of propeller thrust loads. On later engines the one-piece master rod had a silver-lead plain bearing because of Hobbs' investigative work on R-1535 master rod bearing failures. At the rear, a single-speed blower driven at 10-to-1 crank speed fed the cylinders through nine individual intake pipes with a Bendix updraft carburetor. Direct-drive was a feature of all production R-985s, although several experimental engines were built with reduction gearing.

By World War II the most common versions of the R-985, the AN-1 and AN-3, were rated at 450 hp at 2300 rpm and 36.5 in Hg manifold pressure (Refs. 2.5, 6.4, 9.6).

Applications

The 985, like the 1340, did sterling service in secondary duties such as training, liaison, and executive transport.

Beech AT-11 Kansan (Army Air Force Designation) and SNB-1 (Navy Designation)

The Beech AT-11 (Fig. 9.6) was based on the C-45 Expediter light personnel transport and was specifically designed for the training of bombardiers and air gunners. The AT-11, which was powered by two R-985 AN-1s or AN-3s and featured all-metal construction, was modified with a large bulbous, all-Plexiglas nose. Provisions were also made for bomb racks and a flexible gun for its intended training purposes. Mounted in the Plexiglas nose was the top-secret Norden bombsight,

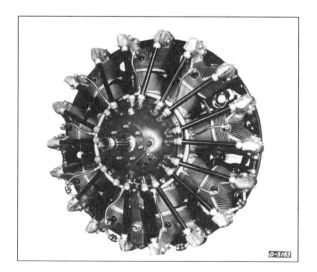

Fig. 9.5 Pratt & Whitney R-985, the smaller sibling to the R-1340 Wasp. (Courtesy of the New England Air Museum and Pratt & Whitney Aircraft.)

Fig. 9.6 Beechcraft AT-11 Kansan used for training of bombardiers. (Courtesy of the National Air and Space Museum, Smithsonian Institution, Photo No. 1A-05959.)

which legend claimed could place a bomb in a pickle barrel from 30,000 ft. In fact, the designer of the bombsight, when confronted with this claim, asked, "Which pickle do you want to hit?" (Ref. 9.7). The vast majority of bombardiers in the Army Air Force of World War II received their training in this aircraft.

Beech C-45 Expediter (Army Air Force Designation) and JRB (Navy Designation)

The Beech C-45, although very similar to the AT-11, had a more streamlined all-metal nose and the interior was configured for passenger transportation (Ref. 2.7).

Chance Vought OS2U Kingfisher

The Chance Vought Kingfisher was built to a Navy specification for a shipborne observation aircraft. It was first flown in March 1938 in a wheeled configuration. In May 1938 the first test flight took place from water. This configuration featured a single-fuselage-mounted main float with wing-mounted stabilizer floats and tandem seating for two pilots (Fig. 9.7).

The plane was of mixed construction of metal and fabric. The load-bearing section of the wing from the spar forward was all metal, creating a classic D-section torsion box. An unusual and advanced feature of the Kingfisher was the use of spoilers for lateral roll control when flaps were deployed. The flaps were full span and encompassed the ailerons. With the flaps retracted, roll control was provided by the more conventional ailerons.

Used extensively in the Pacific operating under the harshest and most primitive conditions, the Kingfisher gave an excellent account of itself.

Fig. 9.7 Vought OS2U Kingfisher. (Courtesy of the National Air and Space Museum, Smithsonian Institution, Photo No. IB-47358.)

The British Fleet Air Arm also received substantial numbers through lend-lease programs and put them to good use in target towing, radar calibration, and general liaison duties (Refs. 2.7, 9.8).

R-1535 Twin Wasp Jr.

The R-1535, the third of the Pratt & Whitney two-row radials (all of which were designed by Luke Hobbs) was a mixture of old and new. The first two-row engine was a one-off R-2270 experimental engine; the second was the R-1830.

Design started in May 1931, and by November an engine was undergoing tests. An indicator to its early 1930s heritage was the use of grease-lubricated valve gear instead of the much more reliable and efficient engine-fed oil-pressure lubrication (Figs. 9.8, 9.9).

Power ratings for the 1535 varied from 700 to a high of 950 hp in the case of the -64. Most were rated at 700 to 800 hp at 2650 rpm. The 1535-in^3 displacement was derived from 14 R-985-size cylinders. Like its predecessors, the R-1535 used rolling-element bearings to support the crankshaft: two roller bearings at the front, a single roller bearing at the rear, and a ball bearing for the center main. Reduction gearing was a six-pinion internal planetary set-up. A one-piece crankshaft design dictated a two-piece master rod, supported on plain bronze bearings, a production first for Pratt & Whitney.

Although it was requested by the Navy, Pratt & Whitney was not convinced that the most efficient way to obtain the required horsepower was through 14 relatively small cylinders. The Navy felt the small frontal area of the R-1535 would offset any disadvantages caused by lack of displacement (Ref. 2.5). Consequently, Pratt & Whitney never put their heart and soul into the development of this

Fig. 9.8 Early production, A-series, Pratt & Whitney R-1535. Note the grease-lubricated valve gear. (Courtesy of the New England Air Museum and Pratt & Whitney Aircraft.)

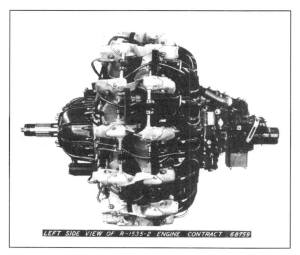

Fig. 9.9 Using 14 R-985-size cylinders, Pratt & Whitney produced the twin-row R-1535. This is a later B-series engine with valve gear lubricated by engine oil. (Courtesy of the New England Air Museum and Pratt & Whitney Aircraft.)

engine. As it was, the only aircraft to take full advantage of the 1535's small frontal area were not even military aircraft; they were racing aircraft exemplified by Howard Hughes' highly successful racer, the H-1 Special, which exhibited beautiful craftsmanship. In typical Hughes style, he spared no expense for its construction. The real focus of Pratt & Whitney's development efforts in the mid 1930s was the R-1830, probably the most-produced aircraft engine in history.

It is a little appreciated fact that Pratt & Whitney was the first to develop and manufacture two-stage superchargers. The first experimental engines with two-stage superchargers were R-1535s, although none were produced in this configuration. R-1535s were also used as the basis for Pratt & Whitney's first sleeve valve experiments (Refs. 2.5, 9.1, 9.9).

Manufacture

Pratt & Whitney built all the R-1535s; 2880—a relatively small number—were built in East Hartford between 1931 and the end of production in 1941.

Applications

Like many other fine aircraft engines that were in service by World War II, the R-1535 suffered the same fate as other engines that lacked displacement. Although the specific power was adequate, 750 hp was totally insufficient for a front-line aircraft engine by World War II standards. Consequently, the R-1535 had a brief career. By 1943, R-1535-powered aircraft were rarely exposed to hostile action.

Several well-known prewar aircraft including the Grumman F2F and F3F, the Navy's last biplane fighters, were powered by R-1535s.

Vought SB2U Vindicator

The Vought Vindicator was designed for a Navy Bureau of Aeronautics competition in 1934 for a carrier-based single-engine dive-bomber.

When introduced in the mid 1930s, the Vindicator represented the state of the art, sporting many new and advanced features such as rearwardly retractable main landing gear, wing folding, and monoplane design. Construction was typical 1930s convention underscored by a mixed-fabric-covered rear fuselage and monocoque forward fuselage. Two seats were provided in tandem. The cowl featured a prominent air scoop on the upper surface, which served the double purpose of supplying air to the supercharger and to the oil cooler.

When the Battle of Midway commenced on the evening of 3 June 1942, the SB2U, along with the Douglas TBD Devastator, were the only carrier-based torpedo bombers available. The SB2U was hopelessly outclassed by its Japanese foe; consequently, appalling losses were suffered. They were phased out of front-line service soon afterward and by 1943 were removed from the Navy inventory (Refs. 5.2, 9.10).

Bristol Bolingbroke

The Canadian Car & Foundry Company was licensed to build a variety of British aircraft. Among them was the Bristol Bolingbroke, a derivative of the Bristol Blenheim, a light twin-engine bomber that was almost obsolete by the start of World War II. Like many aircraft in this category, the Bolingbroke performed sterling duty until it could be replaced by later designs. The only operational use the Bolingbroke saw was in Canada, flown by RCAF pilots, and some limited use in the Aleutians on antisubmarine patrols to protect the islands from attack by the Japanese. Various power plants were installed including the R-1535, along with the Bristol Mercury, for which it was originally designed (Refs. 5.2, 9.11).

R-1830 Twin Wasp

If sheer numbers manufactured were the only judge of the greatest aircraft engine built, then the R-1830 Twin Wasp would win hands down. Approximately 178,000 examples of this truly great engine were built, making a significant contribution to the Allied war effort. Another 1931 design, it was, surprisingly, the largest aircraft engine under development in the United States during much of the 1930s (Ref. 2.5). The displacement was derived from 14 air-cooled cylinders, 5.5-in bore and 5.5-in stroke (Fig. 9.10).

The design team was headed by Luke Hobbs, the brilliant engineer who had cut his teeth in the profession at Bendix, where he made significant contributions to the injection carburetor. Following Pratt & Whitney's two-row radial design practice, the engine was made up of three basic sections: the nose case, which housed the propeller reduction gearing, and in some models the magnetos and governor; the power section, including the crankcase, cylinders, front and rear cam compartments, and crankshaft; and the blower section, which contained the supercharger, intermediate rear section, accessory section, and the carburetor. On most models, the magnetos were housed at the rear of the engine rather than mounted on the nose case.

Large amounts of magnesium were used in an effort to keep weight down. The nose case and intermediate blower sections are two examples of the extensive use of this very light metal.

By the mid 1930s, Pratt & Whitney had developed very sophisticated mounting systems to attenuate, and at the same time dampen, vibration. Eight engine-mounting brackets were located on the intermediate blower section, taking advantage of the development work in engine mounting. The attention paid to this critical aspect of engine design had many beneficial side effects, not the least of which was reduced fatigue on the airframe, the bane of all aircraft designers.

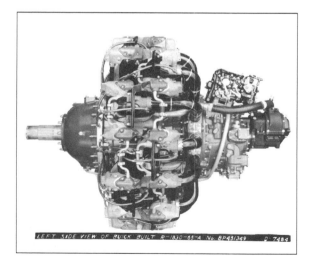

Fig. 9.10 Side view of the Pratt & Whitney R-1830-65A. Tens of thousands of these engines were built by Buick or Chevrolet for Consolidated B-24 production. (Courtesy of the New England Air Museum and Pratt & Whitney Aircraft.)

Single-stage supercharging was the preferred method of boosting the majority of R-1830s, although some models had two-stage supercharging for installation in the Grumman F4F-3 in 1939. This was a world's first—two years ahead of the Rolls-Royce Merlin 60, first of the two-stage Merlins, which made its debut in 1941 (Ref. 2.5). Many R-1830s had two-speed supercharging along with turbo-supercharging for enhanced high-altitude performance.

A two-barrel downdraft Bendix injection carburetor was typically used, mounted on top of the blower and, following usual practice for this magnificent carburetor, fuel was injected into the eye of the supercharger impeller. Some models incorporated updraft carburetion.

A three-piece aluminum forging made up the main crankcase section; these sections were securely held together with substantial bolts. A steel liner pressed into the rear section supported the rear main roller bearing, and a bronze liner similarly pressed into the front section served the same purpose for the front main roller bearing. The front bronze liner was extended forward where it served double duty as the front cam ring bearing, a good example of the ingenuity displayed throughout the engine.

The crankshaft was a one-piece forging with two dynamic counterweights. This naturally dictated two-piece master rods. Three main bearings supported the crank, with the center main a large diameter, narrow, roller bearing. The end mains were also roller bearings, but of more conventional proportions (Fig. 9.11). One exception to this design was the R-1830-75, which used three plain bearings. Master rod bearings were silver-lead-indium, split on the centerline. Two silver-plated shims were fitted between the cap and rod for protection against fretting (see the Vulture description in Chapter 4 on Rolls-Royce engines).

*Fig. 9.11 Pratt & Whitney R-1830-65 crankshaft assembly, propeller reduction gear, oil pump gears, and accessory drive gears. R-1830-65s were used in Consolidated B-24 Liberators. (*Buick Service Manual. *By permission of Buick Division of General Motors.)*

The cams were conventional double-track designs, one for intake and one for exhaust, with four lobes per track, which naturally dictated eight-to-one reduction gearing.

Cylinder design was again conventional, although significant effort was expended in optimizing cooling fin design. Heads were cast, then screwed and shrunk onto the chrome molybdenum steel alloy forged barrel, according to usual Pratt & Whitney practice since the first Wasp. The barrel had cooling fins machined integrally in most cases; some models featured an aluminum cooling muff shrunk onto the barrel. As with most Pratt engines, the combustion chamber was a two-valve (sodium-cooled exhaust) hemispherical affair with pushrod-actuated valves.

The nose case was a magnesium or occasionally an aluminum casting, internally stiffened with ribs, the opposite of the R-1535, which had external stiffening ribs. For the more common 16:9 and 2:1 propeller ratios, Farman reduction gearing was employed with six bevel pinion gears mounted on a cage integral with the propeller shaft, which had the ubiquitous SAE No. 50 spline. Engines fitted with 3:2 reduction gearing had straight planetary pinion gears.

Lubrication was provided by a pressure pump and two scavenge pumps. One scavenge pump, mounted in the nose case, scavenged the cylinder valve gear drain-off, and the other was integral with the pressure pump, which scavenged the rear section. Early engines had a compensating relief valve that allowed higher than normal oil pressure when the oil was at 104°F or less, then reducing down to the normal 85 to 100 psi when the oil reached operating temperature (Refs. 2.5, 4.15, 9.12).

Performance

Like that of many engines that enjoyed a long production life, the power of the R-1830 rose significantly over the years, primarily because of improved fuels, improved supercharger technology, and cooling schemes.

Early production models were rated at 750 hp at 2300 rpm and 7000 ft. This rating was achieved with 80-octane fuel. With the availability of 87-octane, power rose to 800 hp at 2400 rpm. By 1939 the -13 was rated at 900 hp at 2700 rpm and 10,000 ft for installation in the Curtiss P-36. As World War II progressed, power was upped to 1200 and finally the last development of the R-1830, the -94, was rated at 1350 hp at 2800 rpm. Use of high-performance-number fuel and physical improvements allowed this higher horsepower rating, although it has been argued that at this power reliability suffered.

Manufacture

Because the R-1830 was produced in greater numbers than any other aircraft piston engine, several subcontractors were engaged for the production during World War II. Although large numbers were built by Pratt & Whitney in East Hartford, Buick and Chevrolet also manufactured significant numbers, particularly -43s and -65s, for the Consolidated B-24 Liberator along with -94s for the C-87, a derivative of the B-24.

A licensing fee of one dollar per engine was briefly charged for all Pratt & Whitney engines; however, even this nominal amount was soon dropped for the duration of World War II.

R-1830s were also manufactured overseas under licenses by Commonwealth Aircraft in Australia and, after World War II, by Flygmotorbolaget in Sweden (Ref. 4.15).

Applications

As a fighter aircraft power plant the R-1830 lacked horsepower and displacement to be truly competitive, but in the early years of the war some significant fighters were powered by this engine. Bombers and transports were ideally suited to this magnificent power plant. Table 9.1 summarizes the R-1830's performance and applications.

TABLE 9.1—PRATT & WHITNEY R-1830 PERFORMANCE AND APPLICATIONS SUMMARY

Dash Number	Applications	hp/rpm/alt	Comments
-1	XB-14 P-33	800/2400/SL 800/2400/7000	
-7	Northrop XA-16	950/2450/SL 850/2450/8000	Similar to -1 except strengthened crank and rods, forged crankcase, and automatic mixture control
-9	Seversky P-35 Northrop XA-16	950/2450/SL 850/2450/8000	Updraft carburetion. Automatic lubrication for valve gear. Similar to -7 but not fitted with automatic mixture control
-13	Curtiss P-36A/D/E/F	1050/2700/SL 900/2550/10,000	Downdraft carburetion. C series with new type cylinders, long-reach plugs, redesigned rear section, and 11-in-diameter impeller
-17	Consolidated YA-19 Curtiss P-36A/C	1200/2700/SL 1050/2550/6500	Similar to -13 except for silver-lead master rod bearings and strengthened C-type cylinders
-19	Seversky XP-41	1200/2700 1050/2550/6500	Similar to -17 except fitted with two-stage blower and NA-V12A carburetor
-23	Curtiss P-36B	1100/2700/SL 950/2700/14,300	Similar to -17 except for blower ratio
-25	Curtiss P-36B	1100/2700/SL 950/2700/14,300	Similar to -23 except for propeller reduction ratio
-31	Curtiss XP-42 Martin YB-10A Seversky XP-41	1050/2550/SL 1000/2700/14,500	

(continued)

TABLE 9.1, continued

Dash Number	Applications	hp/rpm/alt	Comments
-33	Consolidated RB-24 Consolidated XB-24B Consolidated YB-24 Consolidated PB3Y-3 Martin RB-10B	1200/2700/SL 100/2700/14,500	Similar to -25 except fitted with two-speed blower
-35	Republic YP-43 Republic P-43D	1200/2700/SL 1200/2700/20,000	Performance figures quoted are with turbo. Similar to -21 except for blower ratio
-39	XB-24A AT-12	1050/2700/SL 1050/2700/8700	Similar to -33 except compression ratio and carburetor setting
-41	Consolidated RB-24C	1200/2700/SL 1200/2700/25,000	Similar to -33 except fitted with turbo
-43/-43A	Consolidated B-24D/E/G/H Consolidated XB-24F Consolidated C-87A/B Consolidated F-7 Consolidated XB-41	1200/2700/SL 1200/2700/25,000	Similar to -41 except for reduction gear. Buick and Chevrolet also built -43s. 43As had pressurized magnetos
-45	Republic AT-12 Seversky P-35A	1050/2700/SL 1050/2700/7700	P-35As were sold to Sweden. Also built by Buick and Chevrolet. Similar to -17 except for propeller redution ratio, carburetor, and rating
-47	Republic RP-43 Republic P-43D	1200/2700/SL 1050/2700/25,000	Performance quoted with turbo. Without turbo power is 1050/2700/7500. Similar to -45 except for carburetor and dual vacuum pump drive
-49	P-43B/C	1200/2700/SL 1200/2700/25,000	Similar to -45 except for carburetor, dual vacuum pump drive and fitted with turbo
-57	P-43A/E	1200/2700/SL 1050/2700/7500	Similar to -82 except fitted with turbo. Also built by Chevrolet
-59	Consolidated B-24D	1200/2700/SL 1250/2700/25,000	Improved cylinder barrel design with deeper fins. Similar to -43 except spinner injection, blower drive, pressurized magnetos, and revised nose section

(continued)

TABLE 9.1, continued

Dash Number	Applications	hp/rpm/alt	Comments
-64	Consolidated PBY-1 Consolidated XPBY-1 Consolidated PBY-2	900/2500/SL 850/2450/8000	Updraft carburetion. Heavier rods and pistons allowed a higher rating
-65/-65A	Consolidated B-24B/F/J/L XB-24G XC-109, F-7, C-87 Douglas DC-3/C-47	1200/2700/SL 1200/2700/25,000	-65s built by Buick only. -65s and -65As built by Buick and Chevrolet only. Performance figures quoted are with turbo. -65A fitted with pressurized magnetos. Similar to -43 except fitted with Chandler Evans (CECO) carburetor
-66	Consolidated PBY-3 Grumman XF4F-2	1050/2700/SL 900/2550/12,000	Downdraft carburetion. Automatic valve lubrication. Superseded by -84
-67	Douglas C-47	1200/2700/SL 1200/2700/4900	Similar to -43 except for carburetor and operation without turbo. Built by Chevrolet
-72	Consolidated PBY-4 Consolidated XPBY-5	1050/2700/SL 900/2550/12,000	
-75	Douglas DC-3 YB-24K, B-24N	1350/2800/SL 1100/2600/30,000	Automatic spark advance incorporated. Improved cooling. Plain main bearings. Built by Buick
-76	Grumman F4F-3/-4	1200/2700/SL 1000/2550/19,000	Two-stage, two-speed. Harmonic balancer-type crank. Updraft carburetion.
-78	Consolidated PB2Y-2	1200/2700/SL 1000/2550/19,000	Two-stage, two-speed fitted with torque indicator
-80	Consolidated YPB2Y-1, PBY-4	1200/2700/SL 1050/2550/7500	
-82	Boomerang (Aust.) Consolidated PBY-5A Douglas R4D (Navy DC-3)	1200/2700/SL 1050/2550/7500	Similar to -45 except fitted with Bosch magnetos. Navy engine
-86	Eastern FM-1 Grumman F4F-3, F4F-4/-7	1200/2700/SL 1000/2550/19,000	Nose-mounted magnetos. Two-stage, two-speed
-88	Consolidated PB2Y-3/ -3B/-3R, PB2Y-5, PBY-3, Douglas C-47/DC-3	1200/2700/SL 1000/1550/19,000	
-90	Grumman F4F-3A/-4A, F4F-6	1200/2700/SL 1000/2700/14,500	Superseded by -12 on all Navy F4F-3As

(continued)

TABLE 9.1, continued

Dash Number	Applications	hp/rpm/alt	Comments
-90B	Bristol Beaufort II Boomerang Douglas C-47B Short Sunderland V Vickers Wellington IV	1200/2700/SL 1000/2700/14,500	Similar to -90 but modified for British requirements
-90C	C-47B/D, C-117A/B	1200/2700/SL 1000/2700/14,500	Similar to -43 except for special Army/Navy ignition harness two-speed blower. Navy engine
-90D	C-47B/D C-117A/B/D	1200/2700/SL 1000/2700/14,500	Similar to -90C except blower clutches are removed
-92	Douglas C-47	1200/2700/SL 1050/2550/7500	Most commonly used engine for DC-3/C-47 family of aircraft

Source: Refs. 2.5, 2.7, 4.15, 9.12, 9.13.

Curtiss P-36 and 75 Hawk

Forerunner of the more famous P-40, the Curtiss P-36 went through the remarkably short design period of only seven months (Fig. 9.12). Perhaps this should not be surprising, considering it was designed by Don Berlin. The first flight of the P-36 occurred in April 1935 powered by an R-1830-13, which gave 1050 hp at 2700 rpm. The P-36 was submitted for an Army contract with the Seversky P-35 as competition. The winner of this contract turned out to be the P-35, but the Army felt that there was enough merit in the P-36 to place an order for 210 aircraft. France was also interested in the aircraft and subsequently placed an order for 200 as the Curtiss Model 75 Hawk, which was the name given to the export models.

Although the P-36 did not play as large a role in World War II as other more famous aircraft, the most significant contribution these two orders made was keeping Pratt & Whitney and Curtiss in business during the dark, desperate days of the depression. To fulfill the French order, an additional wing was constructed at the East Hartford manufacturing site.

The French Model 75 Hawks were on their way to France when the Battle of France was lost; consequently these aircraft were diverted to the British for whom they served in North Africa (Ref. 9.14).

Consolidated B-24 Liberator

The Consolidated B-24 Liberator, which was built in larger numbers than any other aircraft by the United States during World War II, made significant contributions to the Allied strategic bombing effort (Fig. 9.13). The design was conceived in January 1939, and the prototype flew on 31 December 1939. Several novel developments were incorporated into the design, the most significant

Fig. 9.12 Curtiss P-36. (Courtesy of the National Air and Space Museum, Smithsonian Institution, Photo No. 1A-30566.)

Fig. 9.13 Consolidated B-24J Liberator. B-24s were the most-produced aircraft in the United States during World War II; more than 19,000 examples were built including subvariants such as LB 30s built for the British. (Courtesy of the National Air and Space Museum, Smithsonian Institution, Photo No. 1A-22540.)

of which was the Davis wing. With the help of the California Institute of Technology's wind tunnel, David R. Davis developed a remarkably high aspect ratio wing that offered improved efficiency. The wing featured stressed-skin construction with an aluminum spar, which may have been its Achilles heel in combat. It had an unfortunate tendency to fold when damaged due to flack or fire. This was in stark contrast to the B-17, which had a main spar fabricated from a Warren truss, thus making it far more resilient to battle damage.

Several manufacturers were brought on board to mass-produce this large and complex aircraft, including Ford Motor Company. Ford had just completed a new state-of-the art assembly line in Willow Run, Michigan, in 1941. The plan was to build 1942 model cars at this facility; the events at Pearl Harbor squashed those plans, and the plant was instead converted over to producing B-24s. As can be imagined, the growing pains were initially severe with many problems requiring resolution before production could get into full swing. When the worst of the production problems were overcome, the rate of production at Willow Run, nicknamed Will-it-Run, was nothing short of prodigious. At one time, B-24s were rolling off the final assembly line at the rate of one per hour. Ford's production total by the close of World War II was 8675. In addition to Ford and Consolidated, Douglas Aircraft Company and North American Aviation also manufactured B-24s.

Early B-24s were powered by R-1830-33s with single-stage, two-speed superchargers. Turbo-superchargers were fitted with the introduction of the B-24B. This had the effect of not only dramatically improving the altitude performance, but also gave the B-24B the distinctive elliptical-shape cowl that the early B-24s did not have. There were two air intakes on the sides of each cowl: the intake on one side fed cooling air to the oil cooler, and the intake on the other side fed cooling air to the intercooler and induction air to the turbosupercharger. The turbosupercharger discharged compressed and heated air through the intercooler. Discharged air from the intercooler fed the carburetor. Internal ducting routed air to the appropriate places at the optimal velocities and pressures. Heated cooling air from the oil cooler and the intercooler along with cooling air for the engine was discharged from the upper and lower portions of the cowl, with cowl flaps controlling the temperatures. As can be imagined from this brief description, the B-24 cowl was a beautiful piece of engineering work, albeit complex!

The turbo unit was mounted at the rear of the nacelle sitting at the bottom. Exhaust from the 14 cylinders was routed through a collector ring and piped to the nozzle box of the turbine unit of the General Electric turbosupercharger.

Operationally, the B-24 was deployed in all theaters of World War II. As combat experience was gained, various modifications and improvements were incorporated. The first major modification was the use of turbosupercharging, which was incorporated on the B-24B and all subsequent B-24s. The B model was the first model ready for combat. All the turbocharged B-24s were rated at the same power, that is, 1200 hp at 2700 rpm, and 25,000 ft. The -41 engines were fitted to the B-24C; the -43, -43A, or -65 engines were fitted to B-24 Ds, Es, Fs, Gs, and C-87As and Bs (transport version of the B-24) (Fig. 9.14). R-1830-65s were fitted with the Chandler Groves carburetor when the supply of Bendix carburetors could not meet demand (Fig. 9.15).

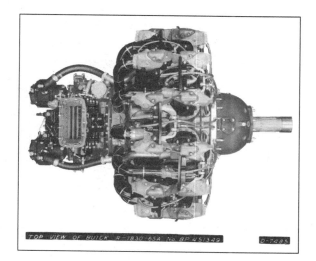

Fig. 9.14 Pratt & Whitney R-1830-65A. All -65A engines were manufactured by Buick or Chevrolet and were installed in most models of the Consolidated B-24 Liberator. Note the Chandler Groves carburetor. This carburetor was developed in case demand for the Bendix PD-12 outstripped production. Pratt & Whitney R-1830-43s and -43As were identical to the -65 engines except for the use of a Bendix PD-12 carburetor. (Courtesy of the New England Air Museum and Pratt & Whitney Aircraft.)

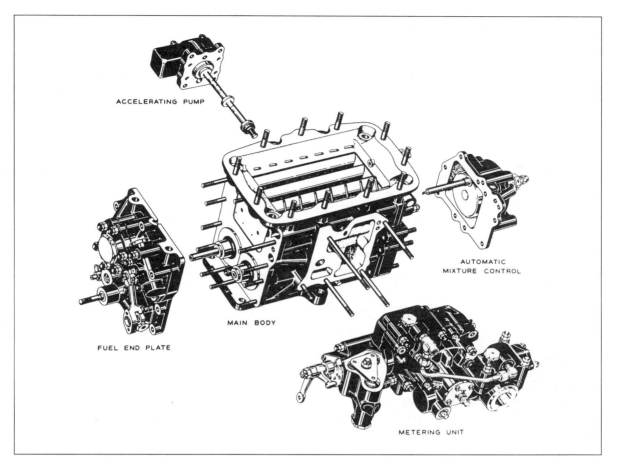

Fig. 9.15 In case the supply of Bendix injection carburetors dried up for Pratt & Whitney R-1830-65s for B-24 production, use of a Ceco (Chandler Evans) carburetor was introduced as a second source. R-1830-43s were the same as a -65 but fitted with a Bendix PD-12 carburetor. (Consolidated B-24 Liberator Erection and Maintenance Manual, *AN 01-5E-2, revised 10 Oct. 1945.*)

The B-24 claimed many significant accomplishments during World War II, not the least of which was the fact it dropped a higher tonnage of bombs than any other allied aircraft (Refs. 2.7, 9.12, 9.15).

Douglas C-47 and DC-3

General Eisenhower felt World War II could not have been won without the ubiquitous Douglas C-47, derived from the DC-3. This jack-of-all-trades was indispensable on numerous occasions in all theaters of the war.

The DC-3 (derived from the DC-1, of which only a single prototype was built, and the DC-2) was the mainstay of the prewar airline industry.

Among the diversified duties it was called upon to perform during World War II were hauling cargo, dropping paratroopers, towing gliders, transporting high-ranking officers, and so forth (Fig. 9.16).

Various power plants were used for the DC-3, such as Wright R-1820s and the Bristol Pegasus; however, the vast majority were powered by assorted models of the Pratt & Whitney R-1830.

The more common military designation was C-47, although many were acquired civilian DC-3s. Officially, they were known as C-48, C-49, C-50, C-51, C-52, C-53 Skytrooper, C-68, C-84, and C-117A. Unofficially, they were called Skytrain, Gooney Bird, and Dakota (the official designation in England). In addition, there were numerous submodels, including an amphibious prototype mounted on floats made by EDO Aircraft Corporation (Fig. 9.17), snow-ski additions to the landing gear, and an engineless glider making a bewildering number of variations on the basic DC-3.

Fig. 9.16 Douglas C-47, usually powered by Pratt & Whitney R-1830-92 or -90s rated at 1200 hp. (Courtesy of the National Air and Space Museum, Smithsonian Institution, Photo No. 1A-38152.)

Fig. 9.17 Amphibian Douglas C-47 mounted on Edo floats. C-47s were also flown with skis, and even an engineless glider version was tested! (Courtesy of the National Air and Space Museum, Smithsonian Institution, Photo No. 1A-38203.)

As with the basic airframe a number of different models of the R-1830 were installed to suit various mission requirements. The majority were fitted with -90s or -92s, both rated at 1200 hp.

Conservatively designed because it was one of the Douglas company's first stressed-skin, monocoque designs, the aircraft was capable of taking tremendous abuse. This feature stood it in good stead for the primitive conditions often encountered in North Africa, the CBI theater, the Pacific, and Europe.

Engine mounting was a chrome molybdenum steel alloy tubular mount attached at four points on the firewall; all loads were then transferred through the monocoque nacelle. Each engine had a 29-gal oil tank mounted behind the firewall with provision for oil dilution.

When a world-beating design like the DC-3 appears it is only natural that other nations take an interest. As a result, the Soviet Union took out a license to build them, powered by Soviet license built Wright R-1820s. Japan also took out a license to manufacture them and used them extensively during World War II.

D-Day (6 June 1944, the Allied invasion of Europe) was, without a doubt, one of the more momentous events of World War II. Without the support of the C-47, the invasion would have been considerably more difficult. This workhorse flew thousands of missions around the clock dropping paratroopers and supplies. C-47s were also used extensively during the ill-fated airborne invasion of Holland at Arnhem, code named "Market Garden." This mission entailed towing hundreds of gliders along with the usual parachute drops.

In the CBI theater, they were used for flying supplies from India to China. This required flying over the Himalayas, possibly the most inhospitable territory in the world. Some of the conditions to be contended with were Japanese fighters, poor weather, and maintaining altitude in overloaded aircraft (Refs. 2.7, 9.12, 9.16).

Consolidated PBY Catalina

One of the unsung heroes of World War II was the Consolidated PBY, another aircraft called upon to perform many diversified missions, many of which it was never designed for (Fig. 9.18).

Pitted against the Douglas XP3Y, the PBY was the winner of a 1935 design competition. The PBY was originally configured as a flying boat, but from the PBY-5A on amphibious landing gear was installed, thus greatly improving its versatility. By 1939 the Navy felt it was obsolete, and consequently the production lines were almost shut down. Orders from Britain saved the day, and the PBY continued in production throughout World War II in various upgraded models. Later models that were fitted with radar were used extensively in the Pacific and were known as the Black Cats because of the all-black paint scheme they sported. Used primarily at night, the Black Cat squadrons wreaked havoc with Japanese installations and shipping.

Fig. 9.18 Consolidated PBY-5A Catalina powered by a pair of 1200-hp Pratt & Whitney R-1830-92s, the same engine that went in many C-47s. (Courtesy of the National Air and Space Museum, Smithsonian Institution, Photo No. 1A-21981.)

Construction of the hull (fuselage) was aluminum monocoque with watertight compartments sealed with bulkheads. The amphibious versions contained the retractable tricycle landing gear in the hull. The main gear retracted into the sides between the wing struts where the wheels lay flush but exposed. The nose gear retracted into a watertight compartment protected with two doors.

Water erosion is always a major challenge for the designer of a flying boat, particularly erosion of the propellers, which may be running at or beyond the speed of sound at the tips. Therefore it was important to keep the propellers as far removed from water as possible. In the case of the PBY, this design challenge was accomplished by mounting the wing on a pylon, parasol-style, above the fuselage. The large, 104-ft span wing was supported by the pylon and two pairs of support struts that terminated at the bottom of the engine nacelle and rear spar. Wing construction was a mixture of a stressed-skin D-section forward of the front spar. The remainder of the wing was fabric covered, as were the control surfaces. The R-1830s were mounted on tubular mounts attached to the firewall with all loads being transferred to the monocoque nacelle.

The prototype XPBY was powered by -58 engines rated at 800 hp. As the PBY underwent modifications and consequently new dash numbers evolved, so did the engines.

PBY-2s had R-1830-64s rated at 850 hp, PBY-3 had R-1830-66s rated at 900 hp (this was the first PBY to feature downdraft carburetion), PBY-4 had R-1830-72s rated at 1050 hp, and PBY-5s—the first ones with the distinctive "blisters"—had R-1830-82s or R-1830-92s rated at 1200 hp (Fig. 9.19). The PBY-5A, the first one with amphibious landing gear, also had R-1830-82s.

PBY production was also undertaken in Canada and the Soviet Union. The Soviet versions were powered by Soviet license built Wright R-1820s (Refs. 2.7, 9.12, 9.17, 9.18).

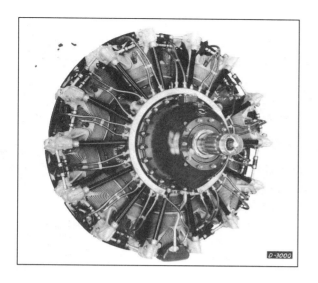

Fig. 9.19 Three-quarter front view of the Pratt & Whitney R-1830-92 Twin Wasp. The -92 engines were installed in a large number of different aircraft including DC-3s and PBY Catalinas. (Courtesy of the New England Air Museum and Pratt & Whitney Aircraft.)

Grumman F4F-3 Wildcat

This pugnacious little fighter bore the brunt of the initial Japanese onslaught after Pearl Harbor (Fig. 9.20). Rather than a revolutionary design, the F4F was an evolutionary design based on the F2F and F3F biplanes of the 1930s.

The prototype XF4F-2 (the XF4F-1 was canceled) was powered by an R-1830-66 fitted with a single-stage, single-speed supercharger rated at 900 hp that yielded a top speed of 288 mph at 10,000 ft. The F4F-3 introduced the most significant development for the R-1830, two-stage supercharging. The R-1830-76 that powered the F4F-3 featured a two-stage, two-speed supercharger with an air-to-air intercooler. This dramatically improved the performance, particularly at altitude, and the maximum speed, which now improved to 335 mph at 21,300 ft. The service ceiling also saw a dramatic improvement, increasing to 33,500 ft. Thus, it is a little-known fact that the F4F-3 was the world's first combat aircraft powered by a two-stage engine. The two impellers faced each other; that is, the two eyes faced each other. The first stage, which was the outboard stage, discharged through the

Fig. 9.20 The world's first production two-stage supercharged engine was the Pratt & Whitney R-1830-76 installed in the Grumman F4F-3 Wildcat, which gained fame at the Battle of Midway. (Courtesy of the National Air and Space Museum, Smithsonian Institution, Photo No. 1B-01128.)

intercooler into the second stage, which was situated in what would normally be considered the usual position for a radial engine supercharger. As it was a pioneer with this type of supercharging, the inevitable problems arose, primarily with surging at high altitude.

The F4F-7 was the last of the R-1830-powered F4Fs, using the R-1830-86 (Fig. 9.21), which featured nose-mounted magnetos but was otherwise similar to the R-1830-76, a two-stage, two-speed engine rated at 1200 hp. All other models were powered by various copies of the Wright R-1820, including later models of the F4F-4. Most were built by Eastern Aircraft and designated FM-2. As a safeguard, an early F4F-3 was fitted with a single-stage, two-speed blown R-1830-90. As can be imagined, the altitude performance was reduced dramatically with a top speed of 312 mph at 21,000 ft.

Construction was conventional aluminum monocoque with fabric-covered control surfaces. Wing folding for carrier storage was incorporated in the F4F-4 and all subsequent aircraft. Main landing gear was a mechanical masterpiece based on a design by Grover Loening. The main wheels folded into the sides of the fuselage with chains and links, and shock absorption was accommodated by oleo struts. Retraction was accomplished by the pilot cranking a handle in the cockpit; 29 turns were required. Pilot workload was heavy during the critical climb-out phase while he was making trim adjustments, adjusting power settings, and cranking up the landing gear. Later F4Fs had the gear retraction chore eased by eliminating the handcrank and replacing it with an electric motor.

By 1942, Grumman had transferred all manufacture of the Wildcat to the Eastern Aircraft Division of General Motors, where it was designated the FM-1 for the R-1830-powered version and FM-2 for the R-1820-powered version.

Many of the early, critical battles in the Pacific were fought with the F4F. The defense of Wake Island depended on F4Fs for air cover. Despite overwhelming odds, the F4Fs put up an incredible defense before being overrun by the numerically superior Japanese.

Fig. 9.21 World's first production aircraft engine with a two-stage supercharger. The Pratt & Whitney R-1830-86 was installed in the Grumman F4F-4, or FM-1 if it was built by Eastern Aircraft. Rated at 1200 hp at sea level, it could maintain 1000 hp at 19,000 ft. Induction air entered the first stage through the oblong-shape port on top of the blower housing. The first stage discharged compressed and heated air through an intercooler and returned to the engine into the updraft carburetor (not shown). The second stage compressed the fuel/air mixture further and discharged into the intake manifold. (Courtesy of the New England Air Museum and Pratt & Whitney Aircraft.)

As with many other U.S. aircraft in the late 1930s, France purchased the G-36A, as the export version of the F4F was known. However, like many of the other purchases of France, they were not delivered in time prior to the German invasion. Consequently, the French order was delivered to the British Fleet Air Arm. The first aerial victory by a U.S.-built aircraft in World War II was achieved by a Fleet Air Arm F4F in December 1940. Two Martlets, the British name for the F4F, patrolling over Scapa Flow protecting the British Fleet, shot down a Junkers Ju88. The British went on to purchase large numbers of F4Fs and used them to good effect throughout World War II in all theaters (Refs. 2.5, 2.7, 9.12, 9.15, 9.19).

R-2000

Based on the R-1830 design, the R-2000 was basically an R-1830 with the cylinder bore increased from 5.5 to 5.75 in, still retaining the 5.5-in stroke. The 0.25-in bore increase gave the 2000 in³ displacement (Fig. 9.22).

Other design changes included the use of plain lead-silver crankshaft main bearings in place of the roller bearings typically used with the R-1830. The magnetos were mounted on the nose case unlike the rear-mounted magnetos of most R-1830s.

It was initially designed for use with 87-octane fuel in case the production 100-octane and higher grades of fuel could not keep up with demand. As it turned out, fears of insufficient supplies of 100-octane or 100/130-grade fuel were ill founded.

The R-2000 was rated at 1300 hp at 2700 rpm on 87-octane fuel; power was increased to 1350 running on 100-octane fuel and later 1450 at 2800 rpm with 100/130-grade fuel.

Manufacture was divided between Buick and Pratt & Whitney (Refs. 2.7, 4.15, 9.12).

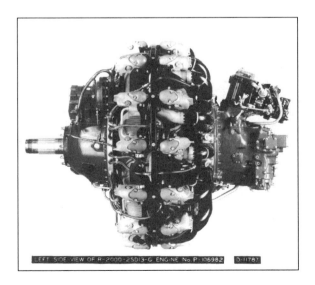

LEFT SIDE VIEW OF R-2000-2SDI3-G ENGINE No. P-106982   D-11787

Fig. 9.22 Based on the R-1830, the Pratt & Whitney R-2000 shared many features with its smaller sibling. Cylinder bore was increased by 0.25 in for the additional displacement. It used plain bearings for the crankshaft main bearings rather than the roller bearings used in most R-1830s. (Courtesy of the New England Air Museum and Pratt & Whitney Aircraft.)

Applications

Douglas C-54 Skymaster

The only application of the R-2000 during World War II was the conversion of the Douglas DC-4 to the Skymaster transport (Fig. 9.23). Although this magnificent aircraft did not have the aura of its smaller stablemate, the DC-3/C-47, it still performed sterling duty as an executive transport for the brass and more mundane duties such as hauling cargo. Its forte was transoceanic transport (Ref. 2.7).

R-2800 Double Wasp

Although not built in the same numbers as the R-1830, the Pratt & Whitney R-2800 was the most significant aircraft engine built in the United States during World War II.

Eighteen air-cooled cylinders were arranged in two rows, and total displacement was 2804 in³ (46 L). Cylinder bore was 5.75 in and stroke was 6.0 in (Fig. 9.24). Several significant deviations were made in the design compared with previous Pratt & Whitney two-row radial philosophy. All bearings were plain, with the exception of the propeller thrust bearing, which was of the ball thrust type and the roller bearings supporting the rocker arms. In addition, the crankshaft was a three-piece built-up unit, allowing the use of one-piece master rods.

Prior to Pratt developing the R-2800 the company was working on the R-2180, another two-row radial; however, that project was dropped in favor of the R-2600. When news came through that Wright Aeronautical was also developing an R-2600, Pratt & Whitney upped the stakes by increasing the displacement of the R-2600 to 2804 in³.

Design commenced on the R-2600 in August 1936; the decision was made to increase displacement to 2804 in³ (46 L) in March 1937. By 1940, the R-2800 was ready for production, rated at 1850 hp.

Fig. 9.23 Douglas C-54 Skymaster powered by Pratt & Whitney R-2000s. (Courtesy of the National Air and Space Museum, Smithsonian Institution, Photo No. 1A-38293.)

Fig. 9.24 Pratt & Whitney R-2800-43 rated at 2000 hp at 2700 rpm. This is a typical B-series engine with a single-stage, two-speed supercharger. The -43 engines were installed in Curtiss C-46s and Martin B-26B/C/E/F/Gs. All R-2800-43s were manufactured by the Ford Motor Company. (Courtesy of the New England Air Museum and Pratt & Whitney Aircraft.)

Design of the early A- and B-series engines was fairly conventional, although several milestones were reached. For the first time, a standard production Pratt & Whitney engine exceeded 100 hp per cylinder. Many engine designers during the 1930s felt 100 hp per cylinder could not be reached, never mind exceeded, primarily because of cooling problems and to a lesser extent fuel quality. With the technology that existed when these statements were made, it was true. However, as casting, manufacturing and design techniques, and materials improved, allowing deeper and more closely pitched cooling fins along with improved baffle technology, the previously insurmountable cooling problems became less of a gating item to ultimate power. At the same time cooling fin design was improving, methods were investigated to obtain the most mileage from the available cooling air. Baffles now received a great deal of scrutiny, resulting in better use of the available cooling air. With the application of these new technologies, the R-2800 started out as a very good engine and ended up as arguably the finest piston engine ever.

Crankcase design was similar to the R-1830, being a three-piece aluminum forging machined all over and bolted together (Fig. 9.25). As mentioned previously, Pratt deviated from its former design philosophy of rolling-element bearings and used plain silver-lead-indium bearings for the crankshaft main and master rod bearings. The three-piece crankshaft used splines and precision bolts to hold this heavily loaded component together. In an effort to dampen second-order vibratory modes caused by the eccentric masses of the master rod assemblies, two counterweights, geared to run at twice crank speed, coaxially but in the opposite direction to the crankshaft, were incorporated, one at the front and one at the rear of the crankcase. The cam plates were also incorporated into the crankcase, one at the front and one at the rear (Fig. 9.26). Following usual Pratt & Whitney practice, four lobe cams driven through 8:1 reduction gears were used, each cam plate featuring two tracks, one for exhaust and one for intake valves. Roller cam followers rode on the cam profiles.

Cylinders were chrome molybdenum steel alloy forgings with aluminum cooling muffs shrunk onto the barrel, a first for Pratt & Whitney. The bore was choked; that is, it tapered in diameter toward top dead center. The cast aluminum cylinder head was screwed and shrunk onto the barrel in the usual way. Cylinder head cooling fin design was similar to the R-1830 but considerably deeper, as manufacturing technology was continually pushed as far as the existing state of the art would allow.

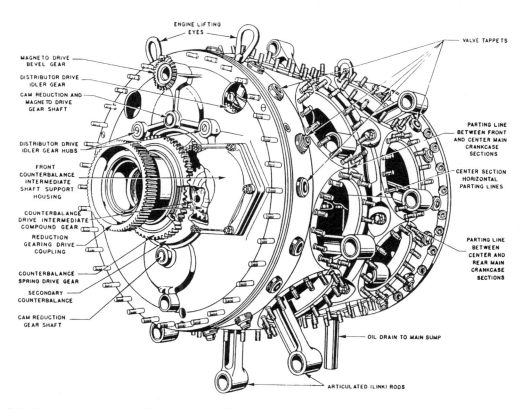

Fig. 9.25 Crankcase section of a Pratt & Whitney R-2800 B-series engine. (Operator's Handbook, *Double Wasp B Series Engines, R-2800-8 and -10.*)

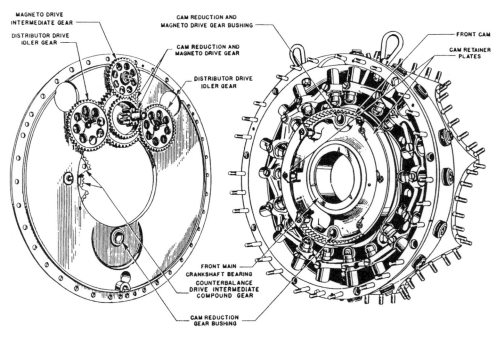

Fig. 9.26 Front cam assembly for a B-series R-2800. (Operator's Handbook, *Double Wasp B Series Engines, R-2800-8 and -10.*)

Combustion chamber design again followed Pratt & Whitney's tried-and-proven philosophy of hemispherical with two inclined valves actuated by tubular pushrods actuating roller-bearing supported rocker arms. A pivoting pad on the valve end of the rocker arm ensured that full-face contact was always maintained between the rocker arm and the valve stem. Valve clearance was set by fitting shims in the pushrods, which featured pressed-in hardened steel ball ends. Although a screw adjustment was provided on the pushrod end of the rocker arm, this was only for fine tuning the clearance. Prior to valve clearance adjustment, the cam ring required centering; this was accomplished by depressing a valve in the opposite cylinder, a time-consuming and laborious process and another example of the meticulous work required of the unsung heroes of World War II, the ground support crew.

A ring of waisted studs secured each cylinder to the crankcase, and the cylinder was sealed with an O-ring at the cylinder barrel flange where it joined the crankcase. Pistons were aluminum forgings, heavily finned inside the skirt. Three compression rings and two oil-control rings were used with the second oil-control ring situated below the wrist pin. Two reliefs for valve clearance were machined into the crown.

A single-piece magnesium casting housed the reduction gearing, magneto drive, distributor drive (all R-2800 models featured nose-mounted magnetos and distributors), propeller governor drive, and a scavenge pump. Reduction gearing was planetary-supported in plain bearings; the more common ratios were 0.350:1, 0.450:1, 0.4:1, and 0.5:1 (Fig. 9.27). Early production A- and B-series engines used SAE No. 50 spline propeller shafts. As the engine was developed and more horsepower was extracted, the C series used the larger diameter SAE No. 60 spline propeller shaft.

The supercharger collector section, mounted at the rear of the crankcase with a ring of studs and nuts—another magnesium casting—contained the supercharger diffuser and nine outlets for the intake manifolds, which were fabricated from thin-wall steel tubing. A Y junction for each intake manifold branched out into two tubes, one feeding a front cylinder and the other feeding a rear cylinder (Fig. 9.28). Six highly sophisticated engine mounts were bolted to the supercharger collector section. As in the R-1830, considerable design effort was spent on shock mounting and damping, resulting in a beautiful piece of engineering. For shock absorption, a circular block of rubber was contained in a two-piece steel forging screwed together set at a dynafocal angle. The damping was accomplished by a clutch arrangement that was similar to an automobile clutch. Pressure was achieved with a diaphragm spring. Each of the six mounts was bolted to the main aircraft engine mount, which was typically a chrome molybdenum steel alloy tubular weldment terminating at four points at the aircraft firewall (Fig. 9.29).

The intermediate rear section contained the supercharger, usually a single-stage unit that could be single speed or two speed. Two-stage, intercooled engines were developed for the Navy. For carburetion, the ubiquitous but beautifully engineered Bendix injection carburetor was mounted on top, although a few models featured updraft carburetion for applications such as the Vought F4U Corsair. Early A- and B-series engines used the Bendix PT-13 three-barrel carburetor, and the later C-series engines used the improved PR-58 (Fig. 9.30). R-2800 supercharger impellers featured an innovative fuel distribution system. Fuel was injected from the fuel feed valve into a "slinger," a sleeve around

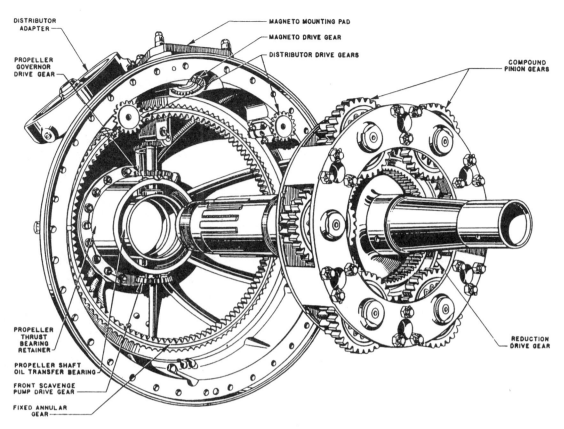

Fig. 9.27 *Two-stage planetary reduction gear for a B-series Pratt & Whitney R-2800. C-series R-2800s deviated from this design by using 15 small pinions in a single-stage planetary reduction unit.* (Operator's Handbook, *Double Wasp B Series Engines, R-2800-8 and -10.*)

the impeller shaft that butted up against the rotating inlet guide vanes. Radially disposed holes around the slinger sprayed the fuel into the impeller eye. The slinger also allowed fuel into radially drilled galleries in the impeller. The galleries, one between each vane, exited at approximately three-quarters the diameter of the impeller. Consequently, considerable centrifugal force was imparted to the fuel, ensuring good mixture distribution and reducing the possibility for induction icing.

At the rear of the engine the supercharger drive gears, clutch, accessory drives for generators, gun synchronizers, tachometer generator, vacuum pump, hydraulic pump, and starter were housed in yet another magnesium casting. In addition to the drives already mentioned, the rear section also contained the two-speed supercharger selector valve assembly, the oil filter, the main oil pressure oil pump, the fuel pump, and the rear scavenge pump (Refs. 2.5, 2.7, 9.20–9.22).

Performance

As in the case of the R-1830, the R-2800 enjoyed a long production life and consequently saw significant development and increase in power.

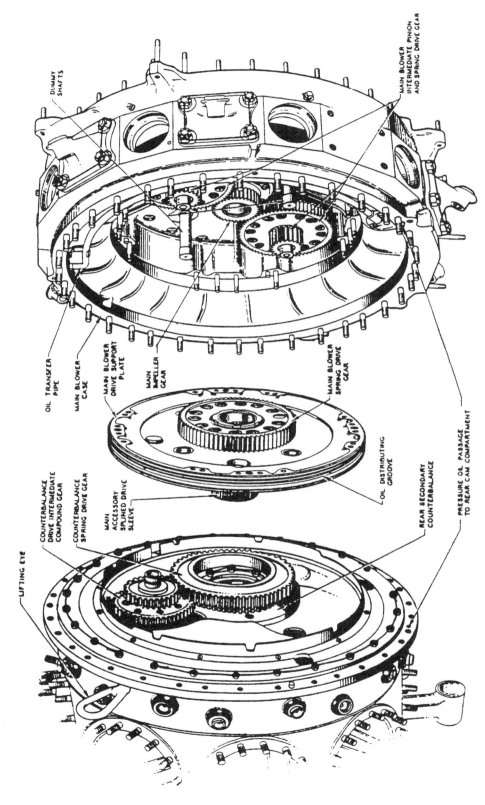

DUMMY SHAFTS

MAIN BLOWER INTERMEDIATE PINION AND SPRING DRIVE GEAR

OIL TRANSFER PIPE

MAIN BLOWER CASE

MAIN BLOWER DRIVE SUPPORT PLATE

MAIN IMPELLER GEAR

MAIN BLOWER SPRING DRIVE GEAR

PRESSURE OIL PASSAGE TO REAR CAM COMPARTMENT

COUNTERBALANCE DRIVE INTERMEDIATE COMPOUND GEAR

COUNTERBALANCE SPRING DRIVE GEAR

MAIN ACCESSORY SPLINED DRIVE SLEEVE

OIL DISTRIBUTING GROOVE

REAR SECONDARY COUNTERBALANCE

LIFTING EYE

Fig. 9.28 Pratt & Whitney R-2800-10 main crankcase, blower drive, and blower section. Note the second-order balancer that runs at twice crank speed. A similar balancer is fitted to the front section of the crankcase. (Operator's Handbook, Double Wasp B Series Engines, R-2800-8 and -10.)

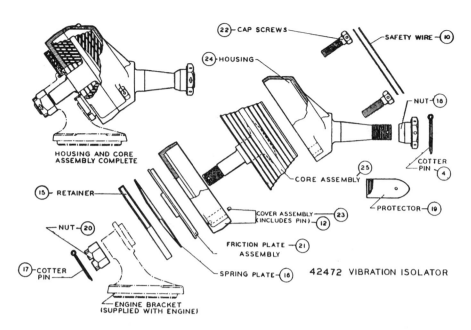

Fig. 9.29 Engine mount for a Pratt & Whitney R-2800. This mount not only provided shock absorption capabilities but shock dampening also. The diaphragm spring-and-clutch plate operated in a similar manner to a modern-day automobile clutch. Six mounts disposed around the blower intermediate housing were used per engine. This level of sophistication was necessary to reduce airframe fatigue. (Overhaul Instructions with Parts Catalog for Vibration Isolators for R-1830, R-2000, R-2800, and R-4360 Aircraft Engines. Author's collection.)

Fig. 9.30 View down the throat of a Bendix injection carburetor. (Courtesy of the National Air and Space Museum, Smithsonian Institution, Photo No. B3-117308-20.)

Early production examples were rated at 1800 hp at 2600 rpm. Power was soon increased to 2000 at 2700 rpm. When the R-2800 was pushed to 2000 hp, the limitations of the cast cylinder head were felt. Additionally, the highly stressed internal parts needed strengthening. Consequently, the definitive C series resulted. The entire engine required redesigning, and the only commonality was the 5.75-in bore and 6.0-in stroke. Although the crankcase remained a three-piece, bolted-together aluminum forging, it saw considerable redesign to strengthen it. Cylinder design was totally revamped. A forged cylinder head now replaced the previously cast cylinder head, allowing deeper, closer-pitched cooling fins. Ganged slitting saws following cams created the correct depth and pitch for the fins. C-series R-2800s were the first Pratt & Whitney production engines with a forged head. The cylinder barrel was still a chrome molybdenum steel alloy forging retaining an aluminum cooling muff shrunk onto the barrel but with more cooling surface area. These modifications substantially increased the cooling fin area and heat rejection capability of the engine. Master rod and link rod strength was increased. In addition the rod ratio was increased, that is, the ratio of the center distance between the wrist pin center and the big end center compared to the stroke. This resulted in longer connecting rods. Crankshaft design was totally revamped, although the three-plain-bearing, three-piece concept was retained. The method of retaining the three-piece crankshaft was revised by using face splines at the joints instead of the previously used male/female splines in the A- and B-series engines. Nose case strengthening again resulted in a total redesign. A two-piece magnesium casting replaced the former one-piece component. The planetary reduction gearing featured far more pinions to distribute the greater loads now imposed on them due to the increase in horsepower. The SAE No. 50 propeller shaft spline was replaced by the larger No. 60 spline. Refinements were made to the supercharger, and the PT-13 series Bendix injection carburetor was replaced by the PR-58 series of carburetor. The result of all these modifications was an engine capable of 2500 hp at 2800 rpm dry and 2800 hp with ADI.

Weights varied from 2150 lb for the earlier single-stage, single-speed engines to 2560 lb for the later models with auxiliary supercharging installed in F4Us and F6Fs. Some experimental models with contra-rotating propellers weighed in at a porky 2650 lb.

Manufacture

With the R-2800, Pratt & Whitney had a world-beater; consequently, numerous subcontractors were employed. The Ford Motor Company was one of the prime subcontractors; in addition, Nash and Chevrolet also manufactured the R-2800.

Construction of a new Pratt & Whitney manufacturing facility in Kansas City, Missouri, was started in July 1942. Although it was initially intended for the production of the B-series R-2800, a gamble was taken that the totally revamped C series would be successful, and the decision was made to tool-up immediately for the C series even though it was still under development at the time. Despite several setbacks, such as the diverting of a number of critically needed Sundstrand centerless grinders to England for Napier Sabre production, which Pratt & Whitney rather uncharitably referred to as "Britain's great white hope," the Missouri facility was soon manufacturing the definitive C-series R-2800 (Ref. 6.9). In retrospect it can be seen that the decision to start immediately with the C engine was correct, even though at the time it was a totally unknown quantity.

When chosen as a subcontractor, Ford naturally sent top manufacturing engineers to East Hartford in order to understand the magnitude of the project. To Pratt & Whitney's surprise, Ford made an exact copy of the East Hartford manufacturing facility in Dearborn. Although Ford built numerous dash numbers of the R-2800, indeed Ford was the only manufacturer of some models, they were all B-series engines.

Applications

Although the R-2800 did not excel in any one area—it did not have the best specific power, lowest specific weight, lowest specific fuel consumption, and so forth—the combination of the right attributes, particularly its reliability, rugged construction, and ability to absorb incredible battle damage made it well suited to the demanding environment in which it operated. Cases have been documented where complete cylinders were shot off, and yet the engine continued to produce sufficient power for a very grateful pilot, enabling him to make it back to base. Table 9.2 summarizes the R-2800's performance and applications.

TABLE 9.2—PRATT & WHITNEY R-2800 PERFORMANCE AND APPLICATIONS SUMMARY

Dash Number	Applications	hp/rpm/alt	Comments
-1	Consolidated XA-19B	1800/2600/SL	A series
X-2	Vought XF4U-1	1800/2600/SL 1500/2400/17,500	Two-stage, two-speed experimental Navy test engine. A series
X-4	Vought XF4U-1	1850/2600/SL 1460/2400/21,500	Same as X-2 with A5-G supercharger. A series
-5	Douglas B-23 Martin B-26A/B Martin XB-26D Curtiss XC-46	1850/2600/SL 1500/2600/14,000	Also built by Ford Motor Company. Similar to -1 except for two-speed blower and carburetor. A series
-8/-8W	Brewster F3A Goodyear FG-1 Vought F4U-1/1C/1P Vought F4U-2	2000/2700/SL 1550/2550/21,500	Updraft carburetion. These engines were also built by Nash. B series
-10/10W	Curtiss P-60A/E Grumman F6F-3/5 Northrop F2T-1 Northrop P-61A	2000/2700/SL 1500/2550/21,500	Downdraft carburetion. Although a Navy engine it was also sold to AAF. B series
-14W	Goodyear FG-3 Northrop XP-61D Republic YP-47M Vought F4U-3	2100/2800/SL 2100/2800/28,500	Built in Kansas City. C series

(continued)

TABLE 9.2, continued

Dash Number	Applications	hp/rpm/alt	Comments
-18/18W	Curtiss YP-60E Vought F4U-4/E/N/P Vought F4U-7 Grumman XF6F-6	2100/2800/SL 1550/2600/26,000	Navy engine but also sold to AAF. C series
-18WA			Similar to -18W but with longer connecting rods and master rods. Counterbalancers redesigned and piston skirt length increased
-21	Republic P-47C/D XP-47E/F/K	2000/2700 1625/2550/25,000	Also built by Ford. B series. Similar to -17 except for different blower ratio and accessory section
-22/-22W	Grumman F7F-2/3 Grumman XF7F-1 Grumman XF8F-1	2100/2800/SL 1450/2600/18,500	All -22Ws were built at Kansas City. C series
-27	Douglas A-26B/C Grumman XF6F-1/-4 Grumman F7F-1N	2000/2700/SL 1450/2600/18,500	Also built by Ford. B series. Similar to -21 except fitted with two-speed blower
-30W	Grumman F7F-5 Grumman XF8F-3	2250/2800/SL 1600/2800/22,000	C series
-31	Lockheed PV-1 Lockheed PV-2	2000/2700/SL 1600/2700/13,500	B series. Also built by Ford. Similar to -27 except different propeller reduction ratio
-32W	Vought F4U-5	2800/2800/SL 1800/2800/30,000	C series with dual first-stage "sidewinder" impellers
-34/-34W	Curtiss C-46F Douglas XA-26D Grumman F7F-4/-3N Grumman F8F-1 Martin PBM-5A	2100/2800/SL 1500/2600/18,500	-34/-34Ws were built in Kansas City only. C series. Similar to -22 except different diffuser section
-43	Martin B-26B/C/E/F/G XB-26D Curtiss C-46	2000/2700/SL 1600/2700/13,500	All -43s were built by Ford. B series. Similar to -27 except rear section employs dual gun synchronizer drives
-51	Curtiss C-46A/D/E/F/G	2000/2700/SL 1600/2700/13,500	All -51s were built by Ford. B series. Similar to -43 except fitted with new type mounting bracket

(continued)

TABLE 9.2, continued

Dash Number	Applications	hp/rpm/alt	Comments
-57	Northrop P-61D/C Republic XP-47J/L/N Republic P-47M/N, P-61C/D	2100/2800/SL 2100/2800/28,500	Built by Chevrolet and Kansas City. C series
-59	Republic P-47D/C Republic XP-47L	2000/2700/SL 1625/2600/25,000	Similar to -21. Only difference was ignition system and fitted with ADI. B series
-63	Republic P-47D/C Republic XP-47L	2000/2700/SL 1625/2550/25,000	Also built by Ford B series. Similar to -21 except fitted with ADI
-65	Northrop P-61A/B Northrop XP-61E	2000/2700/SL 1650/2700/22,500	Similar to -10 but with General Electric ignition. Also built by Nash. B series
-71	Douglas A-26B/C	2000/2700/SL 1600/2700/13,500	Similar to -27 with General Electric tubular harness
-73	Northrop F-15A Northrop P-61C/F Republic P-47N	2100/2800/SL 2100/2800/28,500	Similar to -57 except for ignition system. Also built by Chevrolet
-75	Curtiss C-46A/D/F/G	2000/2700/SL 1600/2700/13,500	Similar to -51 but fitted with General Electric ignition system. Also built by Ford
-77	Republic P-47N Northrop P61C	2100/2800/SL 2100/2800/30,000	Similar to -57. Also built by Chevrolet
-79	Douglas A-26B/C	2000/2700/SL 1600/2700/13,500	Similar to -71 except equipped with ADI. Also built by Ford
-81	Republic P-47N Northrop P-61C	2100/2800/SL 2100/2800/30,000	Similar to -57 except equipped with General Electric ignition
-83	Douglas A-26D/E Martin XB-26F	2100/2800/SL 1700/2800/16,000	Similar to Navy -34W except fitted with General Electric ignition
-87	Republic P-47M/N	2100/2800/SL 2100/2800/30,000	Similar to -73 except incorporates redesigned master rod assemblies and cylinder assemblies

Note: All even dash numbers were Navy-procured engines, and all odd dash numbers were Army Air Corps/Force-procured engines. Several examples exist of Navy engines being installed in Army aircraft. Source: Refs. 2.7, 9.13, 9.20.

Chance Vought F4U Corsair

Possibly the most charismatic of all the R-2800-powered aircraft with its distinctive gull wing lay-out, the Corsair was not only an aesthetically pleasing fighter but also a great performer, proving once again that form follows function.

The first aircraft to go into production powered by an R-2800, the F4U also held the distinction of being the first United States military aircraft to exceed 400 mph in level flight.

Eventually more than 10,000 F4Us were manufactured in numerous subvariants by Chance Vought, Goodyear, and Brewster. The Brewster contract was canceled in July 1944 after 735 had been deliv-ered because of "failure to meet requirements."

Designed in 1938 in response to a Navy design competition, the prototype XF4U celebrated its maiden flight on 29 May 1940 powered by an XR-2800-2 rated at 1800 hp. All the R-2800s installed in production F4Us were unique in that they had two-stage, two-speed supercharging with inter-cooling and updraft carburetion (Fig. 9.31).

Construction was typical of a late 1930s design along with many creative and innovative ideas. At the time of its first flight, the F4U was fitted with one of the world's largest propellers. This dictated the gull wing feature of the design. In order to reduce its length, the landing gear was attached at the lowest point of the "crank" in the wing. Retraction was rearward, rotating through 90° and at the same time the oleo strut was compressed, making for a compact and neat installation. Wing design consisted of a main spar that passed through the fuselage where the firewall was mounted. The hydraulic folding mechanism was installed outboard of the crank in the wing. From the spar forward a D-section box member was created that took all the primary loads. Aft of the spar was fabric cov-ered, and unusual for an aircraft of this era the ailerons were of wood construction, fabric covered. All remaining control surfaces were metal with fabric covering. Rectangular openings mounted in the wing leading edge at the fuselage junction supplied cooling air to twin oil coolers, one in each leading edge. Induction air was also taken from the leading-edge air intakes, ducted to the first stage of the supercharger. Featuring an intercooler for the two-stage supercharger, cooling air was routed from the leading-edge air intakes to the air-to-air intercooler. Flow splitters were an integral part of the air intakes due to the requirement of ducting the air 90° as soon as it entered the air intake plenum. At high speed these flow splitters (six per side) emitted a loud whistling noise, which prompted the Japanese to call the F4U "Whistling Death." Outer wing panels featured the armament, which usually consisted of six .50-caliber machine guns. As the war progressed hard points were designed in for rockets.

Fuselage construction was a monocoque from the firewall aft, with a circular cross section back to the cockpit, where it transitioned to an oval section. At the time of its design gestation, a new tech-nique had been developed for spot welding aluminum that promised lower drag compared with an equivalent riveted structure; Chance Vought took advantage of this new manufacturing technique. Tail construction was conventional stressed skin. The retractable tail wheel went through a complex

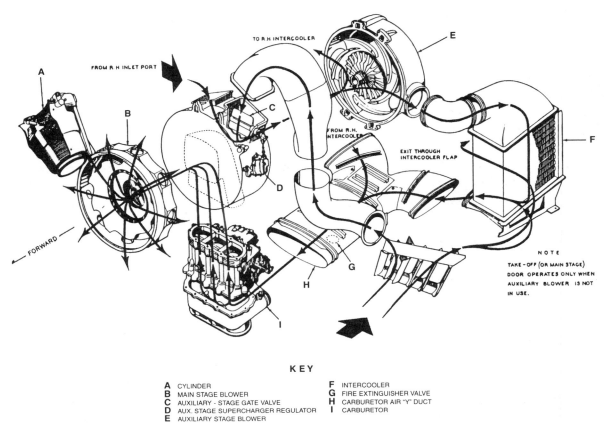

KEY

A	CYLINDER	**F**	INTERCOOLER
B	MAIN STAGE BLOWER	**G**	FIRE EXTINGUISHER VALVE
C	AUXILIARY - STAGE GATE VALVE	**H**	CARBURETOR AIR "Y" DUCT
D	AUX. STAGE SUPERCHARGER REGULATOR	**I**	CARBURETOR
E	AUXILIARY STAGE BLOWER		

Fig. 9.31 Diagram of the Vought F4U-1 induction system. Air entered through the wing leading-edge intakes. Note the six flow splitters that emitted a high-pitched whistling noise. This prompted the Japanese to dub the F4U "Whistling Death." For clarity, only half the intercooler and induction system is shown. Dual intakes and intercoolers were used on the aircraft. (Pilot's Handbook for Navy Model F4U-1, F4U-1C, F4U-1D, F3A, FG-1, F6-1D Airplanes, 15 Oct. 1945. Revised June 1946. Courtesy of the New England Air Museum.)

retraction sequence with the tail hook mounted to the chrome molybdenum steel alloy support structure of the tail wheel. The considerable loads imposed on the tail assembly during an arrested carrier landing were transmitted through the fuselage structure.

Because of the length of the engine, attributable to the auxiliary supercharger stage, a longer-than-usual engine mount was required. This also demonstrates why the firewall was mounted on the wing spar. F4U-1s featured a clean circular cowl with no external protuberances because of the wing leading-edge air intakes for oil cooling, induction, and intercooler cooling requirements. All F4Us were fitted with Hamilton Standard Hydromatic propellers; F4U-1s had three-blade propellers, and all subsequent aircraft had four-blade propellers.

F4U-1s constituted the majority of the Corsairs flown in World War II. Power was provided by the R-2800-8, which was a B-series engine. With the introduction of ADI, R-2800-8W engines were installed (a "W" after the dash number signified the engine was fitted with water/methanol injection). F4U-2s were essentially the same as F4U-1s, but specialized for night fighting featuring a radar pod on the right wing in place of one of the .50-caliber machine guns and a flame-damping exhaust for the six outlets.

The next important variant used during World War II was the F4U-4. (Only three experimental F4U-3s were manufactured. The F4U-3 was basically an F4U-1 powered by an XR-2800-16 with a turbosupercharger from the Turbo Engineering Company of New Jersey and a unique two-stage mixed-flow compressor with air-cooled radial inlet turbine.) Several significant modifications were incorporated into the F4U-4 including the use of the C-series engine in -18W form but still retaining two-stage, two-speed supercharging. The formerly clean, round cowl now featured the first of many bumps and bulges that were to feature prominently in all subsequent F4Us. This was for induction air, now routed from the cowl rather than the wing leading edge as in the F4U-1. F4U-4s were introduced in 1945 and entered combat in May of that year. The last production variant was the F4U-5, which sported the unusual R-2800-32W for power. This engine personified the trend that was occurring with high-performance military aircraft engines. The supercharger was now becoming more and more dominant to the point where it overshadowed the main power section. In the case of the R-2800-32W, two massive "sidewinder" superchargers made up the first stage (Fig. 9.32).

After a protracted development, the F4U was ready for combat in July 1942. However, the problems were not over; the Navy felt the deck-landing characteristics were unsafe due primarily to poor forward vision, and therefore the aircraft was assigned to land-based Marine units. (In some cases, F4Us departed from carriers, landing on an airstrip.) Carrier operations did not commence until December 1944. Interestingly, the British Fleet Air Arm received 2012 F4U-1s, designated Corsair III under lend-lease and used them immediately from carriers, thus getting a nine-month headstart on the U.S. Navy. Different pilot technique was partly responsible for the British success in carrier operations; a

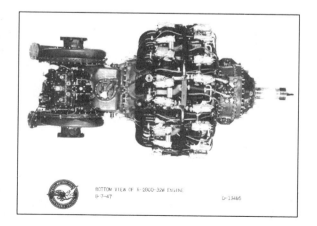

Fig. 9.32 Bottom view of the Pratt & Whitney R-2800-32W. Note the two-side mounted, first-stage supercharger impellers and updraft carburetor. Updraft carburetion was a feature of all F4U Corsairs. This photograph also illustrates well the trend that most high-performance piston engines were following at the end of the piston era. The supercharger was growing to the point where it was as large as the power section. (Courtesy of the New England Air Museum and Pratt & Whitney Aircraft.)

long curving approach to the left (as used by Fleet Air Arm pilots landing Seafires on carriers) afforded the pilot sufficient forward vision to make a successful landing. Modifications to the main gear oleo struts also alleviated the tendency to bounce on landing. Because of the more cramped conditions on board British carriers, the wing tips were clipped by 8 in to facilitate stowage (Fig. 9.33). As a condition of lend-lease, all aircraft were destroyed after V-J Day. This task was accomplished by the simple means of dumping them overboard.

Flying from the usual primitive air strips in the Pacific, Marine units quickly racked up many successes against their Japanese counterparts. Tactics played a crucial part in these successes. Dogfighting a Japanese fighter was inviting trouble; therefore, the preferred and universally successful tactic was hit-and-run without getting tangled up in a slow-speed dogfight against a more maneuverable foe.

The British Fleet Air Arm enjoyed similar success in the Mediterranean and Pacific with their F4Us (Corsairs). In 1943, the Royal New Zealand Air Force also received F4Us and deployed them in the Pacific starting in early 1944.

Goodyear, chosen as a second source, license-built Corsairs and developed a fighter based on the F4U concept with several major changes. Perhaps the most dramatic was the substitution of a Pratt & Whitney R-4360 in place of the R-2800. Other changes included the deletion of the turtleback fuselage design for a bubble canopy; this change was first tried on the FG-1A, Goodyear designation for the F4U-1 (Refs. 2.7, 9.14, 9.22 to 9.24).

Fig. 9.33 Chance Vought F4U-1 Corsair for the British Fleet Air Arm, which flew them from carriers 9 months before the U.S. Navy. A characteristic of the Fleet Air Arm Corsairs was the reduced wing span needed to fit in British carrier hangars, that is, 8 in was removed from each wing tip. At the end of the War, all Fleet Air Arm Corsairs were unceremoniously dumped overboard to meet the lend/lease requirements. (Courtesy of the National Air and Space Museum, Smithsonian Institution.)

Grumman F6F Hellcat

The Grumman F6F, an often overlooked carrier-based fighter of World War II, racked up more victories than any other fighter in the Pacific theater. This pugnacious fighter had all the characteristics of a Grumman product with its rugged construction and ability to sustain considerable battle damage.

The F6F was a contemporary of the F4U Corsair, and even though it was designed after its erstwhile stablemate, it entered service before the F4U, testament to how "right" the design was and to the hard work put in by Grumman employees.

The initial contract with the Navy was signed on 30 June 1941, and the first flight took place in August 1942, a remarkably short gestation period. The first prototype, the XF6F-1, was powered by a Wright R-2600; however, all subsequent aircraft were powered by the Pratt & Whitney R-2800. The first production Hellcat, the F6F-3, flew for the first time in October 1942, and by January 1943 they were being delivered to the Navy. By the end of 1943 more than 2500 had been delivered, by any standards a prodigious production rate. Final production totaled almost 11,000, all of which were manufactured by Grumman (Fig. 9.34).

The design remained almost unchanged for the production life of the aircraft, unlike many other World War II fighters that went through numerous major redesigns. Bearing a family resemblance to the F4F, the F6F was a fresh design, considerably larger, more powerful, and more capable. It was designed with the intent of taking on Mitsubishi Zeros, which it did with incredible success, finally racking up a kill ratio of 19-to-1 against its Japanese adversaries.

Fig. 9.34 The Pratt & Whitney R-2800 powered Grumman F6F Hellcat. One of the unsung heroes of World War II, it accounted for shooting down more Japanese aircraft than any other type. (Courtesy of the National Air and Space Museum, Smithsonian Institution, Photo No. 1B-01182.)

All variants, with the exception of the prototype and the XF6F-6, were powered by the R-2800-10s or water/methanol-injected R-2800-10Ws (Fig. 9.35). Similar in concept to the R-2800s that powered the F4U, with the exception that downdraft carburetion was used, the engine featured two-stage, two-speed supercharging with air-to-air intercooling (Fig. 9.36). Like the engine in the F4U, the second stage of the supercharger was driven at a single speed, the first stage had two speeds, high and low blower, with a third option of neutral for cruising operations. The neutral feature saved fuel and parasitic power loss at altitudes below 7000 ft. At altitudes of 7000 to 22,000 ft the low ratio would be engaged, and at altitudes above 22,000 ft high blower speed would be engaged. When low blower speed was engaged from neutral, the supercharger would accelerate from 0 to as much as 15,000 rpm, placing a tremendous load on the drive. To avoid damage to this heavily loaded gear train, an "accelerating" device, as Pratt & Whitney called it, was used. It was essentially a fluid coupling that brought up the speed of the supercharger impeller in a controlled fashion.

As with the F4U, supercharger surging would occur under some conditions. Surging is the breakdown of airflow across the supercharger impeller, analogous to a wing in the stalled condition. Conditions contributing to surging would be low manifold pressure and high rpm at high altitude. Evidence of it would include engine roughness and a rumbling sound in the supercharger air intake duct. Although not harmful for short periods, it could lead to duct damage and accelerated wear in

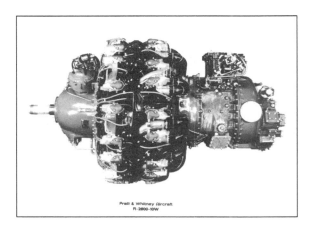

Fig. 9.35 Pratt & Whitney R-2800-10W. First of the production R-2800 two-stage engines. Thousands were manufactured for the Grumman F6F Hellcat and Northrop P-61A Black Widow. The -10Ws were B-series engines identifiable by the one-piece nose section and cast cylinder heads. (Courtesy of the New England Air Museum and Pratt & Whitney Aircraft.)

Fig. 9.36 Pratt & Whitney R-2800-10 two-stage supercharger, first stage is on the right. Induction air enters the port in the middle where the butterfly valve is located. Discharge from the first stage enters an air-to-air intercooler. From the intercooler, air enters the downdraft carburetor then the second supercharger stage. R-2800-10s were installed in Northrop P-61A Black Widows and Grumman F6F Hellcats. (Courtesy of the New England Air Museum and Pratt & Whitney Aircraft.)

the engine if allowed to continue. The condition was usually corrected by shifting to a lower blower speed thus reducing the speed of the supercharger impeller and advancing the throttle, thus allowing more air into the supercharger and "unstalling" the impeller.

Structurally, the F6F deviated from the F4F in several key areas. The wing was mounted at a lower relative position on the fuselage. Consequently a different design of landing gear was required, and it was mounted in the wings rather than the fuselage. Landing gear geometry was similar to the F4U, that is, rearward retracting and rotating 90° during retraction. Monocoque or semimonocoque construction was featured throughout the airframe. All air-intake chores were handled in the design of the cowl. Three main air intakes ducted air to the intercooler radiator, supercharger intake, and oil cooler. Cowl flaps controlled the temperature of the engine, and a separate set of flaps controlled oil and intercooler air temperature. From the F6F-5 on, the oil cooler and intercooler featured individual controls for cooling flap position. Manually operated wing folding was incorporated, with the breakpoint just outboard of the landing gear. Folding geometry followed Grumman's unique and innovative system of positioning the wings alongside the fuselage, making for a very compact package. The outer section of the wings also contained the armament, which usually consisted of six .50-caliber machine guns.

The -10W engine was fitted with water injection (the ADI fluid actually consisted of a 50/50 mix of distilled water and methanol) for war emergency power (WEP). Because of the stress put on the engine because of cylinder head and oil temperature limits being exceeded during WEP, a 5-min limit was imposed, although this limit was understandably exceeded many times during the heat of combat. In extreme emergencies seawater would be used in place of the water/methanol mix, although it can only be conjectured what kind of corrosion would result if the seawater were left in the aircraft for any length of time. When the throttle was advanced past the normal sea-level rating of the engine and into the WEP phase, a microswitch closed, automatically allowing the ADI mixture into the supercharger, and at the same time the fuel mixture automatically "derichened," that is, leaned slightly.

The 22-gal oil tank contained 19 gal of oil and was mounted on the front side of the firewall. This allowed 3 gal of air space.

Used throughout the island-hopping Pacific campaign, the F6F aircraft racked up many successes, the most famous of which was perhaps the "Marianas Turkey Shoot," when they accounted for more than 400 Japanese aircraft for the loss of 18 F6Fs. The highest-scoring Navy ace, Commander David McCampbell, scored his 34 victories in the F6F.

The British Fleet Air Arm received 1182 F6Fs, which they designated Hellcat I and Hellcat II. At the end of World War II all remaining F6Fs were returned to the United States, complying with the lend-lease terms under which they were originally obtained. The Fleet Air Arm put their aircraft to good use including attacks on the German pocket battleship *Tirpitz* in Norway.

When AI radar was developed, it was immediately mounted on the F6F-3E and F6F-5N, housed in a pod on the right wing (Refs. 2.7, 9.14, 9.21, 9.25, 9.26).

Grumman F7F Tigercat

Yet another of the Grumman "Cats," the Tigercat was developed from the earlier XF5F Skyrocket, of which only two prototypes were built. Taking advantage of the emerging radar technology, the F7F was designed from the outset to be a two-seat, twin-engine radar-equipped carrier-based fighter (Fig. 9.37). It was powered by a pair of R-2800-34W single-stage, two-speed, water-injected C-series engines rated at 2100 hp.

Just too late to see action in World War II, the first squadron of F7Fs arrived in Okinawa the day before the war ended (Refs. 9.14, 9.20, 9.27).

Grumman F8F Bearcat

Under development for much of World War II, the F8F Bearcat represented the last of the famous piston engine Grumman "Cat" family (Fig. 9.38). Design started in November 1943, based on the premise of building the smallest, lightest, and most compact fighter possible around the R-2800 (Fig. 9.39). The prototype was ready for its maiden flight less than a year from the commencement of design, flying in August 1944. The first squadron to be equipped with Bearcats, VF-19, was on its way to the Pacific in August 1945 when hostilities ceased. Thus the finest piston-engine-powered aircraft the Navy had just missed combat in World War II by a whisker (Refs. 9.14, 9.20, 9.28).

Republic P-47 Thunderbolt

Possibly no aircraft conjures up the image of the quintessential World War II radial-powered aircraft than the immortal "Jug," so nicknamed because of its resemblance to a milk jug of the 1940s.

Fig. 9.37 The Grumman F7F Tigercat arrived in the Pacific during the waning days of World War II. (Courtesy of the National Air and Space Museum, Smithsonian Institution, Photo No. 1B-01215.)

Fig. 9.38 Grumman F8F Bearcat prototype. The smallest possible airframe fastened to the largest available engine, the Pratt & Whitney R-2800. (Courtesy of the National Air and Space Museum, Smithsonian Institution, Photo No. 1B-01238.)

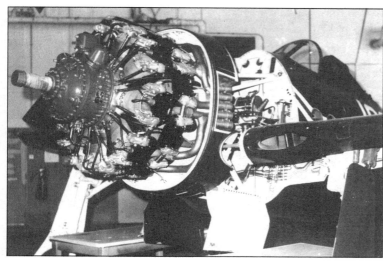

Fig. 9.39 This shot illustrates why the Grumman F8F Bearcat was described as the smallest practical airframe that could handle a Pratt & Whitney R-2800. Note relative position of the firewall compared with the wing leading edge. (Courtesy of the National Air and Space Museum, Smithsonian Institution, Photo No. 1B-01224.)

Like many of its contemporaries, the Republic P-47 was an evolutionary design going back to the 1930s and the Seversky SEV-X-BT designed by Alexander Kartveli for Alexander De Seversky, both of whom were Russian expatriates. The SEV-X-BT evolved into the Seversky P-35, a small number of which were procured by the Army Air Corps. Some were deployed in the Philippines and Pearl Harbor which, along with P-36s and a few P-40s, had to contend with the onslaught of the Japanese surprise attacks on 7 December 1941. Powered by the Pratt & Whitney R-1830, the P-35 was another aircraft overtaken by rapidly emerging new technology. A number of P-35s were exported, primarily to Sweden.

The follow-on to the P-35, the P-41, still retained the R-1830 for power, but in two-stage, two-speed form as the R-1830-19. Only a single prototype was built, but the lineage of the P-47 was now clearly evolving.

The next aircraft in the P-47 evolution were the P-43 Lancer and the P-44 Rocket, which were similar in overall concept and design. The primary difference was the engine, which in the case of P-43 was a turbosupercharged R-1830-35, Seversky's first experience with turbosuperchargers (Fig. 9.40). The P-44 was initially powered by the Pratt & Whitney R-2180, an engine produced in small numbers. The last production versions of the P-44 were powered by the R-2800-7 and redesignated P-47. In 1939 the Seversky company was renamed The Republic Aviation Corporation. For several reasons, the P-44 was abandoned in favor of the XP-47A. During this time, 1940 to 1941, valuable lessons were learned from the war in Europe, particularly with regard to the value of heavy firepower, self-sealing fuel tanks, and armor protection, particularly for the pilot. Consequently, these features were added to the P-47, resulting in what was at the time the world's largest and heaviest single-engine fighter. Contributing to the size and weight of the P-47 was the General Electric Type C turbosupercharger, which was mounted in the underbelly at the rear of the fuselage. The considerable depth of the fuselage was dictated by the requirement for ductwork supplying induction air, cooling air, and exhaust gases to the turbo and the discharge air from the turbocompressor (Fig. 9.41).

All air requirements were supplied by the massive deep oval cowling intake. The upper, circular section supplied cooling air to the engine, and the lower section was subdivided to supply air to the dual circular oil coolers, air to the turbosupercharger compressor, and cooling air for the air-to-air intercooler. The P-47B was the first production variant, entering squadron service in March 1942.

The Jug was powered by the R-2800-21, a B-series engine with single-stage, single-speed supercharging, rated at 2000 hp at 25,000 ft and 2700 rpm. This endowed the Jug with a top speed of 429 mph at 27,800 ft, a good indicator of the effectiveness of the General Electric turbosupercharger, particularly at high altitudes. All subsequent R-2800 B series powered P-47s were powered by the following engines: the R-2800-21 (Scintilla magnetos and no water injection), the R-2800-59 (General Electric magnetos, many of which were manufactured under license by Briggs & Stratton,

Fig. 9.40 Republic YP-43 powered by a Pratt & Whitney R-1830-47/-57 and equipped with a General Electric Type B-1 turbosupercharger. The 100 P-43 Lancers that reached China early in the War were restricted from combat as they lacked adequate armor plating and self-sealing fuel tanks. (Courtesy of the National Air and Space Museum, Smithsonian Institution, Photo No. 1B-33121.)

Fig. 9.41 Republic P-47C powered by the Pratt & Whitney R-2800-59. (Courtesy of the National Air and Space Museum, Smithsonian Institution, Photo No. 1B-33200.)

Milwaukee, Wisconsin), or the R-2800-63 (Scintilla magnetos and water injection), all of which were essentially the same and were consequently rated at the same power (Fig. 9.42). When water injection (ADI) was added, an additional 300 hp became available. This increase in power was critical when a P-47 pilot was facing up to the likes of the Focke-Wulf 190. It was recommended that water had to be used judicially because of the additional loadings placed on the engine. At high altitudes (above the critical altitude), ADI became less effective and offered little, if any, additional power. The same was true at partial throttle settings—no advantage was offered under these operating conditions. As many World War II fighter pilots can attest, overgross take-offs were the norm, rather than the exception; therefore, ADI would often be used to enhance the safety of these harrowing take-offs. At the onset of water injection, a derichment valve leaned out the mixture to compensate for the water/methanol injected into the engine.

With the introduction of the C-series engine a dramatic increase in performance was possible along with a substantial increase in gross weight. The last of the Jugs, the P-47N, weighed in at an incredible 20,700 lb, almost the same as a DC-3! The P-47M was the first production P-47 powered with a C-series engine. Still retaining a single-speed, single-stage supercharger and General Electric type C turbosupercharger, the Ms were powered with the R-2800-57 rated at 2500 hp at 2800 rpm and at 28,500 ft produced 2100 hp. P-47Ns were the last Jugs manufactured and were powered by -57, -73, or -77 engines. All three were very similar; the main differences were the ignition system and the manufacturer. In the case of the -77 and the -73, all were manufactured by Chevrolet, with the -73s featuring General Electric ignition systems.

With the far superior cooling design of the C-series engine, overheating was now eliminated to the point where overcooling was experienced, particularly in cold climates such as that in Europe. The high-altitude capability of the Jug brought on other problems that were never definitively solved. High-altitude engine misfiring became quite common due to the low dielectric strength of the atmo-

Fig. 9.42 Engine change for a Republic P-47. This photograph shows the primitive conditions under which maintenance had to be carried out. Engine is an R-2800-21 or -63, identifiable by the Scintilla ignition system mounted on the nose case and the fact they are B-series engines. The difference between the -21 and -63 was that the latter had ADI and a correspondingly higher rating. (Courtesy of the National Air and Space Museum, Smithsonian Institution, Photo No. 1B-33206.)

sphere at 25,000+ ft. Pressurizing the magnetos helped to a limited degree; the pressurization source was bleed air tapped off from the discharge of the turbosupercharger. Careful maintenance of the entire ignition system was essential: No cracks, foreign material, or moisture could enter; otherwise, high-altitude misfires would result. General Electric ignition systems were somewhat better designed in this regard than Scintilla ignition systems because of the larger diameter and consequently wider spacing of the high tension contacts in the distributor of the General Electric system.

Because of various teething problems found in early squadron service, the P-47B was superseded by the C, and it was this version that entered combat for the first time with the Eighth Air Force in March 1943 flying out of England. Compared with its most formidable adversary, the Focke-Wulf 190, the P-47 had some shortcomings, particularly at medium and low altitudes. Within a short time, tactics were developed to optimize its advantages. Rather than engage in a classic dogfight, Jug pilots evolved the zoom-and-climb tactic, attacking the adversary from above in a dive, and thus taking advantage of the P-47's phenomenal dive capabilities. After the first pass, the pilot would then enter a climb. The ruggedness of the P-47 is legendary. In many cases, overenthusiastic pilots strafing German strongholds flew through trees or other obstacles and lived to tell about it (Fig. 9.43).

In an effort to enhance its performance, water/methanol-injection kits were developed and retrofitted in the field. This offered an additional 300 hp at the push of a button on the throttle quadrant. On later aircraft the water injection was completely automated, requiring no action from the pilot.

The P-47D was the most-produced subvariant of any aircraft built by the United States during World War II: a total of 12,602 were manufactured. The P-47D was similar to the C it replaced; several improvements were incorporated that upgraded the durability of the engine including additional cowl flaps to reduce cylinder head temperatures. The next two production variants, the M and N, were

Fig. 9.43 A good example why the P-47/Pratt & Whitney R-2800 combination gained a reputation for being rugged! (Courtesy of the National Air and Space Museum, Smithsonian Institution, Photo No. 1B-33377.)

built in relatively small numbers: 130 Ms and 1816 Ns. Because of the extra fuel tankage, wingspan, and consequently the extra range of the N, it was used operationally in the Pacific, entering service in early 1945 (Ref. 2.5, 2.7, 9.14, 9.20, 9.29).

Martin B-26 Marauder

Although it was the most maligned U.S. combat aircraft of World War II, the Martin Marauder proved to be one of the most effective Allied medium bombers. It had one of the lowest loss rates, justifying the combat use of this aircraft, which came so close to being scrapped on several occasions (Fig. 9.44).

The Marauder was designed to Specification 39-640; the Army had so much faith in this design that 1131 aircraft were ordered before the first one flew. Interestingly, no formal prototypes were built; instead four preproduction aircraft were constructed. Because of the high performance requirements of the new bomber, new ground was pioneered, particularly in the area of wing loading and landing speed. With a wing span of 65 ft and a take-off weight of 34,000 lb, wing loading was over 50 lb/ft². This was considered very high by the standards of the late 1930s. The Marauder's first flight occurred on 25 November 1940, powered by a pair of R-2800-5 single-stage, single-speed engines rated at 1850 hp at 2600 rpm. Induction air for the downdraft Bendix injection carburetors was fed by a pair of scoops on the leading edge of the cowl, which ducted the air to the Bendix PT-13 carburetor. The B-26B, and all subsequent models, featured much larger scoops that housed air filters. The oil cooler was located in the bottom of the cowl with cooling air fed from the lower leading edge of the cowl. All variants of the B-26 were powered by A- or B-series engines, R-2800-5s (A series) for the preproduction models and R-2800-39s (A series), rated at 1850 hp and 2600 rpm for B-26A, B, and D models. R-2800-41s (B series) rated at 2000 hp and 2700 rpm were also installed in the B-26B with the same rating as the R-2800-39. Again with the same rating as the R-2800-39 and -41, the R-2800-43 powered the B-26B, C, D, E, F, G, and H. All R-2800-43s were built by the Ford Motor Company.

Fig. 9.44 Martin B-26 Marauder, powered by early models of the Pratt & Whitney R-2800. (Courtesy of the National Air and Space Museum, Smithsonian Institution, Photo No. 1B-18350.)

The U.S. Government built a new B-26 assembly plant for Martin in Omaha, Nebraska. Other subcontractors involved in the production of the B-26 were Chrysler, Hudson, and Goodyear.

First deployment of the B-26 occurred in Australia in February 1942. It received rave reviews for its high performance. However, it was being flown by experienced, well-trained crews. When the aircraft was introduced into the European theater, problems surfaced. Because of the high wing loading, the high landing speed of 135 mph, and the unforgiving engine-out characteristics, numerous accidents occurred. At one time the large number of B-26s lost to accidents during training from McDill Air Force Base in Tampa, Florida, brought on the unfortunate reputation of "One-a-Day in Tampa Bay." In reality, the highest accident rate was about one aircraft a week, still an unacceptably high rate even by World War II standards. Several attempts were made to cancel the whole B-26 program, and it was only the glowing reports from combat units, both Army Air Corps and the British RAF, and the sage assessment by Col. Jimmy Doolittle that saved the day for this formidable aircraft.

To correct the handling problems, several fixes were implemented, primarily an increase in the wing span from 65 to 71 ft and an increase in the angle of incidence. This increase in span consequently increased the wing area and reduced wing loading. The increase in the angle of incidence of the wing along with an increase to the thrust angle of the engines also helped. Although these changes made the handling characteristics of the aircraft safer, they resulted in a dramatic reduction in performance—top speed dropped from 323 to 282 mph. At the cease of hostilities, the B-26 was rapidly phased out. At times, it seemed the Army Air Force could not get rid of them fast enough; none of the combat veterans remaining in Europe at the end of World War II were flown back to the United States; instead they were unceremoniously blown up (Refs. 2.7, 9.20, 9.30).

Douglas A-26 Invader

Another twin-engine tactical medium bomber designed by the great Douglas designer Ed Heineman, the Douglas A-26 was a remarkable success from the outset and one of the few aircraft that handsomely exceeded all predicted performance parameters (Fig. 9.45). The weight was 700 lb less than estimated, the bomb load was twice what had been calculated, and the top speed was higher than forecast. Three variations of the A-26 (designed to a 1941 contract) were prototyped: the XA-26, a light bombardment and attack aircraft; the XA-26A, a night fighter version; and the XA-26B, an attack bomber sporting a whopping 75-mm cannon in the nose. Production aircraft dispensed with this unwieldy weapon and replaced it with six and later eight .50-caliber machine guns. The A-26 was introduced into combat with the Ninth Air Force, flying out of England in November 1944, and it immediately racked up a reputation for its remarkable performance, particularly when compared with its contemporaries, the Martin B-26 Marauder and North American B-25 Mitchell.

Construction was fairly conventional, featuring all-monocoque construction with a square section fuselage with rounded corners and a two-spar wing. Power was provided by a pair of R-2800-71s, all of which were built by Ford Motor Company, or R-2800-27s; the only difference was the ignition system. R-2800-71s and -27s were both B-series engines rated at 2000 hp and 2700 rpm at 1500 ft. Single-stage, two-speed supercharging was employed for all B-26 variants.

Engine mounting was unique in that it departed from the ubiquitous chrome molybdenum steel alloy tubular mount typically used for mounting radial engines. The A-26 mount consisted of a sheet metal assembly, formed by spinning, and a stainless steel rear section. Both parts were tied together by six forgings. The six shock and vibration mounts on the intermediate section of the engine picked up the six forgings, a very unique and clever way to hang the engine (Fig. 9.46). Similar thought was shown in the design of the exhaust system. It consisted of nine "fishtail" stacks, each of which terminated

Fig. 9.45 Douglas A-26 Invader powered by Pratt & Whitney R-2800-71s rated at 2000 hp. (Courtesy of the National Air and Space Museum, Smithsonian Institution, Photo No. 1A-37618.)

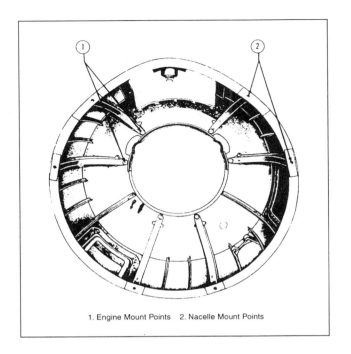

1. Engine Mount Points   2. Nacelle Mount Points

Fig. 9.46 Unique engine mount for Douglas A-26 Invader. The conventional tubular ring mount was dispensed with and replaced with the assembly shown. The engine mount points (1) attached to the R-2800. The loads were transmitted through six forgings (2) that attached to the nacelle. The fireseal was also used as a stressed member. (Douglas A-26 Erection and Maintenance Manual, 01-40AJ-2, 6 May 1944. Courtesy of the National Air and Space Museum, Smithsonian Institution.)

in four outlets at the point were the cowl flaps closed. This configuration thus contributed to the ejector effect for the cooling air, thus forcing additional cooling air through the cowling. Each stack was fed by two cylinders, a front and a rear. An additional advantage of the A-26 exhaust was a limited degree of flame damping. All in all, it was one of the better R-2800 exhaust systems.

Operationally, the A-26 was an immediate success with relatively few mechanical problems; the major problem with early aircraft, nose gear collapse, was soon fixed. The Ford-built R-2800s in particular performed flawlessly. Initially assigned to the 553rd Squadron of the 386th Bomb Group, attached to the Ninth Air Force flying out of England in September 1944, the Invader was fortunate in suffering surprisingly light losses, considering some of the hazardous missions flown. These included support of the Army fighting the German offensive in the Ardennes during the Battle of the Bulge. Flying in the worst winter weather Europe could dish up, the A-26s were used extensively during this critical battle when the Germans made their last desperate attack against the Allies.

Due to a misunderstanding of the potential of the A-26, deployment in the Pacific was delayed until mid 1945; consequently, few offensive missions were flown before the cease of hostilities.

In 1947 the A-26 was redesignated B-26, not to be confused with the Martin Marauder B-26. It soldiered on into the Korean conflict and ended its combat career with the U.S. Air Force in the 1960s in Vietnam! (Refs. 2.7, 9.20, 9.31).

Northrop P-61 Black Widow

The Northrop P-61, the world's first purpose-built, radar-equipped night fighter, looked more like a medium bomber than a fighter (Fig. 9.47). However, looks can be deceiving, as this massive and very capable fighter proved by creating havoc for enemy aircraft in Europe and the Pacific.

The P-61 was designed by John K. Northrop, who formed his company in 1939 after resigning from the Douglas Aircraft Company. Northrop responded to an Army specification for a night fighter in 1940, and by May 1942 the prototype XP-61 was ready for its maiden flight, powered by R-2800-25, two-stage, two-speed engines with downdraft induction. The initial test flights went off with very few problems. The first production aircraft, P-61As, were powered by a Navy engine, the -10, the same as the Grumman F6F Hellcat engine. In this two-stage, two-speed engine, all air intake features were installed on the leading edge of the wing; two long, narrow slots on both sides of the nacelle provided cooling air for the intercooler, oil cooler, and supercharger intake (Fig. 9.48). P-61Bs were similarly powered with R-2800-65s; the only difference from the -10 was the ignition system. The -10s and -65s were B-series engines rated at 2000 hp at 2700 rpm and 1000 ft. With the two-stage, intercooled two-speed blower, 1550 hp could be maintained to 21,500 ft.

Operating from primitive airstrips at night is hazardous duty; therefore in order to reduce the stalling speed to a minimum, large span flaps were incorporated into the design. This obviously necessitated small span ailerons, and consequently spoilers were used on the top surface of the wing to augment lateral control (Fig. 9.49).

Deployed in the Pacific and Europe during May 1944, it quickly racked up victories. Night intruder raids by Japanese aircraft flying out of Iwo Jima were starting to make themselves felt when the P-61 arrived on the scene. Flying standing patrols over Saipan, Tinian, and Guam, they soon eliminated the Japanese night attacks. In Europe they were just as effective; the first victory was a V-1 buzz bomb.

Fig. 9.47 Northrop P-61A Black Widow powered by the Pratt & Whitney R-2800-10s, a Navy engine originally developed for the Grumman F6F Hellcat. (Courtesy of the National Air and Space Museum, Smithsonian Institution, Photo No. 1B-28926.)

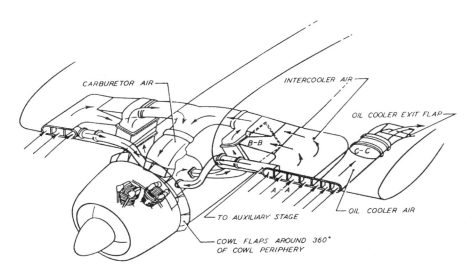

Fig. 9.48 Schematic showing ductwork for induction, intercooler, and oil cooler air for P-61A. Induction air was drawn in through the leading edge of the wing and ducted to the first stage of the supercharger. Compressed and heated air was then ducted through a pair of air-to-air intercoolers from which it then discharged into the carburetor and on into the second stage of the supercharger where full manifold pressure was developed. (Northrop P-61A Erection and Maintenance Manual, AN 01-15FB-2. Courtesy of the National Air and Space Museum, Smithsonian Institution.)

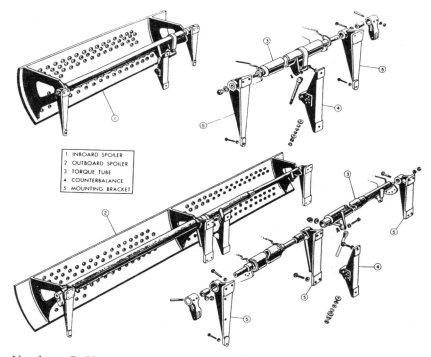

Fig. 9.49 The Northrop P-61 was an early example of the use of spoilers for aerodynamic roll control. (Northrop P-61A Erection and Maintenance Manual, AN 01-15FB-2, 5 May 1944. Courtesy of the National Air and Space Museum, Smithsonian Institution.)

Curtiss C-46 Commando

Transport duties were paramount during World War II, and logistical problems were often times worse than enemy action. Consequently the Curtiss C-46 Commando, with its cavernous cargo hold and weight-carrying abilities, was well suited to the role it played transporting much-needed supplies under very primitive and harsh conditions, whether it was in the CBI theater or the Pacific (Fig. 9.50).

Powered by a pair of R-2800-51s, B-series, single-stage, two-speed engines rated at 2000 hp and 2700 rpm, the C-46 was the largest twin-engine aircraft used by the Allies, spanning 108 ft, larger than a Lancaster, B-17, or B-24!

All-metal monocoque construction was featured throughout, with fabric-covered control surfaces. The fuselage was of the "double bubble concept"; that is, the cross-section consisted of two inter-secting circles. The fuselage floor was constructed at the intersection, thus offering a very stiff and strong construction.

Deployed in all theaters, the C-46 is best remembered for the hazardous flights made between India and China flying the "Hump," so-called because much of the flight was over the Himalayas (Refs. 2.7, 9.20).

Fig. 9.50 Curtiss C-46 Commando escorted by a P-40, another Curtiss product. (Courtesy of the National Air and Space Museum, Smithsonian Institution, Photo No. 1A-31164.)

Northrop XP-56 Black Bullet

Despite the fact that his company mass produced relatively conventional aircraft such as the P-61 Black Widow, Jack Northrop was more interested in designing aircraft using the flying-wing philosophy. Responding to a USAAC design competition for an interceptor, Northrop chose to use the flying-wing concept with a pusher engine buried in the aft fuselage for the XP-56 Black Bullet (Fig. 9.51).

The Pratt & Whitney liquid-cooled, sleeve valve engine, the H-24, X-1800, was the intended power plant. When the USAAF dropped support for this engine, Northrop was forced into using the less suitable R-2800-29 rated at 2000 hp at 2700 rpm. (Curtiss responded to the same design competition and like Northrop used a pusher configuration designed around the Pratt & Whitney X-1800. Suffering the same problem as Northrop—that is, no suitable power plant was available after the cancellation of the X-1800—Curtiss powered the XP-55 Ascender with an Allison V-1710-95.)

In order to improve stability and handling, the R-2800-29 was fitted with a six-blade, contra-rotating propeller. The engine was installed as a pusher to give the pilot an unrestricted field of view and more room for armament in the nose. Cooling a pusher configuration radial is a difficult design issue to resolve. In the case of the XP-56, air scoops in the roots of the wing leading edge fed cooling air through ducts to the engine. An engine-driven, multiblade, axial-flow fan mounted on the nose section increased mass air flow through the engine. Cooling air discharged through adjustable cowl flaps in front of the propeller. As with all propeller-driven pusher aircraft, the question of emergency exit for the pilot was a difficult one to resolve. Pratt & Whitney's solution was a nose case with explosive cord wrapped around it. In case of an emergency, the pilot fired the electrically triggered explosive cord that blew the nose case off, with the potentially lethal propellers attached, clear of the aircraft. Pratt & Whitney destroyed many nose cases testing this device.

Fig. 9.51 Northrop XP-56 Black Bullet. In order to protect the pilot in case of bailout, an emergency ejection system for the contra-rotating propeller was devised. Pratt & Whitney did extensive testing of explosive cord wrapped around the nose case of the R-2800 to blow the propeller clear of the aircraft. (Courtesy of the National Air and Space Museum, Smithsonian Institution, Photo No. 1B-28906.)

Fig. 9.52 Pratt & Whitney R-2800-29. Note the cooling fan, which assisted the reverse-flow cooling for installation in the Northrop XP-56. The -29 was the only D model of the R-2800. Contra-rotating propeller drive was incorporated to improve stability of the XP-56. (Courtesy of the New England Air Museum and Pratt & Whitney Aircraft; from Harvey Lippincott.)

R-2800-29s were the only D-series engines built, and only four were manufactured, all for the XP-56 program (Fig. 9.52). The power section was a B series with modified cooling baffles to accommodate the reversed-cooling flow. A two-stage, two-speed supercharger was used. The power section and supercharger incorporated much of the technology used in the R-2800-10, Grumman F6F power plant.

Just two XP-56s were manufactured and both were beset with handling difficulties. The first was destroyed landing at Muroc Dry Lake where the test flights took place. A burst tire was responsible. Despite modifications to the second prototype, handling was still marginal. The program was abandoned in 1944. Like many unsuccessful projects, all was not lost: Lessons learned on the XP-56 were incorporated into Northrop's later flying-wing designs.

R-4360 Wasp Major

The R-4360 was, without a doubt, the masterpiece of air-cooled radial engine design. Under development throughout World War II, it just missed going into action against the Japanese before the cease of hostilities.

Sharing the same bore and stroke as the R-2800, that is, 5.75-in bore and 6.0-in stroke, the 28 cylinders, arranged in four rows of seven, yielded a whopping displacement of 4363 in^3 (71.5 L).

Several attempts had been made at producing an air-cooled radial with more than two rows; the Armstrong Siddeley Deerhound and Hyena, both of which were three-row radials, are two examples. However, Pratt & Whitney was the first to attempt a four-row radial. Although the Wasp Major was often described as the world's largest aircraft piston engine, in fact there were many development and prototype engines that displaced considerably more than the Wasp Major's 4363 in^3 (71.5 L). It is probably fair to say, however, that the R-4360 was the largest piston engine to see mass production (Fig. 9.53).

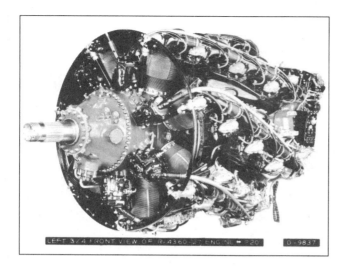

LEFT 3/4 FRONT VIEW OF R-4360-27 ENGINE - P20   D-9837

Fig. 9.53 The largest aircraft piston engine to see mass production, the Pratt & Whitney R-4360. (Courtesy of the New England Air Museum and Pratt & Whitney Aircraft.)

By the late 1930s Pratt & Whitney's developments were becoming diversified to the detriment of valuable programs such as the R-2800. Large amounts of resources were expended on liquid-cooled projects, in particular the H-3130, a liquid-cooled H-24 sleeve valve engine conceptually similar to the Napier Sabre, and its larger brother the H-3730. These engines were under intensive development for the Navy under the leadership of George Mead, who was suffering severe health problems. Considering the Navy's attitude towards liquid-cooled engines, it is surprising they funded this project. The comment was once made by a high-ranking Navy officer that a liquid-cooled aircraft engine made as much sense as an air-cooled submarine! The situation deteriorated to the point were Mead was running the H-3730 program from his sickbed.

In the meantime, Luke Hobbs was investigating the possibility of a four-row air-cooled radial. To this end he built a mock-up engine with 28 B-series R-2800 cylinders and tested it in a wind tunnel. To Hobbs' joy, it turned out that the installed drag was surprisingly low; another feature that contributed to the encouraging results was the layout of the cylinders (Fig. 9.54). Ensuring adequate cooling air to the rear row of cylinders was obviously a prime concern from the outset, so Hobbs arranged the cylinders in a helical configuration, thus allowing sufficient cooling air to be ducted to the rear cylinders.

Hobbs convinced Hap Arnold that the R-4360 could be developed in time to contribute to the Allied war effort, and so the decision was made to drop all the liquid-cooled projects and concentrate all development efforts on the R-2800 and R-4360.

As the R-4360 had the same diameter and frontal area as the R-2800 but offered 50% more power, the initial design concepts were very promising.

Fig. 9.54 First prototype of the Pratt & Whitney R-4360. Major components from existing engines were grafted onto this proof-of-concept engine. Note the R-2800 B-series cylinders and a nose case from the X-1800 program. (Courtesy of the New England Air Museum and Pratt & Whitney Aircraft.)

During the initial design phase of a radial engine several key decisions were required, such as the selection of one-piece master rod(s) with a built-up crank or two-piece master rod(s) with a one-piece crank, plain or rolling-element bearings, manifolding arrangements, mounting, reduction gearing, supercharging, baffling, combustion chamber design, and valve arrangement. In the case of the R-4360, new ground was broken for several of the above-mentioned key design aspects.

The heart of the engine was a one-piece, four-throw forged crankshaft supported in five plain bearings, which obviously dictated the use of split master rods. The split master rods were similar in concept to the R-1830 master rods, that is, split and held together with four fitted, waisted bolts and silver-plated shims between the mating surfaces to reduce fretting. Four link rods were attached to the cap, and the remaining two link rods were mounted on either side of the master rod, which rode in a steel-backed lead-silver bearing. Two bifilar dynamic counterweights were used, one on the front crank cheek and one on the rear crank cheek. The spacing of $192\frac{6}{7}°$ between adjacent crank pin journals gave the required helical "twist" between cylinder rows, that is, $12\frac{6}{7}°$ or $\frac{1}{28}$th of $360°$.

Early in the R-4360 program, Hobbs investigated the use of a built-up crank assembly with one-piece master rods; however, the difficulties were apparently insurmountable. Interestingly, the last development version, the R-4360VDT (variable-discharge turbine) reverted to one-piece master connecting rods and a built-up crank.

Five identical cam plates were required, each featuring three lobes, which naturally dictated 6:1 reduction gearing. The first stage of the reduction gearing was accomplished by a split gear bolted on the crankshaft, which drove the second-stage gear mounted on the main bearing caps.

R-4360 cylinder design deviated from conventional radial engine poppet valve technology in several respects. Although the combustion chamber was a conventional hemisphere with one sodium-cooled exhaust and one inlet valve, the valves were arranged longitudinally along the engine centerline rather than laterally. Consequently, the inlet pushrod was situated at the front and the exhaust pushrod at the rear of each cylinder. The three center cam plates actuated the exhaust valve of the cylinder in front of it and the inlet behind it. The end cam plates thus had a redundant track, the front cam plate actuating the front row inlet valves only and the rear cam plate actuating the rear row exhaust valves (Fig. 9.55).

Inlet port design also deviated from convention by incorporating a downdraft concept between the valves. Consequently the inlet manifold, which was made up from four sections joined by short lengths of rubber hose, was routed over the top of the cylinders, allowing a straight shot for the fuel/air mixture into the cylinder and obviously enhancing the breathing capabilities of the engine. Interestingly, this intake manifold concept was successfully used in the 1960s by several race car engines, the Indy Ford V-8 and the BRM Formula One engines in particular.

Supercharging for the early engines consisted of a single-stage unit with infinitely variable drive up to 7.52:1. The fuel feed valve (a similar fuel "slinger" to that in the R-2800) fed fuel into the impeller through drilled galleries. Carburetion was provided by a massive Bendix PR-100 four-barrel unit (Fig. 9.56).

Propeller reduction gearing was conceptually the same as a C-series R-2800, that is, planetary with a large number of small pinions. In the case of the R-4360, 15 pinions were used. A torquemeter was designed into the nose case that gave readouts for torque produced by the engine, or the torquemeter could be calibrated to read BMEP. This was accomplished by allowing the large-diameter fixed-ring gear in the planetary reduction gearing to "float" back and forth on helical gear teeth. As power was transmitted through the reduction gearing, an end thrust was generated due to the helix angle built into the fixed gear. A number of load cells contained the end thrust; consequently, the pressure generated was translated to read the torque or BMEP being transmitted.

Early engines featured high tension ignition provided by seven magnetos mounted on the nose case, each one supplying the spark for a group of four cylinders.

Fig. 9.55 Complexity of the Pratt & Whitney R-4360 is amply illustrated in this cutaway view. (Courtesy of the New England Air Museum and Pratt & Whitney Aircraft.)

Fig. 9.56 Close-up shot of a Pratt & Whitney R-4360 super-charger cutaway. Note the massive size of the blower drive gears and fuel feed valve. Fuel was injected into the impeller via the slinger ring and centrifuged out through holes drilled into it. (Courtesy of the New England Air Museum and Pratt & Whitney Aircraft.)

Crankcase construction was conventional, that is, a five-piece aluminum forging held together with substantial bolts.

Because of the overwhelming superiority of the R-2800 C-series cylinder design, similar construction was used for the R-4360, that is, a steel barrel with an aluminum muff shrunk on and a forged aluminum cylinder head with closely pitched, machined cooling fins. All cylinders were interchangeable.

Under development throughout World War II, the R-4360 made its initial test runs in April 1941, eight months after work had started on the project. Initial test flights were performed in a Vultee Model 85 (Fig. 9.57).

Facilitating construction of the prototype engine was the fact that R-2800 B series cylinders were used, and a number of R-1830 components were used in modified form such as the forging dies for the crankcase and master rod assembly. An R-2800 rear section and carburetor were also borrowed. The nose section and reduction gear came from one of the liquid-cooled H sleeve valve engines. It was initially rated at 3000 hp and 2700 rpm (Refs. 2.15, 4.15–4.18, 9.19, 9.32).

Applications

By 1944 the Kamikaze menace was creating havoc with the Allied war effort, the U.S. Navy in particular suffering horrendous losses at the hands of the suicidal Japanese Navy and Army pilots. Aircraft carriers were a favorite target, particularly U.S. Navy carriers because of their vulnerable wooden flight decks. Consequently, standing patrols were necessary to fend off the incoming Kamikazes. F6Fs and F4Us were used for this duty; however, a fighter with additional speed was required to adequately defend the Navy.

Fig. 9.57 The first aircraft powered by the Pratt & Whitney R-4360, Vultee Model 85. (Courtesy of the New England Air Museum and Pratt & Whitney Aircraft.)

Goodyear F2G

Pratt & Whitney made the first experimental installation of the R-4360 in a Vought F4U-1 (Fig. 9.58). Goodyear was the primary subcontractor to Chance Vought for the F4U Corsair and incorporated many modifications and improvements. Goodyear-built F4U-1s were designated FG-1, and F4U-4s were designated FG-3. The most radical of all these modifications was the installation of Pratt & Whitney's massive R-4360. Sharing the same basic airframe as the F4U, several modifications were incorporated including the elimination of the turtleback fuselage, replaced with a bubble canopy, and the replacement of the R-2800-8W with the R-4360-2. These modifications resulted in the new designation of F2G.

As the "hot-rodders" know, "there ain't no replacement for displacement," and in the case of the F2G the additional 1560 in³ (25.6 L) and 1000 hp performed as expected.

Fig. 9.58 Pratt & Whitney installed an R-4360 into a Vought F4U-1 Corsair, shown on the left. A standard, R-2800-8-powered F4U-1 is shown on right. Goodyear later produced a production version of the Corsair with the R-4360, designated F2G. (Courtesy of the New England Air Museum and Pratt & Whitney Aircraft.)

The first flight was in May 1944; the intended primary mission for this formidable new fighter was to fend off the Kamikazes (Fig. 9.59). As so often happened during World War II, the F2G did not quite make it into the conflict and neither did the R-4360. After the war, the F2Gs dominated the return of unlimited air racing (Ref. 9.14, 9.23).

Republic XP-72

This very promising fighter was based on the Republic P-47D. A new fuselage that used the wings and tail surfaces from the P-47D was developed to mount the R-4360, and all the associated duct-work for the General Electric turbosupercharger was housed in the aft belly in a similar fashion to the P-47 (Fig. 9.60).

Two prototypes were ordered, the first one flying in February 1944. The second XP-72 featured an Aeroproducts, six-blade contra-rotating propeller driven by an R-4360-13 rated at 3000 hp at 2700 rpm.

The Army was impressed enough with the performance of the aircraft to place an order for 100 aircraft. As usual for promising piston-powered aircraft at this stage, the order was canceled in favor of gas-turbine-powered aircraft.

Summary

By V-J Day Pratt & Whitney were justifiably proud of making an enormous contribution to the Allied War effort. The output of aircraft engines was nothing short of mind-boggling. The rate of production achieved during these difficult years has never been equaled and is unlikely to be surpassed in the future.

Fig. 9.59 The Goodyear F2G, intended to combat the Japanese Kamikaze menace, did not quite get into service prior to the end of hostilities. Powered by a Pratt & Whitney R-4360-2/-4 rated at 3000 hp, it was successfully campaigned in the postwar Thompson Trophy Races. (Courtesy of the National Air and Space Museum, Smithsonian Institution, Photo No. 1B-00249.)

Fig. 9.60 Republic XP-72. Using many P-47 design features, the XP-72 was powered by a Pratt & Whitney R-4360-13 rated at 3000 hp. The two-stage, variable-speed supercharger was augmented by a turbosupercharger. (Courtesy of the National Air and Space Museum, Smithsonian Institution, Photo No. 1B-33501.)

In terms of horsepower delivered, Pratt & Whitney engines supplied 50% of the U.S. air power requirements (Ref. 6.9).

From 1941 to 1945 engines delivered were as follows:

Year	R-985	R-1340	R-1830	R-2000	R-2800	R-4360
1941	4,551	5,418	6,441	9	1,733	0
1942	10,233	7,621	22,655	405	11,840	0
1943	14,357	6,012	59,561	1,449	23,726	11
1944	6,407	5,546	65,060	3,164	45,259	27
1945	488	318	12,787	5,755	31,515	114
TOTALS:	36,036	24,915	166,504	10,782	114,073	152
GRAND TOTAL: 352,462						

The above totals include license-built engines. In addition to the above, 24 R-1535s were built in 1941 terminating production of this engine, a sharp decline from the 1940 production of 1269.

From 1938 to 1945, Pratt & Whitney expanded at an exponential rate. Starting with 3000 employees in 1938, just prior to the big buildup caused by British and French orders, Pratt & Whitney ended up in 1945 with 40,000 employees (Ref. 6.9).

References

2.5 Schlaifer, Robert, and S. D. Heron, <u>Development of Aircraft Engines and Development of Aviation Fuels</u>, Harvard University, Boston, 1950.

2.7 <u>Jane's All The World's Aircraft</u>, McGraw-Hill, New York, 1945/1946.

2.15 Ryder, Earle A., "Recent Developments in the R-4360 Engine," Paper presented at the SAE Summer Meeting (French Lick, Ind.), Society of Automotive Engineers, Warrendale, Pa., June 1950.

4.15 Wilkinson, Paul H., <u>Aircraft Engines of The World 1946</u>, Paul H. Wilkinson, New York.

4.16 Wilkinson, Paul H., <u>Aircraft Engines of The World 1947</u>, Paul H. Wilkinson, New York.

4.17 Wilkinson, Paul H., <u>Aircraft Engines of The World 1948</u>, Paul H. Wilkinson, New York.

4.18 Wilkinson, Paul H., <u>Aircraft Engines of The World 1949</u>, Paul H. Wilkinson, New York.

5.2 <u>Jane's All The World's Aircraft</u>, McGraw-Hill, New York, 1942/1943.

6.4 Wilkinson, Paul H., <u>Aircraft Engines of The World 1941</u>, Paul H. Wilkinson, New York.

6.9 <u>The Pratt & Whitney Aircraft Story</u>, Pratt & Whitney Aircraft Div., United Aircraft Corp., East Hartford, Conn., 1952.

9.1 Harvey Lippincott, retired Pratt & Whitney archivist, correspondence and interviews with author, 1993–1994.

9.2 <u>Index of Wasp & R-1340 Designated Engines</u>, Pratt & Whitney Aircraft, East Hartford, Conn., 15 May 1955.

9.3 Bill Gillette, retired Continental engineer, interview with author.

9.4 Kohn, Leo J., <u>The Story of The Texan</u>, Aviation Publications, Appleton, Wisc., 1975.

9.5 <u>Pilot's Handbook for Army Model AT6, Navy Model SNJ-4</u>, British Model Harvard IIA Airplanes, AN 01-60FE-1.

9.6 <u>Index of Wasp Jr. & R-985 Designated Engines</u>, Pratt & Whitney Aircraft, East Hartford, Conn., revised 2 July 1956.

9.7 *American Heritage of History & Technology,* Summer Edition, Forbes Inc., New York, 1985.

9.8 Adcock, Al, <u>OS2U Kingfisher in Action</u>, Squadron Signal Publications, Carrolton, Tex.

9.9 <u>Index of Twin Wasp Jr. & R-1535 Designated Engines</u>, Pratt & Whitney Aircraft, East Hartford, Conn., revised 1 Oct. 1952.

9.10 Doll, Tom, <u>SB2U Vindicator In Action</u>, Squadron Signal Publications, Carrolton, Tex.

9.11 Mackay, Ron, <u>Bristol Blenheim In Action</u>, Squadron Signal Publications, Carrolton, Tex.

9.12 <u>Index of Twin Wasp & R-1830 Designated Engines</u>, Pratt & Whitney Aircraft, East Hartford, Conn., revised 15 May 1956.

9.13 <u>Model Designations of USAF Aircraft Engines</u>, 9th ed., by authority of Commanding General, Air Materiel Command, U.S. Air Force, 1 Jan. 1949.

9.14 Angellucci, Enzo, with Peter Bowers, <u>The American Fighter</u>, Orion Books, New York.

9.15 Davis, Larry, <u>B-24 Liberator in Action</u>, Squadron Signal Publications, Carrolton, Tex.

9.16 Morgan, Len, <u>The Douglas DC-3</u>, Aero Publishers, Fallbrook, Calif., 1980.

9.17 Scarborough, USN (Ret.), Captain W. E., <u>PBY Catalina In Action</u>, Squadron Signal Publications, Carrolton, Tex.

9.18 Creed, Roscoe, "PBY The Catalina Flying Boat," *Airlife,* England, 1986.

9.19 Linn, Don, <u>F4F Wildcat In Action</u>, Squadron Signal Publications, Carrolton, Tex.

9.20 <u>Index of Double Wasp R-2800 Designated Engines</u>, Pratt & Whitney Aircraft, East Hartford, Conn., revised 15 May 1955.

9.21 <u>Double Wasp (R-2800) CB Series Maintenance Manual</u>, Pratt & Whitney Aircraft Group, East Hartford, Conn., revised Oct. 1977.

9.22 <u>Operator's Handbook</u>, Double Wasp B Series Engines (with Two-Stage Supercharger) (R-2800-8 and -10) 2nd ed., Pratt & Whitney Aircraft, East Hartford, Conn., Nov. 1944.

9.23 Sullivan, Jim, <u>F4U In Action</u>, Squadron Signal Publications, Carrolton, Tex.

9.24 <u>Pilot's Manual For F4U Corsair</u>.

9.25 <u>Pilot's Handbook of Operating Instructions for Navy Models F6F-3, F6F-3N, F6F-5, F6F-5N Airplanes</u>, 15 Oct. 1945, revised June 1946.

9.26 Sullivan, Jim, <u>F6F In Action</u>, Squadron Signal Publications, Carrolton, Tex.

9.27 Scarborough, USN (Ret.), Captain W. E., <u>F7F Tigercat In Action</u>, Squadron Signal Publications, Carrolton, Tex.

9.28 Scarborough, USN (Ret.), Captain W. E., <u>F8F Bearcat In Action</u>, Squadron Signal Publications, Carrolton, Tex.

9.29 Freeman, Roger A., <u>Thunderbolt, A Documentary History of The Republic P-47</u>, Motorbooks International, 1992.

9.30 Birdsall, Steve, <u>B-26 In Action</u>, Squadron Signal Publications, Carrolton, Tex.

9.31 Mesko, Jim, <u>A-26 Invader In Action</u>, Squadron Signal Publications, Carrolton, Tex.

9.32 <u>Index of Wasp Major & R-4360 Designated Engines</u>, Pratt & Whitney Aircraft, East Hartford, Conn., revised 15 May 1955.

Chapter 10

Allison

The United States used just one company for the production of indigenous liquid-cooled aircraft engines. That company was Allison, a division of General Motors Corporation, founded in September 1915 by James A. Allison in Indianapolis, Indiana. Allison was also part owner of the Speedway, initially named the Indianapolis Speedway Company, which started out as a well-equipped precision job shop, building and repairing race cars for the famous annual Memorial Day 500-mile race. Plain bearing technology became one area of expertise early in the career of the fledgling Allison company; this experience not only stood them in good stead for the later development of high-performance aircraft engines, but offered a good source of business.

When the United States was inevitably drawn into the quagmire of World War I in 1917, Allison immediately put a hold on all civilian work in order to concentrate on the war effort. One of the prime requirements by the Allies was a reliable aircraft engine in the 300- to 400-hp range. A team of engineers sequestered themselves in a Washington, D.C., hotel room for five days to design the Liberty, a water-cooled, 1650-in^3 V-12 engine (Fig. 10.1) to meet this demand. As can be imagined, the resulting product of this five-day feverish activity was a totally uninspiring and in some cases poorly thought-out design, for example, the 45° cylinder bank angle and the use of coil ignition, which were influences from the automotive technology that drove the Liberty program.

More than 20,000 Libertys were produced by the end of World War I, of which about 50% percent ended up in Europe prior to the cease of hostilities. Allison was involved with the production of the Liberty, initially making tools, jigs, dies, and fixtures, and later building complete engines. Allison also produced tracked vehicles under license from Caterpillar.

At the cessation of hostilities, Allison remained in the Liberty business, performing engine overhauls. Among the many problems experienced by this engine was failure of the connecting rod bearing, typically after 30 h or even less. A bronze bearing supported the connecting rods, which were of the classic blade-and-fork type. Norman Gilman, Allison's chief engineer at this time, studied the problem and found that under heavy loads the bronze would distort, leading to rapid wear and failure. His solution paved the way for all subsequent plain bearing technology, which continues to this day. Gilman developed a bearing surrounded by a steel shell, rather than manufactured from solid bronze,

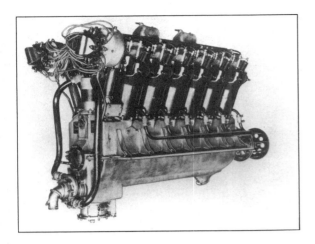

Fig. 10.1 Liberty engine introduced into service at the end of World War I. The vertically mounted generator for the coil ignition is clearly visible mounted between the rear two cylinders. Dual distributors are shown driven off the overhead camshafts. Another typical World War I feature is the use of Mercedes-style fabricated separate cylinders. (Courtesy of the National Air and Space Museum, from the Wilkinson files, Smithsonian Institution, Photo No. A690-E.)

for the high strength and mechanical properties required. A relatively thin layer of bronze was cast onto the steel shell and machined to size. Thanks to this new bearing technology, Libertys now enjoyed a much longer overhaul life measured in the hundreds, instead of tens, of hours. Improved manufacturing techniques and materials would be developed in the subsequent years, but the principle of the steel-backed plain bearing was now born.

Aircraft engine overhaul and modification work kept Allison busy during the lean post–World War I period. Allison exploited the advantages of reduction gearing for the Liberty, which was originally designed and built as a direct-drive engine, in the form of an epicyclic gear modeled after that used in the Rolls-Royce Eagle. Further refinements included an experimental reduction gear with two speeds. Possibly the ultimate on the Liberty theme was an inverted air-cooled 1410-in^3 version of this versatile engine, again developed by Allison (Fig. 10.2).

Requirements for a two-stroke diesel to power a Navy blimp gave Allison its first opportunity to design an aircraft engine from scratch. Through no fault of the engine, the project was canceled primarily because of the difficulty of recovering ballast water from the exhaust of a two-stroke engine.

Fig. 10.2 Inverted air-cooled engine developed by Allison. Based on the water-cooled, World War I era V-12 Liberty. (Courtesy of the National Air and Space Museum, from the Wilkinson files, Smithsonian Institution, Photo No. A692.)

This difficulty may have been caused by the following: The higher exhaust flow from the two-stroke engine created more exhaust that needed to be cooled to below the dew point; consequently, the condensers were larger than those on the alternative otto-cycle engine. The fact that two-cycle engines may not have had enough pumping pressure available, adversely affecting the all-important scavenging, was another problem.

Allison not only gained experience in the areas of transmissions, gears, and bearings, but advanced the state of the art for these critical components during the 1920s. Customers for propeller reduction gearing and crankshaft bearings included Wright Aeronautical and Curtiss.

Jim Allison started to distance himself from the day-to-day operation of the company during the 1920s to concentrate on his considerable real estate holdings in South Florida, where the market was booming during this time. Allison died suddenly following a short illness on 4 August 1928. A period of uncertainty followed his death, although the work of the company continued. As Allison did not have any heirs, the company was put on the block with the stipulation that it remain in the Indianapolis area. On New Year's day 1929, the announcement was made that Fisher & Company of Detroit were the new owners. Interestingly, Eddie Rickenbacker—the famous World War I fighter ace, one-time owner of the Indianapolis Speedway, and later chief executive of Eastern Airlines—was named president. The Fisher era came to an end after just a scant three months when the company was sold to General Motors on 24 March 1929. The purchase price was $600,000 plus $200,000 for improvements. Two buildings plus 14 acres attached to the hallowed speedway were included in the purchase price. The acquisition of Allison was only a small part of General Motors' strategic plans to enter the burgeoning aviation business of the 1920s. The Allison purchase, despite being the smallest, turned out to be one of the most significant as events unfolded. Other aviation-related General Motors' acquisitions during this time included a 24% stake in Bendix and a 40% interest in Fokker Aircraft of America.

A massive 4520-in^3 air-cooled 24-cylinder X engine was Allison's first effort at developing an aircraft power plant. A single prototype was manufactured in 1924 that developed a respectable, for those days, 1200 hp; however, it never went into production or even flew.

Dirigibles seemed to point the way of the future in the early 1930s. The Navy was so enamored with this branch of aviation that several large and ambitious projects were undertaken. The first of these aerial behemoths was the Shenandoah, which featured exquisitely designed and manufactured reversible propeller drives from Allison. The reduction gearing featured 90° drives and extension shafts, the design experience of which would be put to good use in later years.

After the qualified success of the Shenandoah, the Navy embarked on even more ambitious projects, culminating in the Macon and Akron, two massive airborne aircraft carriers that were powered by German Maybach engines. The Navy contracted with Allison to design and build a six-cylinder diesel to replace the Maybach power plant. Final shipping arrangements for the engine were being made when news came through that the Macon had been lost in an accident off the coast of California on 12 February 1935. The Akron had already been destroyed in a thunderstorm 4 April

1933. These disasters effectively ended the Navy's experience with large airships, although smaller blimps were used for many years afterward, particularly for submarine hunting during World War II (Ref. 10.1).

In 1928 Gilman designed an experimental, single-cylinder engine designed to run at high tempera-ture and cooled by ethylene glycol to meet a U.S. Army request. Gilman then developed a six-cylinder monoblock engine for a "family plane" using the tests for an experimental engine's cooling system. The depression killed the "family plane" research, as it did many promising projects. From the seed of the six-cylinder engine sprouted one of the most significant liquid-cooled aircraft engines in U.S. history, the V-1710, also known as the "1710," or simply the "Allison."

In 1930 Gilman laid out the V-1710, endowing it with twelve liquid-cooled cylinders of 5.5-in bore and 6.0-in stroke in 60° V-12 form (Ref. 2.5).

V-1710

Several interesting comparisons between the Rolls-Royce Merlin and the V-1710 have been made over the years. By coincidence, they have similar displacements; they were developed over the same time frame, although the Allison was ahead of the Merlin throughout the 1930s, and most signifi-cantly they both suffered many development problems, many of which were not satisfactorily resolved until the late 1930s and early 1940s.

By the late 1920s and early 1930s, engines had been developed with spectacularly high specific power outputs, in some cases, such as the Rolls-Royce R Schneider Trophy racing engine, exceeding 1.3 hp/in³. Therefore, technology existed for obtaining the power, but the problem lay in maintaining it, that is, for the engine to endure a reasonable time between overhauls and run on available service gasoline instead of the specialized "witch's brews" devised for racing.

The first V-1710, built to a Navy order for one experimental engine, was completed in August 1931 rated at 650 hp at 2400 rpm burning 80-octane fuel and driving through a 3:2 reduction gear. Other details included a compression ratio of 5.8:1, blower ratio of 7.3:1 driving an 8.25-in-diameter impeller that yielded the typically modest 630 ft/s impeller tip speed.

Construction of the V-1710 featured a mixture of the conventional and unusual along with innova-tive design. Two six-cylinder banks were set at the usual 60° for even firing. Monoblock cylinder banks, which featured removable cylinder heads, were retained by 14 long studs secured in the upper crankcase. A classic pent-roof combustion chamber with an included valve angle of 45°, which offered excellent combustion characteristics, was used. The two shrouded spark plugs were disposed on opposite sides of the combustion chamber, one on the inlet side and one on the exhaust side. A narrow circular squish band was formed at an angle around the outer periphery of the combustion chamber which provided the necessary turbulence. This was in direct contrast to the abortive attempt by Rolls-Royce at a similar combustion chamber concept with the early "ramp head" Merlins. A single overhead camshaft actuated the four valves per cylinder; a single rocker opened and closed the paired valves. A single roller cam follower mounted on the rocker rode the cam profile, then the rocker split into a forked configuration. The tips made contact with the valve stems, with valve clearance adjustment provided by a ball-end screw.

Individual exhaust ports were provided for each valve rather than siamesing them, which was the more usual practice. Most applications used six ejector stacks per side (see Fig. 2.8), and the design of the stack siamesed the individual exhaust ports. Some applications used twelve stacks per side or one per valve. This did not apply to turbosupercharged applications, which used a manifold to pipe the gases to the turbine unit.

Cylinder liners, manufactured from carburized hardened forged steel, were shrunk into the cylinder head. Gas loads were sealed by a flange machined on the outside diameter of the liner, which was located on the undersurface of the head. The cast aluminum monoblock cylinder bank assembly was secured to the head by way of six large diameter nuts screwed onto the outside diameter of each liner. Each nut required a whopping 2200 lb-ft of tightening torque. A manifold with metered openings directed coolant flow through the cylinder banks, ensuring even distribution. An interesting feature of the Allison coolant jacket design was the dual turbulent flow and stagnant areas built in. A stainless steel sleeve pressed into the "corrugated" section of the coolant jacket allowed unrestricted, turbulent flow around the wet liners, but severely restricted flow between the jacket and stainless liner (Ref. 10.2). This design protected the cylinder from thermal shock by acting as a "cushion" in the event of sudden and drastic power changes. Support of the 120°, six-throw, seven main bearing crankshaft was unusual and innovative. Main bearing support rigidity is crucial in a high-performance engine, and in the case of the Allison a one-piece cradle incorporating all seven main bearing caps was used. Lower half crankcase functions were incorporated into the main bearing cradle, essentially a semimonocoque structure attached to the upper half crankcase on the main bearing centerline. A narrow magnesium oil pan had the dual function of collecting scavenge oil and allowing access to the main bearing attach bolts. Connecting rod design was of the conventional blade-and-fork concept. Notable features were the size and strength of these highly stressed components, features that did not escape the attention of postwar unlimited air racers, who adapted the Allison connecting rods for use in Rolls-Royce Merlins. Bearing gender for the blade rod was reversed; that is, the journal was the female component formed on the inside of the rod, and the bearing component was created on the center portion of the outside diameter of the steel-backed nickel/silver tin bearing.

Reduction gearing, like many other features, bucked existing trends, but in this case severe problems were experienced that would take years and several total redesigns to satisfactorily resolve. The prototype V-1710 reduction gear featured an overhung pinion off the crankshaft driving an internal type reduction gear. Support for the reduction gear was provided by a large 10-in-diameter journal ground on the outside diameter, which rode in a lead bronze plain bearing. A rolling-element thrust bearing at the front of the extended nose case offered support and handled propeller thrust loads. A more central location of the propeller shaft in relation to the engine offered less installed drag with this reduction gear concept and catered to the 1930s penchant for streamline. Many observers incorrectly assume the early V-1710s (A and C models) had epicyclic reduction gears because of the apparent symmetry of the reduction gear.

The supercharger drive, which tapped off the outside of the propeller reduction gear, was driven by a long quill shaft that extended the length of the engine and ran inside the V. The single magneto, camshafts, and all the accessories were driven from the same quill shaft. Although no reported problems were noted in service, the torsional flexibility of the quill shaft must have adversely affected the critical valve and ignition timing functions.

By 1932 a satisfactory 50-h development test had been run with a rating of 750 hp at 2400 rpm; the increase in power was mainly attributable to an increase in the blower ratio to 8.0:1. At this stage of development, the Navy decided to use the V-1710 for airship use, designating it V-1710B. Several major changes were required for the intended new role, including the requirement for reversing and elimination of the supercharger. Considerable development time was spent designing-in the new requirements, particularly the reversing feature, which involved a shifting mechanism for the camshafts, magneto, and distributor finger. Full reversing could be achieved in 8 seconds.

The airship project was dropped in 1935, after the accidents with the Akron and Macon. At this time, the Army took an interest and resumed funding. (The Army purchased its first V-1710 in December 1932.) Several improvements were incorporated, including lengthening the nose case for improved aerodynamics, stiffening the crankcase, and enlarging the supercharger impeller to a 9½-in diameter. These developments resulted in the V-1710-C, which was to remain in production with various updates until 1940. The first C Model engine, the C1, was rated at 800 hp at 2400 rpm and improved to 1000 hp in 1935. Although some problems surfaced during the initial test runs, they were soon resolved. Encouraged by the promising performance of the revamped engine, Allison submitted the C1 for a type test at 1000 hp at 2650 rpm. The type test required a run of 150 h in a simulated aircraft mounting driving a flight airscrew. This gave the Allison engineers an unexpected and unpleasant surprise. Prior to the type test, engine testing had been conducted with test clubs or on a dynamometer with undeveloped mounting systems. The aircraft engine mount and flight propeller placed unforeseen gyroscopic and fatigue loads on the engine.

Consequently, the remainder of 1935 was spent resolving the problems that surfaced during the abortive attempt at a type test. The major problems centered around the crankshaft and the overhung pinion for the propeller reduction gearing. Legend has it that Fred Duesenberg of automobile fame was brought in as a consultant in an attempt to resolve the crankshaft failures. By 1936 a new engineer, Ron Hazen, who soon rose to be Chief Engineer succeeding Norman Gilman who retired in 1937, was brought in to troubleshoot the difficulties with the V-1710. Failures of the pinion gear were resolved by using an "internal" driveshaft mounted inside the propeller shaft and attached at its end. The torsional flexibility offered by this arrangement dampened the problematic 1½- and second-order vibratory modes that previously created havoc with this component. A friction clutch was provided at the reduction gear, which attenuated first- and second-order vibratory modes caused by the relative movement between the inner driveshaft and the propeller shaft.

As the more serious problems were resolved, other failures bubbled to the surface resulting in design modifications to the combustion chamber, pistons, and piston rings, a change of valve timing, an increase of the compression ratio from 5.8:1 to 6.0:1, and a reduction of the blower ratio from 8.77:1 to 8.0:1. Hazen totally revamped the intake manifold design and gave the V-1710 its classic "Ram's

Horn" configuration, resulting in significantly improved mixture distribution (Fig. 10.3). Hazen's new intake consisted of a short tubular plenum terminating approximately in the center of the cylinder block. Two discharges fed a pair of six-cylinder manifolds that distributed the mixture through two three-cylinder branches (Ref. 10.3). A flame trap situated between the manifold and plenum extinguished any backfires and, according to Hazen, improved mixture distribution. Interestingly and inexplicably, the last production V-1710s manufactured at the end of World War II and later deleted this essential piece of hardware with catastrophic consequences in the case of induction system backfires. The redesigned engine was resubmitted for a 150-hour type-test run. Although dramatically improved, a cylinder head failure occurred 141 h into the run resulting in a penalty run. The other cylinder head suffered the same type of failure during the penalty run. At maximum power, flexing of the crankcase resulted in a cylinder head crack between the No. 3 and No. 4 cylinders, that is, in the middle. The fix was relatively easy; the addition of some appropriate reinforcement to the crankcase consequently improved its beam strength and eliminated the cylinder head cracks (Ref. 2.5). This failure illustrated the importance of how all the major components work together and the impact that a weakness on one of these components has on the rest of the engine. The advantage of a monoblock engine compared to a separate cylinder concept is also illustrated.

Finally, early in 1937, the V-1710-C8 passed its 150-h type test rated at 1000 hp, and it was the first military engine to pass the 1000-hp milestone. Across the Atlantic in England, Rolls-Royce was struggling to get the Merlin through a relaxed type test at 990-hp during the same time frame. Thus it can be seen that the Allison V-1710 was ahead in development at this time (Fig. 10.4).

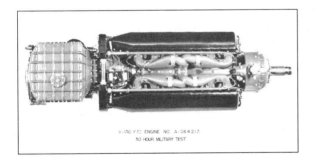

Fig. 10.3 Top view of the Allison V-1710-119 (F32R). Streamlined "ram's horn" intake manifold is shown to good advantage in this shot. (Courtesy of Jack Wetzler.)

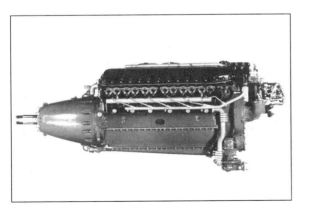

Fig. 10.4 Allison V-1710 C series. The long nose case is evident in this shot. The internal spur reduction gearing gave constant problems. Aircraft powered with the C-series engine were the most aesthetically pleasing; the early P-40s and the XP-38s were two examples. (Courtesy of the National Air and Space Museum, Smithsonian Institution, Photo No. 72-4118.)

With the exception of the B model, *all* V-1710s were supercharged by way of the engine-driven geared supercharger and in some applications supplemented by a General Electric turbosupercharger or an Allison-built auxiliary stage mechanically driven supercharger. Many references to World War II applications refer to "unsupercharged Allisons." This statement is simply not true!

Early Applications

Some limited test flying had taken place during all this frantic development. December 1936 saw the first flight of the new engine in a Consolidated XA-11A, four months prior to its successful type test. The Curtiss XP-37 and Bell XFM-1 (Fig. 10.5) and YFM-1 Airacuda or Fighter Multipurpose followed on the heels of the Consolidated.

Seldom has an aircraft been so misconceived as the Airacuda; fortunately only a relative few were built. Although it was intended as a heavy twin-engine long-range fighter, the performance was so poor that it was slower than the bombers it was supposed to protect. The two V-1710s mounted on top of the wing drove pusher propellers through extension shafts. Modifications required for the pusher configuration demanded a new designation; consequently, the FM-1s were powered by D-model engines, which were essentially the same as the C-model engines except for the extended propeller shaft. Considering that the entire development staff at Allison consisted of only 25 engineers at this

Fig. 10.5 It is fortunate the Bell XFM-1 never saw combat. Although it was an innovative design, performance was abysmal. The General Electric turbosuperchargers were still undergoing development and consequently suffered numerous problems. Emergency exit by crew members in the wing-mounted cupolas was almost impossible. Powered by V-1710-13s rated at 1150 hp, this power could be maintained to 25,000 ft with the engine-driven supercharger supplemented by the General Electric turbosupercharger. (Courtesy of the National Air and Space Museum, Smithsonian Institution, Photo No. 13811AC.)

time, it is remarkable that so many major design changes were incorporated. Turbosupercharging was also introduced with the XFM-1. General Electric was still experiencing problems with the development of the Type B turbosupercharger at this time due to explosions of the turbine and fires; consequently the last YFM-1s had the turbosupercharger removed. By 1942 all remaining YFM-1s had been relegated to nonflying status (Ref. 9.14).

Curtiss XP-37

Curtiss modified the airframe of the Model 75 Hawk to accommodate the V-1710, moving the cockpit aft to balance the longer engine, which was longer than the Hawk's Pratt & Whitney R-1830 engine, thus creating the XP-37. The XP-37 looked more like a 1930s-style race plane than a military fighter, which was not surprising considering it was designed by Don Berlin, who had designed a number of prewar racers.

As in the Bell YFM-1, engine boosting was assisted with a General Electric turbosupercharger, mounted under the cowling for improved altitude performance. Numerous technical problems, primarily with the still undeveloped turbosupercharger controls, forced the cancellation of the P-37 project in 1939 after a total of 13 aircraft (14 including the XP-37) had been delivered (Ref. 9.14).

Manufacture

Orders from the British and French injected new life into the Allison program (just as they had at Pratt & Whitney), and at last economic light was starting to show at the end of the Depression Tunnel. General Motors' management put in place a rapid expansion program that resulted in the construction of a 360,000-square-foot factory in Indianapolis. Production at the new facility started in February 1940. Only 20% of the 7000 parts needed to build a V-1710 were manufactured by Allison. The remaining 80% were manufactured by other General Motors divisions and subcontractors. Cadillac was the biggest contributor, supplying 750 parts including crankshafts, connecting rods, and reduction gears. Delco Remy, another General Motors division, furnished aluminum and magnesium castings and not unnaturally the ignition system (Refs. 2.7, 10.1).

E and F Model V-1710 Engines

V-1710 E

Bell Aircraft embarked on another unconventional aircraft, the P-39, developed concurrently with the FM-1. Two features that distanced this very different fighter aircraft from its peers were the landing gear configuration—it was the first single-engine fighter equipped with tricycle landing gear—and the placement of the engine. The V-1710's position behind the pilot required an 8-ft extension shaft to the propeller reduction gearing mounted in the aircraft's nose. Several advantages were offered by this arrangement, including the fitting of a 20-mm or Oldsmobile 37-mm cannon firing through the hollow propeller shaft (Fig. 10.6).

Fig. 10.6 Allison V-1710 E series. The propeller extension shaft bolted to the front-mounted flange, itself an extension of the crankshaft. The tube running the length of the engine under the spark plugs was a blast tube for cooling the plugs. Also evident are the individual exhaust ports for each exhaust valve. (Courtesy of the National Air and Space Museum, Smithsonian Institution.)

Unlike the C- and D-model engines, the E and F models reverted to more conventional reduction gearing. In the case of the E, a remotely located external spur gear was driven by an extension shaft rotating at crankshaft speed. The governor, gun synchronizer for cowl-mounted rifle caliber guns, hydraulic pump, and reduction gear box oil pump drives were mounted integrally with the propeller reduction gear (Fig. 10.7).

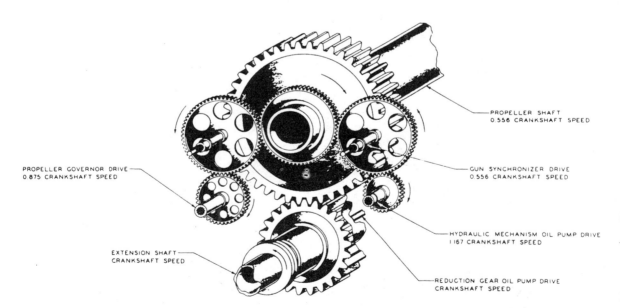

Fig. 10.7 Internal components of the propeller reduction gear for an E-model Allison V-1710. Primarily installed on Bell P-39 and P-63 aircraft. (Allison Service School Handbook, V-1710 Models E and F Engines, revised 15 Sept. 1942. Author's collection.)

Reduction gear lubrication was provided by a dry sump system; one pressure pump supplied oil to the gears at the point of engagement and a scavenge pump for oil return to the remotely mounted tank. Support for the pair of reduction gears was provided by roller bearings, another departure for Allison. A centrally mounted self-aligning bearing supported the pair of 4-ft long, 2½-in-diameter tubular extension shafts which, fortunately for the pilot, gave no trouble (the driveshaft was routed between his legs!). This design was obviously attributable to Allison's vast experience with these kinds of drive arrangements, going back to the 1920s airship days (Figs. 10.8, 10.9).

Supercharger drive for the E and F models differed significantly from the earlier C and D models. Instead of using a quill shaft driven from the front as in the case of C and D models, E and F models drove the single-stage single-speed supercharger from the rear by means of a short torsionally flexible quill shaft through a hydraulic damper/coupling (Fig. 10.10). Camshaft drives and the magneto drive were also taken from the rear, thus relieving the critical timing functions from the torsional excursions experienced by the C and D engines due to the extended quill drive. Ignition was by way of a single magneto mounted in the V at the rear (Ref. 10.4). Ideally, all critical timing functions should have been tapped off the front of the engine with minimal torsional twist in the drive, but Allison, like most other engine manufacturers, chose to tap them off the rear. Dual distributors were mounted, one on each cylinder head, at the rear, driven off the camshaft. Placement of the magneto was not ideal due to the compromise required for routing of the intake manifold.

V-1710 F

The V-1710 F models dispensed with the extension driveshaft (Fig. 10.11), but were otherwise the same as the E model. The opportunity was taken to finally rid the V-1710 of its worst design feature, the overhung propeller reduction gear pinion. A conventional pinion, isolated from the crankshaft and mounted on two steel-backed silver-lead bearings, resulted in a 10-in-higher thrust line. After all the years of grief and heartache Allison suffered with the original overhung pinion and internal gear, it is surprising the engineers did not revert to a more conventional reduction gear sooner than they did.

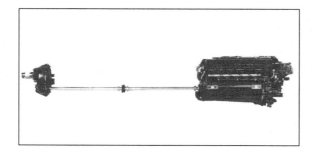

Fig. 10.8 Side view of the E model V-1710 showing the two 4-ft long, 2.5-in-diameter extension shafts terminating at the propeller reduction gear box. Airframe flex and mis-alignment is handled by internally splined flexible couplings. (Courtesy of the National Air and Space Museum.)

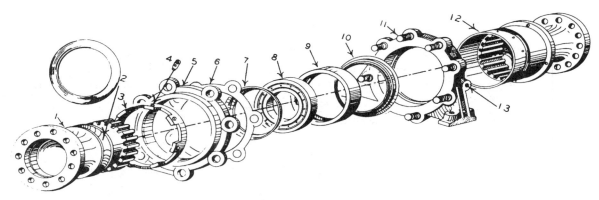

1—Coupling, Ext. Shaft Center Bearing Inner Member
2—Packing, Extension Shaft Coupling
3—Nut, Spanner
4—Pin, Spanner Nut Lock

5—Cover, Ext. Shaft Ball Bearing
6—Gasket, Ext. Shaft Bearing Cover
7—Slinger, Oil
8—Bearing, Extension Shaft, Center
9—Boot, Ext. Shaft Center Bearing

10—Slinger, Oil
11—Housing, Center Bearing
12—Shaft Assembly, Stub
13—Location of Lubrication Fitting

Fig. 10.9 Assembly drawing of the all-important center support bearing for the extension shaft for E-model Allison V-1710s. (Allison Service School Handbook, V-1710 Models E and F Engines, revised 15 Sept. 1942. Author's collection.)

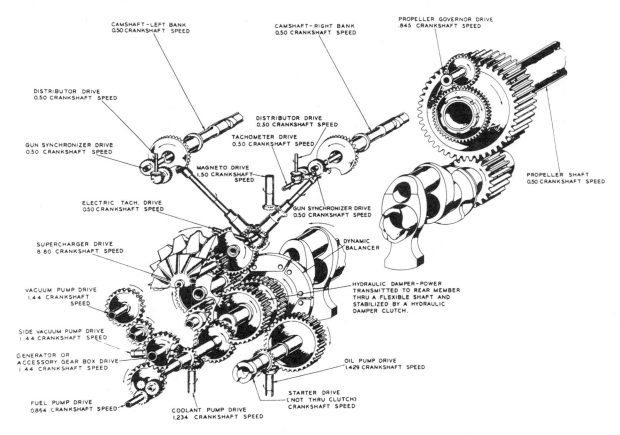

Fig. 10.10 Rear accessory section gear drives for Allison V-1710. Illustration shows F model. E model is similar. Allison Service School Handbook, V-1710 Models E and F Engines, revised 15 Sept. 1942. Author's collection.)

Fig. 10.11 Allison V-1710 F series. This engine eliminated the problems associated with the earlier C-model engine's reduction gear. (Courtesy of the National Air and Space Museum, Smithsonian Institution, Photo No. BA-020650-20.)

Even more surprising is the fact that Allison had been warned by Wright Field engineers in the early 1930s that this type of reduction gear had never been known to succeed! (Fig. 10.12) (Ref. 2.5).

V-1710 G Model

The V-1710 G was the last development version of the V-1710 to see production, and it just missed seeing action in World War II. The only application for this formidable engine was the North American P-82 twin Mustang. The V-1710 G was rated at 2200 hp at 3200 rpm with ADI. An overspeed rating of 3400 rpm was allowed under war emergency conditions, resulting in piston speed of 3400 ft/min, the highest speed attained by any standard production aircraft piston engine before or since.

Two-Stage Engines

The V-1710 was a mixed bag of first-class engineering, ingenuity, and questionable design. Forefront among the complaints leveled against the V-1710 was its lack of altitude performance when boosted only by the single-stage-engine-driven supercharger.

Unfortunately, this lack of altitude performance cost Allison dearly. The NAA P-51 business was lost, and the Lockheed P-38 business would likely have been lost, if lobbying from General Motors had not stopped the Merlin-powered P-38 project (Ref. 4.25). More orders for the P-38 and Bell P-39 from the British might have been received as well. Part of this debacle was caused by the Army's undue influence on the design of the engine and insistence that all applications feature a General Electric turbosupercharger. Consequently, the V-1710 supercharger was designed with the intent that it be supplemented by a turbosupercharger (Ref. 2.5). In practice, this was not always the case. P-51As/A36s, P-39s, Curtiss P-40s, and to a lesser degree Bell P-63s suffered from a lack of altitude performance.

"Too little, too late" best characterizes the efforts by Allison to improve supercharger performance. When Rolls-Royce introduced the two-speed, two-stage intercooled/aftercooled supercharger for the 60-series Merlin, the advantages of this supercharger arrangement were apparent to all concerned.

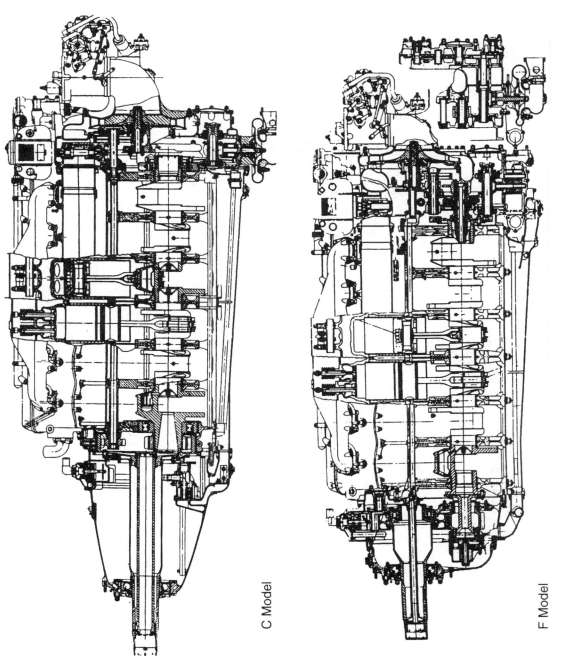

C Model

F Model

Fig. 10.12 Comparison of the C model Allison V-1710 and later F model V-1710. (Courtesy of SAE International.)

Allison followed suit with an "add-on" auxiliary supercharger attached to the V-1710. The supercharger was driven by a jackshaft through a variable-speed hydraulic coupling; the speed was determined by air intake pressure. The auxiliary blower discharged into the engine-mounted supercharger through the Bendix PD-12 injection carburetor. Later developments of this supercharger arrangement shifted the position of the carburetor to the suction side of the auxiliary-stage blower. These two-stage engines operated without the benefit of intercooling or aftercooling with the exception of the -119. Anti-detonation injection offered some degree of charge cooling, which was introduced into the later engines. Bell's P-63 and the experimental P-51J lightweight Mustang were the only recipients of two-stage V-1710s during World War II. The V-1710-119 installed in the NAA P-51J incorporated a large liquid-cooled aftercooler. This engine was also intended for the NAA P-82A, none of which were built (Figs. 10.13, 10.14).

Turbocompounding

In 1941 the first investigations were made into recovering exhaust energy through a gas turbine geared back to the engine crankshaft by means of reduction gearing. Because of the more pressing need of meeting production demand and resolving the remaining development problems, particularly

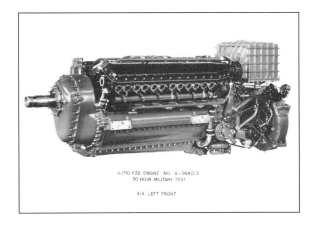

Fig. 10.13 Allison's answer to the 60-series Rolls-Royce Merlin, the V-1710-119. It was installed in the XP-51J, the fastest of the Mustang variants. Two-stage supercharging with a massive liquid-cooled aftercooler to remove 50% of the supercharger compression heat. It used a speed density fuel pump to discharge a precise quantity of fuel into the supercharger, all without a carburetor. This engine was also intended for the P-82A, although none were built. Performance was 1700 hp at 3200 rpm up to 20,700 ft. (Courtesy of Jack Wetzler.)

Fig. 10.14 Three-quarter rear view of Allison V-1710-119. Note the two supercharger stages and the Simmonds control unit for the speed density fuel pump. (Courtesy of Jack Wetzler.)

with the auxiliary supercharger, turbocompounding work was placed on the back burner until 1944. The engine, designated V-1710-E27 or V-1710-127 in Army Air Force terminology, used the two-stage auxiliary supercharger with a gas turbine furnished by General Electric.

The turbine, designated CT-1, was based on the CH-5 turbosupercharger unit. The only major design change to the CH-5 required was the reversal of the rotation direction of the turbine; otherwise it was ideally suited for the purpose. Mounted integrally with the auxiliary supercharger, the CT-1 turbine was fed by dual exhaust pipes, one from each manifold cylinder bank. Output drive from the turbine to the engine was by means of a direct drive through the reduction gearing to the crankshaft; the chosen ratio was 5.953:1; that is, the turbine rotated at 19,049 rpm at 3200 rpm crankshaft speed.

Performance estimates for the E-27 were phenomenal. At 11,000 ft, 3000 hp was estimated at 3200 rpm running on 115/145-PN fuel and 100 in Hg manifold pressure. Actual tests confirmed the estimates; 2800 hp was achieved at 3200 rpm. General Electric stipulated a maximum turbine inlet temperature of 1725°F. In practice, this temperature was easily exceeded. Several remedies were explored, including the injection of excessive ADI to the point where power was falling off. The only solution that offered relief from this problem was water injected directly into the exhaust manifold.

Allison engineers pursued this promising avenue through 1946, when to their dismay the project was canceled. The Bell XP-63H would have been the recipient of this phenomenal hot rod, had it flown (Ref. 10.5).

Diesel Developments

In 1941 and 1942, an investigation was made into manufacturing a diesel V-1710 using as many of the gasoline engine components as possible. Design work was completed, and several single-cylinder test engines were built. The diesel's poor combustion characteristics—the injection pressure required a stratospheric 20,000+ psi—caused the project to be shelved soon (Ref. 10.6).

Design Improvements

Because tooling was in place for mass production of the V-1710, compromises were required in the area of design improvements. If production was not unduly disrupted, changes were made.

Shot blasting is now an accepted method of improving the fatigue life of a highly stressed component, but in 1940 it was state-of-the-art manufacturing technology. Allison was the first engine manufacturer to use shot blasting as a method of improving fatigue life. Crankshafts received this treatment starting in 1941, along with nitriding. These two additional processes made a dramatic improvement to the fatigue strength of this component. As power demands increased, the original crankshaft design, which featured six counterweights, was proving to be inadequate due to excessively high main bearing loads and bending moments imposed on the crankcase. After various design studies had been investigated, a twelve-counterweight crank, "skewed" for economy in material and reduced weight, was designed. The new crank design had the desired results. The main bearing loads and the bending moment on the crankcase structure were lowered, allowing rated operation at 3200 rpm versus the earlier 3000 rpm.

Connecting rods also received similar scrutiny. As power increased and consequently BMEP also increased, the design of the connecting rods started to limit further power increases. The original forked rod featured what was known as the V-type "crotch." With the incorporation of a circular design, the strength of the forked rod saw a dramatic increase. Design improvements at the wrist pin end of both the blade-and-fork connecting rods saw additional and dramatic increases in strength (Fig. 10.15).

Later G-model engines saw the addition of a dynamic pendulum absorber weight fitted to the drive end of the left camshaft, which was a concept similar to the crankshaft dynamic balancer.

With these and other design improvements, the war emergency power of the V-1710 rose to 2200 hp at 3200 rpm with a combat emergency speed of 3400 rpm (Ref. 10.7).

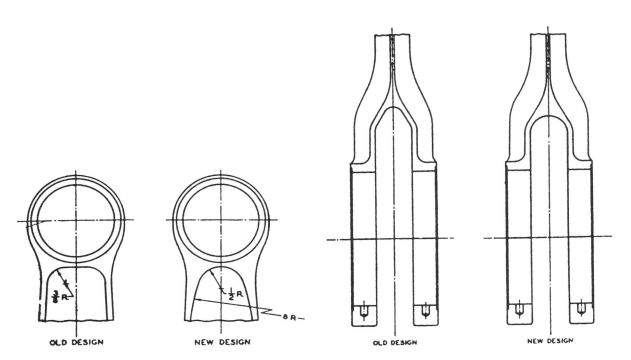

Fig. 10.15 Comparison of connecting rod design improvements for the V-1710. (Courtesy of SAE International.)

Applications

Table 10.1 summarizes the performance and applications of the V-1710 engine.

TABLE 10.1—ALLISON V-1710 PERFORMANCE AND APPLICATIONS SUMMARY

Dash Number[a]	Applications	hp/rpm/alt	Comments
-1	None	750/2400/SL	Designed for rubber mounts and 12-in extension on reduction gear
-3	XB-16	800/2400/SL	Similar to -1 except for relocation of accessories and slightly different carburetor
-5	None	1000/2600/SL	Similar to -3 except for fuel injection
-7 -C4	XA-11A	1000/2600/SL	Similar to -5 except for carburetor replacing fuel injection
-9	None	1000/2600/SL	Similar to -7 except for extended propeller shaft for pusher application
-11 -C8	Curtiss XP-37, YP-37, Lockheed XP-38	1150/2950/SL 1150/2950/25,000	Similar to -7 except for provisions for feathering propeller
-13 -D1	Bell XFM-1	1150/2950/SL 1150/2950/25,000	Similar to -11 except for extended pusher propeller shaft
-15 -C9	Lockheed XP-38	1150/2950/SL 1150/2950/25,000	Similar to -11 except for left-hand rotation; different carburetor
-17 -E2	Bell XP-39	1150/3000/SL 1150/3000/25,000	First of the E series with extended tractor propeller shaft
-19 -C13	Curtiss XP-40	1060/2950/SL 1150/2950/10,000	Similar to -11 except for different carburetor and blower ratio
-21 -C10	Curtiss YP-37	1150/2950/SL 1150/2950/25,000	Similar to -11 except for carburetor
-23 -D2	Bell YFM-1 Bell YFM-1A	1150/2950/SL 1150/2950/25,000	Similar to -13 except for carburetor
-25 -F1	None	1150/3000/SL 1150/3000/12,000	Model designation assigned but none procured
-27 -F2R	Lockheed XP-38A Lockheed YP-38 Lockheed P-38D/E/F	1150/3000/SL 1150/3000/25,000	First of the "short" nose V-1710s. Failure-prone internal reduction gear replaced by more dependable external gear. Other major redesigns incorporated, including strengthened crankcase

(a) Lower designation is Allison's manufacturers designation. (b) 100 in. Hg, ADI, and 150-PN fuel.

(continued)

TABLE 10.1, continued

Dash Number[a]	Applications	hp/rpm/alt	Comments
-29 -F2L	Lockheed F-4 Lockheed XP-38A Lockheed YP-38 Lockheed P-38D/E/F/J	1150/3000/SL 1150/3000/25,000	Similar to -27 except for opposite rotation
-31 -E2	None	1150/3000/SL 1150/3000/12,000	Similar to -17 except for carburetor
-33 -C15	Curtiss P-40/B/C/E/G	1040/2800/SL 1040/3000/14,300	Similar to -19 except for carburetor
-35 -E4	Bell P-39C/D/E/F Bell P-39G/Q	1150/3000/SL 1150/3000/11,800	Similar to -17 except for gun synchronizer and distributor
-37 -E5	Bell YP-39/A/B	1090/3000/SL	Similar to -17 except for blower ratios and different ratings
-39 F3R	NAA F-6A Curtiss P-40D/E Curtiss XP-46 NAA XP-51/P-51A	1150/3000/SL 1150/3000/11,800	Similar to -27 except for blower ratio
-41 -D2A	Bell YFM-1B Bell YP-39A	1090/3000/SL 1090/300013,200	Similar to -23 except equipped with PT-13 E1 carburetor
-43 -F8		1150/3000/SL 1150/3000/12,000	Similar to -39 except improved crankshaft, valve timing, engine cooling, bearing lubrication, and strengthened connecting rods
-45 -F7R		1325/3000/SL 1150/3000/22,400	Similar to -39 except auxiliary second-stage automatic boost control and aneroid unit, PT-13E carburetor
-47 -E9	Bell XP-39E Bell XP-63/63A	1325/3000/SL 1150/3000/21,300	Similar to -45 except E-series engine with extension shaft, remote reduction gear, and independent internal hydraulic system
-49 -F5R	Lockheed F-4A Lockheed P-38F	1325/3000/SL 1325/3000/25,000	Similar to -27 except carburetor, supercharger gear ratio, and ratings
-51 -F10R	Lockheed F-5A/B Lockheed XF-5D Lockheed P-38F/G/H	1325/3000/SL 1325/3000/25,000	Similar to -49 except equipped with PD-12K2 carburetor
-53 -F5L	Lockheed F-4A Lockheed XF-5E Lockheed P-38F	1325/3000/SL 1325/3000/25,000	Similar to -49 except left-hand propeller rotation

(a) Lower designation is Allison's manufacturers designation. (b) 100 in. Hg, ADI, and 150-PN fuel.

(continued)

TABLE 10.1, continued

Dash Number[a]	Applications	hp/rpm/alt	Comments
-55 -F10L	Lockheed F-5A/B Lockheed XF-5D Lockheed P-38F/G	1325/3000/SL 1325/3000/25,000	Similar to -51 except left-hand propeller rotation
-57 -F11R	Lockheed F-5A Lockheed XF-5D Lockheed P-38F	1325/3000/SL 1225/3000/5000 1150/3000/16,000	Similar to -55 except different ratings and carburetor. Equipped with two-speed supercharger and Birmann impeller
-59 -E12	Bell P-39J	1100/2800/SL 1100/3000/15,200	Similar to -35 except supercharger gear ratio, impeller guide vanes, and automatic boost control
-61 -F14		1100/2800/SL 1100/3000/15,200	Similar to -39 except supercharger gear ratio, impeller guide vanes, ratings, and automatic boost control
-63 -E6	Bell P-39D/K/L	1325/3000/SL 1150/3000/11,800	Similar to -35 except propeller reduction gear ratio
-65 -E16		1325/3000/SL 1150/3000/25,800	Similar to -47 except engine stage and supercharger gear ratio. Auxiliary-stage supercharger of Panial design
-67 -E8		1150/3000/SL 1150/3000/11,800	Similar to -63 except larger oil pumps and slight difference in accessory drive
-69 -F18		1325/3000/SL 1325/3000/25,000	Similar to -51 except fuel injection
-71 -F19		1150/3000/SL 1325/3000/25,000	Similar to -69 except fuel injection is made into the combustion chamber
-73 -F4R	Curtiss XP-40K Curtiss P-40K	1150/3000/SL 1150/3000/11,800	Similar to -39 except no provisions for gun synchronizer drives, and increased take-off ratings
-75 -F15R	Lockheed P-38K Curtiss XP-60A/B	1425/3000/SL 1425/3000/27,000	Similar to -51 except propeller reduction gear ratio, increased ratings, water injection
-77 -F15L	Lockheed P-38K	1425/3000/SL 1425/3000/27,000	Similar to -75 except left-hand rotation
-79 -F4L		1150/3000/SL 1150/3000/11,800	Similar to -73 except left-hand rotation. This engine, procured for experimental purposes, was converted to a -73 model

(a) Lower designation is Allison's manufacturers designation. (b) 100 in. Hg, ADI, and 150-PN fuel.

(continued)

TABLE 10.1, continued

Dash Number[a]	Applications	hp/rpm/alt	Comments
-81 -F20R	Curtiss P-40M/N/R NAA P-51A	1200/3000/SL 1125/3000/14,600	Similar to -73 except supercharger gear ratio and equipped with automatic boost control
-83 -E18	Bell P-39L/M/N/Q	1200/3000/SL 1125/3000/14,600	Similar to -63 except supercharger gear ratio and equipped with automatic boost control
-85 -E19	Bell P-39M/N/Q	1200/3000/SL 1125/3000/14,600	Similar to -83 except propeller reduction gear ratio and equipped with automatic boost control
-87 -F21R	NAA A-36/36A	1325/3000/SL 1325/3000/2500	Similar to -51 except equipped with E8 gun synchronizer and different rating
-89 -F17R	Lockheed F-5B/C/F Lockheed XB-38 Lockheed P-38H/J	1425/3000/SL 1425/3000/30,000	Similar to -75 except propeller reduction gear ratio. Also used in P-38J
-89A -F17R		1425/3000/SL 1425/3000/30,000	Similar to -89 except equipped with automatic manifold pressure regulator
-91 -F17L	Lockheed F-5B/C/F Lockheed P-38H/J	1425/3000/SL 1425/3000/30,000	Similar to -89 except left-hand rotation
-91A -F17L		1425/3000/SL 1425/3000/30,000	Similar to -91 except equipped with automatic manifold pressure regulator
-93 -E11	Curtiss XA-42 Curtiss XB-42 Bell P-63A/C	1325/3000/SL 1150/3000/22,400	Similar to -47 except ratings, propeller shaft number, and dimensions
-95 -F23R	Curtiss XP-55	1275/3000/SL 1125/3000/5500	Similar to -81 except special propeller shaft and provision for special propeller jettisoning device
-97 -G1		1200/2700/SL 1245/2700/3500 (7.48:1 blower gears) or: 1245/2700/3500 1150/2700/1500 (9.6:1 blower gears)	First of the G-series engine design. Modified to provide for higher crankshaft speeds, equipped with twelve counterweight crankshaft. Improved rocker arm stud and castings
-99 -F26R	Curtiss P-40N	1200/3000/SL 1125/3000/15,000	Similar to -81 except engine regulator and automatic manifold pressure regulator
-101 -F27R		1325/3000/SL 1150/3000/22,400	Two-stage F-type engine with propeller reduction gear and carburetor between stages

(a) Lower designation is Allison's manufacturers designation. (b) 100 in. Hg, ADI, and 150-PN fuel.

(continued)

TABLE 10.1, continued

Dash Number[a]	Applications	hp/rpm/alt	Comments
-103 -E23		1325/3000/SL 1150/3000/22,400	Two V-1710 power sections connected by shaft to V-3420 reduction gear housing with dual opposite rotating propeller shafts, each with auxiliary-stage super charger: carburetor located between stages, each with automatic boost control regulator
-105 -F29R		1425/3000/SL 1425/3000/30,000	Similar to -75 except counterweighted crankshaft, mechanical accelerating pump on carburetor, automatic engine control, and increased ratings
-107 -F29L		1425/3000/SL 1425/3000/30,000	Similar to -105 except left-hand rotation
-109 -E22	Bell P-63D/E	1425/3000/SL 1100/3000/28,000	Similar to -93 except crankshaft, supercharger gear ratio, supercharger control, and carburetor, located between supercharger stages
-109A -E22		1425/3000/SL 1100/3000/28,000	Similar to -109 except counterweighted crankshaft, and other improvements
-111 -F30R	Lockheed F-5E/F/G Lockheed P-38L/M Lockheed TP-38L	1500/3000/SL 1100/2600//SL 1500/3000/30,000	Similar to -105 except propeller reduction gear ratio, and increased ratings
-113 -F30L	Lockheed F-5G Lockheed P-38L/M	1500/3000/SL 1100/2600/SL 1500/3000/30,000	Similar to -111 except left-hand rotation
-115 -F31R	Curtiss P-40N	1200/3000/SL 1125/3000/15,000	Similar to -99 except counterweighted crankshaft, stronger accessory housing, and wider gears. DFLN-6 magneto and PD-12K8 carburetor
-115A -F31L		1200/3000/SL 1125/3000/15,000	Similar to -115 except automatic manifold pressure regulator.
-117 -E21	Bell P-63A/C	1325/3000/SL 1100/3000/25,000	Similar to -93 except counterweighted crankshaft, stronger accessory housing, and wider gears

(a) Lower designation is Allison's manufacturers designation. (b) 100 in. Hg, ADI, and 150-PN fuel.

(continued)

TABLE 10.1, continued

Dash Number[a]	Applications	hp/rpm/alt	Comments
-119 -F32R	NAA XP-51J NAA XP-82A	1500/3200/SL 1425/3200/SL 1200/3200/30,000	Similar to -101 except lower compression ratio, redesigned accessory housing, aftercooler, speed-density pump in lieu of carburetor
-121 -F28R	Curtiss XP-40Q	1425/3000/SL 1100/3000/26,000	Similar to -101 except auxiliary-stage supercharger gear ratio and fully counterweighted crankshaft. Fitted with PD-12×8 carburetor
-123 -F23L		1425/3000/SL 1100/3000/26,000	Similar to -121 except left-hand propeller rotation. None procured
-125 -E24		1700/3200/SL 1150/3000/22,400	Twin power assembly right and left, each connected by a 24-ft shaft to a remote reduction gear housing, with dual opposite rotating propeller shafts. Each engine equipped with auxiliary-stage superchargers, PD-12 × 12 carburetor, and water injection
-127 -E27	Bell XP-63H	2900/3200/1100[b] 1550/3200/29,000	Similar to -109 except equipped with mechanical feedback exhaust turbine and different propeller gear ratio.
-129		1675/3200/SL 1100/3000/28,000	
-131 -C3	XC-114 YC-116	1600/3200/SL 1300/3000/SL 1360/3000/4750 1220/3000/15,500	Similar to -97 except compression ratio, redesigned accessories section incorporating two-speed single-stage supercharger
-133 -E30	XB-42	1500/3000/SL 1150/3000/27,500	Similar to -109 except 6.0:1 compression ratio and 7.64:1 auxiliary supercharger gear ratio
-135	Bell RP-63G Bell P-63F	1200/3000/SL 1125/3000/15,000	Counterweighted crankshaft (12), outboard reduction gear box, PD13K-8 carburetor, DFLN-5 magneto, with automatic manifold pressure regulator
-137 -E23C		1790/3200/SL 1500/3000/SL 1150/3000/27,500	Two power sections and ratings are the same as -133 and extension shaft and reduction gear arrangement are the same as the -103 engine

(a) Lower designation is Allison's manufacturers designation. (b) 100 in. Hg, ADI, and 150-PN fuel.

(continued)

TABLE 10.1, continued

Dash Number[a]	Applications	hp/rpm/alt	Comments
-139		1500/3000/SL 1150/3000/27,500	Similar to -133 except F-type integral reduction gear is used instead of remote gear box and extension shaft
-141 -F33L		1500/3000/SL 1150/3000/27,500	Similar to -139 except left-hand rotation and slightly different auxiliary supercharger gear ratio
-143 -G6R	NAA P-82E/F/G	1600/3200/SL 1600/3200/SL 1250/3200/30,000	Similar to -101 except change in compression ratio, supercharger gear ratio, larger impeller, addition of water alcohol injection and strengthened parts. All G models featured a dynamic counterweight on drive end of left camshaft
-145 -G6L	NAA P-82E/F/G	1600/3200/SL 1600/3200/SL 1250/3200/30,000	Similar to -143 except left-hand rotation and slightly different auxiliary-stage supercharger gear ratio
-147 -G9R	NAA P-82	1600/3200/SL 1250/3200/32,700	Similar to -143 except cylinder port fuel injection, low-tension high-frequency ignition, redesigned supercharger and supercharger drive, and improved automatic engine control. Right-hand engine
-149 -G9L	NAA P-82	1600/3200/SL 1250/3200/32,700	Similar to -147 except left-hand rotation, slightly different auxiliary-stage supercharger gear ratio of 8.03:1 instead of 8.08:1

(a) Lower designation is Allison's manufacturers designation. (b) 100 in. Hg, ADI, and 150-PN fuel. Source: Refs. 2.7, 4.15–4.18, 6.4, 9.13.

Curtiss P-40

Typical of single-engine fighters of the late 1930s, the Curtiss P-40 was an evolutionary design with roots going back to the YP-37 and P-36. The P-40 was also the first aircraft to see large-scale production powered by the V-1710.

Based on arguments presented by Allison, Curtiss, and Bell Aircraft, the Army was convinced that a medium-altitude fighter should be developed. Among the concerns expressed by Allison were the still unresolved problems with turbosupercharger controls and high-altitude ignition breakdown. In later years these concerns would be alleviated. Improved materials and manufacturing techniques along with revised waste gate controls solved the supercharger control problem, and "supercharging" or pressurizing would offer partial solutions to high-altitude ignition breakdown until the advent of low-tension ignition. Consequently, in 1938 Curtiss converted a P-36A, normally powered by a Pratt & Whitney R-1830-17 to V-1710 power. The engine was a C-model V-1710-C13 sporting a higher-than-normal blower ratio that endowed it with 1090 hp at 2950 rpm and 10,000 ft. Following the concept initiated by the Hawker Hurricane, the XP-40 featured a coolant radiator positioned in the lower fuselage, behind the cockpit. The radiator was soon relocated to the nose, mounted under the engine along with the oil cooler. Induction air was supplied by a simple air scoop positioned just in front of the pilot's windshield. This was later modified by using oversized blast tubes for the twin .50-caliber machine guns mounted on top of the engine. The blast tubes served double duty by supplying induction air to the Bendix injection carburetor.

Although the XP-40 won an Army design competition for fighters in the spring of 1939, competing against not only the turbosupercharged Curtiss YP-37 but other competitive aircraft including the Pratt & Whitney R-1830 powered P-36, its performance was not awe inspiring. Top speed was 327 mph at 12,000 ft, which would have put it at a severe disadvantage compared to contemporary British and German aircraft. The production P-40 improved upon the XP-40's performance with various aerodynamic refinements; the most significant was the use of flush riveting over much of the structure. P-40Bs and Cs were essentially the same, exhibiting a top speed of 345 to 352 mph and powered by a C-model V-1710-33 (Fig. 10.16). The P-40D represented the first major design

Fig. 10.16 Curtiss P-40B powered by a C15-model Allison V-1710-33. The internal pinion gear reduction gear was purposely designed to be streamlined and had a noticeable effect on the appearance of the aircraft. The extended nose case gave the aircraft a sleeker look. Allison-powered P-40Ds and later planes were powered by F-model V-1710s with a more conventional spur reduction gear. Compare with Fig. 10.17. (Courtesy of the National Air and Space Museum, Smithsonian Institution, Photo No. 1A-30972.)

changes not only to the airframe but also to the engine. Introduced in July 1941, the P-40D was the first variant to use the F-model V-1710 (Fig. 10.17). The 10-in-higher thrust line and shorter engine nose case gave the aircraft a very different profile. Deletion of the upper-cowl-mounted .50-caliber machine guns required a new induction ram-air scoop on top of the cowling, which now featured a single opening just behind the spinner.

The V-1710-39 rated at 1150 hp required a larger and deeper chin cowling to house the coolant and oil radiators. All subsequent production P-40s were similar to the P-40D with the exception of the P-40F and P-40L, which were powered by V-1650-1s, Packard-built single-stage Rolls-Royce Merlins. So many variations on the P-40 theme were produced that Curtiss almost went through the alphabet, with the last production example designated P-40R, which were P-40Fs and P-40Ls that had their Packard V-1650-1 engines replaced with V-1710-81s. Although Don Berlin, designer of the P-40, had requested the use of a two-stage Merlin, this request was turned down. However, the P-40Q featured the Allison two-stage engine, the V-1710-121, which endowed it with a respectable 422 mph top speed (Refs. 2.7, 9.14, 10.8).

Construction (V-1710-powered P-40s)

The deep chin radiator location gave the P-40 its characteristic shape and an ideal location for the various "shark's mouth" paint jobs it sported during its operational life. Divided into three sections, the plenum supplied cooling air to the dual coolant radiators and oil cooler. All three coolers were cylindrical and constructed from brass (Fig. 10.18). As a weight-saving measure, later models used aluminum coolant radiators. Coolant and oil temperatures were controlled with multiple cowl flaps in a similar fashion to an air-cooled radial installation, perhaps a throwback to its Pratt & Whitney R-1830 roots in P-36 form. Engine mounting was accomplished by a cantilevered chrome molybdenum steel alloy tubular assembly attached to the four fuselage longerons (Fig. 10.19). Fuselage construction was semimonocoque with flush riveting. Wings were mounted in the lower fuselage and

Fig. 10.17 Curtiss P-40D powered by the 1150-hp Allison V-1710-39 (F4R). This was the first use of the F-model V-1710 with its higher thrust line, created by the new "external spur gear" configured reduction gear. This design was ultimately able to transmit over 2000 hp. (Courtesy of the National Air and Space Museum, Smithsonian Institution, Photo No. 1A-31083.)

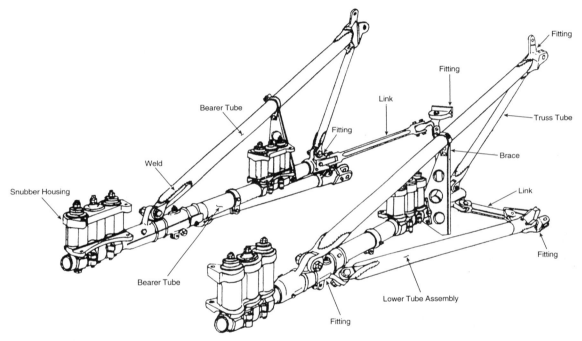

Fig. 10.18 Curtiss P-40 QEC. Note two main coolant radiators and the single, central oil cooler. All Allison V-1710 powered P-40s had this arrangement. The Merlin-powered P-40F had a single, large rectangular coolant radiator and a single circular oil cooler. (Courtesy of the National Air and Space Museum, Smithsonian Institution, Photo No. 1A-31067.)

Fig. 10.19 Tubular steel engine mount for P-40 powered by the in-line Allison V-1710. (P-40 Erection and Maintenance Manual, *01-25CH-2. Courtesy of the National Air and Space Museum, Smithsonian Institution.)*

attached at the centerline, where they were joined. Landing gear assemblies were mounted in the wing leading edge and retracted to the rear, rotating through 90° by means of gear quadrants during the retraction cycle. Prototype P-40s used gear leg mounted fairings, production models dispensed with this vulnerable set-up and opted instead for wing-mounted fairings that folded over the retracted gear leg, leaving the wheel exposed but flush in the trailing edge wheel well. Pilot protection was provided for in the usual fashion with a bulletproof windshield and armor plating behind and in front of the pilot.

The British were the first to use the P-40 in combat after receiving aircraft originally ordered by the French but not delivered because of their capitulation in 1940. As was the case with most U.S. aircraft except for the Mustang, the British were not overly impressed with the P-40C, named Tomahawk 1 in RAF nomenclature, which arrived in early 1941. Among the complaints were lack of armor plating and self-sealing fuel tanks, although this was a result of requirements for the original French order. North Africa proved to be an ideal environment for the British P-40s (Tomahawks) where they accounted for themselves quite well against the Italian Air Force and the Luftwaffe.

General Claire Chennault, leader of the American Volunteer Group (AVG), ensured the P-40's place in the history books when his small team of pilots, no more than 80 at any given time, racked up an incredible kill ratio against the Japanese in China. In the brief time the AVG were operational, a scant eight months, they registered 286 kills against a formidable foe. In July 1942, the AVG became the Twenty-Third fighter group of the USAAF. An interesting footnote to Claire Chennault's P-40s is that they were delivered from England without engines. Allison told him enough spares were in stock to build 150 engines, but they were all out of spec. Consequently the engines were built up and through necessity "hand fitted." These engines then gave better service than "normal" engines!

The 7 December 1941 attack on Pearl Harbor was a total surprise. By the time the Army Air Corps could gather its wits incredible damage had been wrought. All Navy-based aircraft were almost immediately put out of action. The only saving grace was that a few USAAC P-40Cs managed to get airborne and claim some of the attacking Japanese aircraft. Even though it was obsolete by 1941/1942 standards, the P-40 was the best fighter in service with the Army Air Corps at the time.

Production of the P-40 variants carried on until 30 November 1944, by which time, like its counterpart the Hawker Hurricane which also went out of production at this time, it was overdue for retirement.

As history unfolded, the P-40 would be the last Curtiss aircraft procured by the Air Force in large numbers.

Lockheed P-38 Lightning

The Lockheed P-38 made a major contribution to the Allied war effort with a production run of almost 10,000. This large, complex, twin-engine fighter was designed to a 1937 specification, X-603, which, among other things, called out for a twin-engine fighter with a speed in excess of 360 mph at 20,000 ft. Kelly Johnson, along with Hall Hibbard, Vice President and Chief Engineer of Lockheed, designed the P-38 as a twin-boom, twin-engine fighter. Flush riveting, tricycle landing gear, and later in 1944, power-boosted ailerons were just some of the advanced features incorporated into the design. Turbosupercharging was one of the more significant aspects of the new aircraft, even though General Electric was still experiencing problems with the design and manufacture of its Type B unit. As is the case with many aircraft, the prototype (XP-38) was the most aesthetically pleasing of all the variants (Fig. 10.20). The XP-38 used V-1710-C8/C9L engines driving counter-rotating propellers and was the only P-38 to use C-model engines (Fig. 10.21); consequently, Lockheed took advantage of the longer nose case and more central thrust line of these engines compared with the

Fig. 10.20 *Lockheed XP-38 prototype. This aircraft, and the batch of "castrated" (without turbo-superchargers) P-322 versions built for the British before Pearl Harbor, were the only P-38 variants powered by C-model Allison V-1710s. It had a much sleeker nacelle compared with the subsequent F-model V-1710 powered aircraft. Postwar air racers usually deleted the turbos and reverted to these sleek nacelles, even though they retained the F-model engines. (Courtesy of the National Air and Space Museum, Smithsonian Institution, Photo No. 1B-14515.)*

Fig. 10.21 *Right-hand nacelle of the Lockheed XP-38. (Courtesy of the National Air and Space Museum, from the Wilkinson files, Smithsonian Institution, Photo No. 73-817.)*

F model V-1710. The resulting engine installation resulted in almost pencil-slim nacelles. (The British placed an order for 674 Model 322-61-03 Lightnings powered by V-1710-C15 engines, same as the British P-40Cs, which did not have the General Electric turbosuperchargers due to a lack of supply. Both propellers rotated to the right rather than counter-rotating as did the P-38 propellers. These modifications sealed the fate of this bastardized aircraft, resulting in the order being quickly canceled when the RAF realized they had a "lemon" on their hands. Most of the British order ended up as trainers with the USAAF.)

The XP-38's first flight occurred on 27 January 1939 with Lieutenant Ben Kelsey at the controls. Following the first test flights, a transcontinental record run was attempted. Although the record was broken, the XP-38 was destroyed in a crash landing caused by carburetor ice and loss of engine power during the landing approach at Mitchell Field, Long Island, at the end of the flight.

All subsequent P-38s after the XP-38 were powered by different variants of the F-model V-1710. Because of the higher thrust line and shorter nose case of the F model engine, the nacelle took on a very different appearance. The boom-mounted radiators were increased in size and dual oil coolers mounted under the engine were used to improve cooling (Refs. 2.7, 9.14, 10.9).

Construction Details

Layout and configuration of the P-38 were unconventional, although construction techniques followed the by-now almost standard stressed-skin monocoque method. Twin booms supported the engine nacelles, the General Electric turbosuperchargers, the main landing gear, and the horizontal and vertical tail surfaces. The wing was a cantilevered monoplane tapering in chord and thickness and made up in five sections. A main box spar made up the primary structural member for the center section. Front and rear shear members were tied together with corrugated and flat sheet stock, making the whole assembly very strong and stiff. A slotted Fowler flap contributed to the low-speed performance of the aircraft. Later models featured a "maneuvering" flap. The flap was situated between the fuselage and engine nacelle and about mid chord. Maneuverability and dogfighting ability were enhanced by its deployment. One of the reasons the P-38 had a less-than-stellar performance with the Eighth Air Force in England was the lack of maneuvering flaps fitted to their early-model aircraft. A field modification kit was designed by Lockheed to rectify this deficiency. Four hundred kits were flown over to England aboard a C-54. Unfortunately, a British RAF Spitfire mistook the C-54 for a Focke-Wulf Condor and shot it down. By the time a second shipment was ready the decision had been made to phase the P-38 out from the Eighth Air Force.

Pilot accommodation was provided by a central nacelle mounted on top of the wing center section. Armor protection was provided by a bulletproof windshield and armor plating in front, behind, and below the pilot. In addition, later P-38s featured a vertical strip of armor plating alongside the turbine wheel of the General Electric turbosupercharger in case of turbine failure caused by a stuck waste gate. The counter-rotating propellers rotated inward, except for the propellers on the XP-38, which initially rotated outward, and those on the model 322, which were right-hand-rotating propellers on both sides. All three landing gear legs retracted to the rear; the nose gear sat between the pilot's legs when in the retracted position, and the main landing gear retracted into the booms.

Exhaust from each engine was manifolded, joining at a Y junction in front of the firewall. A single pipe routed the exhaust over the top of the wing to the turbine section of the turbosupercharger (Fig. 10.22). The General Electric Type B turbosupercharger was mounted in a horizontal position on top of the boom and supplied air to the downdraft Bendix injection carburetor. An air scoop positioned on the outside of the tail booms, under the wing trailing edge, supplied engine induction air to the suction side of the turbo (Fig. 10.23).

On early P-38s, intercooling was accomplished by ducting the discharge from the turbo through the leading edge of the wing. While this would appear to be an admirable idea as it offered not only the necessary intercooling function at zero drag but offered anti-icing capabilities as well, in practice serious problems were encountered. Insufficient intercooling from the leading-edge intercoolers led to destructive detonation due to high charge temperatures. The solution, incorporated on P-38Js and later models, was an air-to-air intercooler mounted under the engine. A much deeper cowl resulted from this requirement, giving the P-38 yet another profile. Although the new intercooler arrangement solved the problem of high induction temperatures, new problems surfaced. In cold climates, particularly in Europe during winter, overcooling of the induction air resulted in lead-fouling problems for the spark plugs. As much as 8 cm^3 per gallon of tetraethyl lead were used in 115/145-PN aviation fuels during World War II; consequently, lead-scavenging additives were necessary. Bromides were the most common lead-scavenging agents. Even with additives, low induction temperatures would allow lead to "migrate" to the spark plug electrodes, which could cause plug fouling and failure. This was one of the contributing factors to the problems experienced by the Eighth Air Force. Conversely, the P-38 was far more successful in the warmer Pacific climate where low charge temperatures were avoided.

Two lightweight forgings, cantilevered from the firewall, supported each engine along with a pair of chrome molybdenum alloy steel tubular bracing struts. Engine cooling was accomplished by two semicircular, honeycomb-matrix radiators mounted on the sides of the boom, with boundary layer

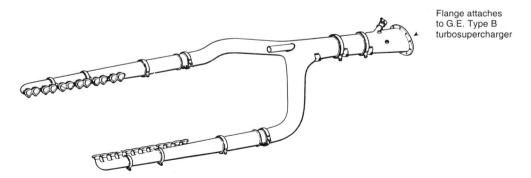

Flange attaches
to G.E. Type B
turbosupercharger

Fig. 10.22 Exhaust manifold system for P-38. Exhaust was ducted to the General Electric Type B turbosupercharger mounted on top of each tail boom. Because of the intense heat from the exhaust, a sophisticated and complex shrouding system (not shown) was installed to protect the airframe from heat damage. (Lockheed P-38 Erection and Maintenance Manual, TO-75F-2, 25 Dec. 1943. Courtesy of the National Air and Space Museum, Smithsonian Institution.)

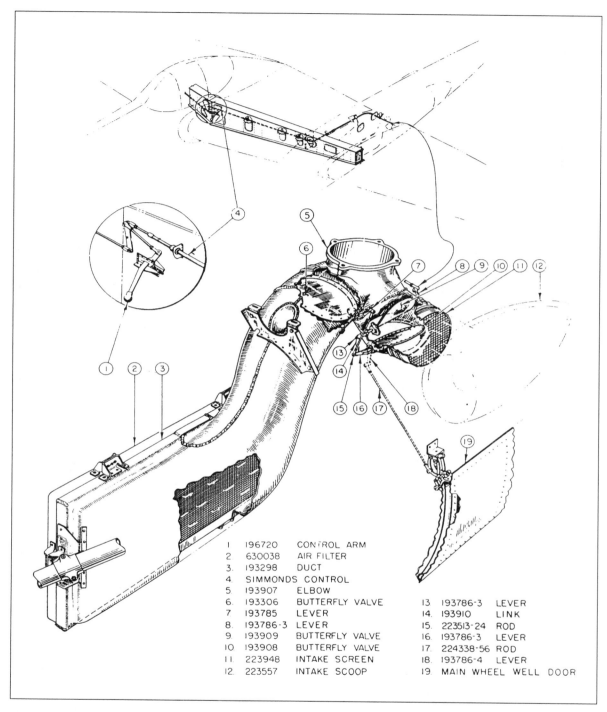

1	196720	CONTROL ARM
2	630038	AIR FILTER
3	193298	DUCT
4		SIMMONDS CONTROL
5	193907	ELBOW
6	193306	BUTTERFLY VALVE
7	193785	LEVER
8	193786-3	LEVER
9	193909	BUTTERFLY VALVE
10	193908	BUTTERFLY VALVE
11	223948	INTAKE SCREEN
12	223557	INTAKE SCOOP
13	193786-3	LEVER
14	193910	LINK
15	223513-24	ROD
16	193786-3	LEVER
17	224338-56	ROD
18	193786-4	LEVER
19		MAIN WHEEL WELL DOOR

Fig. 10.23 Induction air system for Lockheed P-38. Elbow (5) was attached to the suction side of the turbosupercharger compressor. Illustration shows ram air for normal operation and filtered air for dusty conditions. (Lockheed P-38 Erection and Maintenance Manual, AN 01-75F-2. Courtesy of the National Air and Space Museum, Smithsonian Institution.)

control in the inlets. Air was ducted in and airflow controlled by hydraulically actuated exit shutters, one per side. Dual oil coolers under the engine provided the necessary oil temperature control requirements.

Lockheed pioneered the area of power-assisted and power-operated control surfaces. The P-38 was one of the first production aircraft to take advantage of this new technology. In order to improve roll control, power assistance was designed for the ailerons with an 83% reduction in effort by the pilot.

Three-blade constant-speed Curtiss electric propellers were fitted to all P-38s (Refs. 2.7, 10.10).

Service

P-38s contributed to the war effort in all theaters, including the CBI (China-Burma-India), the Aleutians, Pacific, North Africa, Italy, and Europe.

The P-38D was the first variant considered fit for combat by the USAAF. It was first deployed in mid 1941, when it participated in the 1941 Carolinas and Louisiana War Games. After Pearl Harbor, P-38s were assigned to the Aleutians, the West Coast of the United States, and Iceland. The Eighth Air Force was also an early user of Lightnings (Fig. 10.24). Unfortunately, the P-38's career with the Eighth was star-crossed. Severe technical problems made life difficult for pilots and ground crew alike. Cockpit heating was always inadequate; consequently, Eighth Air Force pilots who flew high-altitude missions in temperatures of −60°F below were nearly frozen and often needed assistance getting out of the aircraft after one of these debilitating missions. Extremely low ambient temperatures also caused oil to congeal in the cooler. The high altitudes flown, typically 20,000 to 30,000 ft, compounded the problem, resulting in oil foaming. This could cause bearing failure and in severe cases failed connecting rods due to lack of oil flow and contamination from entrapped air. By October 1944, the Eighth gave up on the P-38 aircraft and replaced them with P-47s or P-51s.

Fig. 10.24 Lockheed P-38H. The supercharger intercooler was designed into the wing leading edges. Limited heat rejection capability from this set-up resulted in high induction temperatures when operating later higher-powered engines at high altitudes. This resulted in detonation and frequent engine damage. From the P-38J on, the leading-edge intercooler was replaced by an air-to-air radiator mounted under the nacelle, giving a much deeper appearance. (Courtesy of the National Air and Space Museum, Smithsonian Institution, Photo No. 1B-14439.)

The Pacific was an ideal theater of operations for the P-38 due to the much milder climate; consequently, many of the problems experienced by the Eighth did not occur. The two U.S. highest-scoring aces, Major Dick Bong with 40 victories and Major Tommy McGuire with 38, flew P-38s in the Pacific theater.

At the cease of hostilities, P-38s were quickly withdrawn from service after almost 10,000 had been built (Fig. 10.25). Still, the P-38 introduced complex aircraft to pilots and maintenance personnel, as well as concepts and criteria that became crucial requirements in the emerging jet age.

North American P-51 Mustang, A-36 Apache, and F-6

In 1940 the British purchasing commission was anxious (one could almost say desperate) to purchase U.S. fighter aircraft. The Curtiss P-40 was already in mass production, and consequently the British approached North American Aviation to build P-40s under license for the RAF. Wisely, North American talked the British out of the P-40 and instead persuaded them to consider a design of their own. Amazingly, the prototype Mustang flew less than 100 days after the contract was signed (Fig. 10.26). Fortunately, much of the up-front aerodynamic work, particularly the use of laminar flow flying surfaces had been done at the California Institute of Technology and by NACA (Refs. 2.7, 9.14).

Construction

Power for the P-51A was provided by a V-1710-39 rated at 1150 hp, the same engine as in the P-40D. Later P-51As used the V-1710-81, again another engine from the P-40, in this case the P-40M. Two box section Y-beams fabricated from aluminum supported the engine from the firewall. Induction air for the downdraft carburetor was supplied by a long scoop on top of the cowling with the opening just behind the spinner. A belly-mounted annular radiator with a circular oil cooler in the center kept

Fig. 10.25 Lockheed P-38 production line in Burbank, California. As the war progressed, final assembly took place outside thanks to the near-perfect southern California weather. The QEC suspended from the overhead crane was for a later model P-38J/L or M. The intercooler was part of the QEC and was mounted under the nacelle. (Courtesy of the National Air and Space Museum, Smithsonian Institution, Photo No. 1B-14410.)

Fig. 10.26 Built to a British RAF specification, the P-51 was one of the finest fighters of World War II. This photograph shows an RAF Mustang I powered by an Allison V-1710-F20R. Aircraft purchased by other than the U.S. Army Air Corps used the engine manufacturer designation for "commercially sold" engines, rather than the Air Corps designation, which for the V-1710-F20R was V-1710-81. (Courtesy of the National Air and Space Museum, Smithsonian Institution, Photo No. 1B-27247.)

temperatures under control. Ductwork for the radiator and oil cooler was carefully configured in order to achieve near-zero net drag or, under ideal conditions, positive thrust. Variable inlet and discharge openings optimized temperatures and drag (Fig. 10.27). Dive-bomber versions of the P-51, designated A-36, had a fixed opening and a variable discharge.

The two-piece, two-spar wing was joined at the center by bolts. The wide-track, inwardly retracting landing gear was mounted on the front spar, and auxiliary doors covered the wheels in the retracted position. A-36 variants featured hydraulically actuated dive brakes on the outer wing panels extending above and below.

The semimonocoque fuselage was made up of three sections: engine, main, and tail (Refs. 2.7, 10.11).

Service

The P-51 (Mustang I) was introduced into service with the RAF in November 1941, and it quickly became apparent that the P-51 was a winner. The British were particularly impressed by the fact that it was powered by a V-1710. Up to this time the British purchases of V-1710-powered aircraft had been less than awe inspiring. Realizing that medium- and high-altitude performance dropped off dramatically due to insufficient supercharger performance with V-1710s, the RAF used the aircraft fitted

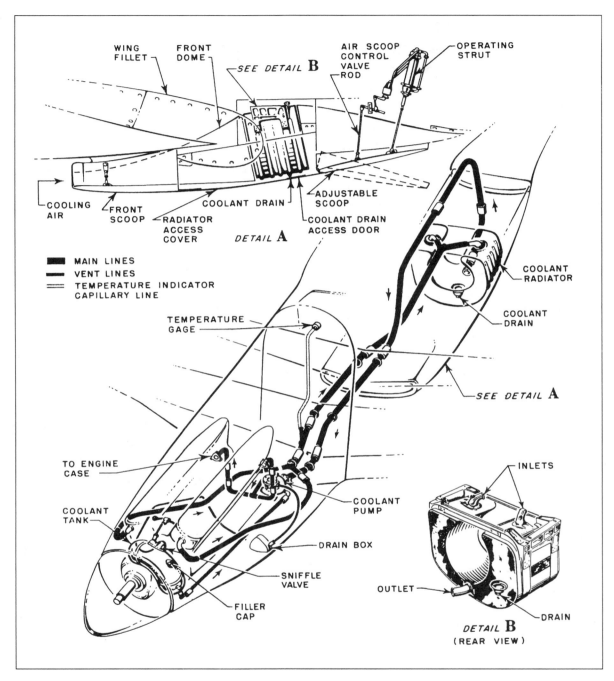

Fig. 10.27 Cooling system for North American P-51A with Allison V-1710-81 engine. Note horseshoe-shape main coolant radiator. A circular oil cooler is mounted in the middle of the radiator. Cooling airflow is controlled by the adjustable front scoop and adjustable rear scoop. The dive-bomber version, the A-36, dispensed with the adjustable feature of the front scoop. The later Merlin-powered versions of the P-51 had a totally revamped cooling and duct system. (North American A-36 Erection and Maintenance Manual, 8 May 1944. Courtesy of the National Air and Space Museum, Smithsonian Institution.)

with two cameras for low-altitude tactical reconnaissance. The British quickly concluded that with a decent high-altitude engine the Mustang's true potential would be realized. Consequently, six RAF Mustangs were flown to Hucknall, the engine installation facility for Rolls-Royce, where Mk. IX Spitfire QECs (power plants) were rapidly cobbled together into the Mustang fuselage for a proof-of-concept experiment. The resulting two stage Merlin powered aircraft transformed the Mustang; all performance parameters saw a dramatic improvement. The outcome was a redesign by North American Aviation to use Packard-built V-1650-3 Merlins.

Understandably, Allison was miffed at losing this substantial business, and this may explain why the Merlin-powered P-38 project was quickly shelved when Allison got wind of it.

Even though a specification was never written for the Mustang, the USAAF realized rather belatedly what the RAF had known for some time: North American Aviation had a real winner on their hands. The P-51 aircraft saw service in Europe with the Eighth Air Force, where it was used for bomber escort, strafing, and photo reconnaissance (designated F-6). P-51s flew alongside A-36As in North Africa, and later the same groups supported the invasion of Sicily. In the CBI theater, A-36s replaced the P-40s used by the USAAC and the AVG.

Overshadowed by the exploits of its more powerful Merlin-powered sibling, the V-1710-powered P-51 Mustang nevertheless made a major contribution, at a critical stage, to the Allied War effort (Refs. 2.7, 10.12).

North American P-51J

North American Aviation installed the Allison V-1710-119 in one of the lightweight Mustang airframes. The P-51J was arguably the most aesthetically pleasing of all the Mustang variants partly because of its very clean cowl design with no induction ram air intake to spoil the lines. Induction air was taken from the main coolant air intake duct. Only two Js were built. It was intended to put the V-1719-119 in the P-82A; however, none were built (Ref. 4.7).

Bell P-39 Airacobra

The P-39 Airacobra was yet another unconventional aircraft from the fledgling Bell Aircraft Company, based in Buffalo, New York. The P-39 was commendable for the innovative ideas incorporated, but unfortunately, the P-39 did not possess the performance of such peers as the Curtiss P-40, itself a somewhat obsolete aircraft by World War II.

Designed to a U.S. Army Air Corps 1937 specification for a single-engine fighter, the Bell Model 4, as it was initially known, showed promise with the creative ideas incorporated.

Defying convention, Robert J. Woods, Bell Chief Design Engineer, placed the V-1710 amidship behind the pilot. Several factors contributed to this decision, which influenced the rest of the aircraft.

In 1935 Oldsmobile developed a 37-mm aircraft cannon. Woods was impressed enough with this weapon to design the P-39 around it. As can be imagined, the recoil from this massive weapon was substantial. Consequently, Woods made the decision to have it fire through the propeller shaft, which in turn dictated a remote drive from the engine. This led to the development of the E-model V-1710, which embodied the power section of an F-model V-1710 and a remote propeller reduction gear box.

At this stage of development, 1937 to 1939, the Army was still enamored with the potential of the turbosupercharger, and as a result the prototype XP-39 had one installed. Mounted directly below the engine, the installation offered good altitude performance as could be expected, with performance dropping off at lower altitudes. The first flight of the XP-39, powered by the V-1710-17, took place on 6 April 1938. Performance was sufficient to impress the Army brass, resulting in a production order for 12 YP-39s. Deletion of the turbosupercharger resulted in a dramatic reduction in performance, particularly in climb rate: 20,000 ft now took 7½ min compared with 5 min for the XP-39. Problems with the General Electric turbosupercharger during the late 1930s contributed to the decision to remove the turbosupercharger; consequently, the P-39 was destined to become a low-altitude interceptor, a role for which it was not originally intended. Even without the weight of the turbosupercharger installation, the aircraft could still not achieve the 400-mph design requirement (Fig. 10.28) (Refs. 2.7, 9.14).

Construction

The two-section fuselage consisted of a rear section that extended from just behind the engine and was a conventional semimonocoque and a forward section of the fuselage made up of two large vertical beams forming the engine mounts, wing attach point, support for the nose wheel assembly, and support for the propeller reduction gearing.

Fig. 10.28 Bell P-39C Airacobra powered by the 1150-hp Allison V-1710-35 (-E4). (Courtesy of the National Air and Space Museum, Smithsonian Institution, Photo No. 94-12675.)

Removable panels gave access to the nose-mounted armament, the cockpit, and the engine (Fig. 10.29). The coolant pump supplied coolant to a single, rectangular radiator mounted under the engine. Cooling air was ducted from two scoops on the leading edge of the wing roots. A single flap controlled mass airflow through the radiator. Two circular oil coolers were also supplied by the coolant radiator air scoops (Fig. 10.30). A 12.8-gal tank mounted behind the engine supplied the oil. Induction air for the supercharger was supplied by an air scoop on top of the fuselage behind the cockpit. Exhaust systems varied from model to model. Some aircraft featured twelve individual ejector stacks per side (in this four-valve engine, each exhaust valve had its own port; that is, they were not siamesed as was the case in some four-valve arrangements); alternatively, six ejector stacks per side were used. Car-style doors on both sides of the fuselage supplied unconventional access to the cockpit. Another car feature was the use of windup side windows.

A three-spar wing mounted the main landing gear and two .50-caliber machine guns. All three gear legs were retracted by a single electric motor by means of shafting and gear quadrants (Refs. 2.7, 10.13).

Service

Although the XP-39 showed promise, primarily due to the turbosupercharger, the early enthusiasm soon cooled down when it was realized that the production versions did not come up to expectations in large part because of the deletion of the turbosupercharger. In retrospect, the fault did not lay with the aircraft design but rather with the continual changes in specifications and roles.

During 1940 the British and French were desperate for any kind of interceptor; consequently, both governments placed substantial orders. Prior to the French delivery, France was overrun by the Germans with the result that Britain received these aircraft. The first deliveries were a bitter disappointment for the British, who, after flying the P-39s on only four missions over occupied France, gave up on them and shipped most of them to the Soviet Union. Australia received the remainder of the British aircraft. The Soviets received huge numbers of P-39s and appear to have made good use of them. The aircraft proved to be ideal, particularly for tank busting, on the Eastern front, which involved a substantial amount of low-altitude tactical support. Finally, the much-maligned P-39 had found its niche. Almost half (4773) of the 9585 P-39s manufactured ended up in the Soviet Union.

At the time of Pearl Harbor, the P-39, along with the P-40, bore the brunt of the Japanese onslaught. Even though it was outclassed by the formidable Mitsubishi Zero, it held the line until later designs could enter service. P-39s saw service in the Aleutians, Australia, and Italy. 1943 saw the end of production in favor of the P-63 (Refs. 9.14, 10.14).

Bell P-63 King Cobra

Although the Bell P-63 is often described as a laminar-flow version of the P-39, this is a gross oversimplification. While the overall configuration was the same as the P-39 (a mid-engine single-seat fighter), significant improvements and design changes were implemented (Fig. 10.31). Like the

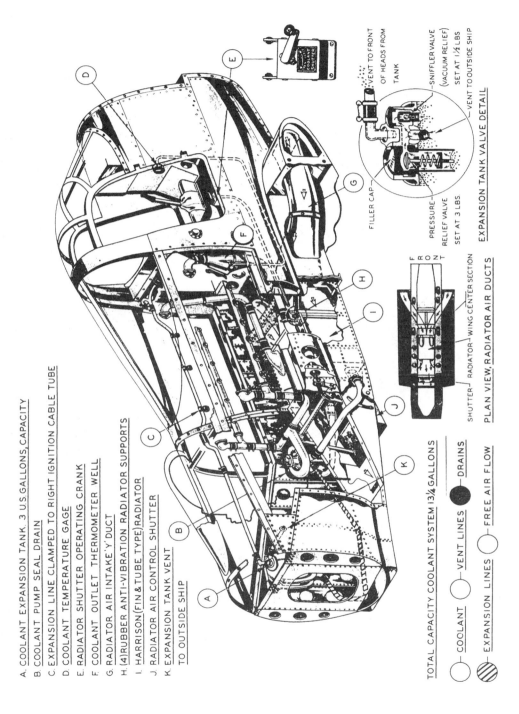

A. COOLANT EXPANSION TANK. 3 U.S. GALLONS, CAPACITY
B. COOLANT PUMP SEAL DRAIN
C. EXPANSION LINE CLAMPED TO RIGHT IGNITION CABLE TUBE
D. COOLANT TEMPERATURE GAGE
E. RADIATOR SHUTTER OPERATING CRANK
F. COOLANT OUTLET THERMOMETER WELL
G. RADIATOR AIR INTAKE 'Y' DUCT
H. (4) RUBBER ANTI-VIBRATION RADIATOR SUPPORTS
I. HARRISON (FIN & TUBE TYPE) RADIATOR
J. RADIATOR AIR CONTROL SHUTTER
K. EXPANSION TANK VENT
    TO OUTSIDE SHIP

TOTAL CAPACITY COOLANT SYSTEM 13¼ GALLONS

COOLANT — VENT LINES — DRAINS

EXPANSION LINES — FREE AIR FLOW

COOLANT SHUTTER

VENT TO FRONT OF HEADS FROM TANK

SNIFFLER VALVE (VACUUM RELIEF) SET AT ½ LBS

VENT TO OUTSIDE SHIP

FILLER CAP

PRESSURE RELIEF VALVE SET AT 3 LBS

EXPANSION TANK VALVE DETAIL

SHUTTER — RADIATOR — WING CENTER SECTION

RADIATOR AIR DUCTS

PLAN VIEW, RADIATOR AIR DUCTS

Fig. 10.29 Allison illustration of the cooling system for the Bell P-39 powered by a V-1710-35 (-E4). For clarity, the illustration does not show the engine installed. (Allison Service School Handbook, V-1710 Models E and F Engines, revised 15 Sept. 1942. Author's collection.)

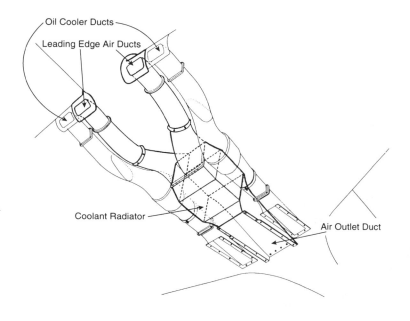

Oil Cooler Ducts

Leading Edge Air Ducts

Coolant Radiator

Air Outlet Duct

Fig. 10.30 Cooling system for the Bell P-39. Dual circular oil coolers were placed on both sides of the main coolant radiator. (Bell P-39 Erection and Maintenance Manual.)

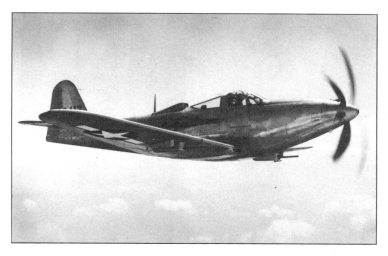

Fig. 10.31 Bell P-63A. The vast majority of P-63s were shipped to the Soviet Union. (Courtesy of the National Air and Space Museum, Smithsonian Institution, Photo No. 1A-07923.)

P-39, all P-63 variants were powered by the V-1710; however, they were usually fitted with two-stage supercharging. This, along with laminar-flow flying surfaces, endowed the P-63 with significantly improved performance.

Fuselage length was increased by 2½ ft to accommodate the auxiliary-stage supercharger. Because of the additional weight of the auxiliary supercharger, the wing was shifted rearward in order to keep the center of gravity where it belonged (Fig. 10.32). For war emergency situations, ADI was provided in the P-63C. Two water/methanol tanks were mounted, one in each wing. Anti-detonation injection allowed a manifold pressure of 76 in Hg, compared with 61 in dry.

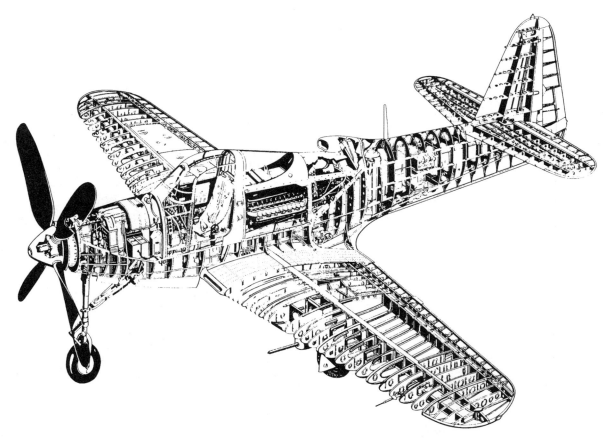

Fig. 10.32 Bell P-63 cutaway. Allison V-1710 sits over wing rear spar, directly behind the pilot. Propeller reduction gear box mounts on circular bulkhead. The structure was very stiff, allowing ± 1 degree of deflection. Still this amounted to a considerable 3.64 inches! (Bell P-63 Erection and Maintenance Manual, AN 01-11OFPE-2. Courtesy of the New England Air Museum.)

With the exception of the XP-63, which was powered by a V-1710-47, all major variants were powered by V-1710-93s, -109s, or -117s. Revisions to the cooling system eliminated the P-39's single coolant radiator. Instead, the P-63 used a pair of rectangular radiators mounted in the wing root area, under the engine. A single, large elliptical oil cooler replaced the pair of circular units used in the P-39. Other construction details followed P-39 practice.

Service

Because of the praise heaped upon the P-39 by the Soviet Union, almost the entire production run of P-63s ended up there. Of the 3303 built, 2421 were shipped there. Few details have emerged as to how effective they were, but considering the significant improvement in performance over the P-39, one can only assume they performed well.

After France was liberated in 1944, the Free French formed an air force with the P-63 as one of their early aircraft. Four hundred that were supplied saw service into the 1950s in Indochina.

One of the most unusual applications for a fighter was the role thrust upon the RP-63 variant. In an effort to realistically simulate gunnery training for waist-and-turret gunners in bombers, specially modified P-63s were used as "targets." Unique .50-caliber ammunition, manufactured from plastic, lead, and graphite, was used. These "frangible" bullets would shatter on impact. To protect the aircraft and pilot, over a ton of armor plating was applied to the aircraft and the engine induction air scoop was redesigned allowing the pilot to raise or lower it by means of a clamshell duct. When a hit occurred, a light illuminated in the cockpit and on the tip of the spinner. This unique feature gave rise to the nickname Flying Pin Ball.

Like its sibling, the P-39, the P-63 was quickly withdrawn from service at the end of hostilities (Refs. 2.7, 9.14, 10.14).

The vast majority of the P-63s were shipped to the Soviet Union, whose government showed absolutely no appreciation as a nation for the massive amount of aid given to them during World War II despite appalling costs in human life getting the equipment to them and the astronomically high material costs.

Lockheed Vega XB-38 Flying Fortress

Lockheed Vega license-built large numbers of the Boeing B-17 Flying Fortresses. Lockheed secured a contract to modify one B-17E airframe, normally powered by four Wright R-1820-65 nine-cylinder radials, to be powered by V-1710-89s (Fig. 10.33). The choice of V-1710-89 made sense as the Lockheed P-38J used this engine on the left side.

The turbosupercharger retained the same position as in the B-17; the primary difference was the requirement for a coolant radiator, which was positioned in the leading edge of the wing. Intercooling requirements were handled by air-to-air radiators under the engine, à la the P-38J.

Fig. 10.33 Boeing XB-38. A Vega-built B-17, the Vega division of Lockheed added Allison V-1710-89 engines. Performance was superior to the Wright R-1820 powered B-17; however, the prototype was destroyed as a result of an in-flight fire, and the project was killed. (Courtesy of the National Air and Space Museum, Smithsonian Institution, Photo No. 1A-12137.)

Initial flights in May 1943 showed great promise, as performance was considerably improved over the R-1820-powered B-17. Speed increased by 10 mph to 327 mph and rate of climb, along with bomb load and range, also saw similar gains. Twenty-nine days after the first flight, tragedy struck when an engine fire caused the loss of the aircraft, at which time the project was terminated (Ref. 10.15).

Curtiss XP-55 Ascender

The Ascender, last of the Don Berlin Curtiss designs, was another attempt by Curtiss to secure a military contract. In 1939 the Army requested proposals for a high-performance fighter. Several manufacturers submitted proposals, all of them unconventional; however, it was Curtiss that won the bid with the Ascender. In retrospect, it would seem Curtiss was on the right track with the canard layout and main wing with a considerable degree of sweepback, but as events turned out the design was a total flop. Several factors went against the airplane almost from the start. First, Don Berlin left Curtiss after he had completed the design but prior to the first flight and therefore was not available for the essential de-bugging. Second, the aircraft was originally designed around the liquid-cooled sleeve-valve Pratt & Whitney X-1800, which promised 2200 hp. After Pratt & Whitney canceled the X-1800 program, Curtiss scrambled to find a suitable replacement, which turned out to be the V-1710-95 (F23R) of 1275 hp.

The V-1710 was mounted in the rear, driving a Curtiss electric three-blade pusher propeller. For cooling and induction, two air scoops were incorporated, one on top of the fuselage, which supplied air for the supercharger, and an air scoop below for supplying air to the coolant and oil radiators (Fig. 10.34).

Three prototypes were constructed, and immediately handling problems became apparent. Brigadier General Ben Kelsey later related that the XP-55 was the only airplane he flew that he could not think of a good thing to say about (Refs. 2.7, 9.14, 10.16).

Fig. 10.34 Allison V-1710-95 (F23R) powered Curtiss XP-55 Ascender. As the Ascender was beset with serious handling difficulties, this project was abandoned in 1944. Allison had proposed development of a V-1710-F16 fitted with contra-rotating propellers. Handling may have improved as a consequence. None were built with the V-1710-F16. (Courtesy of the National Air and Space Museum, Smithsonian Institution, Photo No. 1A-31355.)

V-3420

In 1936 the Army initiated discussions with Allison for an engine in the 2300-hp class. At this time it was felt liquid cooling would be the only way to develop the new generation of high-powered engines coming on-line. Consequently, all the major engine manufacturers including Wright, Pratt & Whitney, Lycoming, Continental, and of course Allison had liquid-cooled projects in the mid to late 1930s.

The Army initially wanted Allison to develop an entirely new multibank engine driving a single crankshaft. Already fighting severe development problems with the V-1710, Allison wisely declined the Army's suggestion and took a more conservative route. With as many existing V-1710 components as possible designed in, the V-3420 was essentially two V-1710s mounted on a common crankcase, a huge and complex aluminum casting for the time (Fig. 10.35). Because of Allison's development problems with the V-1710 during the late 1930s, the V-3420 project was placed on the back burner. This was too bad because this engine turned out to be an excellent performer and one of the few "doubled" engines to work reliably. In contrast, Daimler Benz suffered immense problems with their direct counterpart to the V-3420, the DB 610 series and the DB 613 series of double engines. The entire German strategic bombing capability suffered because of the difficulties associated with the DB 610 and DB 613.

Allison's design study was completed in 1937, and in June 1938 the Army awarded Allison a contract for six engines. Crankshafts were arranged to be 6⅜ in on either side of the engine centerline. The centerlines of each of the pairs of 60° V-12s were set at an angle of 90° to each other, making the outermost cylinder blocks 150° to each other and the inner cylinder blocks 30° to each other. In this fashion, the requirements for evenly spaced power pulses were maintained by providing a cylinder at top dead center every 30° of crankshaft rotation. This firing scheme applied only to the A series, which was not configured for contra-rotating drive, that is, one power output. B-series engines driving contra-rotating propellers and featuring counter-rotating crankshafts fired pairs of cylinders every 60° (Fig. 10.36).

Fig. 10.35 Allison V-3420 A model. The cylinder blocks and crankshafts that were interchangeable with corresponding V-1710 components are evident in this shot. A models had integral reduction gearboxes; B models used extension shafts to remote gearboxes. (Courtesy of the National Air and Space Museum, Smithsonian Institution, Photo No. BA-02077-20.)

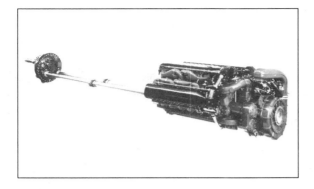

Fig. 10.36 Allison V-3420-23 (B-10) model. Note the two-stage supercharger. These engines were installed in Fisher P-75A Eagles driving contra-rotating propellers. (Courtesy of the National Air and Space Museum, Smithsonian Institution, Photo No. BA-020721-20.)

The versatility of the V-3420 allowed either a direct-connected propeller reduction gear mounted on the front of the engine or a remote reduction gear connected to dual extension shafts as developed for the V-1710 installed in the Bell P-39. In the majority of cases, the extension shaft configuration was used with the V-3420 B series engines, which had counter-rotating crankshafts. In the B engines it was essential to "lock" or "phase" the crankshafts together in order to maintain correct firing sequence. In fact the same cylinders on each crankshaft fired in harmony. This firing scheme demanded "crankshaft timing idler gears," which were installed in the gear case at the front of the engine. The two meshing pinions thus kept everything in time while the crankshafts ran in opposite directions.

A-series engines did not require a "crankshaft timing idler gear" set-up because both crankshafts rotated in the same direction and each crankshaft pinion drove a common propeller reduction gear. This effectively phased the crankshafts together.

A-series engines also had, as a necessity, a different ignition firing order. For smooth operation, it is advantageous to have many cylinders and a corresponding number of evenly spaced power strokes. Deviation from this ideal can, on occasion, induce potentially damaging torsional vibration. Consequently, the power strokes were staggered to alternate between the Vs in the following fashion. For right-hand propeller rotation the banks fire L-R-LC-RC, and for a left-hand engine the banks fire L-RC-LC-R.

For a right-hand engine the firing order is:

> 1L-6R-2LC-1RC-5L-2R-4LC-5RC-3L-4R-1LC-3RC-
> 6L-1R-5LC-6RC-2L-5R-3LC-2RC-4L-3R-6LC-4RC

Allison's cylinder numbering scheme called out for the No. 1 cylinder to be at the rear and the No. 6 at the front, that is, the propeller end.

For a left-hand A-series engine, the firing order is:

> 1L-5RC-6LC-2R-5L-3RC-2LC-4R-3L-6RC-4LC-1R-
> 6L-2RC-1LC-5R-2L-4RC-5LC-3R-4L-1RC-3LC-6R

In the B-series engines, which in most cases featured a remote propeller and contra-rotating propeller drive, the Vs would be timed to fire together with the following firing order:

(1R and 2LC)-(2RC and 5L)-(5R and 4LC)-(4RC and 3L)-(3R and 1LC)-(1RC and 6L)-(6R and 5LC)-(5RC and 2L)-(2R and 3LC)-(3RC and 4L)-(4R and 6LC)-(6RC and 1L)

Accessories Section and Supercharging

The accessories section of the V-3420 was designed to be interchangeable with future configurations and equipment requirements, as was that of the V-1710.

A single-stage, single-speed supercharger, which drove a 10-in-diameter impeller, was situated behind the right-hand V. The balance of the accessories—the generator, the starter, the pumps, and so forth—were then mounted behind the left-hand V (Fig. 10.37). Likewise, the drives were somewhat segregated, except that camshaft, magneto, and distributor drives remained associated with the V they served, as in the V-1710. The rear face of each crankshaft mounted a pendulum-type vibration damper and was connected to the accessory loads by means of a short, torsionally flexible quill shaft, which itself was damped by a hydraulic torsional vibration damper. Supercharger drive requirements were taken from the right-hand crankshaft, as there was no mechanical interconnect between the drives at the rear of the engine. When contra-rotating propellers were used, each was assured of receiving exactly the required power, usually one-half of the total, because of the crankshaft timing idler gears. This would ensure balanced loads on each propeller regardless of what was occurring at the accessory section.

Starting was accomplished by driving the left-hand power section crankshaft through the crankshaft idler timing gears in the case of a B-series engine, or through the propeller pinion gears and reduction gear in the case of an A-series engine. This caused everything to start in concert. Some later models of the V-3420 incorporated an auxiliary-stage supercharger in lieu of a turbosupercharger for maintaining sea-level power to high altitudes. The fairly appreciable power requirements were provided for by a "power take-off" shaft connected to the starter gear, a good selection. The auxiliary-stage supercharger was an enlarged version of the similar unit available for the later versions of the

Fig. 10.37 Three-quarter rear view of Allison V-3420. This example is a single-stage engine; later V-3420s were fitted with two-stage, gear-driven superchargers. The two crankshafts in the V-3420 could be configured to rotate in either direction, hence contra-rotating installations were simple and numerous. (Courtesy of the National Air and Space Museum, Smithsonian Institution, Photo No. BA-02077-20.)

V-1710, featuring a variable-speed drive provided by hydraulic coupling. This ensured maximum supercharger efficiency without incurring a penalty for having the device installed in the induction system when operating at low power or low altitude. This avoided the classic "sawtooth" altitude performance curve of a two- or three-speed supercharger (Ref. 8.2).

Applications

The V-3420 seemed to be the favorite power plant for a plethora of "paper" airplanes designed prior to and during World War II. However, some of these concepts did come to fruition albeit in prototype or preproduction form. Table 10.2 summarizes the performance and applications of the V-3420.

TABLE 10-2—ALLISON V-3420 PERFORMANCE AND APPLICATION SUMMARY

Dash Number	Applications	hp/rpm/alt	Comments
-1		2300/2950 2300/2950/25,000	Four-cycle, double V, super-charged engine equipped with propeller shaft reduction gear and PT-13B carburetors
-3		2300/2950 2300/2950/25,000	Similar to -1 except: different propeller shaft reduction gear ratio
-5		2600/3000 2600/3000/25,000	First of the B series. The propeller shaft is driven by two oppositely rotating extension shafts connected to a remote reduction gear
-7		2600/3000 2600/3000/25,000	Similar to -5 except equipped with two right-angle extension shafts and bevel gears
-9		2300/3000 2300/3000/25,000	Similar to -1 except engineering changes in mechanical design
-11	Douglas XB-19A Boeing XB-39 Lockheed XP-58	2600/3000 2600/3000/25,000	Similar to -9 except propeller reduction gear ratio and super-charger gear ratio
-13	Lockheed XP-58	2600/3000 2600/3000/25,000	Similar to -11 except left-hand rotation and different super-charger gear ratio
-15		2600/3000 2600/3000/25,000	Similar to -11 except different compression ratio, blower ratio, and less weight
-17		2600/3000 2600/3000/25,000	Similar to -11 except carburetor and detailed improvements in structural design

(continued)

TABLE 10.2, continued

Dash Number	Applications	hp/rpm/alt	Comments
-19	Fisher XP-75	2600/3000 2300/3000/20,000	Similar to -5 except two-stage supercharger and contra-rotating propeller shafts
-21		2600/3000 2300/3000/20,000	Similar to -17 except different supercharger gear ratio
-23	Fisher XP-75, P-75A	2600/3000 2300/3000/20,000	Similar to -19 except equipped with twelve counterweighted crankshafts
-25		2600/3000 2600/3000/SL 2600/3000/30,000	Similar to -17 except left-hand rotation
-27		2600/3000 2300/3000/10,000	Experimental project incorporating a -17 and a -25 engine with one engine mounted forward and above the second engine. Connected by two crankshaft extension shafts to a common remote reduction gear housing. Equipped with contra-rotating propeller shafts
-29		2850/3000 2300/3000/25,000	Similar to -23 except provision for 30/70 water glycol coolant. Equipped with auxiliary-stage supercharger, heavier connecting rods, and different rod bearings
-31		3000/3000 3000/3000/30,000	Similar to -17 except increased supercharger gear ratio

Source: Refs. 2.7, 4.15–4.18, 6.4, 9.13.

Douglas XB-19A

In 1935 Douglas embarked on a massive bomber to fulfill the long-range bomber requirements of the Army Air Corps. On 27 June 1941 the aircraft flew with early versions of the troublesome Wright R-3350 radials. The aircraft was flown to the Fisher plant of General Motors in order to replace the Wrights with V-3420-1s (V-3420-As) (Fig. 10.38). Don Berlin, formerly with Curtiss Aircraft and at this time heading up Allison's flight-test department, designed the V-3420 QECs for the XB-19A (Fig. 10.39).

Although a dramatic improvement in performance was gained over the Wright-powered plane, the new airplane lacked the performance of later designs such as the B-29. Consequently, after all useful testing had been concluded, it was used for hauling cargo in the United States, ending its days shortly after World War II by being melted down at Davis-Monthan Air Force Base in Arizona (Ref. 10.15).

Fig. 10.38 Douglas XB-19A after it was re-engined with Allison V-3420-11s. The same QECs were also used in the Boeing XB-39, a derivative of the B-29. (Courtesy of the National Air and Space Museum, Smithsonian Institution, Photo No. 1A-37758.)

Fig. 10.39 Designed by the P-40's designer, Don Berlin, and developed by the Fisher division of General Motors, the Allison V-3420 QEC shown was used in the Douglas XB-19A and Boeing XB-39. (Courtesy of the National Air and Space Museum, Smithsonian Institution, Photo No. 1A-37765.)

Lockheed XP-58 Chain Lightning

Originally conceived as a long-range escort fighter, the Lockheed XP-58 Chain Lightning was another victim of changing priorities and requirements.

Although it was a totally different aircraft, the XP-58 bore a family resemblance to the P-38 Lightning, that is, it had twin booms supporting the turbosupercharged V-3420s and a centrally mounted fuselage pod.

Incredible as it sounds, the V-3420 was actually the eighth (!) choice of power plant for this formidable aircraft. It is surprising in retrospect that the aircraft, ordered in 1940 when the "Hyper" engine program was still in full swing, even got as far as the prototype stage. The XP-58 was originally designed around the Continental IV-1430, an engine that simply did not have the required horsepower for such a large aircraft. The next engine choice was the Pratt & Whitney X-1800, a 24-cylinder liquid-cooled sleeve valve project. When the Navy backed out of this engine in favor of the R-4360, the XP-58 was again left with no engine. The designers went back to the drawing board, and the next engine choices were the Lycoming XH-2470 and the XH-2860. The Pratt & Whitney R-2800 was investigated, but even though this excellent power plant would have been ideal, the aircraft design was not suited to a radial. Consideration was given to the Wright R-2160. Finally, the choice of engine fell on the Allisons V-3420. Sadly, the whole program turned out to be a wasted effort. By the time the XP-58 flew in 1944, the outcome of the war was no longer in doubt. Consequently, the one prototype flew briefly powered by a V-3420-11 and a V-3420-13, both of which were A models driving counter-rotating propellers. After its usefulness as a prototype had been exhausted, it was unceremoniously scrapped (Fig. 10.40).

In retrospect, if Lockheed had been given a more clear direction and delays had not interfered with development, the XP-58 would no doubt have given the Northrop P-61 Black Widow serious competition (Ref. 9.14).

Fisher XP-75 Eagle

Developed by the Fisher division of General Motors, it is not surprising this massive single-engine escort fighter was powered by the V-3420 (Fig. 10.41). Don Berlin, designer of the Curtiss P-40 among many other famous aircraft, had left Curtiss in 1942. Soon after leaving Curtiss, Berlin joined the Fisher division of General Motors and immediately started work on the XP-75. In order to expe-

Fig. 10.40 Lockheed XP-58 long-range escort fighter, powered by two Allison V-3420-11/-13 engines driving counter-rotating propellers, rated at 2600 hp and turbosupercharged for high-altitude operation. (Courtesy of the National Air and Space Museum, Smithsonian Institution, Photo No. 94-12673.)

313

Fig. 10.41 Fisher P-75A Eagle. This view illustrates the F4U landing gear, six-blade contra-rotating propeller, and the ventral duct for the dual circular radiators. The duct also supplied cooling air to the intercooler and induction air. (Courtesy of the National Air and Space Museum, Smithsonian Institution, Photo No. 1A-45320.)

dite the design, major components from existing, successful aircraft were incorporated. The landing gear came from an F4U Corsair, the tail section from a Douglas A-24, and the wings from a P-40 (Berlin originally wanted to use P-51 wings). A purpose-designed fuselage married all these various components together. Power was provided by a V-3420-19, equivalent to the V-3420-B8 in Allison terminology. As a B-model engine, it had two counter-rotating output shafts that drove the six-blade contra-rotating propeller by means of a reduction gear box mounted in the nose. In a similar fashion to the P-39 and P-63, Berlin placed the engine centrally, behind the pilot (Fig. 10.42). Cooling and induction requirements were handled by a beautifully designed duct in the belly of the aircraft. All P-75 V-3420 power plants featured two-stage supercharging. Discharge from the first stage was cooled by an air-to-air intercooler.

Fig. 10.42 Allison V-3420-B, with auxiliary-stage supercharger installed in Fisher P-75 Eagle. (Courtesy of the National Air and Space Museum, Smithsonian Institution, Photo No. 1A-45332.)

Serious handling problems with the prototype resulted in a major redesign, including the elimination of the A-24 tail section in favor of a purpose-designed unit. Even with all the improvements incorporated into the P-75A, performance was mediocre. In a fly-off against a P-47, the P-75 did poorly. Therefore, the fact that P-51s and P-47s now had the necessary range for operations in the Pacific and Europe killed the program, along with an order for 2500 P-75s, in 1944 (Refs. 2.7, 9.14).

Boeing XB-39

Perhaps the best chance the V-3420 saw of getting into a production airplane was the Boeing XB-39. Not long after the prototype Boeing B-29 Superfortress flew, it became apparent that Wright Aeronautical was in serious trouble with the air-cooled, R-3350 18-cylinder radial. Consequently, Boeing delivered the first YB-29 to General Motors for conversion to V-3420 power (Fig. 10.43). As might be expected, performance and reliability were markedly improved; however, by the time the XB-39 was test-flown, the more serious problems with the R-3350 were at least under control, if not resolved.

V-3420-13s (A models) provided the power driving single four-bladed propellers. To expedite development, Douglas XB-19A QECs were incorporated. The engine-driven supercharger was supplemented by turbosupercharging, which offered excellent altitude performance. All coolant radiators and intercoolers were housed in the nacelle under the engine.

Because of the impact on production schedules a changeover in power plant would have made, the decision was made to stick with the R-3350. In retrospect, this may have been a bad decision considering the number of B-29s lost due to mechanical failure (Ref 10.15).

Fig. 10.43 The one-off XB-39 was converted from the first YB-29. When the QEC from the Douglas XB-19 was used, performance markedly improved over the Wright R-3350 powered B-29. The project was not proceeded with because of the impact on production schedules with the B-29. (Courtesy of the National Air and Space Museum, Smithsonian Institution.)

PT-8

One of the more unusual proposals for the V-3420 that actually saw the light of day was the PT-8 patrol boat. A single prototype was built powered by two V-3420s. For reasons not altogether clear, the project was canceled (Ref. 10.1).

DV-6840

An almost infinite number of permutations, variations, and combinations of the basic V-1710 power sections were proposed. One that received serious consideration, although it is doubtful if it reached the stage of hardware being manufactured, was the DV-6840. It was essentially two V-3420s mounted together on a common crankcase, one situated upright, the other mounted inverted. It was a prodigious power plant (Ref. 10.17).

Summary

Unfulfilled potential best summarizes the V-1710. Unfortunately, life can be full of would-haves, could-haves, and should-haves. Poor supercharger performance plagued V-1710 output, and although the auxiliary supercharger alleviated this situation to a degree, the basic problem seems to have been the Army's insistence on turbosupercharging. When this did not materialize in many applications (P-51A/A36, P-40, P-39, P-63) medium- and high-altitude performance declined.

Inevitably, the V-1710 is often compared with the Rolls-Royce Merlin. Apart from obvious design differences, the differences in the British and American cultures show through. Rolls-Royce depended on skilled labor to hand fit many of their engines, resulting in a high parts count with mass production a secondary consideration. Conversely, Allison relied more on mass production techniques that resulted in roughly half the parts count of a Merlin. By the time Rolls-Royce was developing the Merlin, they had accumulated a vast store of knowledge from developing numerous high-power liquid-cooled aircraft engines. The V-1710 was Allison's first foray into the potentially treacherous ground of developing a high-power military aircraft engine. While major blunders were made by both Rolls-Royce in the development of the Merlin and by Allison with the development of the V-1710, Rolls-Royce was able to recover from these setbacks far more rapidly due in part to experience and in part to devoting far more resources and manpower to the project. Numerous Merlins would be on test at any given time, so if an engine failed on test another would be immediately available. On the other hand, Allison struggled along in the 1930s with what amounted to a poverty program; typically fewer than 25 engineers were working on the V-1710 project at any given time and only one development engine was available.

Stronger reciprocating parts resulted in the V-1710 being capable of running up to 3400 rpm representing a piston speed of 3400 ft/min, the highest of any aircraft engine used in World War II. Even today, one of the many modifications performed on the Merlin for racing purposes is to replace the Rolls-Royce connecting rods with V-1710 rods. Innovative features abounded through the engine, such as the crankshaft main bearing support method, the use of advanced manufacturing technologies, and extension driveshaft technology. It has been often stated if the two-stage Merlin supercharger could have been married to the V-1710 it would have been a union made in heaven.

References

2.5 Schlaifer, Robert, and S. D. Heron, <u>Development of Aircraft Engines and Development of Aviation Fuels</u>, Harvard University, Boston, 1950.

2.7 <u>Jane's All The World's Aircraft</u>, McGraw-Hill, New York, 1945/1946.

4.15 Wilkinson, Paul H., <u>Aircraft Engines of The World 1946</u>, Paul H. Wilkinson, New York.

4.16 Wilkinson, Paul H., <u>Aircraft Engines of The World 1947</u>, Paul H. Wilkinson, New York.

4.17 Wilkinson, Paul H., <u>Aircraft Engines of The World 1948</u>, Paul H. Wilkinson, New York.

4.18 Wilkinson, Paul H., <u>Aircraft Engines of The World 1949</u>, Paul H. Wilkinson, New York.

4.25 Colman, P. A., "P-38 Performance Comparison Allison and Rolls-Royce Engines," Lockheed Aircraft Corp., Burbank, Calif., 9 Feb. 1944.

8.2 Dan Whitney, aviation historian, correspondence and interviews with author.

9.13 <u>Model Designations of USAF Aircraft Engines</u>, 9th ed., By Authority of Commanding General Air Materiel Command, U.S. Air Force, 1 Jan. 1949.

9.14 Angellucci, Enzo, with Peter Bowers, <u>The American Fighter</u>, Orion Books, New York.

10.1 Sonnenberg, Paul, and William A. Schoneberger, <u>Allison, Power of Excellence 1915–1990</u>, Coastline Publishers, Malibu, Calif., 1990.

10.2 <u>Allison Service School Handbook</u>, Allison Division General Motors Corp., Indianapolis, Ind., 15 Sept. 1942.

10.3 Hazen, R. M., "The Allison Aircraft Engine Development," *SAE J. (Trans.),* Vol. 49 (No. 5), Society of Automotive Engineers, Warrendale, Pa., SAE Paper No. 410137, 1941.

10.4 Gerdan, Dimitrius, "Late Development of the Allison Aircraft Engine," Paper 450163, Society of Automotive Engineers, Warrendale, Pa., 20 April 1944.

10.5 Gerdan, Dimitrius, and J. M. Wetzler, "The Allison V-1710 Exhaust Turbine Compound Reciprocating Aircraft Engine," Paper presented at the National Aeronautical Meeting (Fall) (Los Angeles, Calif.), Society of Automotive Engineers, Warrendale, Pa., 2–4 Oct. 1947.

10.6 Jack Wetzler, interview with author, 1993.

10.7 Sherrick, E. B., "Design Analysis of the Allison V-1710-G1R Engine 1725 B.H.P. 3400 R.P.M. Power Section Components," Allison Engineering Dept., Report No. 379, 1944.

10.8 McDowell, Ernest R., <u>P-40 In Action</u>, Squadron Signal Publications, Carrolton, Tex.

10.9 Davis, Larry, <u>P-38 In Action</u>, Squadron Signal Publications, Carrolton, Tex.

10.10 Erection and Maintenance Instructions for Army Model P-38L-1 Airplane, 15 Jan. 1945.

10.11 Erection and Maintenance Instructions for Army Model P-51A-1, P-51A-2, P-51A-5 and P-51A-10. British Model Mustang II Airplanes, 15 Feb. 1944.

10.12 Davis, Larry, <u>P-51 Mustang In Action</u>, Squadron Signal Publications, Carrolton, Tex.

10.13 Erection and Maintenance Instructions for Army Model P-39 Series Airplane, 25 April 1943.

10.14 McDowell, Ernie, <u>P-39 Airacobra In Action</u>, Squadron Signal Publications, Carrolton, Tex.

10.15 Jones, Lloyd S., <u>U.S. Bombers 1928 to 1980s</u>, Aero Publishers, Calif., 1980.

10.16 Brigadier General USAF (Ret.) Ben S. Kelsey, Smithsonian Institution Lindbergh Professor, interview with author, Nov. 1980.

10.17 <u>V-3420 and DV-6840 Engine Arrangements</u>, Allison Division General Motors Corp., Indianapolis, Ind., June 1943.

Chapter 11

Wright Aeronautical Corporation

The Wright Martin Company was founded in 1916 and, like many fledgling aircraft engine manufacturers, established itself by building an existing engine under license. For Wright Martin the fortunate choice was the water-cooled Hispano Suiza V-8. In 1919, the Wright Aeronautical Corporation was formed after most of the assets of Wright Martin had been sold off to the Mack Truck Company. Wright Aeronautical continued building derivatives of the Hispano Suiza V-8 into 1922; the last order was from the Army in 1921 for 300 engines. At this time, the Army let Wright Aeronautical know that no additional Hispano Suiza orders would be forthcoming. Suddenly having its bread and butter product made obsolete put Wright Aeronautical in a difficult position. It needed a 200-hp air-cooled radial soon to make up for the lost business from the Hispano Suiza contracts.

Frederick Rentschler, president of Wright Aeronautical and the later founder of Pratt & Whitney, decided the easiest way out of this dilemma would be to purchase an existing company with a successful product. This turned out to be the Lawrence Company, which was building the J-1, a nine-cylinder radial of 200 hp. Although he was initially reluctant, C. L. Lawrence was persuaded to sell the company to Wright Aeronautical, although he stayed on as vice president. The deal went through in May 1923. Soon after the takeover, Wright Aeronautical came out with the J-3, a beefed-up and strengthened version of the J-1. A single J-2 was built but not proceeded with. Cylinder design, particularly cooling, was the most common factor limiting further power increases in the early 1920s. Wright Aeronautical tackled this problem with the J-4 by improving the J-3 cylinder, which had featured an aluminum cylinder with a shrunk-in steel liner. Failure of the aluminum flange where the cylinder attached to the crankcase was just one of several problems with this design. The J-4 engine created the flange feature in the steel liner and used a screwed-and-shrunk aluminum muff over the steel liner for cooling. In 1927, the J-5 Whirlwind, as the smaller radials were now named, created a sensation when Charles Lindbergh won the Raymond Orteig prize of $25,000 for the first person to fly nonstop from New York to Paris (Fig. 11.1). Lindbergh's J-5-powered Ryan NY 1, named *Spirit of St. Louis,* established once and for all the reliability of air-cooled radials.

In the same year, C. L. Lawrence was awarded the Collier Trophy for his work on radial engines.

Fig. 11.1 The engine that got Charles Lindbergh safely from New York to Paris in 1927, the Wright J-5 Whirlwind. Rated at 200 hp at 1800 rpm, it displaced 788 in³. (Courtesy of the New Jersey Aviation Hall of Fame Museum and Gerry Abbamont.)

In 1921, Wright Aeronautical submitted a 1454 in³ nine-cylinder radial for an Army contest for a 350-hp radial. Although the R-1, as the Wright engine was known, came in second, the winning entry failed miserably on test. The Army tested the R-1 at McCook Field, and although the engine developed the promised 350 hp the cylinder design was not up to the task. Sam Heron, who had extensive experience with the design of air-cooled cylinders from his days at the Royal Aircraft Factory working under the famous A. H. Gibson, concluded that the poultice head was the core of many of the R-1's problems. The poultice head design was quite common in the 1920s. It consisted of a closed cylinder liner, with all valve seats incorporated into the closed end of the liner. The cylinder head required a perfect fit over the closed end of the liner for efficient heat transfer and rejection. Because of differences in the coefficient of expansion between steel and aluminum, the necessary contact between the steel cylinder and aluminum head was lost after start-up, consequently heat rejection was poor. A great deal of early Cosmos (later Bristol) Jupiter influence was apparent in the R-1 including the poultice head, the four valves per cylinder, and the compensating device for valve clearance.

Heron incorporated the latest cylinder technology into a cylinder known as the type J. The Army asked Wright Aeronautical to incorporate Heron's cylinder design into the R-1. Exhibiting an early example of NIH, "not invented here," Wright Aeronautical objected to the Army's request, questioning the value of Heron's cylinder design, but reluctantly accepted the Army contract. Although the new cylinders were a vast improvement over their predecessor, new problems now bubbled to the surface including crankshaft failure and other mechanical problems. Correcting the problems with the R-1 resulted in the R-2. Sam Heron made further improvements to the cylinder design including an engine oil pressure lubricated valve gear. The one-piece crankshaft was replaced by a two-piece unit that allowed the use of a one-piece master rod. The designation of the R-2 was changed to R-1454 in 1924 when the Army's new method of engine terminology phased in (Fig. 11.2). Surprisingly, Curtiss bid on the contract and was the low bidder. Heron's influence was also evident

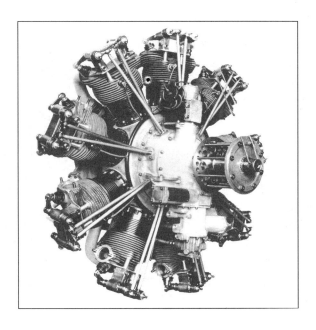

Fig. 11.2 Initially designated R-2, Wright Aeronautical's R-1454 was another victim of the superior Pratt & Whitney Wasp. It was manufactured by Curtiss because they were the low bidder. Rated at 400 hp at 1700 rpm for a weight of 736 lb. (Courtesy of the New Jersey Aviation Hall of Fame Museum and Gerry Abbamont.)

in the supercharger design, which was based on the Armstrong Siddeley Jaguar. Heron had worked on this supercharger design in 1917 along with F. M. Green. Thus the design philosophy for Wright radials for the future was being established, that is, supercharged, one-piece master rods, rolling element-bearing supported crankshafts.

Various delays held up the delivery of the R-2 (R-1454); among them was Curtiss' apparent lack of interest in the project, so it was not until 1926 that it flew in a Curtiss P-1, which had its normal D-12 replaced with the R-1454.

In the ensuing time frame, major events affecting Wright Aeronautical had unfolded, the most profound of which was the resignation of Frederick Rentschler, who went on to found Pratt & Whitney Aircraft Engines. The R-1340 Wasp, Pratt & Whitney's first product, was a world-beater that the R-1454 had no hope of competing with. The superior Wasp, which was almost 200 lb lighter and produced more power, easily outclassed the R-1454.

In the meantime, Wright Aeronautical did not abandon the water-cooled market after the Army decided they would no longer purchase Hispano Suizas. By 1922 the Curtiss D-12 had demonstrated itself as a forerunner in water-cooled V-12 aircraft engine technology.

Consequently, the now technologically obsolete Hispano Suiza was no longer required by the services. Curtiss had gone on to develop the successful V-1570 Conqueror V-12, which was an Army Air Corps mainstay through the 1930s. Wright Aeronautical developed the T-series engines, which were large water-cooled V-12s displacing 1947 in³ (31.9 L). Because of the problems with large aluminum castings at this time, the cylinder blocks were constructed from pairs of three.

The Wright T was intended as a replacement for the obsolete World War I Liberty in Naval aircraft. In fact, the engine mounts used the same spacing as the Liberty, making conversion to the T easier. Development work on the T-1 started in 1921, and by 1922 it was rated at 500 hp, which Wright Aeronautical hoped to increase to 700 hp. The final version, the T-3, was rated at 575 hp (Fig. 11.3).

Like most aircraft engine manufacturers at one time or another, Wright Aeronautical became involved in racing, using the T-series engines boosted beyond their normal rating. Four purpose-built racing aircraft were constructed by Wright Aeronautical and appropriately referred to as "Mystery" ships due to the secrecy surrounding this project. Because the planes were procured by the Navy, they were given the designation NW for Navy-Wright. The NW-1 was flown in the 1922 Pulitzer race, where it crashed because of engine failure caused by overheated oil. NW-2 was entered in the 1923 Schneider Trophy race to be held in England. Despite careful preparation, the effort was as fruitless as the 1922 Pulitzer race. In an attempt to beat the rival D-12-powered Curtiss R3C, the pitch of the propeller was altered to allow an increase in rpm to 2250. Wright Aeronautical had tested the T-2 at this speed and found it was fine for 5 h, then it exploded with no warning. The 1923 Schneider team opted to run at the higher rpm with dire consequences. During testing, the engine exploded causing the aircraft to crash.

Further development produced the T-3 engine with an output of 750 hp under racing conditions. A new aircraft, the F2W-1, was built for the T-3 and entered into the 1923 Pulitzer. Things were no different than in 1922, except that this time the aircraft ran out of gas and was destroyed in a crash landing.

The FW-2, last of the Navy Wright racers, was prepared for the 1924 Schneider Trophy Race to be held at Baltimore. Again, during testing disaster struck when the pilot was scalded by boiling water during his landing approach causing him to lose control of the aircraft (Ref 4.3).

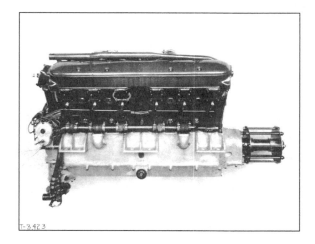

Fig. 11.3 Wright T-3 V-12 water-cooled engine. Intended as a replacement for the World War I vintage Liberty, the T-3 featured the same engine mount spacing as the Liberty. This engine was also used for Wright Aeronautical's foray into racing. (Courtesy of the New Jersey Aviation Hall of Fame Museum and Gerry Abbamont.)

This ended Wright Aeronautical's foray into racing. Unlike many other companies, it did not reap the benefits to be gained from this activity. With the exception of the R-2160, the T series also ended Wright Aeronautical's association with liquid-cooled engines. A total of 264 T engines were built between 1921 and 1926, many of which ended up powering "Rum-Running" speed boats during Prohibition!

After Rentschler's departure in 1924, C. L. Lawrence became Vice President of Wright Aeronautical. Owing to Lawrence's prestige with the Navy, Wright Aeronautical was awarded a contract for another nine-cylinder radial engine known as the P-1 (Fig. 11.4). With a displacement of 1654 in³ (27.1 L), the P-1 was based on a design submitted by Lawrence in 1919 to the Army. In an effort to keep the diameter of the engine to a minimum, it was designed to use a short connecting rod ratio. This forced Wright Aeronautical to position the valves fore and aft with a complex linkage to actuate the rear valves, instead of in the more conventional lateral location. As is usual with engines featuring short rod ratios, high thrust loads were imposed on the pistons, resulting in piston failures. In addition, the unusual valve location also gave problems; consequently, the P-1 was not a success. It was extensively flight-tested in a Douglas DT-2. Another contributing factor to the less-than-stellar performance of the P-1 was the development efforts expended on the water-cooled T series, which drained key personnel from the project.

After the failure of the P-1, Wright Aeronautical embarked on a follow-on, the P-2, which featured the same bore and stroke as the P-1 but with a far less severe rod ratio and conventional, that is, lateral, positioning of the valves in the hemispherical combustion chamber. Again, the cylinder design of the P-2 was influenced by Sam Heron, based on his type J, which surprisingly did not have engine pressure lubrication of the valve gear. It was during the development of the P-2 that Frederick Rentschler had a falling out with his directors and left Wright Aeronautical to form his own aircraft engine company. Rentschler's reason for leaving Wright Aeronautical now has a similar ring to today's corporations; he felt the directors had no understanding of the nature of the business or understanding of the technical aspects (see Chapter 13).

Fig. 11.4 Wright P-1. Note the fore and aft valve location with the awkward linkage for the rear intake valves. A short rod ratio also contributed to the R-1's woes by generating high thrust loads for the pistons. (Courtesy of the New Jersey Aviation Hall of Fame Museum and Gerry Abbamont.)

Rentschler's departure, along with the departure of several key engineering personnel, seriously hurt the P-2 project. Although the P-2 was type-tested at 435 hp and flight-tested, it did not go into production. Instead, the Navy asked Wright Aeronautical to develop a smaller radial for a carrier-based observation aircraft, the Vought O2U. Wright Aeronautical designed the Simoon, based on the P-2, for this Navy requirement. The Navy wanted 350 hp displacing 1176 in³ (19.27 L) at a weight of no more than 650 lb. In the meantime Rentschler introduced the Pratt & Whitney Wasp, which was so superior to anything else then being developed, Wright Aeronautical had no chance against this formidable rival.

However, all was not lost for Wright Aeronautical. In 1926 E. T. Jones, head of the power plant section at McCook Field, and Sam Heron came aboard to replace the recently departed key engineering staff. In 1926 Wright Aeronautical embarked on the R-1750 Cyclone, with the 1750-in³ displacement derived from 6.0-in bores and 6.875-in stroke (Fig. 11.5). The nine-cylinder R-1750 incorporated Heron's type M cylinder and his internally cooled exhaust valves. Initially rated at 500 hp, it passed a type test at this rating in 1927. The Navy purchased a number of R-1750s to power twin-engine flying boats.

Another milestone event in the history of Wright Aeronautical occurred in 1929 when they were merged with Curtiss. Arthur Nutt, designer of the pioneering D-12, became vice president of engineering. After the debacle of the Simoon and the departure of Rentschler and many of the key engineering personnel, Wright then went from strength to strength.

In 1932, the bore of the R-1750 was increased to 6.125 in yielding a displacement of 1823 in³ (29.88 L). Later versions of the R-1820, known as the F model Cyclone, were to make significant contributions to World War II (Fig. 11.6). Douglas Aircraft chose the R-1820 to power the world-beating DC-2 commercial airliner, ensuring the financial success of Wright Aeronautical for the time being.

Fig. 11.5 The R-1750 was the predecessor to the Wright R-1820. This 1927-vintage engine was rated at 525 hp at 1900 rpm. Note the shallow depth of the cooling fins. As casting techniques improved, deeper fins were incorporated, which contributed to increases in horsepower for the follow-on R-1820. (Courtesy of the New Jersey Aviation Hall of Fame Museum and Gerry Abbamont.)

Fig. 11.6 Early Wright R-1820, the largest successful single-row radial. As this engine was developed, many improvements were incorporated that allowed higher horsepower ratings. Cooling was always a factor in radial engine performance; consequently, as the R-1820 was developed, more and deeper cooling fins were incorporated. (Courtesy of the New England Air Museum.)

The introduction of the R-1820 also brought in new features for Wright Aeronautical, including the use of a forged aluminum crankcase. Wright Aeronautical later took this process one step further on later engines by using forged steel crankcases. Power was now up to 700 hp with improved reliability.

Supercharging was becoming more critical to enhance the performance of engines through boosting. Early superchargers offered little if any boost, as their primary purpose was to provide an even mixture distribution; in fact, many period technical articles refer to them as "rotary induction systems." General Electric, as an outgrowth of developing turbosupercharger technology, provided gear-driven superchargers for all the major aircraft engine manufacturers. However, by the mid 1930s it was becoming apparent that the efficiency of the General Electric superchargers lagged behind their British counterparts and that at higher boost pressures the superchargers were limiting engine performance due to internal heat. In 1937 Wright Aeronautical broke away from General Electric and started to design its own superchargers of far greater efficiency (Refs. 2.5, 2.7, 4.3).

R-1820 Cyclone

The F model Cyclone, the first Cyclone with the 1823-in³ displacement, was, by World War II, a conventional nine-cylinder radial. Its ancestry went back to the P-1 of 1923 when it displaced 1652 in³ (27 L).

The forged aluminum crankcase was made up from two sections split on the cylinder centerline. Cylinder construction embodied all of Sam Heron's early work on air cylinder design, that is, a steel barrel with integrally machined-in cooling fins. The cast aluminum cylinder head was screwed-and-shrunk onto the barrel. Two valves were seated in the hemispherical combustion chamber, the exhaust using Heron's sodium-cooling feature.

Because the engine was designed with a one-piece master connecting rod, the crankshaft was made up of two pieces supported by two massive roller bearings. The master rod bearing was steel-backed lead-indium-silver assembly. The F-series R-1820 used two counterweights; the rear one was a pendulum-style dynamic counterweight. Reduction gearing was multipinion planetary housed in a magnesium nose case. The nose case also housed the cam plate and roller tappets.

F-series engines still used the General Electric designed supercharger, a feature that not only held back the performance of this critical engine component but the overall power output of the engine. Carburetion was typically provided by a two-barrel downdraft Holley carburetor.

Performance ranged from 575 to 890 hp at 1900 rpm for a typical weight of 1000 lb.

Ignition was provided by two Scintilla magnetos, which fired the two plugs per cylinder, mounted on the rear cover. Lubrication, as to be expected, was dry sump with one pressure pump and one scavenge pump.

The G series of R-1820 engines incorporated several significant improvements. As usual, one of the main inhibiting factors to increased power was providing adequate heat rejection. Additional cooling fin area was added for the G series; the total was now 2800 in^2 per cylinder.

After realizing that the General Electric furnished gear-driven superchargers were of a low efficiency, no better than 60%, Wright Aeronautical engineers, under the leadership of Kenneth Campbell, developed a single-speed supercharger for the G series that exhibited an efficiency of over 65% at a pressure ratio of 1.5, and by the end of R-1820 production, efficiencies of over 75% were achieved.

The two-piece crankcase was redesigned to take advantage of the mechanical properties of a steel forging. The wall thickness was kept to the minimum to avoid a weight penalty. The remaining design features stayed the same as the F series. Performance for the G series was considerably improved, typically 1200 hp at 2500 rpm (Refs. 2.5, 2.7, 4.16, 4.27, 4.26, 9.13, 11.1).

Manufacture

F-series engines were soon phased out of production after the start of World War II in favor of the G-series engines, which constituted the majority of R-1820 production in World War II.

Most of the G series were manufactured by the Studebaker Corporation, who set up three facilities for the manufacture of the R-1820. The main assembly plant was in South Bend, Indiana. Supporting the South Bend facility, Studebaker's Fort Wayne, Indiana, facility supplied gears and connecting rods. Other precision parts were manufactured in Chicago, Illinois.

Applications

Table 11.1 summarizes the R-1820 Cyclone's performance and applications.

TABLE 11.1—WRIGHT R-1820 PERFORMANCE AND APPLICATION SUMMARY

Dash Number	Applications	hp/rpm/alt	Comments
-1	Keystone Y1B-6 Keystone B-6A Douglas C-11A Y1C-22 C-24	575/1900/SL	First series of 1820 model; improved and redesigned 1750 engine. Also used in O-29A, O-38D, and YP-20.
-3		620/1950/SL	Similar to -1 except propeller shaft reduction gear ratio
-5	C-51A	575/1900/SL	Similar to -1 except redesigned super-charger quill drive shaft, cam, and magneto drive gears. Cuno oil filter
-7	Y1C-14A	620/1950/SL	Similar to -3 except improved engineering changes
-9	YP-20	650/1900/SL	Similar to -1 except improved engineering changes and increased supercharger gear ratio
-11		600/1950/SL	Similar to -3 except higher supercharger gear ratio
-13	Douglas YB-11	670/1950/SL	Redesigned. First series of F-type engine, equipped with downdraft carburetion, 11-inch impeller, forged crankcase and pistons, hollow head exhaust valves
-15	UC-100	730/1950/SL	Similar to -13 except higher supercharger gear ratio and equipped with NA-F7B carburetor and ramming air intake
-17	YA-19 Martin XB-10 Martin B-10 C-27B XO-45	675/1950/SL	Improved design with reinforced crankcase, modified oil pump connection, hot spot, equipped with NA-U8H carburetor, and vacuum pump drive. Also used in O-45
-19	XB-10	675/1950/SL	Similar to -13 except higher propeller reduction and supercharger gear ratio. Commercial engine
-20	Grumman J2F-1	691/1950/SL	First R-1820 for the Navy
-21	A-12	670/1950/SL	Similar to -13 except vacuum pump drive and extended propeller shaft
-22	SBA-1 Grumman F3F-2/3 F2A	950/2200/SL	
-23	YC-30	670/1950/SL	Commercial engine incorporating same features as -17

SL = sea level

(continued)

TABLE 11.1, continued

Dash Number	Applications	hp/rpm/alt	Comments
-25	A-15 Martin YB-10 C-27C XC-31, XC-32	750/1950/SL	Similar to -17 except spur-type propeller reduction gear, equipped with NA-F7C carburetor and ramming air intake. Also used in C-33, C-34, OA-6, and YO-44
-27		670/1950/SL	Similar to -21 except equipped with two-speed supercharger drive and NA-F7C carburetor
-29		800/2100/SL	Similar to -27 except redesigned rear section for adaptation of integral fuel injector, built-in turbosupercharger, automatic regulator, and mixture control
-30	Grumman J2F2/3/4 Grumman F2F2A	790/1950/SL	
-31	Martin YB-10A	675/1950/SL	Similar to -17 except equipped with Farman-type propeller shaft reduction gears, G cylinder heads, and different supercharger gear ratio
-32	Douglas A-24, XBT-2 Douglas SBD-3/2	1000/2350/SL	Similar to -53 except accessory drives, different magnetos, and equipped with Holley 1375 H-type carburetor. Navy engine
-33	Martin B-10B C-32A	740/1950/SL	Similar to -25 except higher supercharger gear ratio and equipped with NA-F7C carburetor, space accessory drive, and stronger gun synchronizer drives
-34	F2A-1	950/2200/SL	
-35		750/1950/SL	Similar to -21 except hydrocontrollable propeller and NA-F7C carburetor
-36	Grumman J2F-3/4		
-37	YA-13 A-13 O-40A, O-40B	690/1950/SL	Similar to -21 except different supercharger gear ratio and carburetor setting
-38	Boeing XSBA-1	950/2200/SL	
-39	Boeing Y1B-17 B-17	930/2200/SL	Similar to -33 except redesigned crankshaft with dynamic damper, cylinder heads, connecting rods, and two-speed supercharger
-41	XO-47	940/2200/SL	Similar to -39 except supercharger gear ratio
-43		1000/2225/SL	Similar to -39 except for supercharger gear ratio and engineering changes

SL = sea level

(continued)

TABLE 11.1, continued

Dash Number	Applications	hp/rpm/alt	Comments
-45	Douglas B-18, B-18M C-38 YOA-5 OA-5	930/2200/SL	Similar to -39 except equipped with smaller diameter impeller and ramming air intake
-47	X1A-18 A-18	930/2200/SL	Similar to -45 except single-speed supercharger
-49	XO-47 O-47A, O-47B	975/2200/SL	Similar to -47 except engineering changes and different ratings
-50	Grumman J2F-5	950/2200/SL	
-51	Boeing YB-17A Boeing B-17B, B-17C Boeing B-17D	1000/2200/SL	Similar to -49 except lower supercharger ratio, requires turbosupercharger to meet take-off and altitude ratings
-53	Douglas B-18A, B-18B, Douglas B-18M C-42 C-58	1000/2200/SL	Similar to -45 except 10.45-in-diameter impeller. Engine is specifically intended for 100-octane fuel
-55	C-39	975/2200/SL	Similar to -49 except equipped with NA-F7K carburetor provision for electric or hydrocontrollable full feathering propeller
-56/W/WA	Eastern FM-2 XFR-1, FR-1	1300/2600/SL	
-57	O-47B	1060/2350/SL	G 100 series, redesigned, higher compression ratio, different reduction gear, and a steel crankcase
-59		1200/2500/SL 1200/2500/1800 1000/2500/13,600	G 200 series, equipped with two-speed supercharger, overall length increased 1 in. Double dynamic damper. Different reduction gear ratio
-60	Douglas A-24B, SBD-5	1200/2500/SL	Similar to -59 except two-speed supercharger and equipped with PD-12K4 carburetor. Navy engine
-62/A	Curtiss XSC-1, SC-1	1350/2700/SL	
-61		875/2100/SL	None procured
-63		1200/2500/SL 1200/2500/25,000	Similar to -65 except redesigned rear section to accommodate fuel injector. Project canceled

SL = sea level

(continued)

TABLE 11.1, continued

Dash Number	Applications	hp/rpm/alt	Comments
-65	Boeing B-17C, B-17D, Boeing B-17E, B-17F, Boeing B-17G	1200/2500/SL 1200/2500/25,000	Similar to -59 except single-speed superchargers. Engines also manufactured by Studebaker. Also used in B-17H, CB-17G, RB-17, FB-17G, H, TB-17G, H, XB-40, and YB-40
-66	Douglas SBD-6	1300/2600/SL	
-67	Grumman XP-50	1200/2500/SL 1200/2500/25,000	Similar to -65 except reduction gear ratio and equipped with torquemeter. Project dropped
-69	Grumman XP-50	1200/2500/SL 1200/2500/25,000	Similar to -67 except left-hand propeller shaft rotation. Project dropped
-70	XF-2M-1	1300/2600/SL	
-71	C-49 C49A, C-49B C-49C, C-49D	1200/2500/SL 1200/2500/25,000	Similar to -65 except different reduction gear ratio. Also used in C-56, C-56A, C-56B, C-56C, and C-84
-72A/WA	Eastern FM-2, Ryan F-21	1350/2700/SL	
-73	Boeing B-17C	1200/2500/SL 1200/2500/25,000	Similar to -65 except does not incorporate a torquemeter nose section
-74W	Eastern FM-2, FR-2, Curtiss SC-2	1425/2700/SL	
-75	A-27	785/2200/SL 1200/2500/25,000	Similar to -33 except propeller shaft reduction gear ratio. These engines were originally intended for Siam (Thailand) but were taken over by the United States
-76	Grumman JR2F1	1425/2700/SL	
-77	NAA P-64	875/2200/SL 1200/2500/25,000	Similar to -41 except supercharger gear ratio and equipped with Holley 1375 carburetor
-79	C-49E C-50 C-50C, C-50D C-110	1100/2350/SL 1200/2500/25,000	Similar to -57 except double dynamic damper, different carburetor, and even-firing magnetos. Commercial engine
-81	C-49F C-50B C-56E C-84	1100/2350/SL 1200/2500/25,000	Similar to -79 except equipped with Holley 1375 F carburetor

SL = sea level

(continued)

TABLE 11.1, continued

Dash Number	Applications	hp/rpm/alt	Comments
-83	C-50 C-51	1100/2350/SL 1200/2500/25,000	Similar to -81 except different reduction gear ratio, magnetos, and rectangular fuel pump drive
-85	C-49F C-50 C-50A, C-50B, C-50C	1100/2350/SL	Similar to -83 except carburetor and even-firing magnetos. Also used in C-56E and C-84
-87	A-29 A-29A, A-29B A-33 AT-18	1200/2500/SL	Similar to -59 except propeller reduction gear ratio, carburetors, and magnetos. Also used in C-60, XC-60A, C-60A, C-60C, and XP-36
-89	C-56 C-60	1100/2350	Similar to -83 except carburetor adapter. Commercial engine
-90	XP2Y-2	785/2200	
-91	Boeing B-17E	1200/2500 1200/2500/25,000	Similar to -65 except special diffuser and two-speed supercharger
-93	Boeing B-17H	1350/2700/SL 1300/2600/25,000	Similar to -65 except forged cylinder heads, modified connecting rod mechanism
-95	Curtiss P-36G	1200/2500/SL	Similar to -87 except accessory drives and cylinder baffles. Engine purchased by Norway, but taken over by United States
-97	Boeing B-17F, B-17G, Boeing B-17H XC-108 YC-108	1200/2500/SL 1200/2500/25,000	Similar to 65 except external oil scavenge and propeller governor control oil lines. Engines also manufactured by Studebaker. Also used in C-108A, D, YC-125A, B, C, C-125A, B, RB-17, A, B, F, and G

SL = sea level
Source: Refs. 2.7, 4.15–4.18, 6.4, 9.13.

Boeing B-17 Flying Fortress

Possibly the most well-known of the R-1820 applications, Boeing B-17s played a major part in the "aluminum overcast" phenomenon that existed during World War II. Raids consisting of as many as 1500 four-engine bombers flown by the Eighth Air Force blasted Germany into defeat.

The B-17's roots go back to Boeing's B-9, the model 247 airliner and the B-15. Responding to a 1934 Army Air Corps competition for a bomber capable of carrying a two-ton bomb load 2000 mi, Boeing designed the Model 299. The 299 was a four-engine aircraft powered by Pratt & Whitney R-1690s developing 750 hp each.

Design was completed in a remarkably short time, and by 28 July 1935 the Model 299 was ready for its first flight. Early test flights gave indications of an aircraft superior to anything in its class. Less than a month later the Model 299 was flown from Seattle, Washington, to Dayton, Ohio, averaging 232 mph for the 2100-mi trip, faster than contemporary fighters. As expected, the Model 299 impressed the Army brass during the competition. However, on 30 October the aircraft attempted a take-off and the worst possible scenario occurred: the Model 299 crashed in flames.

The cause of the accident was determined to be a gust lock left in place on the rudder. The Army contract for which the Model 299 had been bidding was awarded to the Douglas DC-3 based B-18. The contract called for 133 aircraft which, by the standards of this mid depression year, was a plum. Fortunately for Boeing, the Army still had faith in their aircraft and awarded them a contract for 13 aircraft plus an additional airframe for destructive testing.

It was designated YB-17; the name was later amended to Y1B-17. (The "1" means it was purchased with "supplemental" funds from Congress and has nothing to do with the aircraft.) The main departure from the original Model 299 concept was the substitution of Wright R-1820-39 (G-series) engines rated at 930 hp in place of the Pratt & Whitney R-1690 Hornets. Airframe modifications included an increase in fuselage length of 7 ft and an increase in weight of 2000 lbs. Despite the additional weight and size, the additional power offered by the R-1820s increased performance to 256 mph at 14,000 ft and increased range to a maximum of 3400 mi.

The thirteen Y1B-17s amassed an enviable record for reliability and performance, breaking many records including the coast-to-coast record in both directions, the East-to-West taking 12 h, 50 min, and the West-to-East taking 10 h, 46 min. In another remarkable demonstration of this tough aircraft, a fully instrumented Y1B-17 was caught in violent turbulence that would have destroyed any other aircraft of this class. Although the Y1B-17 suffered severe damage, it was repaired to fly again. So convincing was this unintentional test of the structural integrity of the Y1B-17 that plans for destructive testing on the fourteenth airframe were canceled. Instead this aircraft formed the basis of the Y1B-17A, which incorporated the most significant modification of all the B-17 variants, the fitting of General Electric Type B-3 turbosuperchargers. This was also the first application of turbosupercharging to a heavy bomber.

The resulting aircraft was designated Y1B-17A. Rated at 1000 hp, the R-1820-51s (G59) used a single-speed/single-stage supercharger augmented by the turbosupercharger. As would be expected, altitude performance improved dramatically; the service ceiling was now an awesome 38,000 ft, and top speed increased to 300 mph at 25,000 ft. Performance would remain at this level for all subsequent models of the B-17 despite an increase of 200 hp per engine on later models. However, gross weight increased dramatically as the demands of modern warfare called for additional armor, defensive weapons, self-sealing fuel tanks, and so forth. Following the successful trials of the Y1B-17A, an order for 39 of these aircraft was placed, and these aircraft were designated B-17B.

Structure of the B-17 was fairly conventional, although it continued a tradition for all piston-powered Boeing aircraft in that it employed minimal use of hydraulics. The only hydraulic systems were the cowl flap actuation and the brakes. All other functions, including landing-gear retraction, gun turrets, flaps, and so forth, were electrically powered.

Many crews were grateful that they were flying the B-17 rather than the B-24 because of its enviable reputation for absorbing battle damage. Part of this was attributable to the Warren truss main spar for the wing (Fig. 11.7). Luftwaffe fighter pilots much preferred to fly against the more vulnerable B-24 Liberator, which could oftentimes be shot down in one pass, whereas the B-17 invariably took several passes to shoot down. The fuel tanks, housed in the wing, totaling a maximum of 2780 gal for the G model, were originally of the nonself-sealing type. Six tanks in the inner wing section and nine tanks situated between wing ribs, nicknamed Tokyo tanks, supplied the R-1820s. From the B-17D on, self-sealing fuel tanks were incorporated after the bitter experience the British RAF had with their early B-17Cs (Fortress 1s). The circular-section semi-monocoque fuselage was made up of circumferential stiffeners tied together with longerons and longitudinal stiffeners and was covered in a stressed aluminum skin. Tail surfaces were also stressed-skin construction with all control surfaces fabric covered.

The R-1820 was mounted on a chrome molybdenum ring mount that attached to a monocoque nacelle. Oil for each of the four engines was supplied by a 37-gal self-sealing oil tank (incorporated into the F-model B-17). This large quantity of oil was required for the long missions flown by the B-17. The General Electric Type B turbosupercharger was mounted on the underside of the nacelle in a near-horizontal position. Exhaust gases were fed to the turbine unit through an exposed exhaust pipe. Induction air was fed to the compressor by a wing leading edge duct. Discharge air from the compressor was routed through an air-to-air intercooler then to the downdraft carburetor (Fig. 11.8).

Fig. 11.7 Internal wing structure of the Boeing B-17. The Warren truss spar was difficult for Luftwaffe pilots to destroy; consequently, they much preferred to fly against the more vulnerable B-24 with its aluminum spar. (Courtesy of the National Air and Space Museum, Smithsonian Institution, Photo No. 1A-11417.)

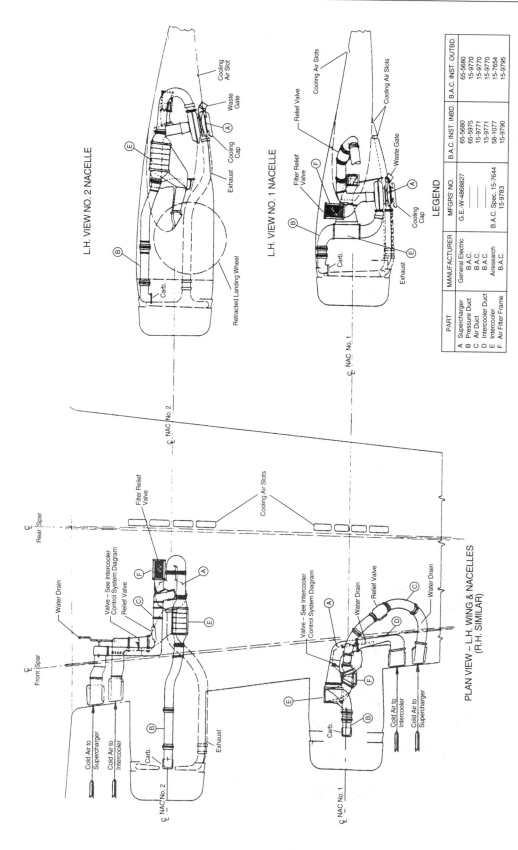

Fig. 11.8 Diagram showing installation of the General Electric turbosupercharger in the Boeing B-17 and associated ductwork for the induction air and intercooler. (Boeing B-17 Erection and Maintenance Manual, T.O. 01-20EF-2, revised 15 Sept. 1943. Courtesy of the New England Air Museum.)

Heated cooling air from the intercooler and oil cooler was discharged over the trailing edge of the wing through the characteristic rectangular slots seen on overhead shots of the B-17. R-1820-65 (G666) engines powered the C, D, E, F, and G models. R-1820-91s were also used in the E model (Fig. 11.9). An upgraded R-1820-93, which incorporated improved features such as forged cylinder heads and modified connecting rods and was rated at 1350 hp, was installed in the B-17H. B-17F, G, and H models could also have the R-1820-97 rated at 1200 hp. The -97s also featured forged cylinder heads. Most of the -97s were manufactured by Studebaker (Refs. 2.7, 9.13, 11.2, 11.3).

Service

The RAF was the first to fly the B-17 (Fortress 1 in British terminology) into combat. Initially the experience was a disaster. Many of the problems were attributable to wrong tactics, but some were due to design deficiencies. Lack of self-sealing fuel tanks and inadequate defensive firepower and armor plating caused the B-17 to easily fall prey to German fighters. After these deficiencies had been corrected, the aircraft proved itself with the Eighth Air Force.

B-17Cs and Ds were very similar, however the B-17E incorporated major design changes, most noticeably to the rear half of the fuselage, which was totally redesigned. One of the more obvious features was considerably larger vertical tail surfaces. The E model incorporated a tail-gunner position for the first time. The Es were also the models initially used by the fledgling Eighth Air Force; the first raid was against Rouen, France (Fig. 11.10). Daylight tactics employed by the Eighth demanded ever-increasing defensive armament and tight flying formation for survival.

The YB-40 was a derivative of the B-17, incorporating additional gun positions and ammunition. The YB-40 failed in its intended mission as a long-range bomber escort. The YB-40s were often flown 15,000 lb over gross, resulting in poor performance compared with the B-17Fs they were escorting. After the main bomber force released their bombs, they were typically 8000 lb lighter, whereas the

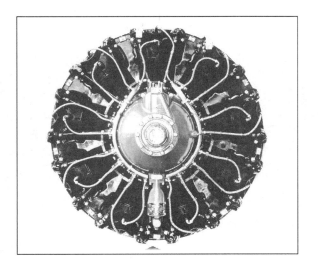

Fig. 11.9 Wright R-1820-91. Thousands of these engines were manufactured for Boeing B-17Es. Studebaker also manufactured them under license. (Courtesy of the New Jersey Aviation Hall of Fame Museum and Gerry Abbamont.)

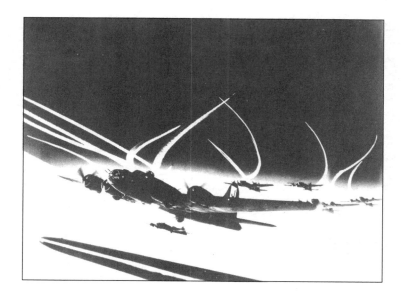

Fig. 11.10 A formation of Eighth Air Force Boeing B-17s over Germany. The condensation trails overhead are from fighters protecting the bomber stream. For each gallon of fuel burned, 1 lb of water vapor was formed in the exhaust gases. At high altitudes where temperatures could dip to –60°F, water vapor in the exhaust condensed almost immediately. (Courtesy of the National Air and Space Museum, Smithsonian Institution, Photo No. 1A-11678.)

YB-40s were still struggling along at a high gross weight. This made them vulnerable to German fighters. The exercise was not a total failure; valuable lessons learned from the YB-40 experience were incorporated into B-17Gs. The most noticeable change was the G model's distinctive chin turret.

Deployment in the Pacific theater was not as successful as in the European theater primarily because of the tactics used. Although intended to be a strategic bomber, the B-17 was put into the role of tactical bomber, resulting in comparatively heavy losses. By late 1942 B-17s were increasingly replaced by B-24s, and by September 1943 they were phased out of Pacific combat missions entirely.

However, the B-17 did not depart from the Pacific theater altogether. Its next role was a critical and much-appreciated one, that of air sea rescue. The B-17H variant incorporated a lifeboat for rescuing Twentieth Air Force crew members forced down in the ocean after attacking Japan. As the B-29 campaign got into full swing, crews were warned to bail out over Japan only as a last resort. At this stage of the war, reports were coming in of Japanese atrocities and mistreatment of POWs.

By war's end, a total of 12,761 B-17s had been built. Manufacture was divided up between Boeing, Douglas Aircraft, and Lockheed Vega. The B-17G was the most-produced variant, with a total of 8680 (Fig. 11.11).

B-17s soldiered on for many years after the war with the U.S. Air Force and Coast Guard along with many foreign air forces.

Fig. 11.11 Boeing B-17 production line. Construction of these bombers was a national priority. A consortium of Boeing-Martin-Vega were each operating production lines at various sites around the United States. (Courtesy of the National Air and Space Museum, Smithsonian Institution, Photo No. 1A-11159.)

Douglas SBD Dauntless

Nicknamed Slow-But-Deadly, the Douglas SBD Dauntless was one of the best known of the U.S. Navy dive-bombers of World War II. Derived from the earlier BT-1 and XBT-2, the SBD (Scout Bomber Douglas) went into production in 1940 (Fig. 11.12). The Army also used it as a dive-bomber, designating it A-24. The A-24 was similar to its Navy sibling; the main difference was the deletion of the tail hook.

Fig. 11.12 Douglas SBD Dauntless powered by a Wright R-1820. (Courtesy of the National Air and Space Museum, Smithsonian Institution, Photo No. 1A-40112.)

By 1941 it was the Navy's standard carrier-borne dive-bomber and consequently bore the brunt of the Battle of Midway, often described as the crucial turning point in the battle of the Pacific. Despite horrendous losses, the Battle of Midway was a qualified success for the United States.

As later aircraft such as the TBM/TBF and SB2C came into service, the SBD was phased out. Production ended in July 1944 after 5936 had been completed.

Construction consisted of a monocoque fuselage that provided accommodation for the two-man crew seated in tandem. Like all Navy-procured aircraft, it did not have turbosupercharging. Instead, the R-1820 relied on single-stage, two-speed supercharging for boosting. The engine was mounted on a tubular steel mount attached to the firewall. Oil cooling was provided by a circular cooler mounted in front of the firewall with cooling air fed by a variable inlet scoop under the cowling. Cooling air was exhausted through two vents on the side of the fuselage. All SBDs were powered by variations of the G-model R-1820. SBD-1s were powered by R-1820-32s rated at 950 hp at 5000 ft and 1000 hp available at take-off. SBD-5s were the next aircraft to benefit from a power increase, with R-1820-60s rated at 1200 hp for take-off. The last production SBDs, the -6s were powered by R-1820-66s rated at 1300 hp.

Wing design was typical Douglas multicellular construction, similar in concept to the DC series of aircraft. The landing gear retracted inward, thus offering a good footprint for stability (Refs. 2.7, 11.4).

Brewster F2A Buffalo

The history of the Brewster company was a long and illustrious one going back to the 1800s when they manufactured carriages. Like many of the early carriage manufacturers, they graduated to the manufacture of automobiles. Brewster entered the aviation field by manufacturing components for other builders, particularly floats for seaplanes.

In June 1936 Brewster responded to a Navy request to start development of its model B-139 fighter, later designated F2A, although actual work on it had started three months prior to this date. The F2A was the Navy's first monoplane fighter with retractable landing gear. Its first flight occurred on 2 December 1937 (Fig. 11.13).

Performance was below expectations; however, this was improved based on results obtained from an F2A installed in the full-size NACA wind tunnel at Langley, Virginia. Speed improved to 295 mph powered by an R-1820-22 rated at 950 hp.

Bearing a striking resemblance to the Grumman F4F Wildcat, the F2A shared similar construction methods. The all-monocoque fuselage featured the classic barrel-shape dictated by a large diameter radial. Wing construction was of one piece and housed the main gear legs, which turned out to be a weak point with numerous gear failures on landing.

Fig. 11.13 Brewster F2A Buffalo. The Navy's first monoplane fighter. (Courtesy of the National Air and Space Museum, Smithsonian Institution, Photo No. 1A-15906.)

Throughout the development period, various modifications were incorporated, including the installation of an R-1820-40 rated at 1200 hp for take-off and modification of the air ducts supplying the carburetor and oil cooler.

Despite the modifications and improvements based on the Langley tests, the Navy was not enthusiastic about the aircraft, possibly due to the F4F, which exhibited superior performance, entering service at the same time. Only one squadron, VF-3, accepted F2A-1s even though the Navy had originally intended to equip more.

The remainder of the Navy order for F2A-1s were diverted to Finland, who in 1939 was fighting the Soviet Union. All Navy equipment such as the arresting hook was removed, and for operations in snow, skis were attached. It was in Finnish service that the F2A saw its moment of glory, arguably because of the inferior equipment the Soviets threw against it.

Because of a shortage of spare parts, the Finns were very innovative in keeping their F2As airworthy. As the R-1820s came due for replacement, captured Soviet M-63s, which were license-built R-1820s, were substituted.

Only one other squadron apart from VF-3 received F2As—VF-2 aboard the USS *Lexington,* which used them briefly from September 1941 to January 1942. All remaining F2As were passed on to the Marines. At Midway, the F2As suffered severe losses, particularly against the formidable Mitsubishi Zero, which totally outclassed it. The rest of the Pacific campaign was a repeat of the performance at Midway; whenever it tangled with Japanese aircraft the outcome was usually a foregone conclusion.

The British, who took over a Dutch order, found the F2A to be an inferior fighter compared to contemporary Bf 109s and Spitfires and consequently shipped them out to the far East.

By 1944, when the surviving F2As had been relegated to training squadrons, they were phased out (Refs. 5.2, 11.5).

Grumman F4F Wildcat

A far more successful R-1820 powered fighter was the Grumman F4F Wildcat. Although all early production Wildcats were powered by Pratt & Whitney R-1830s, later models were powered by the Wright R-1820. Several factors contributed to this engine change. The Pratt & Whitney R-1830-76/86 was the first aircraft engine with a two-stage supercharger. This new technology created new problems, especially surging at high altitude, and that was never satisfactorily resolved with the Pratt & Whitney R-1830-76/86.

The British Fleet Air Arm took delivery of the first R-1820-powered aircraft, which they named Martlet 1 (Fig. 11.14). Rated at 1200 hp, the R-1820-G205A (-40B) did not offer the same performance as the R-1830-86, but it was lighter and easier to maintain. The largest production batch of Wildcats were the FM-2s; 4777 were built. FM-2s were powered by the R-1820-56, with some models offering water injection for a war emergency power of 1350 hp.

General Motors Eastern Aircraft Division built Wildcats under the designation FM (Refs. 2.7, 9.14).

Tank Engines

The reliability, versatility, and ruggedness of the R-1820 was not lost on the Army. A derated R-1820 was installed in the T-1 heavy tank. Two versions were built, the 781C9GC1 rated at 800 hp and 2300 rpm, and the 795C9GC1 rated at 675 hp and 1950 rpm (Fig. 11.15).

Fig. 11.14 Britain received large numbers of Grumman Wildcats for the Fleet Air Arm. Designated Martlet, they were powered by a Wright R-1820-40B. (Courtesy of the National Air and Space Museum, Smithsonian Institution, Photo No. 1B-01076.)

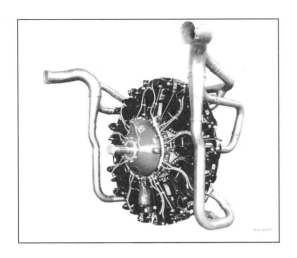

Fig. 11.15 Versatility of the Wright R-1820 is illustrated in this shot of the tank version. (Courtesy of the New Jersey Aviation Hall of Fame Museum and Gerry Abbamont.)

R-2600 Cyclone 14

The R-2600 was Wright Aeronautical's first successful two-row radial. Several attempts at two-row radial design had been attempted in the early 1930s, but none were successful or even flown. It was not until 1935 that the more serious problems of two-row design had been understood and overcome by Wright Aeronautical. In November 1935 Wright Aeronautical embarked upon the R-2600, a two-row 14-cylinder air-cooled radial. The R-2600 shared the same bore as the R-1820, that is, 6.125 in, but its stroke was reduced to 6.3125 in yielding 2603 in^3 (42.7 L) from the 14 cylinders. From the lessons learned on the R-1820, R-2600 development went relatively smoothly (Fig. 11.16). An interesting result of the R-2600 development was the impact it had on Pratt & Whitney. At the time they learned of the R-2600, Pratt & Whitney engineers were also developing an air-cooled radial of 2600 in^3 (42.7 L), although theirs was derived from 18 cylinders rather than 14 as in the case of the R-2600. Pratt & Whitney upped the ante by increasing the displacement of their engine to 2804 in^3 (46 L) (Ref. 2.5).

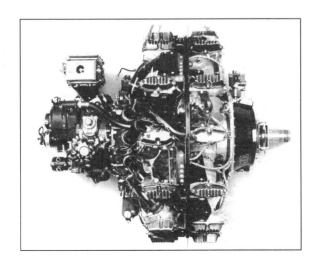

Fig. 11.16 Side view of the Wright R-2600-12. Early R-2600s such as the -12 featured a forged aluminum crankcase; later R-2600s used a forged steel crankcase. (Courtesy of the New Jersey Aviation Hall of Fame Museum and Gerry Abbamont.)

As would be expected, cylinder design was based on the R-1820, incorporating two pushrod-actuated valves per cylinder in a hemispherical combustion chamber. Cylinder barrels initially had cooling fins machined-in integrally. Later models used Wright Aeronautical's patented "W" finning concept, which consisted of an aluminum muff swaged onto the barrel. "W" finning offered additional cooling area plus the opportunity to repair damaged barrels by replacing the muff.

Two cam plates, one at the front and one at the rear of the power section, were driven through 6:1 reduction gearing, thus demanding three lobes per cam track, which actuated roller tappets (Fig. 11.17).

The crankcase was an aluminum forging split vertically on the cylinder centerlines making a three-piece assembly bolted together. Later crankcases were manufactured from steel forgings. The one-piece master rods rode initially in copper-lead bearings; later this was upgraded to silver with a lead flash. Again, this was a case of "not invented here." Pratt & Whitney had demonstrated the superiority of silver bearing over copper-lead, but Wright Aeronautical steadfastly refused to incorporate it until there was no alternative.

One counterweight per crankshaft throw was incorporated, each one featuring a dynamic counterweight. Each crank cheek was attached to the crankpin by a clamp bolt in a similar fashion to the Bristol two-row radials (Fig. 11.18). As in all previous Wright Aeronautical radials, rolling-element bearings supported the crankshaft; in the case of the R-2600, three roller bearings were used.

After realizing the fallacy of relying on General Electric, Wright developed its own supercharger for the R-2600. Initially single-speed, later models offered two-speed supercharging. Manufactured from a magnesium casting, the supercharger housing also served to support the engine mounts. Mounted on top of the supercharger, the downdraft carburetor could be a Holley or Bendix injection carburetor. Drives for the dual magnetos, oil pumps, generator, fuel pumps, and vacuum pumps were mounted on the cast magnesium rear cover (Fig. 11.19).

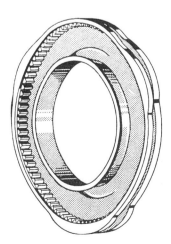

Fig. 11.17 Rear cam ring for a Wright R-2600. Note the three cam lobes, which would dictate a reduction ratio of 6:1 to the crankshaft. (North American B-25 Erection and Maintenance Manual, AN 01-60GE-2. Courtesy of the New England Air Museum.)

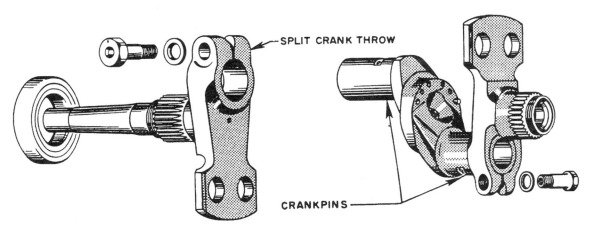

Fig. 11.18 Wright R-2600 crankshaft assembly. The pair of holes in the crank webs are pivots for the dynamic counterweights (not shown). Three roller bearings support the crankshaft. (North American B-25 Erection and Maintenance Manual, AN 01-60GE-2. Courtesy of the New England Air Museum.)

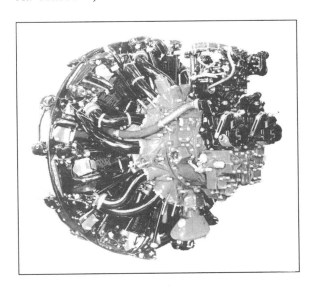

Fig. 11.19 Three-quarter rear view of a Wright R-2600-9 showing the pair of rear-mounted magnetos and the downdraft carburetion. (Courtesy of the Aviation Hall of Fame Museum.)

A cast magnesium nose case housed the reduction gearing, which was similar to that used on the F model and later R-1820s, that is, multipinion planetary.

Weight ranged from 1935 lb for the early single-stage engines with aluminum crankcases to 2045 lb for the later models with two-speed supercharging and steel crankcases.

Introduced in 1937 and rated at 1500 hp and 2400 rpm, the R-2600 was initially used by Boeing for their prewar Pan Am Clipper flying boats; therefore, by World War II it was a well-proven power plant. During the war, power increased from 1500 at 2400 rpm to 1900 hp at 2800 rpm because of improvements such as strengthening the crankcase by substituting steel for aluminum, increasing cooling fin area on cylinder barrels by using "W" finning, replacing copper-lead master rod bearings with silver-lead, increasing the strength of the rods and crank, increasing boost pressure, and so forth.

Three basic series of R-2600 were manufactured during the war: the A, the B, and the BB series, which was put into production in 1944. The As were typically rated at 1500 hp, the Bs at 1700 hp, and the BBs at 1900 hp. All R-2600s were manufactured by Wright Aeronautical at various facilities, primarily at Paterson, New Jersey, and Cincinnati, Ohio. Production of the R-2600 ended at the Cincinnati plant when production was shifted to the manufacture of the R-3350 in 1944. All production of the R-2600 ceased immediately at the end of World War II.

A short-stroke version of the R-2600, designated R-2170, was developed and tested. The R-2170 retained the same bore as the R-2600, but stroke was reduced to 5.25 in. The reduction in stroke contributed to the reduction of the diameter of the engine to 47 in compared with 55-in-diameter of the R-2600. Little effort was expended on this engine; consequently, none got into production (Refs. 2.7, 9.13, 11.6).

Applications

The design and power output of the R-2600 was very similar to the BMW 801, which powered the Focke-Wulf 190. However, despite the similar characteristics, R-2600s were never used in fighter applications. Instead, the R-2600 was used primarily in medium bombers, both single-engine and twin-engine. Table 11.2 summarizes the performance and applications of the R-2600.

TABLE 11.2—WRIGHT R-2600 PERFORMANCE AND APPLICATION SUMMARY

Dash Number	Applications	hp/rpm/alt	Comments
-1	B-22	1500/2300 None	Single-stage, single-speed supercharger
-3	Douglas A-20A Douglas XA-20B, F Douglas B-23 C-67	1600/2400 1600/2400/3000 1400/2400/11,500	Similar to -1 except equipped with two-speed supercharger and different propeller shaft reduction gear ratio
-5		1600/2400	Similar to -3 except equipped with three-speed supercharger
-6/A	Martin PBM-1/2, Martin XPBM	1600/2400	
-7	Douglas A-20 Douglas A-20D Douglas YF-3 Douglas F-3A O-53	1700/2500 1700/2500/...	Similar to -3 except equipped with single-speed supercharger

(continued)

TABLE 11.2, continued

Dash Number	Applications	hp/rpm/alt	Comments
-8/A	A-25 A-25A A-35A Curtiss SB2C-1/2 Grumman/Eastern TBF-1, TBM-1	1700/2800 1700/2600/4500 1450/2400/21,000	Navy engine, used in A35B and A25 airplanes
-9	NAA B-25 NAA B-25A, B-25B Curtiss C-46 O-56	1700/2600 1700/2600/4500 1450/2600/12,000	Similar to -13 except equipped with Stromberg carburetor PT-13E2
-10	Grumman XTBF, TBF/-1/-2 PB2Y-4	1700/2600	Also rated at 2800 rpm
-11	Douglas A-20A, A-20B Douglas XP-70 Douglas P-70	1600/2400 1600/2400/3000 1400/2400/11,700	Similar to -3 except equipped with both type I and II vacuum pump drives
-12	Martin PBM-3	1700/2800	Similar to -11. Navy model
-13	A-24A, A-24B, A-24C A-30A, A-30B Short Stirling	1700/2600 1700/2600/4500 1450/2600/12,000	Similar to -9 except equipped with Holley 1685H or 1685HA carburetor. Also used in XB-25E, F, G, B-25C, D, G, H, J, CB-25J, TB-25J, B-37, F-10, and A-35A, B
-14	Grumman XF7F	1800/2800	Production F7Fs used Pratt & Whitney R-2800s
-15	XB-33 B-33	1800/2800 1750/2600/29,500	Similar to -7 except reduction gear ratio and equipped with torquemeter nose section
-16	Grumman XF6F	1700/2600	Production F6Fs used Pratt & Whitney R-2800s
-17	C-55	1700/2500 1750/2600/29,500	Similar to -13 except engineering changes and power ratings
-19	A-30 A-31 A-35 B-37	1600/2400 1750/2600/29,500	Similar to -11 except higher compression ratio and equipped with roller impeller clutch, I-point priming, and Holley 1685H or 1685HA carburetor
-20	Eastern TBM-3, Curtiss SB2C-3/-4	1900/2800	
-21	Vultee (V-72)	1600/2400 1600/2400/1000 1400/2400/10,000	Similar to -19 except equipped with Holley 1685H carburetor and cylinder baffles. These engines converted to -19
-22	Martin PBM-3D	1900/2800	

(continued)

TABLE 11.2, continued

Dash Number	Applications	hp/rpm/alt	Comments
-23	Douglas A-20C, A-20G, Douglas A-20J, A-20K Douglas F-3A	1600/2400 1600/2400/1000 1400/2400/10,000	Similar to -19 except equipped with Stromberg PD-12K1 carburetor. Also used in P-70A, B, AT-24A, B, C, and D
-25		1600/2400 1600/2400/1000 1400/2400/10,000	Similar to -19 except equipped with Eclipse accessory gear box
-27		1600/2400 None	Similar to -23 except equipped with PD-12J1 carburetor. No engines built with this model designation
-29	Douglas A-20H, A-20K A-30A, A-30B, A-30C	1700/2600 1700/2600/4500 1450/2600/12,000	Similar to -9 and -13 except narrow vane impeller. Also used in B-25C, D, G, H, J, F-10, AT-24A, B, C, and D
-31	British (M-33-C) B-37	1700/2600 1700/2600/4500 1450/2600/12,000	Similar to -13 except valve spring arrangement is designed for 2800 rpm operation

Source: Refs. 2.7, 4.15–4.18, 6.4, 9.13.

North American B-25 Mitchell

The North American B-25 was one of the finest twin-engine medium bombers of World War II. It was named after General Billy Mitchell, who was court-martialed for his zealous advocacy of a strong, independent Air Force.

Responding to a U.S. Army Air Corps request for a twin-engine medium bomber, North American Aviation designed the model NA-40-1. When powered by two Pratt & Whitney R-1830s, the plane's early 1939 performance was poor. To improve the mediocre performance, the R-1830s were replaced by the substantially larger and more powerful Wright R-2600-9, rated at 1700 hp for take-off (Fig. 11.20). Numerous structural changes were also incorporated, including the layout of the cockpit, which went from a tandem seating arrangement for the pilot and copilot to side-by-side.

With the increase in power, performance was now acceptable and the aircraft was designated NA-40-2. First flown in March 1939, the NA-40-2 had a short life when the aircraft was destroyed in a fatal crash during evaluation. However, test flying had demonstrated the value of the NA-40-2. A third prototype designated NA-62 was built, incorporating modifications from the lessons learned from the NA-40-2. The NA-62 was flown in September 1939 and designated XB-25 by the Army Air Corps. By this stage of development the classic B-25 form had emerged and changed little during its production life.

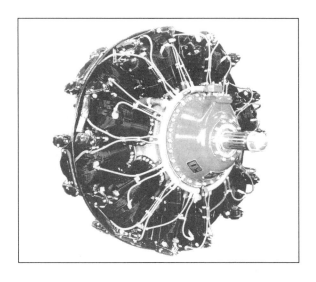

Fig. 11.20 Three-quarter view of the Wright R-2600-9. Early production North American B-25s and B-25As were powered by this engine. (Courtesy of the New Jersey Aviation Hall of Fame Museum and Gerry Abbamont.)

Construction was conventional, although the tricycle landing gear was a new innovation in the late 1930s. Built up from five sections, the two-spar wing was mounted midway up the fuselage. The outer wing panels were sealed to assist flotation in case of ditching. Because of a directional stability problem, the wing was modified from the tenth production aircraft on to eliminate dihedral on the outer wing panels. This altered the appearance of the B-25 and gave it its classic gull-wing look.

The R-2600s were mounted on tubular steel mounts attached to monocoque nacelles. Early model B-25s featured a collector ring exhaust with a single outlet. Later exhausts had improved breathing capability by incorporating individual stacks resulting in an "interesting" exhaust note. An air scoop mounted on top of the cowling supplied induction air to the downdraft carburetor (Fig. 11.21). Oil cooling was accomplished by an oil cooler buried in the leading edge of the wing. The semimonocoque fuselage had four longerons. The section of fuselage above the wing and between the two spars was integral with the wing.

Although initially conceived as a medium bomber, the B-25, like many successful aircraft in World War II, was adapted for roles that its designers never intended. One of the more interesting modifications was the installation of a massive airborne 75-mm cannon in the B-25G and H. Handling difficulties caused by the weight shifting the center of gravity and, more significantly, the recoil, could cause the aircraft to stall if the weapon was fired at low air speed. Other versions featured "solid" noses with large numbers of fixed .50-caliber machine guns in the nose and the fuselage sides firing forward.

Deployed in all theaters of the war, the B-25 created havoc for the enemy. Even when later designs such as the Douglas A-26 were introduced, the B-25 still performed yeoman service (Fig. 11.22). By far the most well-known mission for the B-25 was the Tokyo raid led by Lieutenant Colonel Jimmy Doolittle on 18 April 1942. After the Japanese attack on Pearl Harbor, the United States desperately needed a morale booster. That morale booster came from Doolittle and his soon-to-be-famous raiders. In a short period of time, 16 B-25Bs were prepared for the raid and loaded aboard the aircraft

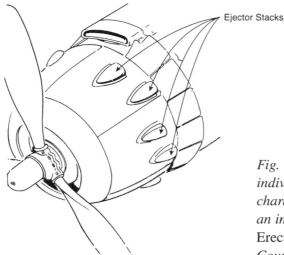

Ejector Stacks

Fig. 11.21 Later North American B-25s featured individual ejector exhaust stacks that produced the characteristics bumps around the cowl along with an interesting exhaust note! (North American B-25 Erection and Maintenance Manual, AN 01-60GE-2. Courtesy of the New England Air Museum.)

Fig. 11.22 North American B-25C Mitchell medium bomber powered by Wright R-2600s. (Courtesy of the National Air and Space Museum, Smithsonian Institution, Photo No. 1B-26102.)

carrier *Hornet*. Additional fuel tanks were installed and weight reduced by the removal of nonessential equipment. A pair of painted broomsticks were placed in the tail to simulate a pairs of .50s! The Holley carburetors fitted to the R-2600-9 engines were modified to allow greater range.

Many felt it would be impossible to get a heavily laden medium bomber airborne from the short confines of a carrier deck. By running the engines at maximum take-off power, that is, 44.5 in Hg manifold pressure and 2500 rpm, the available 1700 hp from each engine got the B-25s airborne with the *Hornet* steaming at full speed into a brisk wind.

Although all 16 aircraft were lost due to emergency landings or to the crew bailing out, the mission was a resounding success, not because of the damage caused, but from the vulnerability the Japanese felt. In a few short years, Wright-powered B-29s would devastate Japan.

B-25s were used extensively in the Pacific in tactical bombing roles at low and medium altitudes and were used for ground strafing with its withering firepower from as many as twelve .50-caliber machine guns. In Europe, it was used to support many critical ground operations, including the controversial bombing of Monte Casino in the Italian campaign.

B-25s soldiered on for many years after the war in U.S. Air Force guise and in many foreign air forces, as well as in many civilian applications (Refs. 2.7, 11.7).

Douglas A-20 Havoc, Boston, P-70, F-3

Another twin-engine medium bomber, the Douglas Havoc followed a surprisingly similar design path and development as the B-25 (Fig. 11.23). Early production versions of the A-20, known as DB-7s, were powered by Pratt & Whitney R-1830's, as was the early B-25.

The concept of the A-20 originated in the 1930s as a private venture. As in many previous cases, the French came through with orders for the DB-7 during the austere depression era. The limited service they saw with the French were not successful because of tactical errors. However, the French experience pointed up some shortcomings, which were corrected. The main requirement was for additional power, which came in the form of Wright R-2600-A5Bs rated at 1600 hp at 2400 rpm for take-off. Only 75 aircraft, designated DB-75As, saw service with the French before the capitulation. These 75 aircraft served with the Vichy Government and conducted several missions against the Allies.

Fig. 11.23 Douglas A-20 Havoc powered by Wright R-2600-11s. (Courtesy of the National Air and Space Museum, Smithsonian Institution.)

The British also took an interest in the DB-7, giving it the type name Boston. Undelivered French orders were diverted to England after the collapse of France in June 1940. During this period, the U.S. Army Air Corps was taking an interest in Douglas' new bomber. The Army took delivery of the prototype, designated A-20, in mid 1940. The plane differed in several significant areas compared with the British and French versions; the most noticeable change was the installation of a turbosupercharger to the Wright R-2600-7. The turbosupercharger installation was dropped on all subsequent A-20 variants. Although several technical difficulties were experienced with this installation, the deciding factor in the decision to drop the turbo was the fact that missions would be flown at medium to low altitudes, and therefore the turbo would offer no benefit. Service aircraft were fitted with single-stage, two-speed superchargers with power increasing from 1600 hp for the early A-20As to 1700 hp from the A-20H on. From the C model on, ejector exhaust replaced the collector ring system previously used.

The single-spar wing was attached to the fuselage at five points, one at the leading edge, two at the main spar, and two at the rear shear web. A monocoque nacelle supported the R-2600s, which were mounted on a tubular steel mount. Various exhaust systems were employed, including collector ring, flame damping for night operations, and individual ejector stacks.

The narrow fuselage housed a single pilot, rear gunner, and bomb-aimer/radio operator. A detachable nose allowed the installation of a "solid" gun nose or Plexiglas bomber nose. The solid nose could house four 20-mm cannon and two .50-caliber machine guns. Because of problems with them, most of the 20-mm cannons were replaced with .50-caliber machine guns. Flush-riveted construction was used throughout the fuselage (Ref. 2.7).

Production ended in September 1944 after 7097 had been built. After the liberation of France, the French Air Force used them extensively. Several thousand were shipped to the Soviet Union via Iran. As usual, very little information is available as to how effective they were on the eastern front, and again the Soviet government showed no appreciation or gratitude to the United States for supplying these aircraft.

Variations on the medium bomber theme made it a versatile aircraft. The British were the first to use it as a night fighter by installing a searchlight in the nose. Other modifications included British style "barbed" exhaust flame dampers and .303-caliber machine guns mounted in the nose. In 1940 British Havocs, or Bostons as the RAF designated them, were fitted with Mk. IV AI (airborne interception) radar to combat the nightly raids by Luftwaffe bombers. The R-2600 in RAF service was capable of taking tremendous abuse and still getting their crews home (Fig. 11.24).

P-70s were USAAF night fighters based on the British experience and converted from A-20As. The F-3 was a photo reconnaissance version of the A-20.

Martin PBM Mariner

By the late 1930's the Navy felt the Consolidated PBY Catalina was becoming obsolete. In hindsight, little did they realize the erstwhile PBY would not only continue in production throughout World War II but would also belie its apparent obsolescence. Martin responded to a Navy request in

Fig. 11.24 An amazing example of the toughness of the Wright R-2600. This engine brought an RAF Boston home after a raid in France. The other engine was shot away. Sadly, three of the crew members were killed on this mission. (Courtesy of the National Air and Space Museum, Smithsonian Institution, Photo No. BW-710900-20.)

1936 for a twin-engine patrol bomber. Designated XPBM-1, it was delivered in to the Navy in 1939. A quarter-scale proof-of-concept flying model was built prior to the first flight of the full-size aircraft. This was quite common in the late 1930s; for instance, Short & Harland built a similar model of the Stirling that was half scale.

The prototype was powered by R-2600-6s, which gave 1600 hp for take-off. Relatively few problems surfaced during flight testing, and by 1940 aircraft were being delivered to Navy squadrons. A single XPBM-2 was built; it was essentially the same as the PBM-1 except fitted with long-range fuel tanks and a strengthened structure to withstand the rigors of a catapult launch.

PBM-3s received additional power in the form of R-2600-12s rated at 1700 hp for take-off. From the PBM-3D on, the power was again increased to 1900 hp from R-2600-22s. Some variants of the -3 incorporated a fan to assist in cooling the R-2600s (Fig. 11.25). Earlier models of the PBM featured retractable wing floats; these were replaced on the -3 and later models with fixed floats. Six hundred seventy-nine PBM-3s would be built, and it would also be the last variant powered by Wright R-2600s (Fig. 11.26). PBM-5s (the PBM-4 was never built) were powered by Pratt & Whitney R-2800-34 engines rated at 2100 hp.

Structurally, PBMs featured a classic two-step hull for the fuselage, which was of monocoque construction. In order to keep the propellers out of the water spray, an inverted gull wing was mounted high on the deep fuselage. Each engine nacelle featured a bomb bay under the wing for internal stowage of depth charges and bombs.

PBMs were built at Martin's Omaha, Nebraska, facility and in Baltimore, Maryland (Refs. 2.7, 11.8).

Fig. 11.25 Engine cooling fan installed on the Wright R-26000-11s in the Martin PBM-3 Mariner. (Courtesy of the National Air and Space Museum, Smithsonian Institution, Photo No. 1B-19162.)

Fig. 11.26 Martin PBM Mariner on the step. (Courtesy of the National Air and Space Museum, Smithsonian Institution, Photo No. 1B-19102.)

Service

The wide open expanses of the Pacific Ocean were ideal for the PBM's long range. Japanese shipping and shore bases felt the effect of PBM bombing missions. The Mariner also played an important role in air sea rescue, rescuing downed pilots and crews from torpedoed ships. Squadrons were also deployed on the Caribbean and the Canal Zone for submarine hunting.

The British received 30 PBM-3Bs, designated Mariner G.R. Mk. 1 for Coastal Command service.

Grumman TBM/TBF Avenger

Another classic aircraft from the Grumman "Iron Works," the Avenger was one of the finest single-engine torpedo bombers of World War II.

The year 1939 was a watershed year for new aircraft. This was understandable considering the level of tension between the United States and Japan as well as the war erupting in Europe. This was the year Grumman responded to a Navy request for a 300-mph torpedo bomber. In 1940 the Navy ordered the XTBF-1, which was delivered in 1941. Considering this was Grumman's first attempt at designing a torpedo bomber, they did a first-class job. Although the aircraft did not reach the required 300-mph top speed, testing went remarkably smoothly. The most noticeable change was the addition of a dorsal fillet for the vertical stabilizer to improve directional stability.

Such was the escalating tension between the United States and Japan that top priority was given to the XTBF program. By early 1942 production examples were entering squadron service.

The single-spar wing was mounted in the mid position of the fuselage. The outer sections folded flush with the sides of the fuselage. TBF-1s were powered by an R-2600-8 fitted with a two-speed supercharger rated at 1700 hp. Later variants, TBM-3 and on, were powered by an R-2600-20 rated at 1900 hp. The additional 200 hp demanded additional heat rejection. This was accomplished by a larger and dedicated oil cooler opening on the bottom edge of the cowl leading edge. To further increase mass airflow through the cowling, additional cowl flaps were incorporated. Induction air for the downdraft carburetor was supplied from a ram air scoop built into the leading edge of the cowl. A collector ring exhaust had two outlets, one on each side of the fuselage. For night operations, some exhaust systems were fitted with a flame damper. Oil was supplied by a 32-gal tank. A tubular steel engine mount attached to the firewall at four points. The oval section fuselage formed a semi-mono-coque. The bomb bay featured two folding doors, with each door pivoted in the middle.

Because of Grumman's commitment to other projects, particularly the F6F Hellcat, production at the Bethpage, Long Island, facility was ended in December 1943. In its place, the Eastern Aircraft Division of General Motors took over production. All Eastern-built Avengers were designated TBMs.

After the Pearl Harbor attack, automobile production came to a screeching halt; consequently, large manufacturing facilities were idled. Eastern Aircraft was established in January 1942 from five General Motors automobile companies based on the eastern seaboard of the United States. The five companies were in Baltimore, Md.; Tarrytown, N.Y.; Linden N.J.; Bloomfield, N.J.; and Trenton, N.J. As can be imagined, General Motors had no idea what they were getting into with the production of a highly complex military aircraft. However, after the initial teething problems had been overcome, production got into full swing to the tune of 77%, or 7546 examples, of the Avenger production run being completed by V-J Day. On V-J Day, all contracts were canceled, and soon after Eastern Aircraft was dissolved. The former Eastern Aircraft plants then got back into automobile production.

Service

Rushed into service, the first six aircraft were delivered just in time for the battle of Midway in June 1942. Unfortunately, they suffered heavy losses against the Japanese in the battle. Despite this inauspicious start, the TBM established an enviable combat record (Fig. 11.27). Various forms of ordnance could be carried, including a single 2000-lb general-purpose bomb, a 1600-lb armor-piercing bomb,

Fig. 11.27 Grumman TBM/TBF Avenger powered by the Wright R-2600. (Courtesy of the National Air and Space Museum, Smithsonian Institution, Photo No. 1B-02004.)

or four 500-lb bombs. The bomb bay could also house a Mk. 13 aircraft torpedo, which initially gave serious reliability problems until various aerodynamic and hydrodynamic fixes were incorporated.

The TBMs were used extensively in the Pacific, against shore targets and Japanese shipping. A young George Bush became a highly decorated pilot in the Pacific theater flying TBMs.

In the North Atlantic, TBMs provided invaluable service hunting the German U-Boat menace, the one weapon that Hitler had at his disposal that nearly crippled the Allied war effort.

At the cease of hostilities, TBMs continued on in service into the 1950s (Refs. 2.7, 11.9).

Curtiss SB2C Helldiver

The last of a long line of Curtiss military aircraft to be ordered in quantity, the Helldiver, designed for the same missions as the TBM, did not initially live up expectations. One of the more maligned Allied aircraft of World War II, the SB2C suffered through a protracted and troubled development phase that delayed its entry into combat. Like the RAF Short Stirling (see next section and Chapter 5), the SB2C was a victim of its specifications (Fig. 11.28).

Because of the less-than-stellar performance of early models, the SB2C quickly gained several unflattering nicknames including "The Beast" and "Son-of-a-Bitch Second Class"!

The U.S. Navy awarded the contract for the Helldiver in May 1939. The first prototype flew in November 1940 powered by an R-2600-8 rated at 1700 hp. Immediately, handling problems became apparent. Part of the reason for the handling problems was the Navy requirement that two of them should fit in a standard 40 × 48 ft carrier elevator. Consequently, compromises were made with the overall design to accommodate the space requirement. Things deteriorated rapidly when the proto-

Fig. 11.28 A victim of unrealistic initial specifications, the Curtiss SB2C later went on to prove its worth after all the problems had been worked out. (Courtesy of the National Air and Space Museum, Smithsonian Institution, Photo No. 94-13740.)

type was severely damaged in an accident caused by engine failure in February 1941. The whole program was delayed for three months while awaiting repairs to the prototype. Modifications were incorporated into the rebuilt aircraft including improvements to the cooling of the R-2600. Additional cowl flaps with a deeper chord and a dedicated chin-mounted air scoop for the oil cooler were added.

During terminal-velocity dive tests in December 1941, the aircraft suffered structural failure resulting in the total loss of the prototype. Again, the program was set back, this time by five months.

With all the delays caused by the mishaps with the prototype aircraft and the required fixes, it was not until June 1942 that the first production version, the SB2C-1, rolled off the production lines. It would be more than a year later, November 1943, before the SB2C saw action, by which time a staggering 880 additional major design changes had been implemented.

With the introduction of the SB2C-3, power was increased to 1900 hp from an R-2600-20, a BB-series engine. Wright Aeronautical's patented "W" cooling fins for the cylinder barrel, which gave far superior heat rejection compared with the machined-in fins of the R-2600-8's barrel, contributed to the additional 200 hp. This allowed top speed to increase from 281 to 294 mph at 12,400 ft. By now, the SB2C was an excellent military aircraft, performing particularly well in many Pacific campaigns. The later SB2Cs, -3 and on, actually outperformed the Grumman TBM (Refs. 2.7, 11.10).

Short Stirling

Most Short Stirlings were powered by the Bristol Hercules (see Chapter 5 on Bristol engines); however, a number were powered by a civilian version of the R-2600, designated GR2600A5B, rated at 1600 hp. Later, up-rated R-2600-13 B-model engines, rated at 1700 hp, were installed in Stirlings. Performance was the same as the Hercules-powered aircraft (Ref. 2.7).

R-3350 Cyclone 18

One of the most troublesome engine projects of World War II and possibly on a par with the Rolls-Royce Vulture or Napier Sabre for the amount of grief and headaches it caused, the R-3350 offered numerous "challenges" to Wright Aeronautical's development engineers and B-29 crews.

Design work started in January 1936. The R-3350 shared the same bore and stroke as the R-2600, that is, 6.125-in bore and 6.3125-in stroke; the additional displacement was obtained from four additional cylinders, that is, two rows of nine (Fig. 11.29).

As would be expected, construction details followed R-2600 practice. The three-piece crankcase was initially an aluminum forging; later, a steel forging replaced it. The three-piece clamping-type crankshaft rode in three roller bearings. Two massive dynamic counterweights, one per row, damped out the usual troublesome second and higher orders of vibration (Fig. 11.30). In early production engines, it was found that this was insufficient because vibration emanating from the crankshaft was transmitted to the propeller shaft, resulting in propeller shaft fatigue failures. Additional second-order counterweights, running at twice crank speed, were designed into the front and rear cam plates. Four counterweights were disposed radially around the crankshaft axis and driven off the cam drive. This offered a very compact solution to the problem without unduly affecting production (Fig. 11.31).

The one-piece master rods ran in silver-lead-indium bearings (Fig. 11.32). Cylinder design was also similar to R-2600 practice, that is, a nitralloy forged barrel with Wright Aeronautical's aluminum "W" finning muff rolled into the outside diameter. The heads were cast, a design feature that was to cost the R-3350 dearly in operation. Total cooling surface on the 18 cylinders amounted to 5850 ft², or 3900 in² per cylinder. Although this was an impressive number, it was still insufficient to keep the R-3350 cool under high-power, climbing conditions.

Fig. 11.29 An early prototype of the Wright R-3350. Note the forward-facing exhaust ports for the front row of cylinders and the transversely mounted distributors on the nose case. (Courtesy of the New England Air Museum.)

Rear Dynamic Counterweight Assembly

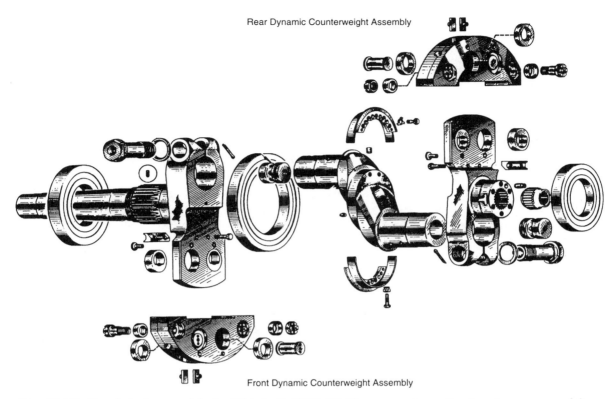

Front Dynamic Counterweight Assembly

*Fig. 11.30 Crankshaft assembly for Wright R-3350-57. Three massive roller bearings are used for the mains. Plain bearings of silver-lead-indium are used for the master rods. Despite the use of two massive dynamic counterweights shown, a serious second-order vibratory mode existed at take-off speed that could induce failure of the propeller shaft. Modifications to incorporate eight (four at the front and four at the rear) second-order counterweights running at twice crankshaft speed resolved this problem. (*Wright Aeronautical Corporation Parts Manual, *R-3350 BA Series. Courtesy of Gerry Abbamont.)*

Combustion chambers were hemispherical with two valves per cylinder, and the exhaust was sodium cooled. Exhaust ports on the front row of cylinders faced forward rather than rearward, which would be the case in normal two-row air-cooled radial practice. Again, this feature caused problems in the service life of the engine. Single-stage, two-speed supercharging was often supplemented by a pair of General Electric type B-11 turbosuperchargers. The R-3350 was one of the first Wright Aeronautical engines to be fitted with a Wright-designed gear-driven supercharger. Previously, all supercharger design work had been performed by General Electric, although General Electric continued to manufacture impellers to Wright Aeronautical's design. Efficiency of the Wright-designed superchargers were on a par with, or in some cases superior to, the Rolls-Royce Merlin XX series and higher, considered to be the state of the art at the time. Wright also learned the same lesson Rolls-Royce had with tight inlet elbows to the supercharger eye; 7½% efficiency was lost through the early inlet elbows. By redesign of the elbow, this loss was reduced to less than 1%. By 1943 the efficiency

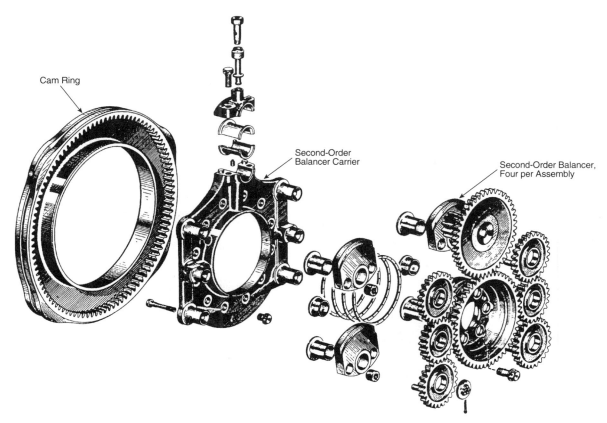

Fig. 11.31 R-3350-57 rear second-order balancers. A similar arrangement was featured at the front of the engine. Four counterweights ran at twice crankshaft speed driven off the cam gears. (Wright Aeronautical Corporation Parts Manual, R-3350 BA Series. Courtesy of Gerry Abbamont.)

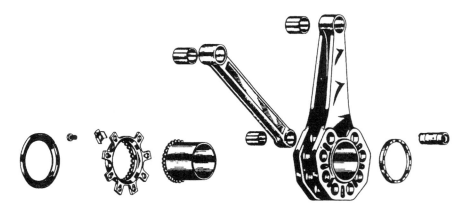

Fig. 11.32 Master connecting rod assembly for Wright R-3350-57 (B-29/B-32 engine). Note the use of an I-section rod rather than the more traditional H-section. Workmanship on these internal engine components was exquisite. All surfaces were polished to a mirror finish for additional fatigue resistance. (Wright Aeronautical Corporation Parts Manual, R-3350 BA Series. Courtesy of Gerry Abbamont.)

of the R-3350 supercharger had risen to 81% at a pressure ratio of 2:1. Carburetion was supplied by a Bendix or Chandler Evans downdraft unit. Due to poor mixture distribution, front cylinders tended to run leaner than the rear cylinders; later engines were fitted with direct fuel injection into the cylinder. Two Bendix Stromberg nine-plunger units supplied an injection pressure of 500 psi. One unit supplied fuel to the front cylinders, and the other supplied fuel to the rear cylinders; this enabled the mixture to be "tweaked" to accommodate the differing mass airflow to the rear and front cylinders (Fig. 11.33). Bosch also developed a similar fuel-injection system for the engine.

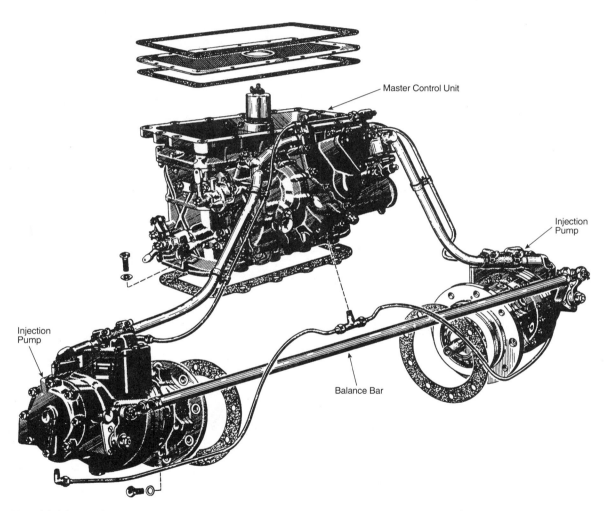

Fig. 11.33 Fuel-injection system fitted to Wright R-3350-57, -57A, -59, and -59A. The two injection pumps were controlled by the master control unit which "read" mass air flow entering the supercharger. Each injection pump fed one row of cylinders. This allowed the mixture to be "tweaked" if one row was running leaner or richer by adjusting the balance bar between the pumps. (Wright Aeronautical Corporation Parts Manual, R-3350 BA Series. Courtesy of Gerry Abbamont.)

Direct fuel injection entered service in 1945, during the waning days of the war. Although no power gain was obtained from direct fuel injection—in fact, there may have been a slight reduction in power—it offered greater safety from the induction fires that plagued the carbureted R-3350s.

Ignition was supplied by a single Bendix Scintilla magneto mounted at the rear, which supplied high-tension current to the dual distributors mounted on the nose case. Reduction gearing followed Wright Aeronautical's multipinion planetary set-up; however, numerous problems were experienced, particularly during the painful, early days of development. Corrections included closer tolerances of the pinions and the carrier. Mounting for the R-3350 was rather unique in that the engine was suspended from the rocker boxes (Fig. 11.34). Although this made for a good suspension system, it could not have been practical, as it made cylinder changes more difficult. Antidetonation injection was considered for the R-3350 in the Boeing B-29; however, it was not incorporated due to the extra weight and complexity involved. In retrospect, it can be seen that this was an error; the B-29 would have benefited from the additional detonation resistance and consequently another 300 to 400 hp per engine from ADI, particularly during the typical overgross take-offs at high temperatures the B-29 was exposed to in the Pacific (Refs. 2.5, 4.15–4.18).

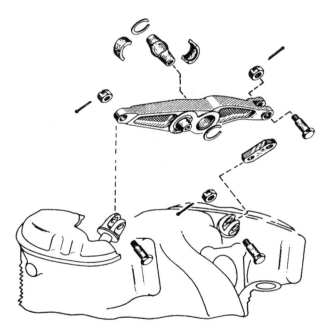

*Fig. 11.34 Unique rocker box engine mount for the Wright R-3350 when installed in a Boeing B-29 or Consolidated B-32. Loads were transmitted through the rocker shaft and rocker box and then through the cylinder head. (*Wright Aeronautical Corporation Parts Manual, R-3350 BA Series. *Courtesy of Gerry Abbamont.)*

Manufacture

The size and magnitude of the R-3350 program was nothing short of mind boggling. Wright Aeronautical built a new plant at Woodridge, New Jersey, solely for R-3350 production. All production at Wright Aeronautical's Cincinnati, Ohio, plant was converted to R-3350 production. The Dodge Chicago Division of Chrysler built a massive new facility in Chicago.

A valuable opportunity was lost when Dodge Chicago built their plant. A decision had to be made on the cylinder head design: should it be forged or cast? The decision was made to keep to the existing cast design due to a delay in delivery of the tooling.

Dodge Chicago supplied the bulk of R-3350s manufactured during World War II—a total of 18,413 compared to 13,791 shipped by Wright Aeronautical. Dodge Chicago was tooling up before the engine passed its type test; consequently they were inundated with 48,500 engineering changes, which naturally impacted production schedules.

One of the major changes was the incorporation of the second-order balancer designed into the front and rear cam plates. Other changes included improving cylinder baffles as combat experience was gained and increasing oil flow from 140 lb/min to 160 lb/min. As experience mounted and engineering changes were incorporated, overhaul times improved from 100 to 400 h by war's end.

New manufacturing techniques were instituted. Though taken for granted today, they were revolutionary in the early 1940s. These techniques included shot peening of the connecting rods and polishing using a high-pressure water/fine-sand mixture that eliminated the previously labor-intensive hand polishing.

Testing involved an initial run of 7½ h starting out at 1400 rpm and culminating in a run at take-off power at 2800 rpm. The 7½-h requirement was reduced to 3¾-h by war's end, as experience demanded. After the initial run, engines were disassembled, checked for inconsistencies, and reassembled for a final test run of 2¾ h (reduced from 3½ h with early production engines). Power recovery was used throughout the testing; that is, the engines drove electric generators feeding power back into the production facility (Ref. 11.11).

Performance

All R-3350s flown in combat were rated at 2200 hp during World War II. This power was obtained at 2800 rpm and 48 in Hg manifold pressure. A war emergency rating of 2500 hp was allowed under extreme conditions (and not necessarily war emergency), for example, during an overgross take-off on an all-too-short strip! (Ref. 9.13)

Applications

Table 11.3 summarizes the performance and applications of the R-3350.

TABLE 11.3—WRIGHT R-3350 PERFORMANCE AND APPLICATION SUMMARY

Dash Number	Applications	hp/rpm/alt	Comments
-3		1800/2205 None	Similar to -1 except different propeller shaft reduction gear ratio and hydromatic propeller control
-5	Douglas XB-19	2000/2400 None	Similar to -3 except dynamic engine suspension from rocker bolts on cylinder heads
-7		2300/2800 2250/2700/20,000	Similar to -5 except single-speed supercharger
-9		2300/2800 2250/2700/20,000	Similar to -7 except equipped with two-speed, dual rotating propeller shafts. Model—for test only
-11	XA-23	2200/2800 2200/2600/2600 1900/2600/16,000	Similar to -5 except different ratings
-13	XA-31C Boeing XB-29 Lockheed XB-30 XB-31 Consolidated XB-32	2200/2800 2200/2400/25,000	Similar to -11 except propeller shaft reduction gear ratio and torquemeter nose section
-15		2200/2800 2200/2400/25,000	Similar to -13 except left-hand propeller shaft rotation. Project canceled
-17	YA-31C Curtiss P-62A Curtiss XP-62	2300/2800 2250/2600/25,000	Similar to -7 except coaxial propeller shafts and torquemeter nose section
-19	A-31C	2200/2800 2200/2600/25,000	Similar to -13 except cylinder head fuel injection and automatic control
-21	Boeing YB-29 Consolidated B-32 C-97	2200/2800 2200/2600/25,000	Similar to -13 except equipped with two each 2.8:1 generator and accessory drives
-21A	Boeing YB-29 Boeing B-29	2200/2800 2200/2600/25,000	Similar to -21 except engineering and design changes
-23	Boeing B-29 Boeing B-29A, B-29B Boeing RB-29A Boeing XB-29E	2200/2800 2200/2600/25,000	Similar to -21 except no torquemeter is provided. Engines also manufactured by Dodge. Also used in B-32, TB-32, XC-97, C-97, YC-97, C-121A, and YC-121B

(continued)

TABLE 11.3, continued

Dash Number	Applications	hp/rpm/alt	Comments
-23A	Consolidated B-32 Boeing B-29 Boeing B-29A, B-29B Boeing RB-29 Boeing RB-29A	2200/2800 2200/2600/25,000	Similar to -23 except engineering changes necessary to make engine suitable for combat use. Engines also manufactured by Dodge. Also used in TB-29, A, B, TRB-29A, C-97, YC-97, C-121A, and VC-121B
-23B	Boeing B-29 Consolidated B-32	2200/2800 2200/2600/25,000	Similar to -23A except incorporated a PR58Q1 or PR58K1 Bendix carburetor in lieu of a Chandler-Evans model 58CPB4. Engine performance or installation was not affected
-25		2200/2800	Similar to -8 except for cylinder head suspension, external gear box, hydraulic starter. None procured. Project canceled
-27		2300/2800 2100/2400/...	Similar to -25 except single-speed supercharger. None procured. No installation
-29		2200/2800 2200/2600/2500 1900/2600/16,000	Similar to -25 except dynamic suspension parts, large diameter mounting ring, and torquemeter. Project canceled
-37A		2200/2800 2200/2600/25,000	Similar to -37 except equipped with a Bosch fuel injector
-39		2200/2800 2200/2600/25,000	Similar to -19 except equipped with Holley fuel injector
-41	Boeing B-29	2200/2800 2200/2600/25,000	Similar to -19 except equipped with Bosch fuel injector
-43	XA-38	2200/2800 2250/2600/2800 1900/2600/14,000	Similar to -31 except equipped with Chandler Evans 58CPB2 carburetor
-45		2300/2800 2250/2600/25,000	Similar to -43 except different rear section, single-speed supercharger of fuel-injection pump type, and double-acting propeller shafts. None procured. Project canceled
-47		2800/2900 2800/2900/...	None procured. Designation canceled and assigned to an R-3350 engine of higher horsepower rating with installation of Bosch fuel-injection system. B-29 proposal

(continued)

TABLE 11.3, continued

Dash Number	Applications	hp/rpm/alt	Comments
-49		2800/2900 2800/2900/...	None procured. Designation canceled and assigned to an R-3350 engine of higher horsepower rating with installation of Bendix fuel-injection system. B-29 proposal
-51		2200/2800 2800/2600/...	None procured. B-29 proposal
-53		2200/2800 2200/2600/25,000	Similar to -23 except equipped with a Bendix fuel injector and low-tension ignition. None procured. B-29 proposal
-55		2200/2800 2200/2600/25,000	Similar to -23 except equipped with a Bosch fuel injector and low-tension ignition. None procured. B-29 proposal
-57	Boeing B-29 Boeing B-29A, B-29B Boeing XB-29E Boeing RB-29 Boeing RB-29A	2200/2800 2200/2600/25,000	Similar to -19 except equipped with a Bendix fuel injector and high-tension ignition. Torquemeter eliminated. Engines also manufactured by Dodge. Also used in TB-29, A, B, TRB-29A, C-97, YC-97, C-121A, and VC-121B
-57A	Boeing B-29 Boeing B-29A, B-29B Boeing RB-29 Boeing RB-29A Boeing TB-29 Boeing TB-29A, TB-29B	2200/2800 2200/2600/25,000	Similar to -57 except incorporates a redesigned fuel-injection line system and redesigned airseal. Performance of engine or airplane not affected. Airplane installation was affected unless the airplane was reworked to accommodate this engine. Also used in TRB-29A, C-97, C-121A, and VC-121B
-59	Boeing B-29 Boeing B-29A, B-29B Boeing XB-29A Boeing RB-29A	2200/2800 2200/2600/25,000	Similar to -41 except equipped with Bosch fuel injector and high-tension ignition. Torquemeter eliminated. Also used in C-121A and VC-121B
-59A	Boeing B-29 Boeing B-29A, B-29B Boeing XB-29E Boeing RB-29A Consolidated B-32	2200/2800 2200/2600/25,000	Similar to -59 except incorporates a redesigned fuel-injection line system and redesigned airseal. Engine or airplane performance is not affected but airplane installation was affected unless the airplane was reworked to accommodate this engine. Also used in C-121A and VC-121B

(continued)

TABLE 11.3, continued

Dash Number	Applications	hp/rpm/alt	Comments
-61		2200/2800 2200/2600/25,000	Similar to -23 except equipped with Ceco carburetor and low-tension ignition
-63		2200/2800 2200/2600/25,000	Similar to -23 except equipped with Stromberg carburetor and low-tension ignition
-65		2500/2800 2500/2800/25,000	Similar to -23A except different cooling system, double-acting propeller shafts, newly designed oil pump, oil sump, supercharger, and overlap cams. Equipped with low-tension ignition and fuel injection
-65A		2500/2800 2500/2800/25,000	Similar to -65 except equipped with spark plug type fuel injection nozzle
-67		2500/2800 2500/2800/25,000	Similar to -57A except incorporated the following revisions: supercharger rear housing, new rear and front oil pumps and sumps; single-track planetary reduction gear; new blower front housing, oil jet manifold; super rear cover with aluminum bearings; internal fuel lines; and Bendix fuel-injection system
-69		2500/2800 2500/2800/25,000	Similar to -59A except incorporated the following revisions: supercharger rear housing, new rear housing; new rear and front oil pumps and sumps; single-track planetary reduction gear; new super front housing, oil jet manifold; super rear cover with aluminum bushings; internal fuel lines; Bosch fuel injection system

Source: Refs. 2.7, 4.15–4.18, 6.4, 9.13.

Boeing B-29 Superfortress

The airplane most associated with the R-3350 and that proved almost as problematic as the engine was the Boeing B-29 (Fig. 11.35).

On 29 January 1940 the Army put out a request for data to be sent out to the major airframe manufacturers for a long-range bomber. Five companies responded: Lockheed with the B-30, Douglas with the B-31, Boeing with the B-29, Martin with the B-33, and Consolidated with the B-32. Interestingly, all five bids called out the R-3350 for the power plant.

Fig. 11.35 Boeing B-29 Superfortress, powered by various dash numbers of the Wright R-3350, some of which featured direct cylinder fuel injection. (Courtesy of the National Air and Space Museum, Smithsonian Institution, Photo No. 1A-11962.)

Because of new information coming in from Europe and the Eastern Front, the initial specification was substantially changed in April 1940. The new specifications included self-sealing fuel tanks, armor plating, multiple-gun turrets, and so forth. Contracts were awarded to Lockheed and Boeing, with Boeing being the favorite. Because of Lockheed's commitments to other aircraft, particularly the P-38, they dropped out. In its place, Consolidated's bid was accepted.

Boeing incorporated many new features in the B-29, or Model 341 as it was originally known when designed to the original specification. When redesigned to the later specification, it received the Boeing designation Model 345.

The B-29 was the world's first strategic bomber with a pressurized fuselage. A cabin altitude of 10,500 ft was maintained to 35,000 ft. It was the first aircraft with a computer-directed gun sighting system. Butt-jointed skins with flush riveting were recently introduced technologies used with the B-29. Tricycle landing gear was among the other new or recent innovations.

In order to get the required performance, Boeing designed a beautiful, 11½:1 aspect ratio, laminar flow wing of 141-ft, 3-in span. As with all Boeing piston engine aircraft, most systems were electrically operated.

Abandoning the Warren truss wing design used on the B-17, Boeing used a web-type structure relying on the skin for a substantial part of the load bearing. At the wing roots, the skin was a substantial ³⁄₁₆ in thick, which was the heaviest used up to that time. The massive electrically operated Fowler flaps were built up in three sections: a center section and two outer sections. The B-29 flap system was the first application of precision ball screws, now taken for granted in industry. The landing gear was also electrically operated.

The circular cross section fuselage was built in five sections. Three pressurized compartments were incorporated into the fuselage: one in the nose section, one aft of the bomb bay, and one in the tail turret. A crawl tunnel over the dual bomb bays was provided between the nose section and the aft section; however, the tail turret was isolated. The vertical tail surface design was an enlarged version of the B-17E. The defensive armament was unique and advanced the state of the art. Gunners (with the exception of the tail gunner) were isolated from their weapons; consequently, they were not exposed to the tremendous recoil and vibration emanating from the weapon when it was fired. Four turrets, each mounting a pair of .50-caliber machine guns, were mounted on the fuselage, two on top and two on the bottom. Five sighting stations were provided: one in the nose, three in the center pressurized compartment, and one in the tail. Although some sighting stations had secondary control over certain other turrets, only one sight could be in control of a given turret at one time.

Power was provided by a variety of R-3350s. The prototype XB-29 used R-3350-5s rated at 2000 hp at 2400 rpm; later this aircraft was fitted with -13 engines rated at 2200 hp at 2800 rpm. The -13 differed from the -5 by having a different propeller reduction gear ratio, 20:7 instead of 16:7. This introduced the use of four-blade propellers, which characterized all subsequent B-29s. The XB-29 had three-blade propellers. YB-29s were powered by R-3350-21s, similar to the -13 except for generator and accessory drives. The -21A was based on the -21 but incorporated numerous design and engineering changes. Production versions of the B-29 had R-3350-21A engines and -23 engines, which were similar to the -21A and were the first versions produced by Dodge. The -23A was also the first "combat" engine (Fig. 11.36). The -23B was similar to the -23A but incorporated a Bendix carburetor instead of the Chandler Evans. The R-3350-41 was the first production engine fitted with a Bosch direct-cylinder fuel-injection system, otherwise it was similar to a -13. Likewise, the -57 was also fuel injected, with Bendix supplying the injection equipment. The -57As incorporated an improved fuel-injection line system (Fig. 11.37). Last of the R-3350 variants fitted to the B-29 were the -59 and -59A, which were similar to the -41 except the Bosch fuel-injection system was used.

Fig. 11.36 Three-quarter view of an early Wright R-3350-23, first of the so-called "combat" engines for the B-29. Note the transversely mounted distributors on top of the nose case. (Courtesy of the New Jersey Aviation Hall of Fame Museum and Gerry Abbamont.)

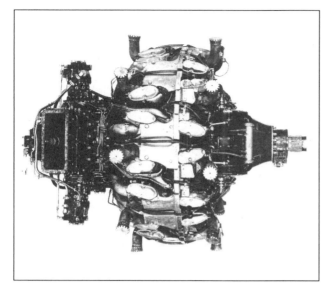

Fig. 11.37 Top view of the Wright R-3350-57. Note the dual Bendix fuel-injection pumps and the balance bar for the pumps. Exhaust stacks shown were for testing purposes only. Aircraft exhaust system was manifolded into collector rings and routed to the dual turbo-superchargers. (Courtesy of the New Jersey Aviation Hall of Fame Museum and Gerry Abbamont.)

In each case, the engine was boosted by a pair of General Electric Type B-11 turbosuperchargers operating in parallel and mounted vertically on the nacelle, behind the firewall. The exhaust from each row of cylinders fed a turbo. The front cylinders exhausted forward in a manner similar to many of the Bristol radials. The collector ring for the front row was situated inside the leading edge of the cowl; the exhaust was then routed under the engine to the turbo. The turbo compressor discharged into an intercooler and then into the downdraft carburetor or master control unit if it featured direct fuel injection.

A large plenum, under the main air cooling intake for the engine, housed the oil cooler, the turbo compressor air intake, and the intercooler. Temperature was controlled by variable cooling flaps.

Development was painful. Not only were new power plants used, but entire new systems were pioneered. In today's terminology, the B-29 would have been referred to as a paradigm shift. The logistics involved in manufacturing it were colossal. Components were delivered to Renton, Washington, from all over the United States. Eventually, five main production plants were turning out B-29s.

The first flight of the XB-29—piloted by Boeing's chief test pilot, Eddie Allen—occurred on 21 September 1942. As a harbinger of things come, 900 engineering changes were made between the spring of 1940 and the first flight.

Tragedy struck on 18 February 1943 when Allen, flying XB-29 No. 2, experienced an engine fire in the No. 1 nacelle. This fire was extinguished with the on-board system; however, a second fire then broke out in the No. 2 nacelle. This time, it was not possible to extinguish the fire. The aircraft crashed into a high-rise building 3 mi from the runway. Allen was killed along with the ten-man test crew and 20 people on the ground. Because of the numerous problems the R-3350 had experienced during the XB-29 test program, the aircraft was grounded and the whole B-29 program put on hold, this at a critical stage of the war. Not only was the B-29 grounded, but all R-3350-powered aircraft were also grounded.

Because of the critical nature of the B-29 program, a Senate investigating committee was formed chaired by Senator Harry S Truman. The conclusion of the committee placed the blame of the XB-29 problems on the R-3350. Cases were cited of poor workmanship and inspection. However, the loss of the XB-29 should not be blamed on the R-3350. The crash investigation determined that the fire started in the leading edge of the wing; the ignition source was thought to have been instrument tubing running through the leading edge that was ignited by contact with the exhaust system. An idiosyncrasy of the XB-29 fuel system allowed fuel to be siphoned from the filler cap into the leading edge under certain conditions. This then led to a major fire from the initial fire caused by the instrument tubing. A redesign of the fuel filler system eliminated this problem.

In the meantime, the R-3350 had reached its nadir as far as development problems went, but it would be a long time before reliability would be acceptable. Due to the plethora of engineering changes on the R-3350, logistics became almost unmanageable. Finally, a "combat" version of the R-3350-23 evolved by which the early production B-29s would be powered.

Wright Aeronautical engineers analyzed 82 engine failures from October to February 1943. Reduction gear failures had featured prominently as a cause; consequently, several changes were incorporated, including closer tolerances for the pinion carrier. When multiple pinions are used in a heavily loaded gear train, close tolerances are critical, but this makes for a very difficult manufacturing job. In other cases, Rolls-Royce resorted to hand-fitting all the pinion gears in the Vulture reduction gear, and Napier designed the brilliant but complex gear balancing system for the Sabre reduction gear.

Overspeeding due to slow response from the governor was another cause for concern. Larger oil galleries in the nose section, which allowed a greater oil flow, corrected this problem. The increased oil flow required a larger scavenge pump.

In the meantime, while Wright Aeronautical was laboring to get some semblance of reliability from the R-3350, aircraft workers were toiling in abysmal conditions in Kansas incorporating the latest modifications into the delivered B-29s.

B-29s entered combat flying from purpose-built strips in China. Each aircraft that departed the United States carried a spare R-3350 slung in its bomb bay. A staging area in India was established and from there the B-29s ferried their own fuel and supplies over the Hump to China.

Problems were rampant, and overheating was the main culprit. Cowl flap position was critical; if the flap was opened too far, the aircraft could not maintain formation due to additional drag; if it was not opened sufficiently, severe overheating resulted. This early experience drove home several important lessons. Loose fitting or damaged cylinder baffles, which could be tolerated in less highly stressed radials, would aggravate the marginal cooling situation.

Field modifications such as blast tubes directed over hot spots on the top cylinders and interconnecting oil lines for the rocker boxes helped.

The first B-29 raid was against Bangkok in June 1944. Early results were disappointing. Many losses occurred due to mechanical failure. Part of the problem was the requirement to bomb from high altitudes. The long climb to 30,000 ft stressed the R-3350 to the limit. On Christmas Eve 1944, a new tactic was tried against a Japanese target, the base at Hankow. The aircraft bombed at a much lower altitude, offering two major advantages. Engine problems were substantially reduced, and, due to the requirement for less fuel, a higher bomb load could be carried. After the capture of the Marianas in August 1944 by the Marines, B-29 bases were immediately built. This eliminated the need to fly from China and the associated logistical problem of flying material over the Hump in support of those operations. The island of Saipan was the first base to support B-29 operations in the Marianas. Although logistics were considerably easier than when operating from China, a long, treacherous over-water flight was required to reach targets in Japan. Tactics were again altered by using incendiaries instead of high-explosive bombs. The destruction wreaked havoc with the Japanese homeland. As many as 500 B-29s would attack a given target. In fact, far more destruction was caused by the "conventional" raids than from the two atomic raids.

On 6 August 1945 the first atomic bomb, carried aloft by a B-29 named *Enola Gay,* was dropped; its target was Hiroshima. The mission went as planned. Three days later, on 9 August, the B-29 *Bockcar* dropped the second atomic bomb. This finally forced the Japanese Emperor to sue for peace, and on 15 August 1945, V-J Day was declared. World War II was over.

Wright Aeronautical engineers analyzed the problems with the R-3350 and found several causes for the unreliability and overheating. Cowl flaps were set for the highest cylinder head temperature allowable: 260°C for take-off and 232°C for cruising in auto lean. This did not allow for discrepancies in thermocouples or instruments or even if the hottest cylinder was being measured. Inspections found that thermocouples were often out of calibration. Damaged intercylinder and head baffles caused overheating of the affected cylinder(s). A maximum of 20 min ground running could be tolerated prior to take-off. During all ground operations, cowl flaps were set at their wide open setting of 26°. For take-off, the cowl flaps were closed down to 8°.

The three top cylinders in the rear row—numbers 1, 3, and 5—were particularly susceptible to exhaust valve seat erosion with subsequent erosion of the valve guide boss. It was found that this condition would occur after approximately 175 h. Some units were aware of the problem and made a practice of changing engines at 150 h. This was obviously a very wasteful and time-consuming practice. Therefore, a scheduled maintenance program was incorporated in which the port was inspected after 150 h and every 15 h thereafter, and if any evidence of port erosion existed, the engine was changed.

Almost as serious as the exhaust port problem was the leaking of the exhaust ball joint for the front cylinders. A leak would allow white-hot exhaust to be blown over the cylinder head, contributing to overheating. Improved design of the exhaust ball joint alleviated this situation.

Improved cooling while on the ground was obtained by the incorporation of cuffs on the root of the propeller blades. Cowl flaps were shortened, and additional cowl flaps on top of the nacelle were added, thus increasing the airflow through the cowl. Improved cylinder baffle designs and seals were incorporated. Inter rocker box lubrication lines were introduced, thus flooding the valve stem, upper guide, and spring with oil to help carry away some of the excess heat. These and many other modifications improved life for the engines and for the flight and ground crews.

Toward the end of the war, the time between overhaul had grown to 400 h, about average for a World War II combat engine.

Despite its rocky start, the B-29 is recognized as one of the most effective strategic bombers of World War II. A total of 4221 were built by the time production ended in 1945 (Refs. 2.5–2.7, 11.12, 11.13).

Consolidated B-32 Dominator

In a parallel effort backing up the B-29 program, the Consolidated B-32 Dominator was also developed (Fig. 11.38). Both aircraft were built to the same specification, and both had the same power plants. The first flight of the B-32 occurred just ahead of the B-29; however, this would be the only time this troubled aircraft would be ahead. The development of the B-32 was even more problematical than the tortuous B-29 program. On several occasions, the program was almost canceled; however, because of the development problems experienced by the B-29, it was felt a backup program should be kept alive as insurance. As the aircraft became mired in technical problems, some of the more complex systems were deleted, such as the requirement for pressurization and the remote-control system for the defensive guns.

Fig. 11.38 Consolidated B-32. (Courtesy of the National Air and Space Museum, Smithsonian Institution, Photo No. 1A-22702.)

Engine nacelle design was very similar to the B-29; the most obvious difference was the orientation of the dual General Electric type B-11 turbosuperchargers. Although they were mounted vertically, they were not flush with the nacelle, as in the B-29.

The XB-32 first flew powered by R-3350-13s, and early production examples had R-3350-13s or -21s. The last B-32s were powered by R-3350-59As. All these dash numbers of R-3350 were also installed in the B-29.

Many of the Consolidated B-24 Liberator landing gear components were used, including the wheels and tires. The main difference was that they were doubled in the B-32 to handle the increased weight. Performance was similar to the B-29.

By the war's end, a total of 144 Dominators had been delivered, and of these very few entered combat. The combat debut was 29 May 1945. After V-J Day, B-32s were quickly withdrawn from service and scrapped. Even brand-new aircraft coming off the production lines in Fort Worth were flown to Reconstruction and Finance Corporation (RFC) disposal centers and scrapped (Ref. 11.14).

R-4090

Another variation on the R-3350 theme was the R-4090. This engine represented one of the few examples of an eleven-cylinder per row radial (Fig. 11.39). Twenty-two 3350-size cylinders were arranged in two rows around a steel forged crankcase. Several engines were completed and test-flown prior to the cancellation of this project.

With the engine rated at 3000 hp at 2800 rpm, at a weight of 3260 lb, performance and weight were comparable to the early Pratt & Whitney R-4360s that were being developed at the same time (Ref. 9.13).

Fig. 11.39 One of the rare occasions when a 22-cylinder radial was built. The Wright R-4090 used 22 R-3350-size cylinders in two rows. Rated at 3000 hp at 2800 rpm, it was under development during World War II. Specifics compared favorably with the Pratt & Whitney R-4360 under development at the same time. It developed the same power for less weight. Photograph shows an R-4090-1; a -3 was built that featured contra-rotating propeller drive. (Courtesy of the New Jersey Aviation Hall of Fame Museum and Gerry Abbamont.)

References

2.5 Schlaifer, Robert, and S. D. Heron, <u>Development of Aircraft Engines and Development of Aviation Fuels</u>, Harvard University, Boston, 1950.

2.6 Johnson, Robert E., "Why the Boeing B-29 Bomber and Why The Wright R-3350 Engine?" *J. American Aviation Historical Society,* Fall 1988.

2.7 <u>Jane's All The World's Aircraft</u>, McGraw-Hill, New York, 1945/1946.

4.3 Foxworth, Thomas G., <u>The Speed Seekers</u>, Doubleday & Co., New York.

4.15 Wilkinson, Paul H., <u>Aircraft Engines of The World 1946</u>, Paul H. Wilkinson, New York.

4.16 Wilkinson, Paul H., <u>Aircraft Engines of The World 1947</u>, Paul H. Wilkinson, New York.

4.17 Wilkinson, Paul H., <u>Aircraft Engines of The World 1948</u>, Paul H. Wilkinson, New York.

4.18 Wilkinson, Paul H., <u>Aircraft Engines of The World 1949</u>, Paul H. Wilkinson, New York.

5.2 <u>Jane's All The World's Aircraft</u>, McGraw-Hill, New York, 1942/1943.

9.13 <u>Model Designations of USAF Aircraft Engines</u>, 9th ed., By Authority of Commanding General Air Materiel Command, U.S. Air Force, 1 Jan. 1949.

9.14 Angellucci, Enzo, with Peter Bowers, <u>The American Fighter</u>, Orion Books, New York.

11.1 <u>Parts Catalog, Wright Cyclone 9 Aircraft Engines</u>, Wright Aeronautical Corp., Paterson, N.J., 15 Aug. 1940.

11.2 Freeman, Roger, <u>B-17 Flying Fortress</u>, Bonanza Books, 1984.

11.3 Willmott, H. P., <u>B-17 Flying Fortress</u>, Chartwell Books, 1980.

11.4 Stern, Rob, <u>SBD Dauntless in Action</u>, Squadron Signal Publications, Carrolton, Tex.

11.5 Maas, Jim, <u>F2A Buffalo in Action</u>, Squadron Signal Publications, Carrolton, Tex.

11.6 <u>Overhaul Manual, Wright Cyclone 14 Aircraft Engine</u>, Wright Aeronautical Corp., Paterson, N.J., Nov. 1940.

11.7 McDowell, Ernest R., <u>B-25 Mitchell in Action</u>, Squadron Signal Publications, Carrolton, Tex.

11.8 Smith, Bob, <u>PBM Mariner in Action</u>, Squadron Signal Publications, Carrolton, Tex.

11.9 Scrivner, Charles L., <u>TBM/TBF in Action</u>, Squadron Signal Publications, Carrolton, Tex.

11.10 Stern, Robert, <u>SB2C Helldiver in Action</u>, Squadron Signal Publications, Carrolton, Tex.

11.11 Stout, Wesley W., <u>Great Engines and Great Planes</u>, Chrysler Corp., Detroit, Mich., 1947.

11.12 Berger, Carl, <u>B-29 The Superfortress</u>, Ballantine Books, New York, N.Y., 1970.

11.13 Johnson, Robert E., "Why the Boeing B-29 Bomber, and Why the Wright R-3350 Engine?," *American Aviation Historical Society,* Santa Ana, Calif., Fall 1988.

11.14 Harding, Stephen, and James I. Long, <u>Dominator—The Story of the B-32 Bomber</u>, Pictorial Histories Publishing Co., Missoula, Mont., 1983.

Chapter 12

Hyper Activity and Other Near Misses

The term "hyper" in reference to aircraft engines was never well defined, but in the early 1930s the U.S. Army and, to a lesser degree, the Navy financed several "high-performance" (hyper), high-horsepower engine projects. The aim was to approach or obtain 1 hp/in³. This milestone had been achieved with purpose-built racing engines, but no production engine had managed to reach this goal. Although later air-cooled radials were able to meet and even exceed 1 hp/in³, all the hyper developments were liquid cooled.

Two early participants in the hyper sweepstakes were Continental and Lycoming. Initially, they both pursued similar technological paths, that is, twelve (separate) horizontally opposed cylinders and one-piece cylinder heads (Ref. 2.5).

Continental

The beginnings for the hyper program go back to 1930 when Sam Heron, head of development engineering at Wright Field, conducted some experiments on a single-cylinder engine converted to liquid cooling from a modified air-cooled Liberty cylinder. By pushing engine power and temperatures to the limit, Heron determined that a BMEP of 480 psi and coolant temperatures of 300°F were feasible. Based on Heron's findings, the Army contracted in 1932 with Continental Aviation and Engineering Corporation, a division of Continental Motors Corporation, to build an engine incorporating these features. The initial purpose of the contract called for Continental to be an engineering and testing vendor; consequently Continental was at the mercy of the Army for funding and development direction. This set the scene for a protracted and painful ten-year development period, the end of which resulted in huge expenditures of resources and an engine that did not produce sufficient power for the then-contemporary aircraft.

As a starting point, the original 4⅝-in cylinder bore from the air-cooled Liberty was retained; however, the stroke was substantially reduced to 5.0 in from the original 7.0 in in order to accommodate the high rotational speed of 3400 rpm. Even at 3400 rpm, the piston speed was a modest 2833 ft/min.

The resulting displacement of 1008 in³ (16.5 L) from twelve cylinders was totally inadequate even by the standards of the early 1930s; consequently, the Army requested a displacement increase to 1425 in³ (23.36 L) or 118 in³ (1.93 L) per cylinder derived from a bore of 5.5 in and a stroke of 5.0 in.

Continental spent the next six years, 1932 to 1938, working on single-cylinder development, or, to put it in perspective, more time than Rolls-Royce spent on the Merlin development and more than Allison spent on the V-1710. While it was normal practice to build single-cylinder development engines prior to building a complete engine, Continental lost valuable time by not building the full-size engine sooner. It is a good possibility that the Depression had an effect on the slow progress, particularly when it is realized Continental relied entirely on the Army for funding. Exacerbating the problem was the fact a new contract was drawn up for each phase of development, and then funds were released, a prime example of what today would be termed micromanagement. Insistence by the Army of the 300°F coolant temperature added to Continental's woes; it was not until 1938 that cooler heads prevailed, and the requirement was dropped to 250°F. The fact was that at coolant temperatures of 300°F additional heat was rejected into the oil, and consequently any drag reduction advantages in the reduced size of the coolant radiator were wiped out by the requirement for a larger oil cooler. The Army insisted on separate-cylinder construction, which was another retrograde step that caused problems with cracked crankcases later on when the full-size engine was test-run. Separate-cylinder construction also caused the engine to be longer than a comparable monoblock design, borne out by the fact that the single-stage Merlin of 18% greater displacement was shorter.

In the early 1930s conventional wisdom held that for multiengine applications, engines should be buried in the wing. Supporting this argument was a study of the B-17 that determined that a surprisingly high 34% of the total drag was attributable to the engine installation. Consequently, the first design studies of the Continental engine called out for a flat, horizontally opposed cylinder arrangement. When it was realized that a stronger and heavier wing construction was required, landing-gear storage would have been difficult if not impossible, and valuable fuel storage space was eliminated, the buried-engine concept was dropped. The tactical officers of the Army Air Corps were now convinced that an inverted V configuration would be the optimal cylinder arrangement. Unfortunately, this forced Continental to redesign the engine in early 1939 into an inverted V (Fig. 12.1). This was an arrangement similar to those in the German Daimler Benz and Junkers engines. At the same time, the propeller reduction gear was redesigned as a two-stage unit. A spur gear reduction unit from the crankshaft drove a Farman planetary reduction unit mounted on the propeller shaft axis (Fig. 12.2).

The result of all this intensive development activity was a fairly conventional engine, an inverted 60° V-12, but with separate-cylinder construction, and two valves per cylinder actuated by a single-shaft-driven overhead camshaft in a hemispherical combustion chamber. Mixture was fed by a single-stage, single-speed supercharger. The first engine was completed in 1938, and in 1939 it completed a 50-h development test rated at 1000 hp. For all this effort, the IV-1430 was installed in just two prototype aircraft; the McDonnell XP-67, of which two examples were built, and the single Lockheed XP-49.

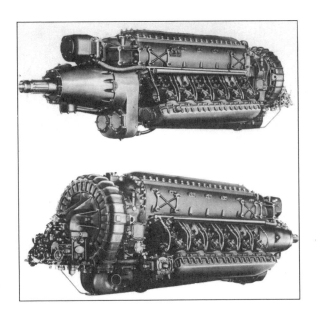

Fig. 12.1 One of the early Hyper engine contenders, the Continental IV-1430. Incredible resources were spent on this project, including construction of a new manufacturing facility in Muskegon, Michigan. The Muskegon facility ended up building Pratt & Whitney R-1340s and Rolls-Royce Merlins under license. (Courtesy of the National Air and Space Museum, Smithsonian Institution, Photo No. BC-401000-20.)

Because it used the wings and the fuselage pod from the P-38, it is not surprising that the XP-49 looked similar to the P-38. After a few test flights, the first of which occurred on 11 November 1942, the whole project was abandoned (Fig. 12.3).

The McDonnell XP-67 single-seat, twin-engine interceptor fighter (Fig. 12.4) fared little better than the Lockheed XP-49. The XP-67 incorporated many new aerodynamic features, such as the fairing-in of the nacelles to the fuselage, which gave the aircraft a unique and attractive appearance. The General Electric turbosuperchargers were vertically mounted in the tail section of the nacelle, thus offering some residual jet thrust from the exhaust. Problems with the Continental IV-1430s plagued the program. The hoped for 1350 hp never materialized; instead it was estimated that engines were only delivering 1060 hp. Consequently, performance suffered and the estimated top speed of 472 mph at 25,000 ft never occurred. Instead, it turned out to be 406 mph, which was totally inadequate by 1943 when testing took place. The first prototype was destroyed due to an engine fire after just 43 flight hours. The second prototype was planned to be powered by Merlins; however, the whole project was canceled prior to its completion.

Curtiss designed yet another variation on the P-40 theme, designated XP-53, which was intended for IV-1430 power. It was basically very similar to the ubiquitous P-40; the primary difference was the employment of laminar flow flying surfaces. Because of the unavailability of the IV-1430, the first two prototypes were powered by a Packard Merlin V-1650 and an Allison V-1710 and redesignated P-60. Again, the project was not proceeded with.

Bell Aircraft also designed a single-engine fighter around the Continental IV-1430, the XP-52. Like the Curtiss XP-53, the project was canceled prior to construction of the prototype. Several innovative design features with the XP-52 included a nose-mounted radiator/oil cooler assembly. The engine was designed to drive a contra-rotating pusher propeller (Refs. 2.5, 4.15, 9.13, 9.14).

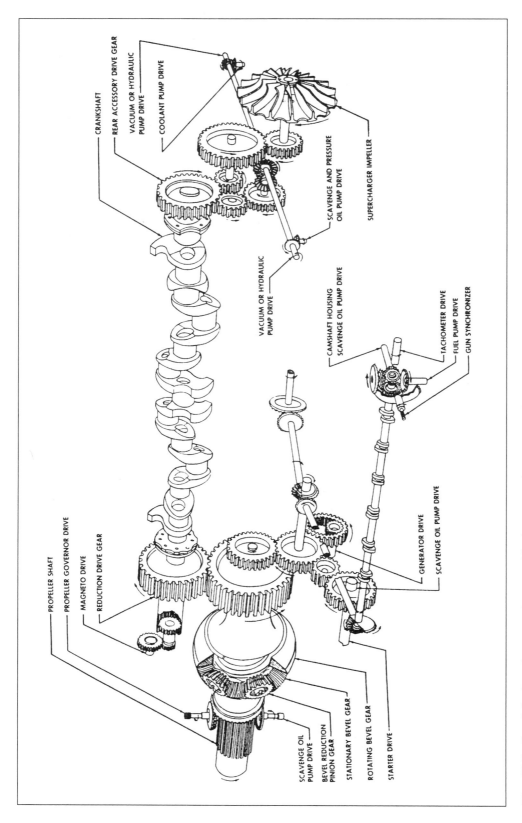

PROPELLER SHAFT
PROPELLER GOVERNOR DRIVE
MAGNETO DRIVE
REDUCTION DRIVE GEAR

SCAVENGE OIL PUMP DRIVE
BEVEL REDUCTION PINION GEAR
STATIONARY BEVEL GEAR
ROTATING BEVEL GEAR
STARTER DRIVE

GENERATOR DRIVE
SCAVENGE OIL PUMP DRIVE

TACHOMETER DRIVE
FUEL PUMP DRIVE
GUN SYNCHRONIZER

CAMSHAFT HOUSING
SCAVENGE OIL PUMP DRIVE

VACUUM OR HYDRAULIC PUMP DRIVE

CRANKSHAFT
REAR ACCESSORY DRIVE GEAR
VACUUM OR HYDRAULIC PUMP DRIVE
COOLANT PUMP DRIVE

SCAVENGE AND PRESSURE OIL PUMP DRIVE
SUPERCHARGER IMPELLER

Fig. 12.2 Crankshaft and gear train assembly for inverted Continental IV-1430. Note the two-stage propeller reduction gear. First stage was a spur reduction gear; which drove a Farman planetary reduction gear; the output of which drove the propeller shaft. (Maintenance Manual for the Continental I-1430-11 Engine, AN 02-40CA-2.)

Fig. 12.3 Lockheed XP-49 powered by a pair of Continental IV-1430-13/15. Although the engines were rated at 1600 hp, it is doubtful they ever delivered this power. Performance of the XP-49 was no better than Lockheed's P-38; consequently, the project was abandoned soon after the first flight in November 1942. (Courtesy of the National Air and Space Museum, Smithsonian Institution, Photo No. 94-4254.)

Fig. 12.4 McDonnell XP-67 twin-engine fighter powered by the Continental IV-1430, one of the early engines in the Hyper program. The IV-1430s gave constant problems in the XP-67 program due to their early development status. (Courtesy of the National Air and Space Museum, Smithsonian Institution, Photo No. 1B-20768.)

Lycoming

Lycoming also jumped into the hyper sweepstakes. Started just several months after the Continental Hyper in 1932, Lycoming's engine shared many design features with the Continental. Displacement, at 1234 in³ (20.23 L), fell between Continental's original concept at 1008 in³ (16.5 L) and the final version at 1434 in³ (23.5 L). The 1234-in³ (20.23 L) displacement was derived from a bore of 5.25 in and a stroke of 4.75 in.

The twelve cylinders were horizontally opposed, thus giving the required minimum height for a buried installation. Separate cylinders with a one-piece cylinder head featured hemispherical combustion chambers with two valves per cylinder actuated by a single overhead camshaft.

Part of the rationale for the design similarities lay with the fact that several key Continental engineers jumped ship in 1935 and joined Lycoming. Development of the Lycoming was far smoother than the Continental for several reasons. Unlike Continental, Lycoming was willing to risk its own money until 1935, when the Army took an interest and supplied limited funds. As it was, Lycoming spent $500,000 of its own money on the O-1230 project, a fortune by the standards of the 1930s. The O-1230 passed its single-cylinder development test in 1936, and by 1937 the full-size engine was bench-tested and passed a 50-h development test rated at 1000 hp (Fig. 12.5). First flight occurred in 1938 installed in a Vultee XA-19A. By 1938 it was increasingly apparent that 1000 hp was insufficient for future fighter aircraft; consequently, Lycoming doubled the size of the engine by the simple expedient of creating an H engine by pancaking two O-1230s on top of each other, thus creating the H-2470. The engine ran in this configuration in July 1940.

The performance of the XH-2470 (2300 hp at 3300 rpm for a weight of 2430 lb) was still inadequate when compared with a Pratt & Whitney R-2800, which produced the same power for considerably less installed weight. The XH-2470-5 featured two-speed propeller reduction gearing, and the XH-2470-7 went one step further by having two-speed propeller reduction gearing with contra-rotating propeller shafts.

Support for the H-2470 came from the Navy in 1939 after Pratt & Whitney backed out of the X-1800 program. A factory was constructed in Toledo, Ohio, for the purpose of building H-2470s.

Vultee responded to a USAAC request for a new fighter with the XP-54 (Fig. 12.6). The resulting aircraft, like most of the other hyper-powered aircraft, was an innovative design featuring a pusher propeller, twin-boom construction, and an interesting cooling system that incorporated the radiators in the wing leading edge and exhausted the air through the engine compartment. Bailout from a pusher propeller aircraft was always a major concern. Several solutions were incorporated by different manufacturers such as the Dornier Do 335 "Pfiel," which incorporated a device to detach the pro-

Fig. 12.5 The twelve-cylinder Lycoming O-1230 was under development throughout most of the 1930s. When it was realized that 1235 in³ was insufficient, the engine was stacked and built as an H-configured 24-cylinder engine, doubling in size to create the H-2470. (Courtesy of the National Air and Space Museum, Smithsonian Institution, Photo No. BL-34000-20.)

Fig. 12.6 Vultee XP-54 powered by the Lycoming XH-2470. (Courtesy of the National Air and Space Museum, Smithsonian Institution, Photo No. 1A-23295.)

peller by means of explosive bolts. In the case of the XP-54, the pilot's seat was released downward though the bottom of the fuselage. Performance was far short of the predicted 510 mph; only 381 mph at 28,500 ft could be coaxed from it. Two prototypes were constructed, and the second aircraft suffered the ignominy of making only one flight before being scrapped.

Curtiss designed and built a single-seat carrier-based fighter around the H-2470 designated XF14C-1. Due to problems with the H-2470, a Wright R-3350 was substituted in the XF14C-2. The fact that Curtiss felt the R-3350 was more reliable than the H-2470 really puts things in perspective, as the R-3350 at this stage of development (in 1943) was far from dependable. The XF14C-2 did not come close to performance expectations, effectively killing the H-2470 program after huge expenditures in resources and materials (Refs. 2.5, 2.7, 6.4, 9.13).

The last hurrah in the Lycoming Hyper sweepstakes was possibly the boldest piston engine project ever undertaken—the incredible XR-7755 (Figs. 12.7, 12.8). Design work started in 1943; the XR-7755 could lay claim to being the largest aircraft piston engine ever built. Cylinder dimensions were 6.375-in bore and 6.75-in stroke. The displacement from 36 cylinders was 7755 in³ (127.1 L). The four rows of nine cylinders were liquid cooled. An overhead camshaft featured two sets of cam lobes that could be shifted in flight in order to optimize economy. Another throwback to its "hyper" heritage was the use of separate cylinders that incorporated two valves per cylinder in a hemispherical combustion chamber. The nose case housed a complex propeller reduction gear that incorporated contra-rotating drive and two speeds. The two-speed mechanism was hydraulically operated from engine oil boosted to 300 psi. A five-piece steel forged crankcase supported the four-throw, four-piece crankshaft. The crankshaft was supported in five roller bearings. A single-stage, single-speed supercharger was supplemented by dual turbosuperchargers.

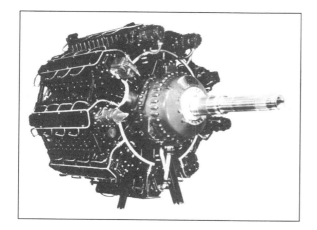

Fig. 12.7 Lycoming's magnificent monster. The XR-7755 was arguably the largest aircraft piston engine built. It was intended for the Consolidated (later Convair) B-36. Politics interfered, and consequently, production B-36s were powered (underpowered?) by six Pratt & Whitney R-4360s, and later supplemented by four General Electric J-47 jet engines. (Courtesy of the National Air and Space Museum, Smithsonian Institution, Photo No. BL-350000-20.)

Fig. 12.8 Rear three-quarter view of the Lycoming XR-7755 illustrating the intake manifolds and supercharger. (Courtesy of the National Air and Space Museum, Smithsonian Institution, Photo No. BL-350000-20.)

Some of the "gee-whiz" figures associated with this beautiful piece of mechanical engineering were a fuel consumption of 580 gal/h at take-off power (or as Lycoming mentioned in their publicity with this engine, enough to run the average family automobile for one year), a coolant flow of 750 gal/min, and an oil flow of 71 gal/min.

The engine, rated at 5000 hp, weighed 6050 lb, which gave a specific weight of 1.21 lb/hp, not particularly good by the standards of the mid 1940s; however, it made up for this weight with a good specific fuel consumption of 0.43 lb/hp/h.

The XR-7755 was designed for Consolidated's new long-range bomber, which was under development during World War II, later designated B-36, and built by Convair after World War II. Production B-36s were powered by six Pratt & Whitney R-4360s, not because of any shortcoming with the excellent XR-7755, but because of politics. Early B-36s were grossly underpowered with the R-4360 and were soon modified with a Band-Aid fix of adding four J-47 jets (Refs. 4.17, 12.1, 12.2, 12.5, 12.6).

Chrysler

A latecomer in the hyper sweepstakes was the Chrysler IV-2220, which shared many similarities with the Lycoming and Continental engines, that is, liquid-cooling, separate-cylinder construction, two valves per cylinder, and hemispherical combustion chambers. The primary difference was the displacement and number of cylinders. The inverted, 90°, V-16 displaced 2219 in³ derived from 5.8-in bores and 5.29-in strokes (Fig. 12.9).

Power take-off for the reduction gearing was in the center of the engine, rather than in the more typical position of the front. This offered the advantage of substantially reducing torsional twist in the crankshaft. Supercharger and accessories drive was also taken from the center of the engine to the rear by a quill shaft. The two-piece crankshaft was joined in the center with the reduction gear pinion sandwiched between. A single overhead camshaft actuated the two valves per cylinder.

Mounting differed from the norm. Two massive aluminum forged beams were pivoted at the center of the engine on both sides (Fig. 12.10). The beams attached to the aircraft firewall and were supported by two tubular struts. A tubular, third mount supported the rear of the engine at the accessory section (Fig. 12.11).

Although the IV-2220 exhibited commendably low frontal area the length, at 125 in, almost 10½ ft, was a result of the wide, separate-cylinder construction. A Rolls-Royce Griffon displaced almost the same as the IV-2220 at 2239 in³ (36.7 L) and yet was only 71 in long for the comparable single-stage version.

Design work started in 1939, and in 1941 an Army contract was awarded. Work continued until 1944, when the project was canceled. At its own expense, Chrysler test-flew the IV-2220 in the one-off Republic XP-47H (Fig. 12.12). Performance was no better than the equivalent Pratt & Whitney R-2800 powered P-47 (Refs. 2.5, 4.15, 9.14).

Wright Aeronautical Corporation

Wright Aeronautical also had a contender for the hyper business. The Wright Aeronautical effort ranks as one of the most complex aircraft piston engines ever attempted and, as can be imagined, was buried in its own complexity (Fig. 12.13).

The engine, designated R-2160 Tornado (35.4-L displacement), derived its displacement from 42 cylinders of 51 in³ (0.836 L) derived from a bore of 4.25 in and a stroke of 3.625 in (Fig. 12.14).

Designed on 14-cylinder modules, the R-2160 consisted of three of these modules. Plans were in place and design completed for a 70-cylinder version to be built up from five modules. Good design features characterized the R-2160, even though it deviated from Wright Aeronautical's area of expertise by being liquid-cooled. Wright Aeronautical had designed and built a number of water-cooled engines up to the late 1920s but since then had concentrated on air-cooled radials.

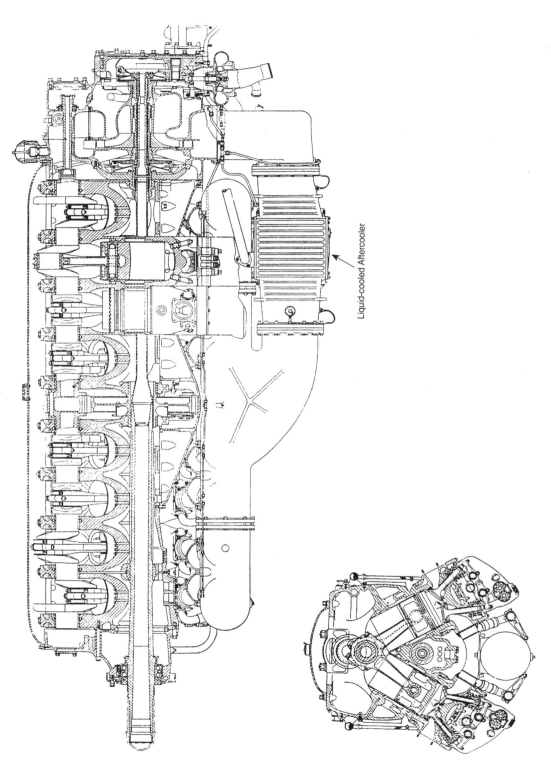

Fig. 12.9 Chrysler IV-2220 cutaway. Wide cylinder spacing is evident from this illustration. This explains why the Rolls-Royce Griffon of almost identical displacement was 71 in long and the IV-2220 was a whopping 122 in long. Liquid-cooled aftercooler is incorporated into the intake manifold. (Automotive and Aviation Industries, 15 Apr: 1946.)

Liquid-cooled Aftercooler

Fig. 12.10 Chrysler IV-2220 mounted in the Republic XP-47H. Performance was no better than that of the Pratt & Whitney R-2800 powered variants. Engine-driven supercharger was boosted by a General Electric Type CH-5 turbo-supercharger mounted in the rear fuselage. The liquid-cooled after-cooler is evident, mounted in the intake manifold. (Courtesy of the National Air and Space Museum, Smithsonian Institution, Photo No. BC-4010.)

Fig. 12.11 Rear support mount for the Chrysler IV-2220. Similar in principle to the three-point mounting used for most front engine, rear wheel drive cars. (Courtesy of the National Air and Space Museum, Smithsonian Institution, Photo No. BC-4010.)

Fig. 12.12 One-off Republic XP47H powered by the inverted liquid-cooled Chrysler IV-2220 V-16. After the engine program was canceled, Chrysler continued on with the project at its own expense. The XP-47H showed no performance improvement over the Pratt & Whitney R-2800 powered variants. (Courtesy of the National Air and Space Museum, Smithsonian Institution, Photo No. 1B-33440.)

Fig. 12.13 The Wright R-2160 Tornado. One of the most fascinating (and complex) aircraft engines developed. The engine went through extensive testing, yet it was never flown. (Courtesy of the National Air and Space Museum, Smithsonian Institution, Photo No. 94-13743.)

Six cylinders per row (total of seven) featured monoblock construction. Two-valve hemispherical combustion chambers and overhead camshafts were part of the cylinder head design. An unusual feature of this grandiose engine was the propeller reduction gearing. Seven pinions, each one driven from the cylinder head of a cylinder row, drove the reduction gear by means of a layshaft (Fig. 12.15).

The radial engine ancestry of the R-2160 was featured in the crankcase design, which was formed from nine bolted-together steel forgings. A built-up crankshaft allowed the use of one-piece master rods with six articulated rods attached (Figs. 12.16, 12.17). All crankshaft bearings were plain.

For take-off, the R-2160 was rated at 2350 hp at 4145 rpm. The weight was 2400 lb. These figures compare quite favorably with a two-stage Rolls-Royce Griffon, which had similar displacement but was considerably less complex.

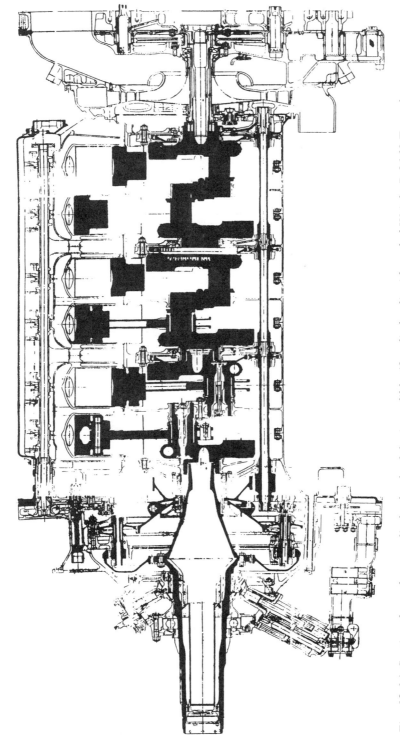

Fig. 12.14 Section through one cylinder bank of the incredible 42-cylinder, liquid-cooled Wright R-2160 Tornado. (Courtesy of the New Jersey Aviation Hall of Fame Museum and Gerry Abbamont.)

Fig. 12.15 Propeller reduction gear layshafts from Wright R-2160 Tornado. Seven layshafts were employed to drive the propeller reduction gear. (Courtesy of the New Jersey Aviation Hall of Fame Museum and Gerry Abbamont.)

Fig. 12.16 Crankshaft section from the Wright R-2160 Tornado. Crank was made up of three of these sections. (Courtesy of the New Jersey Aviation Hall of Fame Museum and Gerry Abbamont.)

One consequence of the compact design of the engine was the close proximity of the cylinder rows to each other. This allowed very little room for the intake manifold, the design of which was necessarily compromised resulting in less-than-ideal flow characteristics through the intake system. Follow-on designs addressed this issue, but none were built.

Because of the pressing need to correct the serious problems with the R-3350, engineering personnel were drained from the project, and by 1943 the R-2160 was abandoned.

Although several aircraft were designed around it, no complete R-2160 was delivered to the AAF. Republic designed the XP-69 single-engine fighter for the R-2160. Although a mock-up was completed, the aircraft was not built. Non-delivery of the power plants forced Lockheed into powering the one prototype of the XP-58 after numerous changes in engine choice during the development phase of this ill-fated aircraft (Refs. 2.5, 9.14, 12.3, 12.4).

Fig. 12.17 Master rod assembly for Wright R-2160 Tornado. Note the exquisite workmanship. (Courtesy of the New Jersey Hall of Fame Museum and Gerry Abbamont.)

Pratt & Whitney

Considering the opposition the Navy had to liquid-cooled aircraft engines ("a liquid-cooled aircraft engine makes as much sense as an air-cooled submarine"!), it is surprising how many liquid-cooled projects they funded directly or in conjunction with the Army.

Pratt & Whitney was enamored with the liquid-cooling concept in the mid 1930s because of George Mead's influence. After learning of the benefits of sleeve valve technology and particularly the work being done in England, Mead, at that time Vice President for Engineering, visited there in 1937. Many prominent English engineers, particularly Roy Fedden of Bristol and Harry Ricardo, were convinced the poppet valve had reached the limits of its technology, and consequently they led the sleeve valve campaign.

The results Napier was getting from the Sabre convinced Mead that liquid-cooled sleeve valve technology was the wave of the future. Upon his return, Pratt & Whitney signed a contract with the Navy for an 1800 hp engine, which Pratt designated X-1800, X for experimental and 1800 for 1800 hp. It was conceptually similar to the Napier Sabre, that is, liquid-cooled, 24-cylinder H-configuration using sleeve valve technology. The X-1800 shared an almost identical displacement to the Sabre: 2240 in³ (36.7 L). This was later increased to 2600 in³ (42.6 L) with a projected 2000 hp.

As Mead's health deteriorated, he ran the X-1800 program from his sickbed at home. In mid 1939, Mead resigned from Pratt & Whitney, leaving development of the liquid-cooled projects to Luke Hobbs. Not surprisingly, Hobbs canceled the X-1800 program in 1940 in concert with the Air Corps' interest in the R-4360 and the limited resources of the company. The H-3730, a Navy request for an outgrowth of the X-1800, was continued through 1943, when it was also canceled (Fig. 12.18).

The cancellation of the H-3730 was delayed because Pratt & Whitney had no engine in the 3000-hp class in the early 1940s, as development of the R-4360 was in its infancy. As the R-4360 progressed, it was apparent this would be a more suitable engine for them to concentrate on (Refs. 2.5, 6.9).

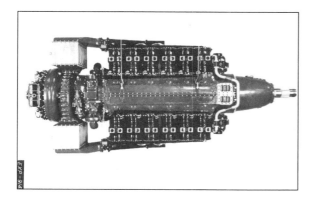

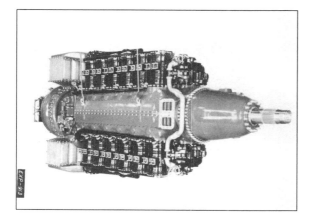

Fig. 12.18 Pratt & Whitney H-3730 built for the Navy. Although several engines were built, none flew. This one is a later development version with two-stage supercharging and a pair of liquid-cooled aftercoolers. Company and contemporary documents refer to this engine family as the X-1800, that is, Experimental-1800 hp. (Courtesy of the New England Air Museum and Pratt & Whitney Aircraft.)

Summary

In retrospect, it could be argued that the hyper program was a wasted effort; none of the engines described in this chapter saw volume production. In fact, compared to other countries such as Germany and England, relatively little effort was expended on these engines. Although it could be argued that a plethora of engine designations were manufactured during World War II, the majority were simply minor changes to existing designs. For example, several ignition systems were used on Pratt & Whitney engines that resulted in a different dash number even though everything else on the engine was the same. In a similar vein, even a difference in generator drive ratio would result in a different designation.

Valuable lessons were learned, such as the fallacy of the buried-engine concept and the 300°F coolant temperature requirement. Although Continental built a new facility for the production of the IV-1430, this factory was put to good use manufacturing license-built Pratt & Whitney R-1340s and Rolls-Royce Merlin V-1650s. In a similar vein, Lycoming built a new factory at Toledo, Ohio, for the manufacture of its O-1230. Again this facility was put to good use during the war. Chrysler's project incorporated excellent engineering, but was too late. George Heubner, head of the IV-2220 program, later went on to design the company's V-8 automobile engines, including the Chrysler "hemi" engines culminating in the ultimate "muscle" car engine, the awesome 426 hemi. The auto engine combustion chambers were a direct descendent from the IV-2220s.

Pratt & Whitney was like a fish out of water designing liquid-cooled engines. To the surprise of no one, these projects were canceled when Luke Hobbs took over from George Mead.

Although the Wright R-2160 showed great promise and with sufficient development time would have been an excellent power plant, the decision to shelve it in favor of a more concentrated effort on the R-3350 paid dividends early in the war.

References

2.5 Schlaifer, Robert, and S. D. Heron, <u>Development of Aircraft Engines and Development of Aviation Fuels</u>, Harvard University, Boston, 1950.

2.7 <u>Jane's All The World's Aircraft</u>, McGraw-Hill, New York, 1945/1946.

4.15 Wilkinson, Paul H., <u>Aircraft Engines of The World 1946</u>, Paul H. Wilkinson, New York.

4.17 Wilkinson, Paul H., <u>Aircraft Engines of The World 1948</u>, Paul H. Wilkinson, New York.

6.4 Wilkinson, Paul H., <u>Aircraft Engines of The World 1941</u>, Paul H. Wilkinson, New York.

6.9 <u>The Pratt & Whitney Aircraft Story</u>, Pratt & Whitney Aircraft Div., United Aircraft Corp., 1952.

9.13 <u>Model Designations of USAF Aircraft Engines</u>, 9th ed., By Authority of Commanding General Air Materiel Command U.S. Air Force, 1 Jan. 1949.

9.14 Angellucci, Enzo, with Peter Bowers, <u>The American Fighter</u>, Orion Books, New York.

12.1 Bill Witmer, retired Lycoming engineer, interview with author, 1994.

12.2 <u>Introducing Lycoming XR-7755 The World's Largest Reciprocating Aircraft Engine</u>, Lycoming Div., The Aviation Corp., Williamsport, Pa., 31 Oct. 1946.

12.3 <u>Tornado Engine Model Variations</u>, Wright Aeronautical Corp., Paterson, N.J., 4 Oct. 1939.

12.4 "Summary of 150 Hour Endurance Test on Wright Aeronautical Corporation T-14 Tornado Test Unit Engine," Wright Aeronautical Corp., Paterson, N.J., 18 Nov. 1941.

12.5 Paul D. McBride, Manager—Promotions & Trade Shows, Textron Lycoming, Reciprocating Engine Division, interview and correspondence with author, 1994.

12.6 Ed Pease, retired Lycoming engineer, interview and correspondence with author, 1994.

Chapter 13

Conclusion

In the relatively short time span of 1903 to 1945, aircraft piston engine technology reached its zenith. Today the so-called high-tech piston engines owe a great deal to the technology that was developed prior to 1945.

Even before the end of hostilities on V-J Day, 15 August 1945, the writing was on the wall for these magnificent creations of the practicing engineer. The gas turbine was already making giant strides in displacing the piston engine. In a few short years, no new piston engine projects would be embarked upon, although the engines soldiered on in secondary roles for another 50 years.

The contribution to victory by air power was incalculable. He who ruled the skies decided the outcome of victory. In the ensuing years of relative peace, the jet has ruled supreme, but the clean efficiency of the gas turbine lacks the charisma of the noisy, leaky, temperamental piston engine. The magnificent roar of these multiple-thousand horsepower, high-performance aerial hot-rod engines that displaced several thousand cubic inches has been all but silenced.

The days of the so-called aluminum overcast, when raids of more than 1000 bombers streaking the sky with condensation trails were commonplace, are now gone. Gone forever. Indeed one wag is reported to have said, "We couldn't afford the gas bill today!" There is more than a grain of truth to this statement. The average 1000-bomber raid would consume over 3,000,000 gallons of fuel alone. Other logistics were just as impressive, including the oil consumed, ammunition, bombs, spare parts required, maintenance, and human suffering.

The effects of World War II have been long and far reaching. The following years saw profound changes in industry and society. The days of the great, powerful, and charismatic industry leaders like Rentschler, Royce, Fedden, Hobbs, Henry Ford, Sam Heron, Eddie Rickenbacker, Frank Halford, Sir Harry Ricardo, and countless others like them, have gone forever. In their place are committees who now carry on from their illustrious predecessors in a quiet and efficient manner with precious little vision or love for their companies' products, services, or history.

Exciting new products under development are now held back according to the whims of Wall Street or the London Stock Exchange, or worse yet, litigation attorneys. Today, apparently simple deals involve armies of attorneys. This is in stark contrast with the time when Hives of Rolls-Royce picked up the development of gas turbines from the Rover Car Company. An agreement was reached over lunch in which Rolls-Royce gave Rover the tank engine business in exchange for the gas turbine project and, more importantly, the services of Frank Whittle and his team. A similar deal today would involve protracted negotiations and the exchange of huge sums of money.

On the rare occasion when a successful corporation is established by a CEO who possesses the characteristics of a bygone era, that corporation is rewarded with not only high monetary returns, but also the rewards of that individual's vision, leadership, and compassion for the product or service being offered. Sadly, this is now a rarity that has been replaced by leveraged buyouts, corporate raiders, and junk bond manipulators.

Still, the achievements of a generation or two of dreamers, engineers, technicians, machinists, pilots, and entrepreneurs have left us with a history and artifacts chronicling how they focused their energies and solved the problems of their day. They did it with their hands and minds; today we use microchips and software. The old methods may no longer be appropriate, but the way they met the challenges certainly is. We can learn a lot from these accomplishments of the past.

Index